T0190394

Communications in Computer and Information Science 1618

More information about this series at https://link.springer.com/bookseries/7899

Leonid Sokolinsky · Mikhail Zymbler (Eds.)

Parallel Computational Technologies

16th International Conference, PCT 2022
Dubna, Russia, March 29–31, 2022
Revised Selected Papers

 Springer

Editors
Leonid Sokolinsky [iD]
South Ural State University
Chelyabinsk, Russia

Mikhail Zymbler [iD]
South Ural State University
Chelyabinsk, Russia

ISSN 1865-0929   ISSN 1865-0937 (electronic)
Communications in Computer and Information Science
ISBN 978-3-031-11622-3   ISBN 978-3-031-11623-0 (eBook)
https://doi.org/10.1007/978-3-031-11623-0

This Springer imprint is published by the registered company Springer Nature Switzerland AG
The registered company address is: Gewerbestrasse 11, 6330 Cham, Switzerland

Preface

This volume contains a selection of the papers presented at the 16th International Scientific Conference on Parallel Computational Technologies, PCT 2022. The PCT 2022 conference was held in Dubna, Russia, during March 29–31, 2022.

The PCT series of conferences aims at providing an opportunity to report and discuss the results achieved by leading research groups in solving practical issues using supercomputer and neural network technologies. The scope of the PCT series of conferences includes all aspects of the application of cloud, supercomputer, and neural network technologies in science and technology such as applications, hardware and software, specialized languages, and packages.

The PCT series is organized by the Supercomputing Consortium of Russian Universities and the Ministry of Science and Higher Education of the Russian Federation. Originating in 2007 at the South Ural State University (Chelyabinsk, Russia), the PCT series of conferences has now become one of the most prestigious Russian scientific meetings on parallel programming, high-performance computing, and machine learning. PCT 2022 in Dubna continued the series after Chelyabinsk (2007), St. Petersburg (2008), Nizhny Novgorod (2009), Ufa (2010), Moscow (2011), Novosibirsk (2012), Chelyabinsk (2013), Rostov-on-Don (2014), Ekaterinburg (2015), Arkhangelsk (2016), Kazan (2017), Rostov-on-Don (2018), Kaliningrad (2019), Perm (2020), and Volgograd (2021).

Each paper submitted to the conference was scrupulously evaluated by three reviewers based on relevance to the conference topics, scientific and practical contribution, experimental evaluation of the results, and presentation quality. The Program Committee of PCT selected the 22 best papers to be included in this CCIS proceedings volume.

We would like to thank the respected PCT 2022 platinum sponsors, namely Intel, RSC Group, and Karma Group, and the conference partner, Special Technological Center, for their continued financial support of the PCT series of conferences.

We would like to express our gratitude to every individual who contributed to the success of PCT 2022. Special thanks to the Program Committee members and the external reviewers for evaluating papers submitted to the conference. Thanks also to the Organizing Committee members and all the colleagues involved in the conference organization from the Joint Institute for Nuclear Research, the South Ural State University (national research university), and Moscow State University. We thank the participants of PCT 2022 for sharing their research and presenting their achievements as well.

Finally, we thank Springer for publishing the proceedings of PCT 2022 in the Communications in Computer and Information Science series.

June 2022

Leonid Sokolinsky
Mikhail Zymbler

Organization

The 16th International Scientific Conference on Parallel Computational Technologies (PCT 2022) was organized by the Supercomputing Consortium of Russian Universities and the Ministry of Science and Higher Education of the Russian Federation.

Steering Committee

Berdyshev, V. I.	Krasovskii Institute of Mathematics and Mechanics, UrB RAS, Russia
Ershov, Yu. L.	United Scientific Council on Mathematics and Informatics, Russia
Minkin, V. I.	South Federal University, Russia
Moiseev, E. I.	Moscow State University, Russia
Savin, G. I.	Joint Supercomputer Center, RAS, Russia
Sadovnichiy, V. A.	Moscow State University, Russia
Chetverushkin, B. N.	Keldysh Institute of Applied Mathematics, RAS, Russia
Shokin, Yu. I.	Institute of Computational Technologies, RAS, Russia

Program Committee

Dongarra, J. (Co-chair)	University of Tennessee, USA
Sokolinsky, L. B. (Co-chair)	South Ural State University, Russia
Voevodin, Vl. V. (Co-chair)	Moscow State University, Russia
Zymbler, M. L. (Academic Secretary)	South Ural State University, Russia
Ablameyko, S. V.	Belarusian State University, Belarus
Afanasiev, A. P.	Institute for Systems Analysis, RAS, Russia
Akimova, E. N.	Krasovskii Institute of Mathematics and Mechanics, UrB RAS, Russia
Andrzejak, A.	Heidelberg University, Germany
Balaji, P.	Argonne National Laboratory, USA
Boldyrev, Yu. Ya.	St. Petersburg Polytechnic University, Russia
Carretero, J.	Carlos III University of Madrid, Spain
Gazizov, R. K.	Ufa State Aviation Technical University, Russia
Glinsky, B. M.	Institute of Computational Mathematics and Mathematical Geophysics, SB RAS, Russia
Goryachev, V. D.	Tver State Technical University, Russia

Il'in, V. P.	Institute of Computational Mathematics and Mathematical Geophysics, SB RAS, Russia
Kobayashi, H.	Tohoku University, Japan
Kunkel, J.	University of Hamburg, Germany
Kumar, S.	Rudrapur, India
Labarta, J.	Barcelona Supercomputing Center, Spain
Lastovetsky, A.	University College Dublin, Ireland
Likhoded, N. A.	Belarusian State University, Belarus
Ludwig, T.	German Climate Computing Center, Germany
Lykosov, V. N.	Institute of Numerical Mathematics, RAS, Russia
Mallmann, D.	Julich Supercomputing Centre, Germany
Malyshkin, V. E.	Institute of Computational Mathematics and Mathematical Geophysics, SB RAS, Russia
Michalewicz, M.	A*STAR Computational Resource Centre, Singapore
Modorsky, V. Ya.	Perm Polytechnic University, Russia
Pan, C. S.	Cloudflare, UK
Prodan, R.	Alpen-Adria-Universität Klagenfurt, Austria
Radchenko, G. I.	Silicon Austria Labs, Austria
Shamakina, A. V.	HLRS High-Performance Computing Center Stuttgart, Germany
Shumyatsky, P.	University of Brasilia, Brazil
Sithole, H.	Centre for High Performance Computing, South Africa
Starchenko, A. V.	Tomsk State University, Russia
Sterling, T.	Indiana University, USA
Sukhinov, A. I.	Don State Technical University, Russia
Taufer, M.	University of Delaware, USA
Tchernykh, A.	CICESE Research Center, Mexico
Turlapov, V. E.	Lobachevsky State University of Nizhny Novgorod, Russia
Wyrzykowski, R.	Czestochowa University of Technology, Poland
Yakobovskiy, M. V.	Keldysh Institute of Applied Mathematics, RAS, Russia
Yamazaki, Y.	Federal University of Pelotas, Brazil

Organizing Committee

Koren'kov, V. V. (Chair)	Joint Institute for Nuclear Research, Russia
Podgaynyi, D. V. (Deputy Chair)	Joint Institute for Nuclear Research, Russia
Derenovskaya, O. Yu. (Secretary)	Joint Institute for Nuclear Research, Russia
Antonov, A. S.	Moscow State University, Russia
Antonova, A. P.	Moscow State University, Russia

Contents

High Performance Architectures, Tools and Technologies

VGL Rating: A Novel Benchmarking Suite for Modern Supercomputing Architectures

Ilya Afanasyev[1,2]([⊠]) [iD] and Sviatoslav Krymskii[1]

[1] Research Computing Center, Lomonosov Moscow State University,
Moscow 119234, Russia
afanasiev_ilya@icloud.com
[2] Moscow Center of Fundamental and Applied Mathematics, Moscow 119991, Russia

Abstract. This paper presents a novel project aimed to rank modern supercomputing architectures. The proposed rating is based on an architecture-independent Vector Graph Library (VGL) framework. The initial integration with VGL greatly simplifies the process of ranking new supercomputing architectures due to the fact that VGL provides a convenient API for developing graph algorithms on a large variety of supercomputing architectures. Unlike existing projects (such as Graph500), the proposed rating is based on a larger number of graph algorithms and input graphs with fundamentally different characteristics, which makes it significantly more representative when certain architectures have to be compared for a specific real-world problem. Moreover, the proposed flexible software architecture of our rating allows one to easily supplement the rating with new graph algorithms and input data, if necessary.

Keywords: Graph Algorithms · Graph Framework · Benchmarking · Rating systems · Graph500 · NVIDIA GPU

1 Introduction

The ranking of modern supercomputing systems and computational platforms is an important problem of modern computer science. With a large variety of architectures that exist and are widely used nowadays, it is crucial to understand which systems are capable of solving a specific real-world problem faster, frequently taking into account the properties of input data.

There exist multiple projects such as Top500 [14], Graph500 [15], HPCG [13], Algo500 [5], which are aimed to rank the performance of supercomputing systems based on algorithms used in different fields of application. The purpose of this study is to develop a ranking of modern shared memory systems that is more representative than existing systems. Our research extends the approach of using graph algorithms to rank modern supercomputing architectures using a family of graph algorithms, which is important due to the fact that graph algorithms are used in a wide range of applications: solution of infrastructure and biological problems, analysis of social and web networks, etc.

L. Sokolinsky and M. Zymbler (Eds.): PCT 2022, CCIS 1618, pp. 3–16, 2022.
https://doi.org/10.1007/978-3-031-11623-0_1

We have developed a novel rating system named as the VGL-rating project[1], which is designed to achieve two main goals: (1) broader the group of graph algorithms and input data used in the benchmarking core to make the rating more representative and (2) make the benchmarking and submission process as simple as running a single script on the target architecture (with all the required action being automatized).

Thus, our project has the following advantages over existing solutions such as Graph500 or Algo500. Firstly, our rating takes into account a larger group of graph algorithms with drastically different characteristics, as well as input data from various fields of application, which makes it more representative than existing counterparts. Secondly, its native integration with the VGL framework greatly simplifies the process of benchmarking a new architecture. Previously, when submitting to a rating project, such as Graph500 or Algo500, the user has to follow the following relatively complex steps: (1) develop optimized implementations of a specific graph algorithm, (2) obtain input data, (3) run the implementation and measure performance metrics correctly and (4) fill multiple forms to get into the rating list.

On the contrary, our rating makes the benchmarking process as simple as running a single script that automatically performs the described steps. This is achieved by the native integration of the rating with the VGL framework, which provides highly optimized implementations for a large variety of modern CPUs and GPUs. Thus, the development of an optimized implementation is covered by VGL developers and hardware vendors, who are allowed to extend VGL on their platforms, while all the remaining steps (downloading input data, compiling optimized implementations, submitting performance results) are performed automatically by a convenient script provided in VGL.

The rating system described in this paper is currently intended for shared memory architectures. For this reason, at the current stage of the project, it cannot be considered as a full replacement of Graph500. However, the VGL rating can easily be extended for clusters and systems containing multiple NVIDIA GPUs (DGX) or vector engines (Aurora8) due to outgoing updates of the VGL framework, which currently enables distributed graph processing using MPI as a beta version [3].

2   Related Work

At the moment of this writing, many solutions aimed to benchmark and consequently rank supercomputing systems exist. Examples of such solutions include the Top500 [14], Graph500 [15], Green500 [7] lists, the Algo500 [5] project based on Algowiki [17], the HPCG [13] benchmark, and some others. Typically, these solutions are based on applying a specific frequently used algorithm and its implementation, such as solving SLE, doing SPMV, etc., and using some performance metrics to rank various supercomputing systems. Such a variety of

---

[1] The VGL rating is currently available at vgl-rating.parallel.ru.

existing ratings is explained by the fact that different algorithms used as a benchmarking core stress different parts of the supercomputing hardware (for example, Graph500 – memory subsystem). At the same time some approaches, such as Algo500, are more general, since they are capable of benchmarking supercomputing systems based on any algorithm described in the Algowiki project.

The most related to our project is the Graph500 rating, which also uses the implementations of the Shortest Paths and Breadth-First Search (BFS) graph algorithms launched on RMAT [6] graphs of different scales as a benchmarking core. However, this rating, in our opinion, has the following drawbacks:

– Only 2 graph algorithms are used. At the same time, there are many other graph algorithms with different properties, which usually demonstrate a drastically different performance on different evaluated architectures and result into significantly different ratings based on these algorithms;
– Similarly, using only one type of synthetic input graphs leads to the same problem, i.e. architectures can potentially be ranked drastically differently when some other graph is used;
– Graph500 provides only generic MPI and OpenMP implementations, forcing users to develop their own highly optimized implementations;
– Graph500 targets large supercomputing systems, while it is also interesting to compare single-node (and single-GPU) systems.

Thus, we decided to build our own rating system on top of the VGL framework. This rating is mostly aimed to benchmark single-node systems, at the same time using graphs and algorithms with different properties, which allows creating a more general and balanced rating.

As a benchmarking core we use our own VGL framework. There exist potentially other CPU-based or GPU-based graph-processing systems, such as Gunrock [18], cuSha [9], Ligra [16], etc. However, as we will show in the following sections, VGL suites these purposes better since it is architecture-independent and supports a large variety of modern architectures.

3   Proposed Benchmarking Method

When developing a novel rating designed to rank systems based on the performance of graph algorithm implementations, we had to decide three main features of the developed rating:

1. which graph algorithms should be used as the basis of the rating;
2. which input graphs should be used as the basis of the rating;
3. which mathematical model should be used to create a rating based on the selected graph algorithms and input graphs.

The next three subsections describe each of these three features in detail.

3.1   Selecting Graph Algorithms

Firstly, we conducted a detailed study of the characteristic properties of a wide set of graph algorithms, which was aimed at identifying fundamentally different graph algorithms with fundamentally different computational characteristics. In the course of this study, a number of basic mathematical properties of graph algorithms (complexity, computing power, structure of information graphs), as well as the properties of typical programs that implement these algorithms, were examined.

Based on the analysis, we decided to form our rating on top of the following graph algorithms:

Breadth First Search (BFS) is an algorithm designed to find the shortest paths from one vertex of an unweighted graph to other vertexes. In a parallel version, the algorithm traverses the graph by "layers", starting from the initial layer, which consists of the source vertex. The Breadth First Search algorithm is the basis for many other graph algorithms, such as searching for connected and strongly connected components, transitive closure, etc. This algorithm differs from others in its "sparsity": on each iteration, BFS typically processes only a certain subset of graph vertexes (which can be rather small for the currently processed "layer").

Page Rank (PR) is a graph algorithm that is applied to a collection of hyperlinked documents and assigns to each of them some numerical value measuring its "importance". This algorithm can be applied not only to web pages, but also to any set of objects interconnected by reciprocal links, for example, to any graph. This algorithm differs from others in that the processing of each vertex requires loading information from multiple indirectly accessed arrays, thus causing a larger latency compared to other algorithms (BFS, SSSP), which indirectly access only a single array.

HITS (search for topics by hyperlinks) is a graph algorithm designed to find Internet pages that match the user's request based on the information contained in a hyperlink. The idea of the algorithm relies on the assumption that hyperlinks encode a significant number of hidden authoritative pages (an authoritative page is a page that corresponds to the user's request and has a greater proportion among documents of a given topic, i.e. a larger number of pages linking to this page). The HITS algorithm is similar to the Page Rank algorithm. They both use the link relationship in web graphs to determine the importance of pages. However, unlike Page Rank, HITS only works with small subgraphs of a large web graph. This algorithm differs from others as it changes the traversal direction (visiting either incoming or outgoing edges) twice on each iteration.

The Bellman-Ford algorithm of shortest paths in a graph from a source node (Shortest Paths from a Single Source, SSSP) is a graph algorithm that finds the shortest paths from the starting node of the graph to all the others. This algorithm goes through all the edges of the graph at most $|V-1|$ times and tries to improve the value of the shortest paths. This algorithm differs from others due to (1) its larger computational complexity and the (2) fact that it processes weighted graphs.

The main comparative characteristics of the algorithms (including those already mentioned during the algorithm description) are provided in Table 1. An analysis of these characteristics enables to conclude that we selected a representative set of graph algorithms. Our additional conducted experiments demonstrated that the performance of graph algorithms solving other problems, including Maximum Flow, Strongly Connected Components, Coloring, quite resembled one or several algorithms that we used as the basis of our benchmark. Thus, these four algorithms form the basis for a representative rating reflecting the features of a wide range of graph algorithms. However, our implementation makes it easily to extend the set of algorithms used in the rating (as will be shown in the other section), in case we need to add another drastically different algorithm in the future.

Table 1. Main comparative characteristics of the algorithms used in the rating basis.

	BFS	SSSP	PR	HITS
Sequential complexity	$O(|E|)$	$O(|V| * |E|)$	$O(|E| * N)$	$O(|E| * N)$
Parallel complexity	$O(d)$	$O(|V|)$	$O(N)$	$O(N)$
Computing power	1	$|V|$	N	N
Working with sparse vertex lists	yes	no	no	no
Working with inbound and outbound edges at the same time	yes	no	no	yes
Working with weighted graphs	no	yes	no	no
Necessity to use atomic operations	no	no	yes	yes
Necessity to check convergence	no	no	yes	no
Fixed number of iterations	no	no	yes	yes

3.2   Selecting Input Graphs

Secondly, we had to decide which input graphs should form the basis of the rating. Unlike existing ratings (e.g. Graph500), which use a single type of input graphs, we used a wide set of real-world and synthetic graphs of different size, the main characteristics of which are provided in Table 2.

Table 2. Graphs used in the project. Each graph is described by the Name, Number of Vertexes, Number of Edges triple. The columns and rows of the table correspond to the different sizes and categories of these graphs.

	Social	Infrastructure	Internet	Rating	Synthetic
Tiny	YouTube friendships (1.13 mln, 3 mln)	Texas (1.38 mln, 1.9 mln)	Stanford (282k, 2.3 mln)	Netflix (498k, 1B)	RMAT (2^{18}, 2^{23})
Small	LiveJournal links (5.2 mln, 49 mln)	Western USA (6.2 mln, 15 mln)	Zhishi (7.83 mln, 66 mln)	Amazon ratings (3.4 mln, 5.8 mln)	RMAT (2^{22}, 2^{27})
Medium	-	Central USA (14 mln, 34 mln)	UK domain (18.5 mln, 262 mln)	-	RMAT (2^{24}, 2^{29})
Large	Twitter (41.6 mln, 1.5B)	Full USA (24 mln, 57.7 mln)	Web trackers (40.4 mln, 140 mln)	Amazon (31 mln, 82.6 mln)	RMAT (2^{25}, 2^{30})

Table 2 demonstrates the graphs from four important application fields (social, infrastructure, internet, rankings), which differ in:

1. Number of vertexes (from 133 thousand to 105 million).
2. Number of edges (from 144 thousand to 3.3 billion).
3. Maximum number of edges outgoing from one vertex (from 9 to 20.7 million).
4. Average number of edges outgoing from one vertex (from 2.13 to 496).
5. Size of the largest connectivity component (from 75 to 104 million).
6. Diameter (from 4 to 8000).
7. Number of cycles in the graph (from 0 to 5.6 million).

Based on the data presented, we can conclude that the developed rating uses different classes, the parameters of which significantly impact the performance of graph algorithm implementations on different architectures.

3.3   Principles Used to Form the Rating

The rating has a large number of parameters that allow one to specify weights for the category of graphs (social, infrastructure, Internet, rating, synthetic), algorithms (Page Rank, HITS, Shortest Paths, BFS), graph size (tiny, small, medium, large). By default, all parameters have the same weight (equal to 0.5) and, therefore, the same contribution to the final result, however, the user can select a weight for each parameter in order to give preference to one or another parameter. Each selected weight (from 0.0 to 1.0) indicates how strongly a particular parameter should affect the generated rating.

Two approaches to the formation of the rating were implemented. First, for both approaches, all algorithms are launched on all graphs. Further, for each pair {graph, algorithm}:

1. The performance values are sorted among all architectures; after sorting, each architecture receives a sequential number, i.e. an index in the sorted array. For each architecture, a value equal to the difference of the number of architectures and the sequential number of the architecture, multiplied by the weight, is added to the final rating.
2. The maximum performance value among all architectures is found, and all results are divided by this value (normalization is performed). After that, for each architecture, the normalized values multiplied by weights are added to the final rating value.

Let us denote the set of graph types (social, infrastructure, etc.) used as the basis of the rating as I, the set of graphs as G, the set of used graph algorithms as J, the set of graph scales as K, the set of tested architectures as A. In addition, let us denote the weights of these sets (which are specified by users) as x_i, x_j, x_k.

In the first implementation, we first fix the graph $g \in G$, the graph algorithm $j \in J$, and for all $a \in A$ we obtain an array of performance values M_{gja} corresponding to the triple {g, j, a}. Then we sort these values, and each architecture gets the value p_{gja} corresponding to the index of the value M_{gja} in the sorted array. Let N be the number of architectures, then the final rating is formed according to the following equation:

$$R_a \ (Rating \ of \ architecture \ a) = \sum_{\forall g \in G, \forall j \in J} (N - p_{gja}) * x_i * x_j,$$

In the second implementation, the rating is formed according to the following equation:

$$R_a \ (Rating \ of \ architecture \ a) = \sum_{\forall i \in I, \forall j \in J, \forall k \in K} \frac{\forall p \in A \ M_{ijk\_p}}{\max_{\forall t \in A} M_{ijk\_t}} * x_i * x_j * x_k.$$

where M_{ijk_a} is the performance of the implementation of the graph algorithm j on graphs of type i of size k on the architecture a.

The essence of the first approach is that the architecture that is often better in efficiency on fixed graphs and algorithms will have a higher rating; while the second approach calculates the sum of normalized efficiency values. The problem of the second approach may be that one architecture works much better than others on a small number of fixed graphs and algorithms, while it is slightly worse on all others. In this case, this architecture can be ranked higher than others, although it shows less efficiency on most graphs.

In the second approach, the normalization by the maximum performance value obtained among all architectures on a certain combination of input parameters i, j, k, t is required to avoid situations when performance differences on different sets of input data are drastically different due to some properties of input data. For example, the shortest paths algorithm on a road graph performs many more iterations compared to social graphs (due to their different diameters). Without this normalization, the performance input of road graphs will be much lower compared to social ones, which should not be the case.

4   Using VGL as a Benchmarking Core

As mentioned in the introduction, we decided to use the architecture-independent graph-processing framework VGL [2,4] as a benchmarking core; it currently supports many modern supercomputing architectures: NVIDIA GPUs [10], NEC SX-Aurora TSUBASA vector engines [1], A64FX with HBM memory, as well as multicore CPUs of different models and vendors (Intel Xeon, Intel KNL, Arm Kunpeng, AMD EPYC, etc.). The architectural independence of VGL [2] is achieved by using the same data and computation abstractions for all supported architectures (in terms of interfaces, but not implementations). The use of optimized implementations with generic interfaces is achieved by means of C++ object oriented programming, inheritance and templates.

Using VGL as a benchmarking core requires the development of implementations of the graph algorithms selected in Sect. 3.2 on the basis of VGL computational and data abstractions. Thus, the developed high-performance implementations of the PR, SSSP, BFS, HITS graph algorithms based on the VGL API will be able to operate on different VGL-supported architectures with the specification of proper compilation flags.

Scripts to perform the automatic downloading of input data, the compilation of the required algorithms for the target architecture, as well as the submission of performance measurements and performance results, were added to the VGL build. These modifications will be described in the following section in detail.

5   Developed Benchmarking System

During the course of this project, the VGL framework was extended with a set of interfaces for automatically collecting performance data. These interfaces execute the selected graph algorithms (PR, BFS, SSSP, HITS) on specified input data on VGL-supported architectures. Afterwards, the interfaces automatically send the results to the rating server, which in turn creates a rating based on the ranking method described in Sect. 3.

The general scheme of the developed benchmarking system is illustrated in Fig. 1.

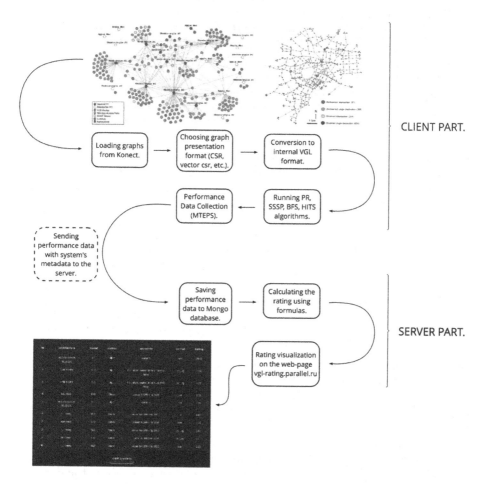

Fig. 1. Scheme of the developed benchmarking system: the client side is implemented via VGL scripts and interfaces, while the server part is responsible for data storage and rating visualization.

As shown in Fig. 1, the developed system has client and server parts.

Client Part: On the architecture being benchmarked, the user launches a Python script provided inside VGL, which downloads graphs from the Konect collection [12], converts them into the internal VGL format, launches four graph algorithms and then collects performance data in TEPS [15]. Afterwards, the performance data is uploaded to the rating server.

Server Part: The server executes two scripts: the first is responsible for receiving data from the client and storing the received data in MongoDB [8], while the second is responsible for calculating the rating based on user-specified parameters and visualizing it as an HTML page.

Next, we will describe these two parts in detail, following the process of benchmarking a specific architecture chosen by the user, submitting the obtained benchmarking results and processing these results by the rating system.

First of all, the user launches the Python script submit.py on the client side, which automatically performs the following actions.

At the beginning, the type of the architecture is determined: presence of GPUs, vector edges of the SX-Aurora TSUBASA system [11], vendor, type and generation of the CPU, etc. Depending on the obtained values, the evaluated graph algorithm implementations are compiled according to the obtained information (using specific compilers, optimizations flags, etc.). To achieve this, we implemented in VGL a fairly large database of recommended compilation and optimization settings for many widely used supercomputing architectures.

Afterwards, all graphs needed for testing are downloaded from the Konect collection, and synthetic graphs are generated using random graph generators implemented in the VGL framework.

After downloading, all graphs are divided into groups by the categories defined in Sect. 3.1. When generating a rating, the user will be able to specify influence weights for each of the groups.

The user can provide additional parameters to the submity.py script to launch graph algorithms on specific subsets of input graphs: Tiny, Tiny + Small, Tiny + Small + Medium, Tiny + Small + Medium + Large (in other words, a gradual increase in the graphs used). These modes allow one to accelerate the benchmarking process, as well as to solve the problem when certain large graphs cannot be stored in the memory of the evaluated architecture, which can be the case for NVIDIA GPUs or personal computers where the memory is limited by around 16–32 GB. It is important to emphasize that if some graph is not used for testing, the obtained rating of the benchmarked architecture will be lower as if the performance obtained on these graphs was equal to zero.

Once downloaded, the graphs are converted to an edge list format and stored on the disk as binary files. Then, the optimized routines of the VGL framework are used to load and convert these graphs into a specific optimized representation, namely, CSR, VectorCSR [4], segmented or clusterized CSR [19], etc. Using the optional parameters of the submit.py script, the user can select a specific graph storage format for the evaluated architecture, which they think would be more suitable. By default, VGL also provides a recommendation database, which format should be used for a specific architecture (similarly to compilation and optimization options).

Afterwards, all four algorithms are executed on all converted graphs, the performance data is collected and saved as an array of dictionaries. Finally, this performance data is packed and sent to the rating server. An offline export of the performance data is implemented as an option. This is necessary in the case when the benchmarked system does not have access to the Internet, which is a frequent situation for supercomputer nodes. In both cases, the generated array of dictionaries containing the performance results is converted to a stream of bytes using the pickle library and sent by the client to the server using the socket library, where the received stream of bytes is converted back to a Python dictionary.

The rating server processes the received performance data in the following way.

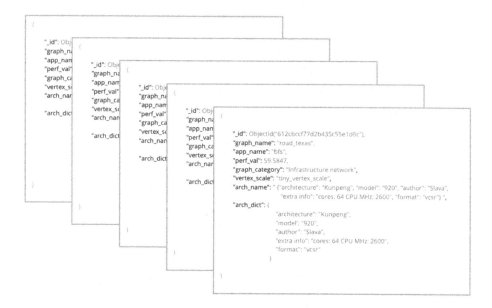

Fig. 2. Structure of the data saved in the Mongo database.

The received data is saved to the Mongo database in the format shown in Fig. 2. We decided to use a non-relational (NoSQL) Mongo database due to the fact that in MongoDB, each collection object can contain different fields, while in SQL databases, tables have a strongly typed schema. In our project, it allows providing additional information, i.e. new graphs, algorithms, types of the evaluated system during the development of the project, while remaining back compatibility with older data.

After the data is saved, a specific method for calculating the rating (described in Sect. 3) is used. The developed system is very flexible, and additional rating formulas can be easily provided. In the future, we plan to support data visualization based on various rating formulas according to the user's choice.

A web page[2] written in html, css and javascript is used to visualize the results. The interaction of Python scripts and web pages is implemented using the Flask web framework.

---

[2] vgl-rating.parallel.ru.

6 Using the Developed Benchmarking System to Rank Modern Supercomputing Platforms

Table 3. Rating results used to make observations. Each cell after the name of the architecture provides its rating value, which shows how often the given architecture is better than the others.

Rating position	Overall rating	BFS algorithm	LARGE size
1	NEC SX-Aurora TSUABSA, 37.4	NEC SX-Aurora TSUABSA, 32	NVIDIA GPU V100, 36.25
2	NVIDIA GPU V100, 31.23	Intel Xeon 6140, 22.75	NVIDIA GPU P100, 31
3	NVIDIA GPU P100, 19.86	NVIDIA GPU V100,16.25	Intel Xeon 6140, 25.5
4	Intel Xeon 6140, 12	Kunpeng 920, 16	Kunpeng 920, 22
5	Kunpeng 920, 8.81	NVIDIA GPU P100, 15	NEC SX-Aurora TSUABSA, 19
6	Intel Xeon 6240, 5.45	Intel Xeon 6126, 10.75	Intel Xeon 6240, 7.75
7	Intel Xeon 6126, 4.35	Intel Xeon 6240, 9.25	Intel Xeon 6126, 7.5

Based on the developed rating, the following modern supercomputer architectures were ranked:

1. Vector processors NEC SX-Aurora TSUBASA
2. Graphics accelerators NVIDIA (P100, V100, etc.)
3. Central processing units Intel Xeon (Skylake, Cascade Lake)
4. Central processing units A64FX
5. Central processing units ARM Kunpeng.

The following observations were made according to the results provided in Table 3:

1. Kunpeng 920 works faster on infrastructure graphs than Intel Xeon 6140, but slower on all the others.

2. NVIDIA GPUs process social graphs faster than NEC SX-Aurora TSUBASA v1.0 and all the others slower.
3. NVIDIA GPUs work faster with the PR, SSSP algorithms than NEC SX-Aurora TSUBASA v1.0 and slower with the other algorithms.
4. Intel Xeon 6140 is faster on the BFS algorithm than NVIDIA GPU P100 and V100 and slower on the other algorithms.
5. Kunpeng 920 is faster on BFS than Intel Xeon 6140 and slower on all the others.
6. NVIDIA GPUs are faster on Large graphs than NEC SX-Aurora TSUBASA v1.0 and slower on the other graph sizes.
7. Kunpeng 920 and Intel Xeon 6140 are faster on Large graphs than NEC SX-Aurora TSUBASA v1.0 and slower on the other graph sizes.

7 Conclusion

In this paper, we proposed a novel rating system that evaluates the performance of target architectures based on the performance of multiple graph algorithms: PR, SSSP, BFS and HITS. At the same time, our rating uses different types of input graphs: infrastructure, social, rating, synthetic, which in aggregate makes the proposed rating more representative than its existing counterparts.

The proposed rating system is implemented on top of the architecture-independent VGL framework, which makes the benchmarking and submission process as simple as running a single script provided in VGL.

Information about our rating is currently available on the vgl-rating.parallel.ru website. In addition, everyone can easily contribute to the VGL framework, freely available at vgl.parallel.ru, by implementing support for new architectures. We strongly believe that the proposed rating will be frequently used to compare modern supercomputing architectures, gradually turning into a larger project.

Acknowledgements. The reported study presented in all sections, excluding Sect. 5, was funded by RFBR and JSPS according to research project No. 21-57-50002 and Grant number JPJSBP120214801. The work presented in Sect. 5 was supported by the Russian Ministry of Science and Higher Education, agreement No. 075-15-2019-1621.

References

1. NEC SX-Aurora TSUBASA C/C++ compiler user's guide. https://www.hpc.nec/documents/sdk/pdfs/g2af01e-C++UsersGuide-016.pdf. Accessed 12 May 2020
2. Afanasyev, I.V.: Developing an architecture-independent graph framework for modern vector processors and NVIDIA GPUs. Supercomput. Front. Innov. **7**(4), 49–61 (2021). https://doi.org/10.14529/jsfi200404
3. Afanasyev, I.V., Voevodin, V.V., Komatsu, K., Kobayashi, H.: Distributed graph algorithms for multiple vector engines of NEC SX-aurora TSUBASA systems. Supercomput. Front. Innov. **8**(2), 95–113 (2021)

4. Afanasyev, I.V., Voevodin, V.V., Komatsu, K., Kobayashi, H.: VGL: a high-performance graph processing framework for the NEC SX-Aurora TSUBASA vector architecture. J. Supercomput. **77**(8), 8694–8715 (2021). https://doi.org/10.1007/s11227-020-03564-9
5. Antonov, A., Nikitenko, D., Voevodin, V.V.: Algo500-a new approach to the joint analysis of algorithms and computers. Lobachevskii J. Math. **41**(8), 1435–1443 (2020)
6. Chakrabarti, D., Zhan, Y., Faloutsos, C.: R-MAT: a recursive model for graph mining. In: Proceedings of the 2004 SIAM International Conference on Data Mining, pp. 442–446. SIAM (2004). https://doi.org/10.1137/1.9781611972740.43
7. Feng, W.C., Cameron, K.: The green500 list: encouraging sustainable supercomputing. Computer **40**(12), 50–55 (2007)
8. Győrödi, C., Győrödi, R., Pecherle, G., Olah, A.: A comparative study: MongoDB vs. MySQL. In: 2015 13th International Conference on Engineering of Modern Electric Systems (EMES), pp. 1–6. IEEE (2015)
9. Khorasani, F., Vora, K., Gupta, R., Bhuyan, L.N.: CuSha: vertex-centric graph processing on GPUs. In: Proceedings of the 23rd International Symposium on High-Performance Parallel and Distributed Computing, pp. 239–252 (2014)
10. Kirk, D., et al.: Nvidia CUDA software and GPU parallel computing architecture. In: ISMM, vol. 7, pp. 103–104 (2007)
11. Komatsu, K., Watanabe, O., Musa, A., et al.: Performance evaluation of a vector supercomputer SX-Aurora TSUBASA. In: Proceedings of the International Conference for High Performance Computing, Networking, Storage, and Analysis, Dallas, TX, USA, 11–16 November 2018, SC 2018, pp. 54:1–54:12. IEEE (2018). https://doi.org/10.1109/SC.2018.00057
12. Kunegis, J.: Konect: the koblenz network collection. In: Proceedings of the 22nd International Conference on World Wide Web, pp. 1343–1350 (2013)
13. Marjanović, V., Gracia, J., Glass, C.W.: Performance modeling of the HPCG benchmark. In: Jarvis, S.A., Wright, S.A., Hammond, S.D. (eds.) PMBS 2014. LNCS, vol. 8966, pp. 172–192. Springer, Cham (2015). https://doi.org/10.1007/978-3-319-17248-4_9
14. Meuer, H.W.: The top500 project. looking back over 15 years of supercomputing experience (2008)
15. Murphy, R.C., Wheeler, K.B., Barrett, B.W., Ang, J.A.: Introducing the graph 500. Cray Users Group (CUG) **19**, 45–74 (2010)
16. Shun, J., Blelloch, G.E.: Ligra: a lightweight graph processing framework for shared memory. In: ACM SIGPLAN Notices, vol. 48, pp. 135–146. ACM (2013)
17. Voevodin, V., Antonov, A., Dongarra, J.: AlgoWiki: an open encyclopedia of parallel algorithmic features. Supercomput. Front. Innov. **2**(1), 4–18 (2015)
18. Wang, Y., Davidson, A., Pan, Y., et al.: Gunrock: a high-performance graph processing library on the GPU. In: Proceedings of the 21st ACM SIGPLAN Symposium on Principles and Practice of Parallel Programming, pp. 1–12. ACM (2016). https://doi.org/10.1145/2851141.2851145
19. Zhang, Y., Kiriansky, V., Mendis, C., Zaharia, M., Amarasinghe, S.P.: Optimizing cache performance for graph analytics. arXiv abs/1608.01362 (2016)

HPC TaskMaster – Task Efficiency Monitoring System for the Supercomputer Center

Pavel Kostenetskiy[✉], Artemiy Shamsutdinov, Roman Chulkevich,
Vyacheslav Kozyrev, and Dmitriy Antonov

HSE University, 11, Pokrovsky boulevard, Moscow 109028, Russia
pkostenetskiy@hse.ru

Abstract. This paper is devoted to the monitoring system *HPC Task-Master* developed at the HSE University for the *cHARISMa* cluster. This system automatically evaluates the efficiency of performing tasks of HPC cluster users and identifies inefficient tasks, thereby significantly saving the expensive machine time. In addition, users can view reports on completing their tasks, along with inferences about their work and interactive graphs. Particular attention in this paper is paid to determining the effectiveness of the task – the system allows the administrator to personally configure the criteria for evaluating the effectiveness of the task without the need for changes in the source code. The system is developed using open-source software and is publicly available for use on other clusters.

Keywords: HPC cluster · efficiency · monitoring

1 Introduction

A task efficiency monitoring system is essential for detecting incorrectly started calculations that entail the insufficiently efficient use of cluster resources. This paper describes a new task performance monitoring system, *HPC TaskMaster*, developed at the HSE University for the *cHARISMa (Computer of HSE for Artificial Intelligence and Supercomputer Modeling)* cluster.

The developed system allows users to view reports on the performance of their tasks together with interactive execution schedules and automatically identify tasks that worked inefficiently. Having access to the results of the analysis, users can run their tasks more efficiently in the future, which will significantly save the machine time of the cluster.

In addition, the system will allow the administrators of the cluster to collect statistics about user tasks, which was previously unavailable.

L. Sokolinsky and M. Zymbler (Eds.): PCT 2022, CCIS 1618, pp. 17–29, 2022.
https://doi.org/10.1007/978-3-031-11623-0_2

The most common examples of the inefficient usage of cluster resources are:

- allocation of insufficient or excessive resources for a task;
- running a non-parallel task on multiple CPU cores or GPUs;
- allocation of the compute node capacity without starting calculations.

The following requirements were defined for the design of the task performance monitoring system.

1. The system should collect the following data for each task:
   - utilization of specific CPU cores allocated for the task;
   - utilization of GPUs allocated for the task;
   - GPU memory utilization;
   - GPU power consumption;
   - utilization of RAM created by the task;
   - file system usage.
2. The system must analyze the collected data and use it to determine whether the task worked effectively.
3. The system must provide users with access to the list of completed tasks and reports on their completion using a web application.

The rest of this paper is organized as follows. A comparison of different monitoring systems is carried out in Sect. 2. In Sect. 3, the architecture of the system is described. The detection of inefficient user tasks is considered in Sect. 4. User statistics are provided in Sect. 5. Finally, Sect. 6 shows the conclusions of this work.

2   Related Work

The key feature of the HSE cluster is how it allocates resources for user tasks. Instead of allocating the entire compute node for one task, the user is given a certain number of processor cores and GPUs. As a result, several dozen tasks can be performed on the compute node at once, thus optimizing cluster resources. Due to this feature, ready-made solutions for monitoring system resources, such as Nagios and Zabbix, are not suitable for this cluster. *cHARISMa* already has a monitoring system of its own [4], however, it is designed to display only the global usage across the whole cluster and its nodes.

Since one of the HSE University goals is to provide cluster users with a secure system in the HSE University environment, a new monitoring system was built using open-source monitoring tools. Chan [3], Wegrzynek [11], Kychkin [6], Safonov [10] describe how using a combination of programs such as *Telegraf*, *InfluxDB* and *Grafana* allows one to quickly set up and run a cluster resource monitoring system. In [2,3], it is also described how the *Slurm* plugin acct_gather enables to collect metrics for *Slurm* tasks, which is precisely the data required for a task efficiency monitoring system. Since all programs, except *Telegraf*, are already installed on *cHARISMa*, this approach can be used to monitor tasks on the cluster.

The development of LIKWID Monitoring Stat [9], a task monitoring system using InfluxDB, Grafana and built-in LIKWID tools for monitoring tasks on the cluster, also draws attention. For each task, a dashboard is created from ready-made JSON templates, which allows creating personalized graphs for each task. The disadvantages of using the LIKWID Monitoring Stack on the HSE Cluster include the need to use LIKWID tools for the system to operate and the lack of a web interface for the system in addition to Grafana, which makes the system inconvenient for using on a cluster with a large number of users and tasks.

In addition to monitoring cluster resources, the system must analyze the effectiveness of user tasks. A well-known system for creating reports on the effectiveness of tasks is JobDigest [7,8]. It analyzes the collected integral values and, based on them, applies a tag to the task describing the property of the task (for example, "low GPU utilization"). Although using tags is convenient for searching and filtering tasks, it is not always possible to provide an overall picture of the effectiveness of the task using tags alone.

Summarizing all the above, we can conclude that there is no ready-made task monitoring system fitting the individual characteristics of the cHARISMa cluster, which can be integrated into the HSE University environment. It is necessary to develop its own software system for evaluating the effectiveness of tasks, which can be flexibly configured for specific types of user tasks, delimit access for cluster users, and take into account the compliance of tasks with registered scientific and educational projects. As the basis of the system, it is worth using the open-source software *Telegraf*, *InfluxDB* and *Grafana*.

3   System Architecture

This section describes the monitoring infrastructure of the *HPC TaskMaster* system, shown in Fig. 1.

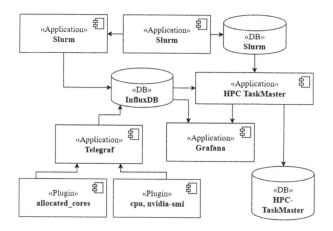

Fig. 1. Diagram of the system components

The *Slurm* task scheduler is used to run tasks on the cluster. The main data of *Slurm* tasks is stored in the *MySQL* relational database using the background process *slurm database (slurmdbd)*, and the task metrics are written to the *InfluxDB* time series database using the plugin *acct_gather*. This plugin collects memory and filesystem usage (read/write) for each task.

The required metrics of utilizing specific CPU cores and GPUs are collected with the *Telegraf* daemon, which has built-in plugins for these metrics. Thus, having the CPU and GPU IDs assigned to the task, the system can collect metrics for the components and, therefore, distinguish utilization for different tasks on one node. Additional metrics are collected using developed plugins in Python.

The collected metrics are stored in the *InfluxDB* database. InfluxDB was chosen as a time-series database because of Telegraf support and Slurm acct_gather plugin support, which allows one to store all the required metrics in one database.

Grafana is used as a tool for visualizing graphs on the *cHARISMa* cluster. *Grafana* provides great opportunities for configuring and formatting charts and also has support for creating them using the API. This API allows automating the creation of graphs for each task. New graphs for each task are created using JSON templates. Based on the available data about the task, when the user requests it, graphs are automatically built in Grafana. The created graphs are displayed on the system's website using iframe technology, where the user can interactively view the graphs for the period of task execution. In addition, the system creates graphs for both completed and running tasks. Thereby, the user can observe the work of his task in real time.

The advantage of using a combination of *Telegraf*, *InfluxDB* and *Grafana* is the ability to install and configure these tools on any cluster. Moreover, these tools make the monitoring system quite flexible – additional data for the system can be collected using the built-in plugins of *Telegraf* or developed ones.

It is important to pay attention to the fact that the *HPC TaskMaster* system has a negligible impact on the performance of compute nodes; the installed Telegraf daemon uses only 0.03% of the overall CPU performance. In addition to Telegraf, another source of the computing cluster load is InfluxDB. Installed on the head node, InluxDB uses an average of 5 GB of storage per month. To free up storage, a retention policy that compresses metrics older than 6 months is used.

The *HPC TaskMaster* system is developed on Django, a Python web framework that has a large number of available packages and a wide range of tools for developing web applications, which allows one to develop a monitoring system using Telegraf, InfluxDB and Grafana. In addition, Django has a built-in administration panel through which the administrator can configure the monitoring system himself without making changes to the source code of the program.

The task performance monitoring system works according to the following principles:

- metrics are collected on each compute node using Telegraf and stored in the InfluxDB database on the head node. Metrics from the *acct_gather* plugin are also stored in InfluxDB;
- the system updates its local MySQL database by comparing its tasks with those from the Slurm database;
- while the task is running, aggregated metrics are collected for it from the InfluxDB database with a certain period;
- if the task is completed, its aggregated metrics are collected for the last time;
- the collected aggregated metrics are analyzed by the system, and an inference about the efficiency of the task is generated.

4 Detecting Inefficient Tasks

The user interacts with the HSE high-performance computing cluster [4] by launching tasks through the SLURM workload manager. A task is a set of user processes for which the workload manager allocates computing resources (compute nodes, CPUs, GPUs, etc.) Each launch of the user's program for execution generates a new task, which is collected in the database and analyzed.

Here we define task efficiency as the usage of allocated resources above a certain threshold.

4.1 Collected Data

HPC TaskMaster collects two types of data about running tasks on the HPC cluster:

1) parameters characterizing the running task;
2) metrics that characterize the execution of the task.

Parameters. Table 1 shows the task parameters and their type.

Metrics
Table 2 shows the metrics collected during the execution of the task. The metrics form a time series θ_i. $\Theta = \{\theta_i\}$ denotes the set of all-time series of the task.

The frequency of collecting metrics can be adjusted and selected in such a way as to obtain sufficiently detailed information about the task without overloading the system with data collection and storage.

4.2 Data Processing

Aggregated Metrics
To simplify the analysis, aggregated metrics $\Lambda^k = (\lambda_1^k, \cdots, \lambda_m^k)$ are calculated for each time series [5]. They include the minimum, maximum, average, median and standard deviations. In addition to them, the tuple Λ includes the average load of each node and the combined average load of the nodes.

Table 1. Parameters of the task

№	Parameter	Type
1	ID	Integer
2	Task name	String
3	Status	
4	Launch command	
5	Type of compute nodes	
6	Number of compute nodes	Integer
7	Number of CPU cores	
8	Number of GPUs	
9	Exit code	
10	User ID	
11	Project ID	
12	Start date and time	Date
13	End date and time	

Table 2. Collected metrics and collection frequency

№	Metrics	Frequency, seconds	Units of measurement
1	CPU cores usage by the user		percentages
2	CPU cores usage by the system		
3	GPU usage		
4	RAM usage	10	
5	GPU memory usage		kilobyte
7	GPU power consumption		watt
8	File System access	60	megabyte

Tags

Since the task parameters are a heterogeneous set of data (integers, strings, dates), to simplify their analysis, a system of tags, i.e., "labels" indicating the type of task, execution time, and other properties of the task, is introduced. Table 3 contains a list of tags currently available in the system. Additional tags can be developed and implemented into the system.

The tuple $T^k = (\tau_1^k, \ldots, \tau_n^k)$ is assigned to the task with the ID k, where n is the number of tags in the system. The τ_i element corresponds to the indicator of the i tag and takes the value 1 if all conditions are met and the tag is assigned to the task, and 0 otherwise.

Indicators

To determine if the task is working inefficiently, it is necessary to evaluate the disposal of the components involved in the task. To do this, the concept of *indicator of problems* is introduced.

Table 3. List of tags

№	Tags	Type
1	Jupyter-notebook task	
2	LAMMPS task	
3	VASP task	
4	Allocation of resources for calculations	String
5	The task lasted less than a minute	
6	The task was completed with an error	

Indicators, dimensionless values inversely proportional to the value of the metrics, are used to evaluate the disposal of the components involved in the task.

Indicators take a value from 0 (with the full use of allocated resources) to 1 (otherwise). For example, the value of the indicator l_j is calculated from the aggregated metric $\lambda_j^k \in \Lambda^k$ using formula (1).

$$l_j^k = 1 - \frac{\lambda_j^k - a_j}{b_j - a_j}, \quad l_j \in [0, 1], \tag{1}$$

where a_j, b_j are the admin defined parameters referring to the minimum and maximum possible values of the j-th element of the aggregated metrics.

Indicators are placed in the tuple of indicators $L^k = (l_1^k, \ldots, l_m^k)$.

The list of currently available indicators is presented in Table 4. Additional indicators can be developed and implemented into the system. The number of indicators for a specific task depends on the number of cores, compute nodes and GPUs used.

Table 4. List of indicators

№	Indicators
1	Low average CPU usage
2	Low average CPU core usage
3	Low average GPU usage
4	Low GPU memory usage
5	The task was completed with an error

4.3   Inferences

To help users to interpret the results, the system has a set of inferences $\Phi = (\phi_i)$. Inferences are the result of the analysis of the task.

Different requirements for tags and indicator values are set for each inference. An inference is assigned to the task when all the conditions are met. Several inferences can correspond to one task at once.

Denote the union of tuples of indicators L and tags T as

$$N^k = (l_1^k, \ldots, l_n^k, \tau_1^k, \ldots, \tau_m^k). \tag{2}$$

Let Ω_i be a set of conditions for the output of ϕ_i to the elements of the tuple N^k.

Then we can match the set C^k to each problem:

$$C^k = \{\phi_i \in \Phi : \Pi_{\omega \in \Omega_i} \mathbb{1}_\omega(N^k) = 1\}, \tag{3}$$

where $\mathbb{1}_\omega$ is the indicator function equal to 1 if the condition $\omega \in \Omega_i$ is met. In other words, the tuple C^k contains the inferences assigned to the task.

4.4   Example

Let us consider a computational task performed on the *cHARISMa* supercomputer using 176 cores and 16 NVIDIA Tesla V100 GPU accelerators on 4 compute nodes. Table 5 shows the parameters of the task.

Table 5. Parameters of the task

№	Parameter	Value
1	ID	405408
2	Task name	SimpleRun
3	Status	Successful
4	Exit code	0
5	Launch command	sbatch run_task.sh
6	User ID	2000
7	Project ID	32
8	Start date and time	November 11, 2021 10:13:28
9	End date and time	November 12, 2021 13:19:09
10	Type of compute nodes	type_a
11	Number of compute nodes	4
12	Number of CPU cores	176
13	Number of GPUs	16

The aggregated metrics across all compute nodes for the example task are shown in Table 6.

Table 6. Aggregated metrics by node

№	Metrics	Value
1	Avg. load of cores on comp. node cn-001	99.36
2	Avg. load of cores on comp. node cn-002	99.11
3	Avg. load of cores on comp. node cn-003	99.15
4	Avg. load of cores on comp. node cn-004	99.51
5	Avg. load of comp. nodes	99.28
7	Avg. utilization of GPUs on comp. node cn-001	71.62
8	Avg. utilization of GPUs on comp. node cn-002	71.6
9	Avg. utilization of GPUs on comp. node cn-003	71.15
10	Avg. utilization of GPUs on comp. node cn-004	71.8
11	Avg. utilization of GPUs	71.54

Table 7 shows the aggregated metrics of the time series for compute node cn-001. Data for compute nodes cn-002, cn-003, cn-004 are not shown to save space.

Table 7. Aggregated metrics of compute node cn-001

	Node cn-001	Min	Avg	Max
	CPU usage by the **system**			
1	Core 1	0	0.12	11.4
⋮	⋮	⋮	⋮	⋮
44	Core 44	0	0.13	7
	CPU usage by the **user**			
45	Core 1	0	98.9	100
⋮	⋮	⋮	⋮	⋮
88	Core 44	0	99.8	100
89	Average usage of cores on the node		99.36	
	GPU usage №:0			
90	Utilization	0	71.62	99
91	Memory usage, MB	0	7095.3	8780
92	Power consumption, Watt	66	128.9	156.1
⋮	⋮	⋮	⋮	⋮
	GPU usage №:3			
99	Utilization	0	71.61	99
100	Memory usage, MB	0	7095.3	8780
101	Power consumption, Watt	66	129	155.9
102	RAM usage, MB	0.35	128.29	715.44
	File system access, GB			
103	Read	0	141389.39	288706.41
104	Write	0	1302.76	2753.31

Tags of the Task

Based on the parameters of the task from Table 5 and the tags from Table 3, no tag will be assigned to task *405408*, since it is completed without an error and is not the launch of one of the packages. Therefore, the tuple of task tags will have the form $T^{405408} = (0, 0, 0, 0, 0, 0)$.

Indicators of the Task

Based on the data from Tables 6, 7, the system calculates the values of the indicators shown in Table 8.

Table 8. List of indicators

N	Indicator	Value
Compute node **cn-001**		
1	Core 1	0.011
⋮	⋮	⋮
44	Core 44	0.002
207	GPU №:0 utilization	0.284
⋮	⋮	⋮
210	GPU №:3 utilization	0.284
223	GPU №:0 memory usage	0.778
⋮	⋮	⋮
226	GPU №:3 memory usage	0.778
⋮	⋮	⋮
Compute node **cn-004**		
205	Core 1	0.011
⋮	⋮	⋮
206	Core 40	0.002
207	GPU №:0 utilization	0.279
⋮	⋮	⋮
208	GPU №:4 utilization	0.28
209	GPU №:0 memory usage	0.779
⋮	⋮	⋮
210	GPU №:3 memory usage	0.778
Summary		
239	Avg. load of cores on node **cn-001**	0.006
240	Avg. load of cores on node **cn-002**	0.009
241	Avg. load of cores on node **cn-003**	0.008
242	Avg. load of cores on node **cn-004**	0.005
243	Avg. load of nodes	0.007
244	Avg. utilization of GPUs on node **cn-001**	0.284
245	Avg. utilization of GPUs on node **cn-002**	0.284
246	Avg. utilization of GPUs on node **cn-003**	0.289
247	Avg. utilization of GPUs on node **cn-004**	0.282
248	Avg. utilization of GPUs	0.285

Inferences of the Task

After the previous steps, we get a tuple

$$N^{405408} = (l_1, \ldots, l_{202}, \tau_1, \ldots, \tau_6)$$

As an example, let us consider the three outputs presented in Table 9.

Table 9. Inferences

ϕ_i	Inference	Conditions	Cond. is met
1	Successful task	$l_i \le 0.5$, $i = 1, \cdots, 248$	Yes
		$\tau_i = 0$, $i = 5, 6$	Yes
2	Task completed with an error	$\tau_5 = 1$	No
3	Inefficient CPU usage	$l_i > .5\, i = 1, \cdots, 206, 239, \cdots, 243$	No
4	GPU is not used	$l_i \le 0.5$, $i = 1, \cdots, 206, 211, \cdots, 215$	No
		$l_i > 0.8$, $i = 207, \cdots, 238, 244, \cdots, 248$	No

Based on the tuple N^{405408}, the system will associate the set $C^{405408} = \{\phi_1\}$ with task *405408*, since the task is executed without errors and all resources are used.

An example of the task report with an inference of inefficient salloc usage is shown in Fig. 2.

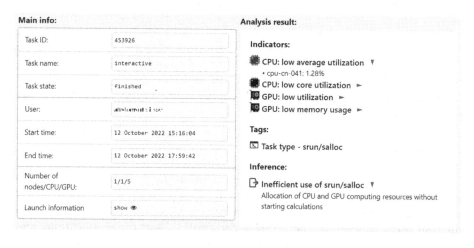

Fig. 2. Task report

5 User Statistics

System administrators have access to inference statistics for each cluster user for a selected period of time. An example of statistics is shown in Fig. 3. Using this pie chart, administrators can understand which types of tasks are causing difficulties for the user. After determining the problem that the user has encountered, he can get a personal consultation to solve this problem.

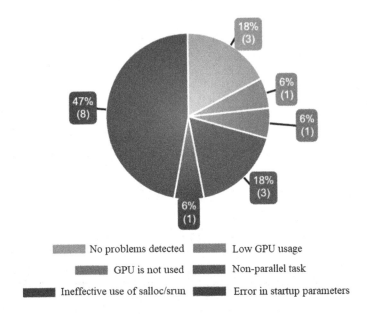

Fig. 3. Graphs of the utilization of computing resources by the task

Statistics of the most active users of the cluster with the lowest percentage of effective tasks are compiled monthly; personal consultations are held on the basis of the statistics. By tracking trends in user efficiency by month, we can conclude how the *HPC TaskMaster* system can increase the efficiency of using cluster resources.

6   Conclusions

The developed task performance monitoring system, *HPC TaskMaster*, is a powerful tool that provides all the necessary information (main information, aggregated metrics, graphs, and inferences) about tasks in one place. This system will help users to identify the problem for existing scientific applications and applications of their development, thereby simplifying work with the cluster for users, allowing them to perform scientific calculations faster and more efficiently in the future.

HPC TaskMaster is constantly evolving and improving. Among the future directions for development are:

– monitoring the effectiveness of individual categories of applications using machine learning tools;

- adding new types of indicators and tags to generate new inferences;
- smart recognition of the type of running application;
- development of a module for notifying users about the launch of inefficient tasks by them.

HPC TaskMaster is available to all cluster users of *cHARISMa* via the personal account of the supercomputer complex. *HPC TaskMaster* is also available for public use [1], and any suggestions for improving the project are greatly appreciated.

The research was performed using the *cHARISMa* HPC cluster of the HSE University [4].

References

1. Open Source/HPC TaskMaster GitLab. https://git.hpc.hse.ru/open-source/hpc-taskmaster
2. Slurm Workload Manager - acct_gather.conf. https://slurm.schedmd.com/acct_gather.conf.html
3. Chan, N.: A resource utilization analytics platform using grafana and telegraf for the Savio supercluster. In: ACM International Conference Proceeding Series. Association for Computing Machinery (2019). https://doi.org/10.1145/3332186.3333053
4. Kostenetskiy, P.S., Chulkevich, R.A., Kozyrev, V.I.: HPC resources of the higher school of economics. J. Phys. Conf. Ser. **1740**, 012050 (2021). https://doi.org/10.1088/1742-6596/1740/1/012050
5. Kraeva, Y., Zymbler, M.: Scalable algorithm for subsequence similarity search in very large time series data on cluster of phi KNL. In: Manolopoulos, Y., Stupnikov, S. (eds.) DAMDID/RCDL 2018. CCIS, vol. 1003, pp. 149–164. Springer, Cham (2019). https://doi.org/10.1007/978-3-030-23584-0_9
6. Kychkin, A., Deryabin, A., Vikentyeva, O., Shestakova, L.: Architecture of compressor equipment monitoring and control cyber-physical system based on influxdata platform. In: 2019 International Conference on Industrial Engineering, Applications and Manufacturing, ICIEAM 2019 (2019). https://doi.org/10.1109/ICIEAM.2019.8742963
7. Nikitenko, D., et al.: JobDigest - detailed system monitoring-based supercomputer application behavior analysis. In: Voevodin, V., Sobolev, S. (eds.) Supercomputing. Communications in Computer and Information Science, vol. 793, pp. 516–529. Springer, Cham (2017). https://doi.org/10.1007/978-3-319-71255-0_42
8. Nikitenko, D.A., Voevodin, V.V., Zhumatiy, S.A.: Deep analysis of job state statistics on Lomonosov-2 supercomputer. Supercomput. Front. Innov. **5**(2), 4–10 (2018). https://doi.org/10.14529/jsfi180201
9. Rohl, T., Eitzinger, J., Hager, G., Wellein, G.: Likwid monitoring stack: a flexible framework enabling job specific performance monitoring for the masses (2017). https://doi.org/10.1109/CLUSTER.2017.115
10. Safonov, A., Kostenetskiy, P., Borodulin, K., Melekhin, F.: A monitoring system for supercomputers of SUSU. In: Proceedings of Russian Supercomputing Days International Conference, vol. 1482, pp. 662–666. CEUR-WS (2015)
11. Wegrzynek, A., Vino, G.: The evolution of the ALICE O 2 monitoring system. In: EPJ Web of Conferences, vol. 245 (2020). https://doi.org/10.1051/epjconf/202024501042

Constructing an Expert System for Solving Astrophysical Problems Based on the Ontological Approach

Anna Sapetina[1], Igor Kulikov[1], Galina Zagorulko[2], and Boris Glinskiy[1]([✉])

[1] Institute of Computational Mathematics and Mathematical Geophysics SB RAS, Novosibirsk, Russia
kulikov@ssd.sscc.ru, gbm@opg.sscc.ru
[2] A.P. Ershov Institute of Informatics Systems SB RAS, Novosibirsk, Russia
gal@iis.nsk.su

Abstract. The current state of the methods for solving computational problems of mathematical physics and supercomputer systems poses a complicated task for the researcher associated with the choice of numerical methods and a multicore computer architecture for efficiently solving the problem in a reasonable time with the required accuracy. We are developing an intelligent support system for solving mathematical physics problems on supercomputers. The system includes a knowledge base and an expert system based on the ontological representation of numerical methods, computing architectures, and inference rules that connect them. This paper discusses in detail the issues related to the formation of inference rules for solving astrophysical problems. The formalization of these rules is described, and their application for constructing a solution scheme of the problem according to the user's specification is shown. An example of solving the problem of modeling the spiral instability evolution in a protostellar disk based on the proposed approach is given.

Keywords: Intelligent decision support · Inference engine · Inference rules · Astrophysics · Compute-Intensive Problems

1 Introduction

Modern astrophysics studies the physical processes of the Universe, the evolution of astronomical objects and their interaction. Mathematical models of evolving astronomical objects and their mutual influence are constructed on the basis of the observed information taking into account the gravitational and magnetic fields. It should be noted that mathematical modeling is the primary theoretical method for studying astrophysical processes. It becomes necessary to solve a numerous class of problems associated with the study of the structure, dynamics

L. Sokolinsky and M. Zymbler (Eds.): PCT 2022, CCIS 1618, pp. 30–42, 2022.
https://doi.org/10.1007/978-3-031-11623-0_3

and evolution of stellar systems, the Sun and stars, with the study of variable stars, multiple stellar systems and the physics of the interstellar medium.

A large number of parallel codes have been developed for the solution of astrophysical problems. We distinguish the following groups of codes: codes based on Smoothed Particle Hydrodynamics [1–3], grid codes [4–6], including codes using adaptive [7–9] and moving [10–12] meshes. Each implemented numerical method and code focus on a certain type of problems and are often limited to the use of classical supercomputer architectures. There are also codes adapted on graphics accelerators [13–15] and Intel Xeon Phi accelerators [16]. However, the use of any of these codes for solving a specific astrophysical problem requires significant improvement. Currently, there are no universal systems for generating astrophysical codes. Nevertheless, attempts to create such systems exist, for example, at the University of Costa Rica [17] on the basis of the EXCALC package. An intelligent system for generating astrophysical codes has not yet been created, although there are attempts to develop such a system, including those based on the ontological approach [18] and the ontological approach practice [19].

In [20,21], we presented the concept of intelligent support for solving compute-intensive problems of mathematical physics using ontology. Let us briefly list the main blocks of the proposed system and their purpose (Fig. 1). The main block of the system is a knowledge base, which includes the ontology of numerical methods and parallel algorithms and the ontology of parallel architectures and technologies, and inference rules. Based on these ontologies, an information-analytical web resource is built, it allows the user to study objects included in the knowledge base, to view the connections between them, and also add new objects to the base. The next block is an expert system, at the input of which the user submits the specification of the problem to be solved. Based on this information, the inference engine builds a scheme for solving the problem using ontology objects from the knowledge base and inference rules formulated by experts. When the solution scheme is determined, the next step is to build a parallel program for solving the problem. In this step, modules from the software library are used. If there is no suitable module, then the user will have to develop it himself. Thus, a parallel code is generated taking into account the computational algorithm and architecture of the selected computing system. The system also includes a block for simulation, which allows one to determine the optimal number of computing cores for solving the problem.

To work with ontological models, inference machines are used, they allow one to check the correctness of the ontology, operating with the names of classes, properties and entities. They can also be used to display information that is not explicitly contained in the ontology based on inference rules. There are several inference machines, the most famous of which are Pellet, HermiT, FaCT++. These inference engines are installed as plugins for the Protege ontology editor [22].

The goal of this work is to develop a crucial component for solving astrophysical problems using the ontological approach: the assignment of a group of inference rules that determine the choice of a numerical method, computing

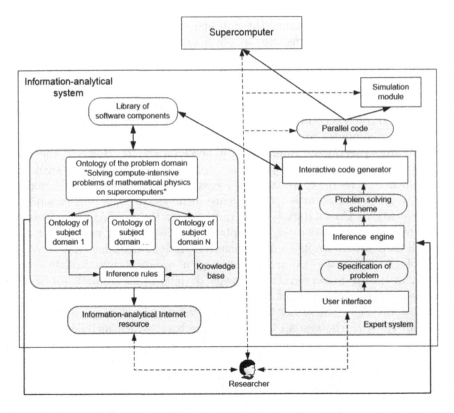

Fig. 1. Main blocks of the intelligent support system for solving compute-intensive problems of mathematical physics.

system architecture and parallel programming technology from the knowledge base. It should be noted that making these decisions depends on the user solving his problem. Therefore, speaking about a system of intelligent support, we consider only such support for decision-making that consists in the best provision of the user with the information required for its conscious adoption, as well as in the prediction of the consequences of certain options for solving the problem. In this paper, we consider inference rules for solving astrophysical problems using an intelligent support system.

2   Scheme Construction and Rules Formalization for Solving Compute-Intensive Astrophysics Problems

The general approach to constructing an ontology for intelligent support of solving compute-intensive problems of mathematical physics is described in detail in [20,21,23]. In [23], the upper level of the ontology for solving compute-intensive problems of cosmic plasma hydrodynamics is shown with templates for describing objects of the main ontology classes. The base objects of each class are listed.

In [20], an example of choosing a chain of objects from the main classes of such an ontology to solve an astrophysical problem associated with the collision of galaxies is given. This work does not consider in detail how this chain should be built to solve the problem, including the questions of setting a group of rules, on the basis of which the numerical method and architecture of the computing system are selected from those available in the ontology.

In [24], we considered a conceptual model for constructing a scheme for solving a mathematical physics problem based on the ontology approach (Fig. 2). The main blocks for the specification of the problem (user interface), the main blocks of the solution scheme, as well as the groups of rules that must be set for the automatic construction of the scheme are highlighted. These are groups of rules determining a system of equations, a numerical method, the implementation of a parallel algorithm, the properties of this algorithm, parallel computing architectures and technologies. Essentially, these are user decision points where intelligent support is needed to select the optimal solution, including from the point of view of parallel implementation. Therefore, for each subject area, it is necessary to develop a set of such rules that will allow the user to avoid mistakes when developing a parallel algorithm and a program for solving his problem.

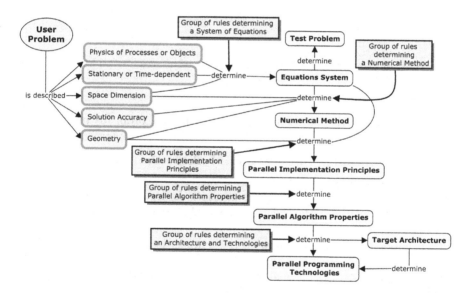

Fig. 2. Scheme of relationships between the main blocks of the user interface (highlighted in blue), problem-solution scheme blocks (highlighted in yellow), and rule groups (highlighted in green). (Color figure online)

Let us consider these issues in more detail in relation to the solution of astrophysical problems. Figure 3 demonstrates the main ontology objects at each point of choice, which can be used to solve astrophysical problems.

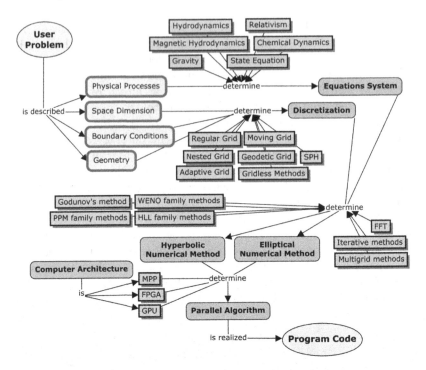

Fig. 3. Basic ontology objects for constructing a scheme of an astrophysical problem solution.

Let us formulate the rules for solving astrophysical problems in a language familiar to an expert in the mathematical modeling of astrophysical processes.

Rules for Determining Physical and Mathematical Models

1. The hydrodynamics model is used by default.
2. If there is a magnetic field, then the magnetic hydrodynamics model is used.
3. If there are velocities of the order of the speed of light, then relativistic hydrodynamics is used.
4. If it is important to take into account the composition of astrophysical objects, then chemical dynamics is added.
5. If the velocities of gravitational interaction are of the order of hydrodynamic ones, then gravity is added.
6. If radiation or a special composition of the gas is taken into account, then a special equation of state is constructed.

Rules for Determining Discretization (Grid)

1. The regular grid is used by default.
2. If a collapse-based process is modeled, then nested grids are used.
3. If the collapse process is multiple, then adaptive grids are used.

4. If it is important to take into account the angular momentum, then moving grids are used.
5. If a spherical object is modeled, then geodetic grids are used.
6. If it is necessary to take into account the collisionless component, then Smoothed Particle Hydrodynamics is used.
7. If it is important to take into account shock hydrodynamic waves, when modeling the collisionless part, gridless methods are used.

Rules for Determining a Hydrodynamic Solver

1. Godunov's method is used by default.
2. If it is necessary to take into account "carbuncle free" effects, then the method of the HLL (Harten, Lax and van Leer) family is used.
3. If it is necessary to reproduce the solution with low dissipation, then the PPM-type (piecewise parabolic method) method is used.
4. If the piecewise parabolic representation is insufficient, then the WENO-type (weighted essentially non-oscillatory) scheme is used.

Rules for Determining a Poisson Equation Solver

1. The method based on the fast Fourier transform (FFT) is used by default for regular grids.
2. If the FFT-based method is long, then multigrid methods are used.
3. If the grid is not regular, then iterative methods are used.

Rules for Determining a Parallel Architecture and Programming Technology

1. The MPP architecture is used by default as the most cross-functional.
2. For the parallel implementation of HLL family methods, Advanced Vector Extensions (AVX) for Intel processors are used.

The rules presented above were formulated by an expert and then formalized using Semantic Web tools [25]. For this purpose, in the ontology there was created the class "Problem Solving Scheme", as well as the relations "includes Mathematical Model", "includes Method", "includes Parallel Algorithm", "includes Technology", "includes Architecture Element", "includes Software Product" for linking the constructed Problem Solving Schemes with specific systems of equations, numerical methods, parallel algorithms, parallel programming technologies, parallel architectures and their elements, program codes. The description of the classes "System of Equations", "Numerical Method", etc., and examples of their entities for solving compute-intensive problems of cosmic plasma hydrodynamics are detailed earlier in [23].

The properties of the classes "Astrophysical Problem" (Fig. 4), "Astrophysical object", "Astrophysical phenomenon/process", allowing one to specify the problem to be solved by the user, were also added to the ontology.

The inference rule was formalized in the SWRL language [26], the support for which is built into the Protege editor.

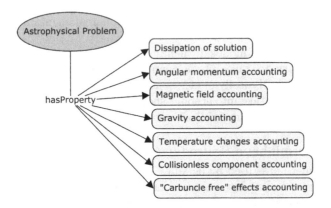

Fig. 4. Properties of an Astrophysical Problem.

3   Using Inference Rules for Intelligent Support

The developed rules were tested when constructing a scheme for solving star formation problems. Below, in an unformalized form, the specification of this class of problems is presented, and it is indicated what conclusions the system should draw.

1. The process of star formation is weakly dependent on changes in gas temperature. The main one is dynamics due to gravity. Thus, we will use the isothermal gravitational hydrodynamics model.
2. The peculiarity of the star formation problem is that it has a strong different scale: 12 orders of magnitude in spatial scales and 15 orders of magnitude in density. Thus, we will use multi-level nested grids.
3. The peculiarity of nested grids leads us to the use of iterative numerical methods for solving the Poisson equation based on the Krylov subspace. For example, the conjugate gradient method.
4. The processes of star formation are supersonic flows with reversed flotation, which leads to the need to use HLLC-type methods.
5. For the parallel implementation of such methods, a convenient solution would be to use the Fortran language and its Coarray Fortran (CAF) feature. The CAF implementation provides a sufficiently compact parallel code with a simple syntax and comparable performance to the equivalent MPI version.
6. The use of HLL family methods makes it possible to use vector calculations quite well, first of all, AVX technology. Since the isothermal hydrodynamics model is used, the conservative variables are density and the three components of the angular momentum. Thus, to organize computations, it is enough to use 4 elements in a vector implemented in AVX-256 or AVX-2 technology.

Let us note an important point of discussion regarding the use of graphics cards. Traditionally, vector computing is considered to be well suited for implementation on graphics cards. This is true for simple vector operations, however, it is important to take into account that graphics cards are primarily aimed at the vector organization of calculations, the elementary operation of which is a simple subtask, which does not imply vectorization. In the case of a family of methods like HLL, it is vector calculations with short vectors that become important, which makes the use of technologies like AVX the most promising.

A "Problem 2" object was added to the system, and its properties were set. Figure 5 shows how these properties are set in the Protege editor.

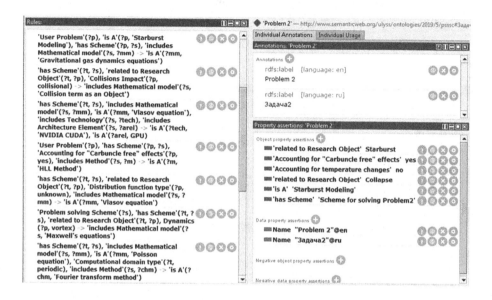

Fig. 5. Star formation problem specification.

As can be seen from Fig. 5, the problem of modeling star formation is considered. It is associated with such physical processes as Star formation and Collapse. When solving it, the temperature change is not taken into account, and "carbuncle free" effects are taken into account.

To construct the scheme, the following objects were added to the ontology: "Scheme for solving Problem2", as well as objects associated with the scheme by the inclusion relation – "Mathematical model for solving the problem", "Numerical method for solving the problem", "Parallel algorithm for solving the problem", "Parallel programming technology for solving the problem", "Architectural element for solving the problem", "Software product for solving the problem". The specific properties of these objects will be determined as a result of the operation of inference rules. Below, in a formalized form, the rules elaborated when constructing the scheme for solving the problem under consideration are presented in Fig. 6

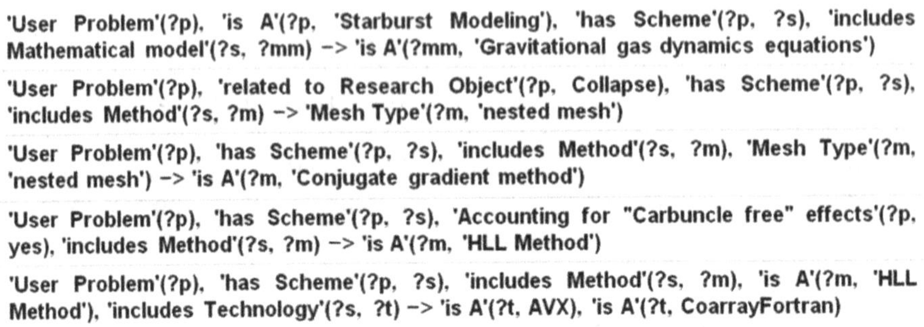

'User Problem'(?p), 'is A'(?p, 'Starburst Modeling'), 'has Scheme'(?p, ?s), 'includes Mathematical model'(?s, ?mm) --> 'is A'(?mm, 'Gravitational gas dynamics equations')

'User Problem'(?p), 'related to Research Object'(?p, Collapse), 'has Scheme'(?p, ?s), 'includes Method'(?s, ?m) --> 'Mesh Type'(?m, 'nested mesh')

'User Problem'(?p), 'has Scheme'(?p, ?s), 'includes Method'(?s, ?m), 'Mesh Type'(?m, 'nested mesh') --> 'is A'(?m, 'Conjugate gradient method')

'User Problem'(?p), 'has Scheme'(?p, ?s), 'Accounting for "Carbuncle free" effects'(?p, yes), 'includes Method'(?s, ?m) --> 'is A'(?m, 'HLL Method')

'User Problem'(?p), 'has Scheme'(?p, ?s), 'includes Method'(?s, ?m), 'is A'(?m, 'HLL Method'), 'includes Technology'(?s, ?t) --> 'is A'(?t, AVX), 'is A'(?t, CoarrayFortran)

Fig. 6. The rules elaborated when constructing the scheme for solving the star formation problem.

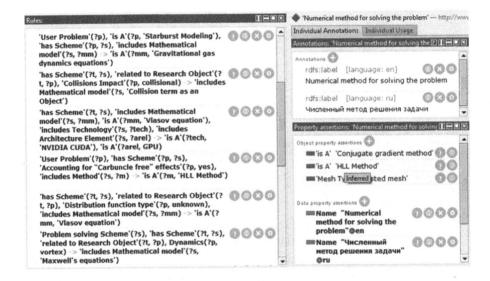

Fig. 7. Determination of methods for solving the problem.

Figure 7 shows which numerical methods and some of their properties were defined in the results of the rules operation in the Protege editor. Similarly, one can see the descriptions of other elements of the Problem Solving Scheme.

As already mentioned, the intelligent problem-solving support system includes the Information-analytical Internet resource built on the basis of the considered ontology. It allows one to present information to the user in a structured, visual form.

4 Codes and Computational Experiments

The expert rules presented in Sect. 2 are based on the author's extensive experience in developing parallel program codes for solving astrophysical problems on various computer architectures. It includes codes such as:

1. GPUPEGAS (GPU-accelerated Performance Gas Astrophysical Simulation) for the simulation of interacting galaxies [14]. A speedup of 55 times was obtained within a single GPU accelerator. The use of 60 GPU accelerators resulted in 96% parallel efficiency.
2. AstroPhi for the simulation of the dynamics of an astrophysical object on hybrid supercomputers equipped with Intel Xenon Phi KNC accelerators [16]. A single Xeon Phi yielded a 27-fold speedup. The use of 32 Xeon Phi accelerators resulted in 94% parallel efficiency.
3. Hydrodynamics code to simulate astrophysical flows on Intel Xeon Phi KNL and Intel Xeon Scalable processors based on multicomponent gravitational hydrodynamics [27]. The parallel implementation is based on a multilevel decomposition of calculations between the MPI process, OpenMP threads, and the Vectorization of one cell calculation. A performance of 173 Gflops and a 48-fold speedup are obtained on a single Intel Xeon Phi processor. 97% weak scalability is reached with 16 Intel Xeon Phi 7290 processors. 200% performance growth is achieved due to the vector instructions usage.
4. Code to simulate special relativistic hydrodynamic flows on supercomputer architectures with distributed memory based on a combination of Godunov's method and the piecewise parabolic method with a local stencil [28]. The code scalability is 94% on the NKS-30T (Intel Xeon X5670) cluster with 768 cores.

As a result of the example from Sect. 3, we present computational experiments on the spiral instability development in a protostellar disk (Fig. 8). For the calculation, we used one node with Intel Xeon Phi Knights Landing (KNL) processors (with support of vector calculations) as part of the Siberian Supercomputer Center. The calculation results agree with the observations [29].

For the computational experiment, a cold Bonnor-Ebert sphere, rotating with an equilibrium differential rotation, with a mass equal to several solar masses is considered. At the initial moment of time, a collapse occurs with an order density of one particle per cm^3. For sixty years, the sphere collapses with an increase in the central density by five orders of magnitude. For six thousand years, the core of the disk is formed with a density of 10^8 particles per cm^3, while the size of the core is on the order of two AU. For the next thousand years, the density rises by another two orders of magnitude, and the development of spiral instabilities takes place. At the time of 15 thousand years, a fairly stable core of the disk with spirals and a characteristic stellar density of the order of 0.1 g/cm^3 is formed, and the density contrast is 12 orders of magnitude.

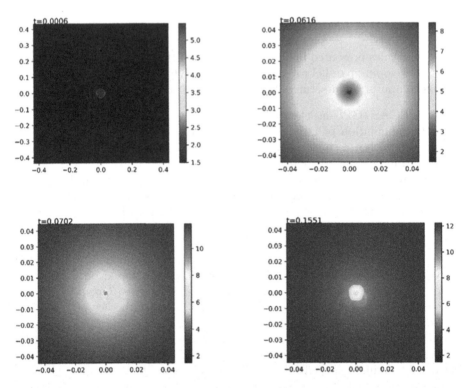

Fig. 8. Logarithm of the density distribution (g/cm^3) in the equatorial plane of the disk. Distances in thousands of AU are plotted along the axes, the unit time is chosen equal to one million years.

5   Conclusion

The article discusses inference rules for constructing a scheme to solve astrophysical problems using an intelligent decision support system based on the ontological approach. The inference rules generalize and formalize the authors' long-term experience in the development of parallel astrophysical codes for multicore computing systems. The basic rules are formulated in a common expert language and formalized using Semantic Web tools with the introduction of additional objects into the ontology. Using the example of solving the problem of the spiral instability development in a protostellar disk, the results of the inference engine operation in the Protege editor are shown. The results of numerical modeling carried out on the basis of the recommendations proposed by the system are presented. An important feature of this approach is the ability of the user to quickly select a suitable solution to the problem.

Acknowledgments. This research was conducted within budget project No. 0251-2021-0005 for ICMMG SB RAS.

References

1. Volker, S.: The cosmological simulation code GADGET-2. Mon. Not. R. Astron. Soc. **364**, 1105–34 (2005). https://doi.org/10.1111/j.1365-2966.2005.09655.x
2. Wadsley, J.W., Stadel, J., Quinn, T.: Gasoline: a flexible, parallel implementation of TreeSPH. New Astron. **9**, 137–58 (2004). https://doi.org/10.1016/j.newast.2003.08.004
3. Steinmetz, M.: GRAPESPH: cosmological smoothed particle hydrodynamics simulations with the special-purpose hardware GRAPE. Mon. Not. R. Astron. Soc. **278**, 1005–1017 (1996). https://doi.org/10.1093/mnras/278.4.1005
4. The Pencil code. pencil-code.nordita.org/references.php
5. Stone, J.M., Norman, M.L.: ZEUS-2D: a radiation magnetohydrodynamics code for astrophysical flows in two space dimensions. I. The hydrodynamic algorithms and tests. ApJS **80**, 753–90 (1992). https://doi.org/10.1086/191680
6. Stone, J.M., Gardiner, T.A., Teuben, P., Hawley, J.F., Simon, J.B.: Athena: a new code for astrophysical MHD. ApJS **178**, 137–177 (2008). https://doi.org/10.1086/588755
7. Mignone, A., Bodo, G., Massaglia, S., Matsakos, T., Tesileanu, O., Zanni, C., Ferrari, A.: PLUTO: a numerical code for computational astrophysics. ApJS **170**, 228–42 (2007). https://doi.org/10.1086/513316
8. Bryan, G.L., Norman, M.L., O'Shea, B.W., et al.: ENZO: an adaptive mesh refinement code for astrophysics. ApJS **211**, 19 (2014). https://doi.org/10.1088/0067-0049/211/2/19
9. Teyssier, R.: A new high resolution code called RAMSES. A&A **385**, 337–64 (2002). https://doi.org/10.1051/0004-6361:20011817
10. Springel, V.: E pur si muove: Galilean-invariant cosmological hydrodynamical simulations on a moving mesh. Mon. Not. R. Astron. Soc. **401**, 791–851 (2010). https://doi.org/10.1111/j.1365-2966.2009.15715.x
11. Hopkins, P.F.: GIZMO: a new class of accurate, mesh-free hydrodynamic simulation methods. Mon. Not. R. Astron. Soc. **450**, 53–110 (2015). https://doi.org/10.48550/arXiv.1409.7395
12. Murphy, J.W., Burrows, A.: BETHE-hydro: an arbitrary Lagrangian-Eulerian multi-dimensional hydrodynamics code for astrophysical simulations. ApJS **179**, 209–41 (2008). https://doi.org/10.1086/591272
13. Schive, H.-Y., Tsai, Y.-C., Chiueh, T.: Gamer: a graphic processing unit accelerated adaptive-mesh-refinement code for astrophysics. ApJS **186**, 457–84 (2010). https://doi.org/10.1088/0067-0049/186/2/457
14. Kulikov, I.: Gpupegas: a new GPU-accelerated hydrodynamic code for numerical simulations of interacting galaxies. ApJS **214**, 12 (2014). https://doi.org/10.1088/0067-0049/214/1/12
15. Schneider, E.E., Robertson, B.E.: Cholla: a new massively-parallel hydrodynamics code for astrophysical simulation. ApJS **217**, 24 (2015). https://doi.org/10.1088/0067-0049/217/2/24
16. Kulikov, I.M., Chernykh, I.G., Snytnikov, A.V., Glinskiy, B.M., Tutukov, A.V.: AstroPhi: a code for complex simulation of the dynamics of astrophysical objects using hybrid supercomputers. CPC **186**, 71–80 (2015). https://doi.org/10.1016/j.cpc.2014.09.004
17. Frutos-Alfaro, F., Carboni-Mendez, R.: Magnetohydrodynamic equations (MHD) generation code. Rev. Mat. **23**, 41–61 (2016). https://doi.org/10.15517/rmta.v23i1.22343

18. Goedbloed, J., Keppens, R., Poedts, S.: Computer simulations of solar plasmas. Space Sci. Rev. **107**, 63–80 (2003). https://doi.org/10.1023/A:1025551117617
19. Sapetina, A., Ulyanichev, I., Glinskiy, B.: The grid codes generation for solving problems of the cosmic plasma hydrodynamics on supercomputers. J. Phys. Conf. Ser. **1336**, 012012 (2019). https://doi.org/10.1088/1742-6596/1336/1/012012
20. Glinskiy, B., Zagorulko, Y., Zagorulko, G., Kulikov, I., Sapetina, A.: The creation of intelligent support methods for solving mathematical physics problems on supercomputers. Commun. Comput. Inf. Sci. **1129** 427–38 (2019). https://doi.org/10.1007/978-3-030-36592-9_35
21. Zagorulko, G., Zagorulko, Y., Glinskiy, B., Sapetina, A.: Ontological approach to providing intelligent support for solving compute-intensive problems on supercomputers. Commun. Comput. Inf. Sci. **1093**, 363–375 (2019). https://doi.org/10.1007/978-3-030-30763-9_30
22. Protege. protege.stanford.edu
23. Sapetina, A., Glinskiy, B., Zagorulko, G.: Content of ontology for solving compute-intensive problems of the cosmic plasma hydrodynamics. J. Phys. Conf. Ser. **1640**, 012019 (2020). https://doi.org/10.1088/1742-6596/1640/1/012019
24. Glinskiy, B., Sapetina, A., Snytnikov, A., Zagorulko, Y., Zagorulko, G.: The automated construction of a scheme for solving compute-intensive problems based on the ontological approach and Semantic Web technologies. J. Phys. Conf. Ser. **2099**, 012022 (2021). https://doi.org/10.1088/1742-6596/2099/1/012022
25. Hitzler, P., Krotzsch, V., Rudolph, S.: Foundations of Semantic Web Technologies. Chapman Hall, CRC, London (2009)
26. SWRL: A Semantic Web Rule Language Combining OWL and RuleML. www.w3.org/Submission/SWRL/
27. Kulikov, I., Chernykh, I., Tutukov, A.: A new hydrodynamic code with explicit vectorization instructions optimizations that is dedicated to the numerical simulation of astrophysical gas flow. I. Numerical method, tests, and model problems. ApJS **243**, 4 (2019). https://doi.org/10.3847/1538-4365/ab2237
28. Kulikov, I.: A new code for the numerical simulation of relativistic flows on supercomputers by means of a low-dissipation scheme. Comput. Phys. Commun. **257**, 107532 (2020). https://doi.org/10.1016/j.cpc.2020.107532
29. Elbakyan, V.G., Johansen, A., Lambrechts, M., Akimkin, V., Vorobyov E.I.: Gravitoviscous protoplanetary disks with a dust component - III. Evolution of gas, dust, and pebbles. A&A **637**, A5 (2020). https://doi.org/10.1051/0004-6361/201937198

HPC Resources of South Ural State University

Natalya Dolganina$^{(\boxtimes)}$ (iD), Elena Ivanova, Roman Bilenko, and Alexander Rekachinsky

South Ural State University, Chelyabinsk, Russia
{dolganinani,elena.ivanova,bilenkorv,alexander.rekachinsky}@susu.ru

Abstract. Currently, South Ural State University (SUSU) has significant achievements in supercomputer modeling, artificial intelligence and Big Data. The high-performance resources of SUSU include an energy-efficient supercomputer "Tornado SUSU" and a specialized multiprocessor complex "Neurocomputer". The "Tornado SUSU" supercomputer and the "Neurocomputer" complex are at the center of the scientific life of the University and enable complex calculations for engineering, natural and human sciences, artificial intelligence. The high-performance resources of SUSU are used in education and for calculating the tasks of the University's partners. The paper describes the "Tornado SUSU" supercomputer and "Neurocomputer" complex technical features, system and application parallel software, scientific and engineering tasks solved with the help of the SUSU resources.

Keywords: Supercomputer · Neurocomputer · Parallel storage system · Supercomputer administration · Supercomputer modeling · Neural networks

1 Introduction

South Ural State University has achieved significant results in the field of digital industry creation. Research is actively developing with the use of supercomputer modeling, artificial intelligence and Big Data. Currently, SUSU has an energy-efficient supercomputer "Tornado SUSU", which ranks 15-th in the TOP50 list of the most powerful CIS supercomputers (September 2021). Tasks in the field of artificial intelligence require high parallelism on shared memory, however, a supercomputer with a cluster architecture does not provide it. To create artificial neural networks, SUSU acquired a specialized multiprocessor complex "Neurocomputer". The neurocomputer uses powerful advanced graphics accelerators to train neural networks. SUSU's high-performance computing resources are used by more than 500 people, these are not only employees and students of South Ural State University, but also employees of external educational, scientific and industrial organizations (industrial enterprises, universities, institutes of the Russian Academy of Sciences). SUSU established the Scientific and Educational Center "Artificial

L. Sokolinsky and M. Zymbler (Eds.): PCT 2022, CCIS 1618, pp. 43–55, 2022.
https://doi.org/10.1007/978-3-031-11623-0_4

Intelligence and Quantum Technologies" (SEC AIQT) [32]. SEC AIQT employees are engaged in the administration of the high-performance resources of SUSU and scientific research in the field of supercomputer technologies, as well as provide user support.

The paper is structured as follows. Section 2 introduces the main high-performance SUSU resources installed in the SEC AIQT, such as the "SUSU Tornado supercomputer", the "Neurocomputer" complex, Panasas ActiveStor 11 data storage systems, OceanStor Dorado 3000 V6, Huawei OceanStor 5300 V5. Section 3 contains an overview of the system software used in the SEC AIQT. The application of equipment monitoring and control systems and software systems in the SEC AIQT is described. Section 4 presents the application software available to users of SUSU's high-performance resources and provides an overview of the scientific and engineering tasks being solved. Finally, Sect. 5 contains the final conclusions.

2 High Performance Resources

2.1 "Tornado SUSU" Supercomputer

The "Tornado SUSU" supercomputer is a fully liquid-cooled computing system with a performance of 473.6 Teraflops, ranked 19-th in the TOP50 list of the most powerful supercomputers in Russia (March 2022). Liquid cooling improves system energy efficiency (40–50% energy savings compared to air-cooled systems) and maximizes electronics packaging density. This makes it possible to get rid of moving parts in the computer, noise and vibration, thereby increasing the reliability and ergonomics of the system [1]. The technical features of the "Tornado SUSU" supercomputer are presented in Table 1.

The "Tornado SUSU" supercomputer is equipped with a high-performance parallel data storage system Panasas ActiveStor 11. It is designed to store initial data and user calculation results. Its peak performance is 30,886 IOPS, the write speed is 2402 MB/s, and the read speed is 3239 MB/s. Currently, more than 500 users of the supercomputer successfully use the storage; the system has been in continuous use since its installation in 2013 and has proven to be fault-tolerant and reliable.

The Panasas ActiveStor 11 storage system consists of five shelves. Four shelves contain 10 storage nodes (StorageBlade) with a capacity of 4 TB each and one control node (DirectorBlade), the fifth one consists of 11 storage nodes. The storage capacity is 204 TB, part of which is reserved for data replication. Control nodes perform the task of storing metadata and provide access to data using protocols such as NFS and CIFS. The system is configured with 7 virtual hot spare nodes, allowing to achieve operational stability in the case of a failure of up to seven disks inclusive.

The shelves in Panasas ActiveStor 11 only support the 10 Gigabit Ethernet interface. Three Panasas Ininiband routers are used to connect the system to the 40 Gb/s Infiniband QDR network, they route packets from the Infiniband QDR network to the storage network. Network load balancing is performed on compute nodes via routes to the storage system network with the same metric.

Table 1. Technical features of the "Tornado SUSU" Supercomputer

Technical features	Value
Quantity of compute nodes/ processors/coprocessors/cores	480/960/384/29184
Type of processor	Intel Xeon X5680 (Gulftown, 6 cores, 3.33 GHz)
Type of coprocessor	Intel Xeon Phi SE10X (61 cores, 1.1 GHz)
RAM	16.9 TB
Disk memory	204 TB, Panasas ActiveStor 11; 700 TB, Huawei OceanStor 5300 V5
System network	InfiniBand QDR (40 Gbit/s)
Control network	Gigabit Ethernet
Peak performance	473.6 TFlops
Operating system	Linux CentOS 6.2

2.2 "Neurocomputer" Complex

The architecture of the "Neurocomputer" complex is based on heterogeneous graphics accelerators. Thus, the "Neurocomputer" structure allows one to flexibly choose the appropriate equipment for the most efficient calculation of any task related to neural networks. The complex consists of six servers united by a common task queue, with the help of which the user gets access to the server with the architecture required for his task. The technical features of the "Neurocomputer" complex are presented in Table 2.

The architecture of the "Neurocomputer" complex is shown in Fig. 1 and consists of two Dell PowerEdge R750 GPU servers based on NVIDIA Ampere A100, three Dell PowerEdge R750 GPU servers based on NVIDIA Ampere A30, one HPE Apollo ProLiant XL270d Gen10 GPU server based on NVIDIA Tesla V100, and three Dell PowerEdge R640 management servers.

The Dell PowerEdge R750 GPU server features two NVIDIA Ampere A100 GPUs with 80 GB of VRAM, two Intel Xeon Silver 4314 processors, 192 GB of RAM and 1.9 TB of SSD storage. The Dell PowerEdge R750 GPU server based on NVIDIA Ampere A30 consists of two GPUs with 24 GB VRAM, two Intel Xeon Silver 4314 processors, 192 GB RAM and 1.9 TB SSDs. These servers are best suited for video-memory-demanding tasks and tasks that require exclusive access to the resources.

The HPE Apollo ProLiant XL270d Gen10 GPU Server is a server with eight NVIDIA Tesla V100 SXM2 GPUs (32 GB VRAM) connected by NVLink,

Table 2. Technical features of the "Neurocomputer" complex

Technical features	Value
Quantity of GPUs/ CUDA cores	18/91432
Types of GPUs	NVIDIA Ampere A100 80 GB PCI-E – 4 pcs.
	NVIDIA Ampere A30 24 GB PCI-E – 6 pcs.
	NVIDIA Tesla V100 SXM2 – 8 pcs.
Quantity of processors/cores	18/268
Types of processors	Intel Xeon Gold 6254
	(Cascade Lake, 18 Cores, 4 GHz) – 2 pcs.;
	Intel Xeon Silver 4314
	(Ice Lake, 16 Cores, 3.4 GHz) – 10 pcs.;
	Intel Xeon Silver 4214
	(Cascade Lake, 12 Cores, 3.2 GHz) – 6 pcs.
RAM	1920 GB
Storage systems	700 TB, Huawei OceanStor 5300 V5;
	46 TB, Huawei OceanStor Dorado 3000 V6 –
	Storage system based on Solid State Drives (SSD)
Communication network	Mellanox Infiniband QSFP28, Mellanox Infiniband
	SFP28, Gigabit Ethernet
Peak performance	276.4 TFlops
Operating system	Linux Centos 7.8

two Intel Xeon Gold 6254 processors, 192 GB of RAM, and 7.68 TB of SSDs in total. The server allows one to achieve maximum efficiency when parallelizing tasks on several graphics accelerators.

The complex also includes three Dell PowerEdge R640 control servers required to organize the operation of the complex. Each control server contains two Intel Xeon Silver 4214 processors and 256 GB of RAM.

Large data sets, which usually consist of many small files (images, audio and video files), are used to train neural networks. The Huawei OceanStor Dorado 3000 V6 data storage system based on solid state drives is connected to the "Neurocomputer" complex. The storage system provides maximum performance when working with files for training neural networks. This storage system performs reads, writes two orders of magnitude faster than hard drives and does not lose performance when working with a many small files.

Huawei OceanStor Dorado 3000 V6 contains two controllers that can replace each other in the event of a failure of one of them, thus ensuring uninterrupted storage operation. Each controller has one Kungpeng 920 processor and an Ascend 310 coprocessor. The processor is developed by Huawei on top of the ARM architecture, with 96 GB of cache memory. The coprocessor is designed to support service neural networks built into the storage.

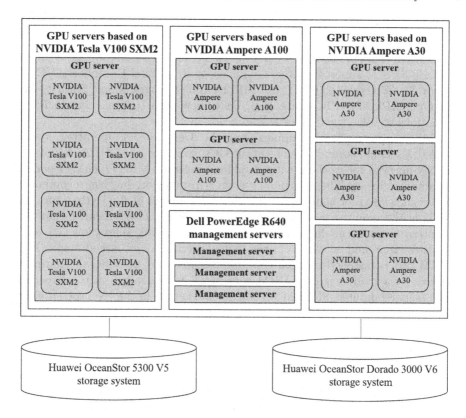

Fig. 1. Architecture of the "Neurocomputer" complex

The storage includes 12 Enterprise SSDs of 3.84 TB each. All storage components are Huawei's own design. The storage capacity is 46.08 TB with 192 GB cache memory. The effective amount of storage that users can use for their data is at least 35 TB, the rest of the space is used for storage fault tolerance.

The "Neurocomputer" complex uses the Huawei OceanStor 5300 V5 data storage system with 700 TB for long-term storage of user data and calculation results. The Huawei OceanStor storage architecture contains two controllers, each controller has one Kungpeng 920 processor with 64 GB of cache memory, data mirroring between the controllers is carried out via a 100 Gb/s network. The storage system includes 50 NL-SAS hard drives, 14 TB each. Support for the most popular protocols, such as NFS, CIFS, iSCSI, etc., makes it possible to use this storage for both the "Neurocomputer" complex and the "Tornado SUSU" supercomputer.

3   System Software

The CentOS 6.2 operating system is installed on each compute node of the "Tornado SUSU" supercomputer. Compilers such as Intel Compiler (C/C++, Fortran 77, Fortran 90), GCC, the MPI2 parallel programming library (Intel MPI, OpenMPI, MVAPICH) are used. They allow users to implement their own applications to solve their tasks.

The "Neurocomputer" complex has the CentOS 7.8 operating system installed. Users use several versions of the GCC compiler, the CUDA, NCCL and CUDNN libraries for working with graphics accelerators, the OpenMPI parallel programming library. The Anaconda system is installed on the "Neurocomputer" complex. It is used for configuring the user environment of the Python program (installing the required version of Python, installing related libraries that provide interaction with artificial neural networks, Keras [13], Tensorflow [34], etc.). A fault-tolerant and scalable cluster management and job scheduling system SLURM [27] is installed on each computer complex for the efficient sharing of resources by a many users. SLURM version 2.5.3 is installed on the "Tornado SUSU" supercomputer, SLURM version 20.02.4 is used in the "Neurocomputer" complex.

3.1   Monitoring Systems

One of the main tasks of a system administrator is to ensure the correct and uninterrupted operation of the equipment, for example, the Infiniband and Ethernet networks, data storage systems, etc. The Nagios and Zabbix systems are used for system monitoring at the Scientific and Educational Center "Artificial Intelligence and Quantum Technologies" (SEC AIQT). We also developed our own supercomputer load monitoring system. It is designed to generate reports on the load and activities of users from the structural divisions of the university [15].

The *Nagios* system provides information about the health of hardware and software services and generates a status change message sent by e-mail to the administrator [5]. The main approach to writing checks in Nagios is the description of checks in the form of scripts using a self-written code, as well as using a standard set of basic checks that are not suitable for organizing monitoring of all resources. Nagios gives the flexibility to perform checks on various services by allowing one to write simple checks yourself; however, this is also a serious drawback. You must independently describe all non-standard checks that require you to analyze the SNMP commands of the equipment. Notification via e-mail is also an inconvenient mechanism since letters often get into the spam folder or arrive later than necessary to respond quickly to problems. We use Nagios to check the status of services such as mail, task queues, networking, communications, and other types of the equipment (Fig. 2).

The Zabbix [6] monitoring system started to be used later than Nagios, but we use it more widely, since Zabbix has the ability to monitor systems actively and passively. In addition, it can be installed on Windows and Linux. Zabbix

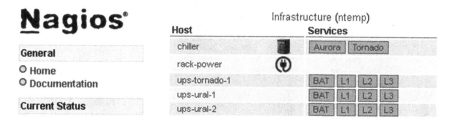

Fig. 2. Monitoring the equipment status using the web interface of the Nagios system

allows creating graphs for individual groups of the equipment (Fig. 3). It has a large and growing base of standard equipment checks (for example, for the Dorado storage system, etc.). This feature of Zabbix enables the setup of new equipment monitoring in the short term.

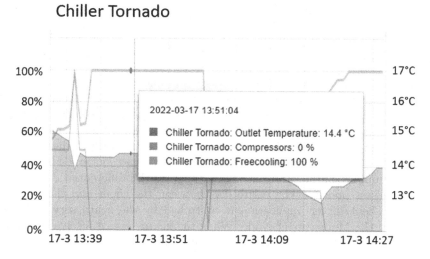

Fig. 3. Monitoring the state of the chiller of the "Tornado SUSU" supercomputer using the web interface of the Zabbix system

Graphs are also a useful Zabbix tool, they allow comparing parameters that have been monitored at different time intervals, identifying dependencies and problems. In addition to the above, a significant advantage of the Zabbix system is the ability to integrate with popular instant messengers and corporate systems, which enables to achieve almost instant response to a change in the state of the equipment or software service. Currently, Zabbix is being actively implemented. It replaces most of the functionality of Nagios, however, the Zabbix system cannot fully cover the functionality of Nagios yet. The SEC AIQT infrastructure diagram in the Zabbix monitoring system is shown in Fig. 4.

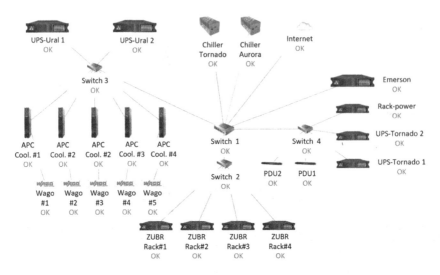

Fig. 4. SEC AIQT infrastructure diagram in the Zabbix monitoring system

3.2 Control Systems

We use specialized software control systems, xCAT and Puppet, to install and configure software on a many compute nodes of the "Tornado SUSU" supercomputer.

xCAT (Extreme Cluster Administration Tool) is a scalable toolkit for deploying and maintaining large clusters [18]. xCAT provides a unified interface for hardware management, the discovery and deployment of diskful/diskless operating systems. All commands are client-server, logged and controlled by policies. They also support authentication. xCAT supports the differentiation of rights based on access policies. The entire flow between the client and the server in the xCAT client/server application is controlled by the xcatd service (xCAT daemon) on the Management Node. When the xcatd service receives an XML-packaged command, it checks the sender's credentials against the ACLs in the policy table.

The service also receives information about the state and status of the nodes from the moment they start working. xCAT is designed to scale very large clusters. Hierarchy support allows one control node to have any number of stateless or stateful service nodes, which improves performance and enables the management of very large clusters. xCAT is used for installing a clustered operating system on compute nodes, by PXE booting over DHCP, with the initial installation and configuration of the operating system, and running the Puppet system background process for further configuration.

Puppet is a configuration management system and a language for describing configuration tasks. System administrators use Puppet to effectively manage a many systems and ensure a single configuration. We set up all compute node configurations with Puppet after its basic installation with xCAT. Namely, we install SLURM task queues, packages for working with the high-speed

Infiniband network, storage and system packages. This organization of the system installation enables to make changes to the system configuration if necessary.

4 Application Software

The high-performance computing resources of SUSU have both proprietary and free application software installed [33], including:

- ANSYS, CAE/multiphysics engineering simulation software for product design, testing and operation [3];
- LS-DYNA, a general-purpose multiphysics simulation software package [19];
- FlowVision, complete, integrated CFD software [9];
- SFTC DEFORM, engineering software that enables designers to analyze metal forming, heat treatment, machining and mechanical joining processes on the computer [25];
- MATLAB, a programming and numeric computing platform used by millions of engineers and scientists to analyze data, develop algorithms, and create models [20];
- OpenFOAM, free, open source CFD software. It has a large user base across most areas of engineering and science, from both commercial and academic organizations [24].

More than 250 scientific tasks are annually performed on the computing resources of SUSU. These are tasks from the fields of artificial intelligence, mechanical engineering, metallurgy and metalworking, the fuel and energy complex, light industry, the production of supercomputers and software, including:

- forecast of the passage time of the queue of highly automated vehicles based on neural networks in the services of cooperative intelligent transport systems [26]
- tigris basin landscapes: sensitivity of the ndvi vegetation index to climate variability derived from observation and reanalysis data [2]
- simulation of the compressibility of isostructural halogen containing crystals on macro- and microlevels [4],
- quantum electronic pressure and crystal compressibility for magnesium diboride under simulated compression [21],
- reaction mechanism and energetics of the decomposition of tetrakis-(1,3-dimethyltetrazol-5-imidoperchloratomanganese(II)) from quantum-mechanics-based reactive dynamics [36],
- ab initio calculation of the total energy of a bcc iron cell containing three dissolved carbon atoms, and internal friction in Fe–C solid solutions [23],
- duplexer based on volumetric modular technology [10],
- VaLiPro: linear programming validator for cluster computing systems [29],
- A parallel computation model for scalability estimation of iterative numerical algorithms on cluster computing systems [28],
- in-RDBMS industrial sensor data analysis [39],

- parallel similarity search [16] and discovery of time series motifs [40], anomalies [38,41], and snippets [37],
- aramid fabric surface treatment and its impact on the mechanics of the frictional interaction of yarns [11],
- development of a supercomputer model of needle-punched felt [7],
- plastic deformation at the dynamic compaction of aluminum nanopowder: molecular dynamics simulations and mechanical model [22],
- micromechanical model of representative volume of powder material [12],
- towards the fog computing PaaS solution [35],
- fog computing state of the art: concept and classification of platforms to support distributed computing systems [14],
- transfer learning for Russian speech synthesis [17],
- model of compound eye vision for machine learning [30],
- student attendance control system with face recognition based on a neural network [31],
- traffic flow estimation with data from a video surveillance camera [8].

5 Conclusions

In this article, we reviewed the high-performance resources of South Ural State University, i.e., the "Tornado SUSU" supercomputer, the "Neurocomputer" complex, the Panasas ActiveStor 11 data storage systems, OceanStor Dorado 3000 V6, Huawei OceanStor 5300 V5. Access to the resources is provided by the Scientific and Educational Center "Artificial Intelligence and Quantum Technologies" established at SUSU. Currently, the HPC resources are used by more than 500 people. These are students and employees of SUSU and external educational, scientific and industrial organizations. Employees of the SEC AIQT maintain the operability of the SLURM task queue, ensure the correct and uninterrupted operation of the Infiniband and Ethernet networks, storage and other equipment using specialized monitoring and management systems. Modern parallel software is installed on the high-performance resources of SUSU, which allows performing research and development work from different fields of knowledge.

Acknowledgments. The work was supported by the Ministry of Science and Higher Education of the Russian Federation (government order FENU-2020-0022) and by the Russian Foundation for Basic Research (grant No. 20-07-00140).

References

1. Abramov, S.M., Zadneprovskiy, V.F., Lilitko, E.P.: Supercomputers "SKIF" series 4. Inf. Technol. Comput. Syst. **1**, 3–16 (2012)
2. Alhumaima, A., Abdullaev, S.: Tigris basin landscapes: sensitivity of vegetation index NDVI to climate variability derived from observational and reanalysis data. Earth Interact. **24**(7), 1–18 (2020). https://doi.org/10.1175/EI-D-20-0002.1
3. ANSYS. http://ansys.com

4. Bartashevich, E.V., Sobalev, S.A., Matveychuk, Y.V., Tsirelson, V.G.: Simulation of the compressibility of isostructural halogen containing crystals on macro- and microlevels. J. Struct. Chem. **62**(10), 1607–1620 (2021). https://doi.org/10.1134/S0022476621100164

5. Borghesi, A., Molan, M., Milano, M., Bartolini, A.: Anomaly detection and anticipation in high performance computing systems. IEEE Trans. Parallel Distrib. Syst. **33**(4), 739–750 (2022). https://doi.org/10.1109/TPDS.2021.3082802

6. Borisov, S.N., Zima, A.M., Dyachenko, R.A., Elizarov, P.V.: Review of modern information monitoring systems for data networks. Modern science: actual problems of theory and practice. Series: Nat. Tech. Sci. (5), 29–34 (2019). (in Russian)

7. Dolganina, N.Y., Teleshova, E.A., Semenikhina, P.N.: Development of supercomputer model of needle-punched felt. In: 2020 Global Smart Industry Conference (GloSIC), Chelyabinsk, Russia, 17–19 November 2020, pp. 1–6. IEEE (2020). https://doi.org/10.1109/GloSIC50886.2020.9267856

8. Fedorov, A., Nikolskaia, K., Ivanov, S., Shepelev, V., Minbaleev, A.: Traffic flow estimation with data from a video surveillance camera. J. Big Data **6**, 73 (2019). https://doi.org/10.1186/s40537-019-0234-z

9. FlowVision. https://tesis.com.ru/own_design/flowvision/

10. Fomin, D.G., Dudarev, N.V., Darovskikh, S.N.: Duplexer based on volumetric modular technology. In: 2021 IEEE 22nd International Conference of Young Professionals in Electron Devices and Materials (EDM), Souzga, the Altai Republic, Russia, 30 June–4 July 2021, pp. 97–100. IEEE (2021). https://doi.org/10.1109/EDM52169.2021.9507637

11. Ignatova, A.V., Dolganina, N.Y., Sapozhnikov, S.B., Shabley, A.A.: Aramid fabric surface treatment and its impact on the mechanics of yarn's frictional interaction. PNRPU Mech. Bull. **4**, 121–137 (2017)

12. Ivanov, V.A.: Micromechanical model of representative volume of powders material. Bulletin of the South Ural State University. Series: Metallurgy **21**(3), 67–81 (2021). https://doi.org/10.14529/met210308

13. Keras. Documentation. https://keras.io/guides/

14. Kirsanova, A.A., Radchenko, G.I., Tchernykh, A.N.: Fog computing state of the art: concept and classification of platforms to support distributed computing systems. Supercomputi. Front. Innov. **8**(3), 17–50 (2021). https://doi.org/10.14529/jsfi210302

15. Kostenetskiy, P., Semenikhina, P.: SUSU supercomputer resources for industry and fundamental science. In: 2018 Global Smart Industry Conference (GloSIC), Chelyabinsk, Russia, 13–15 November 2018, pp. 1–7. IEEE (2018). https://doi.org/10.1109/GloSIC.2018.8570068

16. Kraeva, Y., Zymbler, M.L.: Scalable algorithm for subsequence similarity search in very large time series data on cluster of Phi KNL. In: Data Analytics and Management in Data Intensive Domains - 20th International Conference, DAMDID/RCDL 2018, Moscow, Russia, 9–12 October 2018, Revised Selected Papers, pp. 149–164 (2018). https://doi.org/10.1007/978-3-030-23584-0_9

17. Kuzmin, A.D., Ivanov, S.A.: Transfer learning for the Russian language speech synthesis. In: 2021 International Conference on Quality Management, Transport and Information Security, Information Technologies (IT QM IS), Yaroslavl, Russian Federation, 6–10 September 2021, pp. 507–510. IEEE (2021). https://doi.org/10.1109/ITQMIS53292.2021.9642715

18. Lascu, O., Brindeyev, A., Quintero, D.E., Sermakkani, V., Simon, R., Struble, T.: xCAT 2 Guide for the CSM System Administrator. https://www.redbooks.ibm.com/redpapers/pdfs/redp4437.pdf

19. LSTC LS-DYNA. http://www.ls-dyna.com/
20. MATLAB. https://www.mathworks.com/
21. Matveychuk, Y.V., Bartashevich, E.V., Skalyova, K.K., Tsirelson, V.G.: Quantum electronic pressure and crystal compressibility for magnesium diboride under simulated compression. Mater. Today Commun. **26**, 101952 (2021). https://doi.org/10.1016/j.mtcomm.2020.101952
22. Mayer, A.E., Ebel, A.A., Al-Sandoqachi, M.K.: Plastic deformation at dynamic compaction of aluminum nanopowder: molecular dynamics simulations and mechanical model. Int. J. Plast. **124**, 22–41 (2020). https://doi.org/10.1016/j.ijplas.2019.08.005
23. Mirzoev, A.A., Ridnyi, Y.M.: Ab initio calculation of total energy of a bcc iron cell containing three dissolved carbon atoms, and internal friction in Fe-C solid solutions. J. Alloys Compd. **883**, 160850 (2021). https://doi.org/10.1016/j.jallcom.2021.160850
24. OpenFOAM. https://www.openfoam.com/
25. SFTC DEFORM. https://tesis.com.ru/cae_brands/deform/
26. Shepelev, V., et al.: Forecasting the passage time of the queue of highly automated vehicles based on neural networks in the services of cooperative intelligent transport systems. Mathematics **10**(2), 282 (2022). https://doi.org/10.3390/math10020282
27. Slurm. Documentation. https://slurm.schedmd.com/documentation.html
28. Sokolinsky, L.B.: BSF: a parallel computation model for scalability estimation of iterative numerical algorithms on cluster computing systems. J. Parallel Distrib. Comput. **149**, 193–206 (2021). https://doi.org/10.1016/j.jpdc.2020.12.009
29. Sokolinsky, L.B., Sokolinskaya, I.M.: VaLiPro: linear programming validator for cluster computing systems. Supercomput. Front. Innov. **8**(3), 51–61 (2021). https://doi.org/10.14529/jsfi210303
30. Starkov, A., Sokolinsky, L.B.: Building 2D model of compound eye vision for machine learning. Mathematics **10**(2), 181 (2022). https://doi.org/10.3390/MATH10020181
31. Strueva, A.Y., Ivanova, E.V.: Student attendance control system with face recognition based on neural network. In: 2021 International Russian Automation Conference (RusAutoCon), Sochi, Russian Federation, 5–11 September 2021, pp. 929–933. IEEE (2021). https://doi.org/10.1109/RusAutoCon52004.2021.9537386
32. SUSU Scientific and Educational Center "Artificial Intelligence and Quantum Technologies". https://supercomputer.susu.ru/
33. SUSU REC AIQT. Application software. http://supercomputer.susu.ru/users/simulation/
34. Tensorflow. Documentation. https://www.tensorflow.org/
35. Vetoshkin, N., Radchenko, G.: Towards the fog computing PaaS solution. In: 2020 Ural Symposium on Biomedical Engineering, Radioelectronics and Information Technology (USBEREIT), Yekaterinburg, Russia, 14–15 May 2020, pp. 0516–0519. IEEE (2020). https://doi.org/10.1109/USBEREIT48449.2020.9117791
36. Zybin, S.V., Morozov, S.I., Prakash, P., Zdilla, M.J., Goddard, W.A.: Reaction mechanism and energetics of decomposition of tetrakis(1,3-dimethyltetrazol-5-imidoperchloratomanganese(II)) from quantum-mechanics-based reactive dynamics. J. Am. Chem. Soc. **143**(41), 16960–16975 (2021). https://doi.org/10.1021/jacs.1c04847
37. Zymbler, M., Goglachev, A.: Fast summarization of long time series with graphics processor. Mathematics **10**(10), 1781 (2022). https://doi.org/10.3390/math10101781

38. Zymbler, M., Grents, A., Kraeva, Y., Kumar, S.: A parallel approach to discords discovery in massive time series data. Comput. Mater. Continua **66**(2), 1867–1878 (2021). https://doi.org/10.32604/cmc.2020.014232

39. Zymbler, M., Ivanova, E.: Matrix profile-based approach to industrial sensor data analysis inside RDBMS. Mathematics **9**(17), 2146 (2021). https://doi.org/10.3390/math9172146

40. Zymbler, M.L., Kraeva, Y.A.: Discovery of time series motifs on intel many-core systems. Lobachevskii J. Math. **40**(12), 2124–2132 (2019). https://doi.org/10.1134/S199508021912014X

41. Zymbler, M., Polyakov, A., Kipnis, M.: Time series discord discovery on intel many-core systems. In: Sokolinsky, L., Zymbler, M. (eds.) PCT 2019. CCIS, vol. 1063, pp. 168–182. Springer, Cham (2019). https://doi.org/10.1007/978-3-030-28163-2_12

Parallel Numerical Algorithms

Comparative Analysis of Parallel Methods for Solving SLAEs in Three-Dimensional Initial-Boundary Value Problems

V. S. Gladkikh[1], V. P. Ilin[1], and M. S. Pekhterev[1,2(✉)]

[1] Institute of Computational Mathematics and Mathematical Geophysics SB RAS,
Novosibirsk, Russia
[2] Novosibirsk State University, Novosibirsk, Russia
maxim-pekhterev@mail.ru

Abstract. Iterative methods for solving systems of linear algebraic equations with high-order sparse matrices that arise in absolutely stable implicit finite-volume approximations of three-dimensional initial-boundary value problems for the heat and mass transfer equation on unstructured grids in computational domains with a complex configuration of multiply connected piecewise smooth boundary surfaces and contrasting material properties are considered. At each time step, algebraic systems are solved using parallel preconditioned algorithms for conjugate directions in Krylov subspaces. To speed up the iterative processes, variational methods for choosing initial approximations are applied using numerical solutions from previous time steps. It is discussed how the proposed approaches can be more general formulations of problems, as well as how to increase the productivity of computational methods and technologies in the multiple solution of algebraic systems with sequentially determined different right-hand sides and with the scalable parallelization of algorithms based on the additive methods of domain decomposition. The efficiency of the proposed approaches is investigated for the implicit Euler and Crank–Nicholson schemes based on the results of numerical experiments on a representative series of methodological problems.

Keywords: initial-boundary value problem · implicit schemes · iterative processes · Krylov subspaces · least squares method · numerical experiments

1 Introduction

The numerical solution of multidimensional initial-boundary value problems for partial differential equations of parabolic type is an urgent practical problem in the mathematical modeling of processes and phenomena in many applications, including interdisciplinary ones [7]. A typical example is non-isothermal multiphase filtration [11] in porous media with different-scale geometric and material characteristics. Modern numerical algorithms and technologies for solving the

L. Sokolinsky and M. Zymbler (Eds.): PCT 2022, CCIS 1618, pp. 59–72, 2022.
https://doi.org/10.1007/978-3-031-11623-0_5

considered computational problems of thermal conductivity are presented, for example, in [1,3,10,13–15]. Implicit approximations of the original statements on adaptive unstructured grids, necessary to ensure the absolute stability of numerical integration in time and high-resolution calculations, require the construction of high-performance algorithms for multiprocessor computing systems (MCS). The most resource-intensive stage here is the solution of systems of linear algebraic equations (SLAEs), which take up to 80 % and more computer time when implementing non-stationary and nonlinear models, since at this stage the volume of arithmetic operations performed grows nonlinearly with an increase in the number of degrees of freedom. An existing technological feature of algorithms for solving problems with real data is the storage of matrices of large algebraic systems (with orders $10^8 - 10^{10}$ and higher) in sparse compressed formats.

The purpose of this work is to analyze the features of the application of parallel preconditioned iterative methods in Krylov subspaces in relation to a three-dimensional linear initial-boundary value problem with mixed-type boundary conditions for a non-stationary heat equation. It should be noted that in classical iterative processes, algorithms that converge regardless of the nature of the initial approximation are studied. The main emphasis in our studies is placed on the choice of initial approximations, which make it possible to significantly reduce the number of iterations when solving the SLAE at each time level, due to the use of the results obtained at the previous steps. In contrast to the approximation approaches in common methods of predictor-corrector type [8], we propose a variational algebraic principle based on minimizing the initial residual. Incomplete factorization methods in Krylov subspaces are used as iterative solvers. Solvable algebraic systems are formed using barycentric finite volume methods on a tetrahedral grid, described in [3]. For approximation in time, parametrized two-layer schemes are used, with an emphasis on the implicit Euler and Crank–Nicholson schemes (for further research, the discontinuous Galerkin methods of various orders of accuracy in space and time proposed in [2] are of considerable interest). We also discuss a possible generalization of the results to the solution of initial-boundary value problems in the presence of convection and/or nonlinearity, as well as the possibility of accelerating computations when repeatedly solving SLAEs with different right-hand sides and using the parallelization of algorithms based on the additive method of domain decomposition, see [4,6,9].

The present work is structured as follows. Section 2 describes the features of the continuous and discrete formulations of the problems under consideration, including the study of the stability and additional error of the grid solution due to the approximate nature of the iterative implementation of implicit schemes. Section 3 is devoted to the presentation of the proposed parallel iterative algorithms with the analysis of different approaches to the choice of initial approximations at different time steps. Section 4 presents the results of experimental studies of the effectiveness of algorithms based on the results of calculations for a series of methodological problems. In conclusion, the results obtained and plans for further research are discussed.

2   Continuous and Discrete Problem Setting

Consider the formulation of the three-dimensional initial-boundary value problem of heat conduction in the computational domain

$$(x, y, z, t) \in \Omega \times [0, T], \quad \Omega \in R^3, \quad T \in R^1,$$

with a piecewise smooth boundary Γ, in general, multiply connected, and a closure $\overline{\Omega} = \Omega \cup \Gamma$. The heat conduction equation can be written as

$$c\frac{\partial u}{\partial t} = div(\lambda \cdot grad u) + f(x, y, z, t), \tag{1}$$

where λ is the thermal conductivity coefficient, c is the heat capacity coefficient, and $f(x, y, z, t)$ is the continuous sufficiently smooth source function. On different sections of the boundary Γ_D and Γ_N, $\Gamma_D \cup \Gamma_N = \Gamma$, the Dirichlet and Neumann boundary conditions are imposed on the sought solution, respectively:

$$u|_{\Gamma_D} = u_D(x, y, z, t), \quad \lambda \left.\frac{\partial u}{\partial n}\right|_{\Gamma_N} = \sigma_N(x, y, z, t). \tag{2}$$

Here u_D and σ_N are the given functions of temperature and heat flux distribution. Relations (1), (2) are supplemented by the initial conditions for $(x, y, z) \in \Omega$:

$$u(x, y, z, 0) = u^0(x, y, z). \tag{3}$$

We assume that the initial data of problem (1)–(3) have properties that ensure the existence, uniqueness, and sufficient smoothness of the solution necessary to justify the approximation, stability, and convergence of the approximate methods used below for solving the initial-boundary value problem.

Relations (1)–(3) are approximated on the space-time grid $\Omega^h \times \Omega^\tau$, where the time steps are generally different, i.e.,

$$\Omega^\tau = \{t_{n+1} = t_n + \tau_n, \quad n = 0, 1, \cdots, N_t\},$$

and the spatial mesh with the number of nodes N_h is adaptive and unstructured. For simplicity, we consider it static, i.e., not changing over time. The process of discretizing the initial continuous statement is carried out in two stages. First, using the barycentric finite volume method [3], we approximate the partial differential equation and boundary conditions, as a result of which we obtain a system of ordinary differential equations (ODEs)

$$C_h\frac{d(u)^h}{dt} + A_h(u)^h = g^h + \psi^h,$$
$$u^h, g^h, \psi^h \in \Re^{N_h}, \quad C_h, A_h \in \Re^{N_h, N_h} \tag{4}$$

where $(u)^h = \{u_k(t)\}$ is the vector of values of the desired solution at grid nodes, ψ^h is the spatial approximation error, and C_h and A_h are some independent from time to time symmetric matrices, traditionally called mass and stiffness matrices, respectively, see [7]. At the second stage, we approximate the ODE system using the parameterized one-step scheme

$$C_h((u)^{n+1}-(u)^n) = \tau_n[\theta(g^{n+1}-A_h(u)^{n+1})+(1-\theta)(g^n-A_h(u)^n)+\psi_n^h+\psi_n^\tau]. \quad (5)$$

Here $(u)^n = \{u_k(t_n)\}$ are the vectors of exact values of the sought solution at the nodes of the space-time grid, $\theta \in [0,1]$ is the parameter of the approximating scheme, and $\psi^\tau = O(\tau^\gamma)$ is the time approximation error vector ($\gamma = 2$ for $\theta = \frac{1}{2}$ and $\gamma = 1$ for the rest cases). Note that the algorithms defined by relation (4) for $\theta = \frac{1}{2}, 0, 1$ are called Crank–Nicholson, explicit Euler and "strictly implicit" Euler schemes, respectively. Discarding the approximation terms ψ_n^h and ψ_n^τ in (4), we arrive at a system of linear algebraic equations for the vectors of approximate grid solutions $u^n = \{u_k^n\}$:

$$\begin{aligned}(C_h + \theta\tau_n A_h)u^{n+1} &= (C_h - (1-\theta)\tau_n A_h)u^n + \tau_n g^{n+\theta}, \\ g^{n+\theta} &= \tau_n(\theta g^{n+1} + (1-\theta)g^n).\end{aligned} \quad (6)$$

It is noteworthy that if at each n-th time step SLAE (3) is solved approximately using some iterative process, then u^{n+1} is replaced by the iterative approximation $\tilde{u}^{n+1}$, for which the residual vector is determined

$$r^{n+1} = g^{n+\theta} + \tau_n^{-1}(C_h - (1-\theta)\tau_n A_h)\tilde{u}^n - (C_h + \theta\tau_n A_h)\tilde{u}^{n+1} \quad (7)$$

As shown in [10], for $\theta \geq 1/2$ and a sufficiently small residual norm $\|r^{n+1}\|$ for the implicit schemes under consideration, the absolute stability of numerical integration with respect to time follows.

In this paper, we restrict ourselves to considering the simplest approximations in time, which can be called one-stage Runge-Kutta (R-K) methods. More accurate approximations can be built using multistage R-K algorithms, both explicit and implicit, see [8].

3   Methods for Solving SLAEs in Implicit Schemes

System of equations (6), solved at each time step, can be rewritten as

$$\begin{aligned}\overline{A}u^{n+1} &= \overline{f}^{n+1}, \quad n = 0, 1, \cdots, N_t, \\ \overline{A} = C_h + \theta\tau_n A_h, \quad \overline{f}^{n+1} &= \tau_n g^{n+1} + (C_h - (1-\theta)\tau_n A_h)u^n.\end{aligned} \quad (8)$$

It is natural to solve SLAE (8) for $\theta > 0$ using iterative algorithms for two reasons. The first is related to the spectral properties of the matrix $\overline{A}$. Since for the most common spatial approximations considered by us, the mass matrix C_h has eigenvalues $\nu = O(1)$, i.e., independent of the characteristic mesh steps tau, h, and the eigenvalues of the stiffness matrix A_h lie in the interval $\lambda \in [\lambda_1, \lambda_N]$, $\lambda_1 = O(1)$, $\lambda_N = O(h^{-2})$, see [7], for the eigenvalues of the matrix $\overline{A}$ we obtain the following relations:

$$\mu(\overline{A}) \in [\mu_1, \mu_N], \quad \mu_1 = O(1), \quad \mu_N = O(1 + \theta\tau h^{-2}). \quad (9)$$

Hence, for the corresponding condition number, we have
$cond(\overline{A}) = \frac{\max_k\{\mu_k\}}{\min_k\{\mu_k\}} = O(\theta\tau h^{-2})$, which for small values of τ means a sufficiently fast convergence of iterations.

The second feature of the problems under consideration is that when solving
the SLAE at the current time step, the previous solutions are already known,
which can be used to find a good initial approximation and reduce the number
of iterations. Let us describe some possible approaches here.

3.1   Choice of an Initial Approximation for Solving a SLAE

a) The simplest trick is to choose an arbitrary initial approximation, for example $u^{n+1,0} = 0$. However, this means that the specifics of the initial-boundary
value problem being solved is not taken into account in any way.

b) The most natural way is to put $u^{n+1,0} = u^n$, which formally means the use
of zero-order interpolation (we denote this approach by I^0). This approximation principle can be generalized to higher orders if one remembers the
solutions $u^{n-1}, u^{n-2}, \cdots$ from the previous time steps. For example, using
linear extrapolation gives

$$u^{n+1,0} = u^n + (u^n - u^{n-1})\tau_n/\tau_{n-1}. \tag{10}$$

c) The predictor-corrector method [8], which is implemented in two stages, is
widespread, especially when solving ordinary differential equations. At the
first stage, a preliminary (prognostic) approximation is calculated, for which,
in fact, the explicit scheme obtained from (6) is used for $\theta = 0$:

$$\hat{u}^{n+1} = C_h^{-1}[(C_h - \tau_n A_h)u^n + \tau_n g^n]. \tag{11}$$

At the second stage, the calculated value is corrected with the determination
of the initial approximation by the formula

$$u^{n+1,1} = C_h^{-1}[(C_h - (1-\theta)\tau_n A_h)u^n + \tau_n g^{n+\frac{1}{2}} - \theta\tau_n A_h \hat{u}^{n+1}]. \tag{12}$$

Obviously, procedure (14) can be interpreted as the application of a simple
iteration algorithm. This correction can be repeated any given number of m
times, resulting in a method denoted as PC^m (PC for $m = 1$):

$$\hat{u}^{n+1,k} = C_h^{-1}[(C_h - (1-\theta)\tau_n A_h)u^n + \tau_n g^{n+1} - \theta\tau_n A_h \hat{u}^{n+1,k-1}],$$
$$k = 1, \cdots, m; \quad \hat{u}^{n+1,0} = \hat{u}^{n+1}; \quad u^{n+1,0} = \hat{u}^{n+1,m}. \tag{13}$$

Obviously, for sufficiently small τ_n, this iterative process converges, but
slowly. If we formally restrict ourselves here to the case $m = 0$, i.e., no
correction, and set $u^{n+1,0} = \hat{u}^{n+1}$, then we denote this method as P. Note
also that the PC^m methods can be applied both for the Crank–Nicholson
schemes, and for the implicit Euler method ($\theta = \frac{1}{2}, 1$, respectively), but
these, naturally, will be different algorithms. It is important to bear in mind
that predictor-corrector methods are traditionally used without iterative
refinement.

64 V. S. Gladkikh et al.

d) Reducing the number of iterations at each time step can be ensured if fast preconditioned methods in Krylov subspaces are used to solve SLAE (5), and the initial approximation $u^{n+1,0}$ is determined not from approximation, but from optimization algebraic approaches. For example, in the PC method, instead of correction stage (14), one can use a linear combination of the vectors $u^n, \hat{u}^{n+1}$ according to the condition of minimizing the initial discrepancy $r^{n+1,0} = \overline{f}^{n+1} - \overline{A}u^{n+1,0}$, determined from equation (10):

$$u^{n+1,0} = u^n + cv^n, \quad v^n = \hat{u}^{n+1} - u^n,$$

$$r^{n+1,0} = r^n - c\overline{A}v^n, \quad c = \frac{(r^n, \overline{A}v^n)}{(\overline{A}v^n, \overline{A}v^n)}. \tag{14}$$

Note that in this case, the condition $\overline{A}$, the orthogonalization of the vectors $r^{n+1,0}$ and v^n, is satisfied, i.e., $(r^{n+1,0}, \overline{A}v^n) = 0$. Since formulas (16) implement the simplest version of the least squares method, the corresponding algorithm is further denoted as P-LSM1. It can be generalized in an obvious way if in formulas (16) the vector $\hat{u}^{n+1}$ is replaced by $\hat{u}^{n+1,m}$ from (15), obtained after m corrections, which formally defines the PC ^{m}-LSM1 method.

e) The natural development of the considered least squares method is an increase in the number of solutions stored and used to select $u^{n+1,0}$ from the previous time steps $u^{n-1}, \cdots, u^{n-s}$. We describe this algorithm without using a predictor, denoting it as LSMs:

$$u^{n+1,0} = u^n + c_1 v_1^n + \cdots + c_s v_s^n = u^n + V_n \vec{c},$$

$$\vec{c} = (c_1, \ldots, c_s)^T, \quad V_n = (v_1^n, \ldots, v_s^n) \in \Re^{N,s}, \tag{15}$$

$$r^{n+1,0} = r^n - W_n \vec{c}, \quad W_n = \overline{A}V_n.$$

Here the vectors $v_k, k = 1, \ldots, n$, can be defined in different ways as the differences of the already calculated approximations. For example, in the P-LSM2 method considered further in Sect. 4, we define $v^1 = \hat{u}^{n+1} - u^n$, $v^2 = u^{n-1} - u^n$. Hence, we obtain that the minimization of the norms $\|r^{n+1,0}\|_2$ is equivalent to the orthogonality relation $W_n^T r^{n+1,0} = 0$. This formally leads to the problem of calculating the normal solution of the overdetermined joint algebraic system $W_n \vec{c} = r^n$:

$$B\vec{c} \equiv W_n^T W_n \vec{c} = W_n^T r^n, \quad \vec{c} = (W_n^T W_n)^+ W_n^T r^n, \quad B \in \Re^{s,s}. \tag{16}$$

Here B^+ means the generalized inverse matrix [12], which in this case coincides with the inverse matrix B^{-1}, if W_n has full rank, which means the linear independence of the vectors $v_1^n, \ldots, v_s^n$. It should be noted that instead of (18), to determine the vector $\vec{c}$, one can use the relations obtained from the orthogonality condition $V_n^T r^{n+1,0} = 0$:

$$\tilde{A}\vec{c} \equiv V_n^T \overline{A}V_n \vec{c} = V_n^T r^n, \quad \vec{c} = \tilde{A}^+ V_n^T r^n. \tag{17}$$

Moreover, the matrix $\tilde{A} \in \Re^{s,s}$ is called a low-rank approximation to $\overline{A}$. After calculating the vector $\vec{c}$ by formulas (18) or (19) (the question of their preference is still open), the initial approximation is determined from (17).

3.2   Iterative Algorithms for Implicit Schemes

We represent the matrix of system of equations (8) as the sum $\overline{A} = D + L + U$, where D, L and U are the diagonal (or block-diagonal), lower and upper triangular matrices, respectively. Following the method of symmetric sequential upper relaxation SSOR (or its block version BSSOR, see [5]), or incomplete factorization, to speed up iterations at each time step, we define preconditioning matrices:

$$B = \check{B}\hat{B}, \quad \check{B}^{-1} = \check{G}(G+L)^{-1}, \quad \hat{B}^{-1} = (G+U)^{-1}\hat{G}, \quad G = \check{G}\hat{G}. \quad (18)$$

Here $G, \check{G}, \hat{G}$ are the easily invertible matrices selected for the optimization of the algorithm. In the simplest case, when D is a diagonal positive definite matrix, it is assumed

$$\hat{G}^{\frac{1}{2}} = \check{G}^{\frac{1}{2}} = G = \omega^{-1}D, \quad (19)$$

where $\omega \in [1,2)$ is the upper relaxation parameter.

Consider Aizenshtat's modification for two-way SSOR preconditioning in the following form:

$$\tilde{A}\tilde{u} \equiv \check{B}^{-1}\check{G}A\check{G}^{-1}\hat{B}^{-1}\hat{B}^{-1}\tilde{u}\hat{B} = \tilde{f} \equiv \check{B}^{-1}f, \quad \tilde{u} = \hat{B}u. \quad (20)$$

Then the matrix of the preconditioned SLAE is written as

$$\tilde{A} = (I + \overline{L})^{-1} + (I + \tilde{U})^{-1} + (I + \overline{L})^{-1}(\tilde{D} - 2I)(I + \tilde{U})^{-1},$$
$$\tilde{D} = \hat{G}^{-1}D\check{G}^{-1}, \quad \overline{L} = \hat{G}^{-1}L\check{G}^{-1}, \quad \tilde{U} = \hat{G}^{-1}U\check{G}^{-1}. \quad (21)$$

Here, for the parameter ω from (21) selected from the condition of approximate minimization of the condition number $cond(\tilde{A})$, the following formula demonstrates good practical results, confirmed in the simplest cases by theoretical estimates:

$$\omega = b - \frac{\sqrt{b^2 - 4ab}}{2a}, \quad a = (LD^{-1}Ue, e), \quad b = (De, e), \quad (22)$$

where $e = (1, \ldots, 1)^T$ is the vector with unit components. The corresponding approach, according to [5], will be called the incomplete Aizenshtat factorization IFE. Its distinguishing feature is the efficiency of implementing each iteration, since the multiplication of a vector by the matrix $\tilde{A}$ by the formula

$$\tilde{A}v = (I + \tilde{L})^{-1}[v + (D - 2I)w] + w, \quad w = (I + \tilde{U})^{-1}v \quad (23)$$

requires almost as many arithmetic operations as multiplying by the original matrix A.

To solve preconditioned algebraic system (22), consider the iterative process of conjugate directions (see [5])

$$p^0 = r^0 = \tilde{f} - \tilde{A}u^0, \quad n = 0, 1, \cdots :$$
$$u^{n+1} = u^n + a_n p^n, \quad r^{n+1} = r^n - a_n \tilde{A} p^n, \tag{24}$$

where u^0 is the arbitrary initial approximation, r^n is the residual vector, and p^n are the direction vectors with respect to which we assume that the following orthogonalization conditions are satisfied:

$$(A^\gamma p^k, A p^n) = \rho_n \delta_{k,n}, \quad \rho_n = (A^\gamma p^n, A p^n), \tag{25}$$

where $\delta_{k,n}$ is the Kronecker symbol and $\gamma = 0, 1$ for the conjugate gradient and conjugate residual methods, respectively. It is easy to check that when determining in (26) the iterative parameters by the formula

$$a_k = (r^0, A^\gamma p^k)/\rho_n, \quad k = 0, 1, \ldots, n, \tag{26}$$

residual functionals $\psi_\gamma^n = (\overline{A}^{\gamma-1} r^{n+1}, r^{n+1})$ are minimized in Krylov subspaces

$$\mathfrak{K}_{n+1}(p^0, \tilde{A}) = Span\{p^0, \tilde{A}p^0, \ldots, \tilde{A}^n p^0\}. \tag{27}$$

Due to the symmetry of the matrix $\tilde{A}$, orthogonality conditions (27) are satisfied if the direction vectors are determined using the two-term recursion

$$p^{n+1} = r^{n+1} + \beta_n p^n = \sigma_{n+1}/\sigma_n, \quad \sigma_n = (A^\gamma r^n, r^n), \tag{28}$$

in this case, it is expedient to calculate the iterative parameters α_n instead of (26) by the formula $\alpha_n = \sigma_n/\rho_n$. The criterion for the termination of iterations is the fulfillment of the condition

$$\|r^{n+1}\|_2^2 = (r^{n+1}, r^{n+1}) \leq \varepsilon^2 (\tilde{f}, \tilde{f}), \tag{29}$$

where $\varepsilon << 1$ is the priori given value, the optimal definition of which, strictly speaking, requires a special analysis of the final error of the numerical solution in accordance with formula (9). The number of iterations $n(\varepsilon)$ required to satisfy condition (31) is determined by the inequality

$$n(\varepsilon) \leq \frac{1}{2} |ln\frac{\varepsilon}{2}| cond(\tilde{A}^{\frac{1}{2}}) + 1. \tag{30}$$

3.3   Some Questions of Generalization of the Considered Approaches and Speed-up of Computations

Above, we presented the main directions for improving the efficiency of absolutely stable implicit grid approximations of resource-intensive multidimensional initial-boundary value problems based on the application of the universal least squares method. The above algorithms for the classical heat conduction equation can naturally be transferred to more general formulations: diffusion-convective processes, nonlinear problems with phase transitions, interdisciplinary problems, an example of which is nonisothermal filtration in porous media. Generally speaking, the question of the optimal choice of initial approximations in the iterative implementation of implicit schemes is relevant when modeling any non-stationary processes and phenomena.

The second side of the issue is to apply the proposed approaches to grid equations of a higher order of accuracy, in relation to both spatial and temporal approximations. Here, in particular, promising discontinuous Galerkin algorithms [2,7] are actively developing. Such methods will lead to more complex calculations at each step in time, but also to a reduction in their total number and, as a consequence, to a decrease in communication losses, which is highly important in the light of the evolution of computer platforms.

Another potential opportunity to improve performance in the considered computational models is the use of known technologies for the multiple solution of SLAEs with different sequentially determined right-hand sides. Here, similarly, one can successfully apply the least squares method, using previously stored information to speed up iterations in Krylov subspaces (see the review on deflation algorithms in [4]).

Finally, we emphasize that all the approaches outlined above are based on vector operations that allow scalable parallelization by means of hybrid programming on various computer architectures with distributed and/or hierarchical shared memory. When solving large sparse SLAEs with orders of $10^{10} - 10^{11}$ and higher, additional calculations due to least squares methods are parallelized almost ideally with linear acceleration. This is achieved by means of either MPI message passing (here, the additive methods of the decomposition of areas are natural [9]), or multithreading (OPEN MP), or the vectorization of operations (command systems of AVX type). Results for specific applications here require special experimental applications, and general principles can be found in [6,9].

4   Examples of Numerical Experiments

We investigate the efficiency of the above algorithms experimentally using the results of the numerical solution of three-dimensional initial-boundary value problems for Eq. (1) with constant coefficients c, λ and with Dirichlet boundary conditions. The main goal in this case is to carry out a comparative analysis of the efficiency of the iterative algorithms described in clauses 3.1 and 3.2 for various methods of choosing the initial approximations. All calculations were carried out for a cubic computational domain $\Omega = [0,1]^3$ on a cubic grid with the number of steps along each coordinate $N_x = 16.32.64$. The time steps τ were also chosen constant, and their values and quantities were selected from the conditions of visual representations of the characteristics of the algorithms. All arithmetic operations in the experiments were performed with standard double precision. We do not dwell on the issues of the performance of software implementations and the execution time of the algorithms, since the main goal of research in this case is the mathematical characteristics of the methods, i.e., accuracy and asymptotic estimates of their resource intensity.

The studies were carried out on two test examples with well-known analytical solutions, which were used to determine the initial and boundary conditions. In the first test, the exact solution is

$$u(x, y, z, t) = x(1 - x) + y(1 - y) + z(1 - z) + \frac{t^2}{2},$$

for which the spatial approximation error is zero, and the right-hand side of Eq. (1) is written as

$$f(x, y, z, t) = 2t + 6.$$

For the second example, the sought solution and the corresponding right-hand side are described by the following formulas:

$$u(x, y, z, t) = \sin(\pi x) \sin(\pi y) \sin(\pi z) t (T - t),$$
$$f(x, y, z, t) = (2(T - 2t) + 1.5\pi^2 t (T - t)) \sin(\pi x) \sin(\pi y) \sin(\pi z).$$

The tables below show the results of applying the preconditioned iterative conjugate gradient method described in Sect. 3.2 ($\gamma = 0$ in formulas (26)–(30)).

Table 1 shows the results of calculations for the 1st test problem for nine different space-time grids: $N_x = 16, 32, 64$; $N_t = 10, 20, 40$, using the iteration end criterion in (31) $\varepsilon = 10^{-3}, 10^{-5}$. We consider five ways of choosing the initial iterative approximations described in subparagraphs (a)–(e) from Sect. 3.1: O corresponds to $u^{n+1,0} = 0$, I^0 is the extrapolation of the form $u^{n+1,0} = u^n$, see item b), PI is the predictor with the definition $u^{n+1,0} = \hat{u}^{n+1}$, P-LSM1, P-LSM2, each of which in this case applies to the Crank–Nicholson scheme. The values n_1 and n_2 indicated in the cells of the table are the number of iterations averaged over time steps for $\varepsilon = 10^{-3}$ and $\varepsilon = 10^{-5}$, respectively, and $delta = \max_n \|u(t_{n+1}) - u^{n+1}\|_\infty$ is the uniform norm (maximum vector component) of the numerical solution error for $\varepsilon = 10^{-3}$. The content of Table 2 is similar, but for the second test problem.

The content of Tables 3 and 4 repeats Tables 1 and 2, but only for the implicit Euler scheme.

The analysis of the above results allows us to draw the following preliminary conclusions:

- the use of the least squares method LSM1 and even more so LSM2 can significantly reduce the number of iterations at time steps, with the fundamental possibility of constructing implicit non-iterative approximations;
- the effect obtained from the variational (algebraic) choice of initial approximations has approximately the same character for different values of the steps of the space-time grid and for different types of implicit schemes.

Table 1. Calculation results for the first test, $\varepsilon = 10^{-3}$, $\varepsilon = 10^{-5}$, Crank–Nicholson scheme

Methods \ N_h		16			32			64		
		δ	n_1	n_2	δ	n_1	n_2	δ	n_1	n_2
O	Nt=10	8,45E-07	10	16	2,35E-06	15	24	4,62E-06	23	36
	Nt=20	4,44E-07	9	14	1,32E-06	13	21	2,66E-06	20	33
	Nt=40	2,25E-07	8	12	3,32E-07	12	18	3,01E-06	17	28
I^0	Nt=10	4,99E-07	9	15	1,42E-06	13	22	2,70E-06	19	33
	Nt=20	1,07E-06	7	13	4,99E-07	11	19	4,17E-06	16	29
	Nt=40	1,43E-06	6	10	1,71E-06	9	15	3,22E-06	13	23
PI	Nt=10	8,52E-07	7	13	1,88E-06	11	20	3,11E-06	16	30
	Nt=20	1,75E-06	6	11	1,38E-06	8	16	4,38E-06	12	25
	Nt=40	6,58E-07	4	9	1,06E-06	6	13	6,97E-06	9	19
P-LSM1	Nt=10	1,35E-06	3	3	7,97E-06	5	5	5,63E-06	10	8
	Nt=20	1,27E-06	2	2	1,44E-06	4	4	3,79E-06	8	8
	Nt=40	1,50E-06	2	2	3,56E-06	3	3	6,63E-06	6	6
P-LSM2	Nt=10	9,07E-07	1	2	6,04E-06	1	2	6,30E-06	2	5
	Nt=20	1,13E-06	0	2	2,54E-06	1	2	5,00E-06	1	2
	Nt=40	1,42E-06	0	1	1,46E-06	1	1	4,97E-06	1	1

Table 2. Calculation results for the second test, $\varepsilon = 10^{-3}$, $\varepsilon = 10^{-5}$, Crank–Nicholson scheme

Methods \ N_h		16			32			64		
		δ	n_1	n_2	δ	n_1	n_2	δ	n_1	n_2
O	Nt=10	7,46E-04	8	13	1,86E-04	12	20	4,65E-05	18	30
	Nt=20	7,48E-04	7	11	1,87E-04	10	17	4,67E-05	15	26
	Nt=40	7,49E-04	6	9	1,87E-04	8	14	4,68E-05	12	20
I^0	Nt=10	7,46E-04	8	13	1,86E-04	11	19	4,65E-05	17	29
	Nt=20	7,48E-04	6	10	1,87E-04	9	16	4,67E-05	13	24
	Nt=40	7,50E-04	5	8	1,87E-04	6	12	4,68E-05	9	18
PI	Nt=10	7,46E-04	7	12	1,86E-04	10	18	4,65E-05	15	28
	Nt=20	7,48E-04	5	9	1,87E-04	7	14	4,67E-05	11	21
	Nt=40	7,50E-04	3	7	1,87E-04	5	10	4,68E-05	7	15
P-LSM1	Nt=10	7,46E-04	2	6	1,86E-04	4	9	4,66E-05	9	15
	Nt=20	7,48E-04	2	4	1,87E-04	3	6	4,67E-05	6	9
	Nt=40	7,49E-04	1	3	1,87E-04	2	4	4,68E-05	5	6
P-LSM2	Nt=10	7,46E-04	1	5	1,86E-04	2	7	4,65E-05	3	12
	Nt=20	7,48E-04	0	3	1,87E-04	1	5	4,67E-05	1	8
	Nt=40	7,49E-04	0	2	1,87E-04	0	3	4,68E-05	0	5

A further increase in the performance of algorithms for solving SLAEs in multidimensional initial-boundary value problems can be developed in various directions. The first is the optimization of the considered initial approxima- tions $u^{n+1,0}$. The second is to use the SLAE solution with different right-hand sides, see the overview in [4]. The third is the parallelization of algorithms by

Table 3. Calculation results for the first test, $\varepsilon = 10^{-3}$, $\varepsilon = 10^{-5}$, Euler's scheme

Methods \ N_h		16			32			64		
		δ	n_1	n_2	δ	n_1	n_2	δ	n_1	n_2
O	Nt=10	1,88E-06	11	17	1,56E-06	17	25	5,05E-06	26	38
	Nt=20	1,61E-06	10	16	4,46E-06	15	24	8,78E-06	23	36
	Nt=40	8,86E-07	9	14	2,50E-06	13	21	5,17E-06	20	33
I^0	Nt=10	1,56E-06	10	16	4,63E-06	14	24	7,64E-06	21	36
	Nt=20	1,10E-06	8	14	2,61E-06	12	21	3,55E-06	18	32
	Nt=40	9,78E-07	7	12	2,85E-06	10	18	6,67E-06	15	28
PI	Nt=10	3,89E-07	8	14	2,19E-06	12	21	7,78E-06	17	32
	Nt=20	9,29E-07	6	12	1,95E-06	9	19	4,98E-06	13	28
	Nt=40	3,57E-06	5	10	1,81E-06	7	15	5,83E-06	10	22
P-LSM1	Nt=10	8,00E-07	3	4	2,91E-06	5	6	6,38E-06	9	9
	Nt=20	1,75E-06	2	2	2,76E-06	4	4	5,74E-06	7	6
	Nt=40	1,84E-06	1	1	3,01E-06	3	3	4,34E-06	5	5
P-LSM2	Nt=10	2,98E-06	1	3	9,8E-06	1	4	1,07E-05	2	8
	Nt=20	2,03E-06	0	2	3,14E-06	0	3	2,05E-05	0	4
	Nt=40	2,55E-06	0	1	6,25E-06	0	2	1,80E-05	0	2

Table 4. Calculation results for the second test, $\varepsilon = 10^{-3}$, $\varepsilon = 10^{-5}$, Euler's scheme

Methods \ N_h		16			32			64		
		δ	n_1	n_2	δ	n_1	n_2	δ	n_1	n_2
O	Nt=10	0,032	10	15	3,18E-02	14	22	3,18E-02	21	33
	Nt=20	1,74E-02	8	13	1,71E-02	12	20	1,71E-02	18	30
	Nt=40	9,15E-03	7	11	8,90E-03	10	17	8,84E-03	15	26
I^0	Nt=10	0,032	9	14	3,18E-02	12	21	3,18E-02	18	31
	Nt=20	1,74E-02	7	12	1,71E-02	10	18	1,71E-02	15	28
	Nt=40	9,15E-03	6	10	8,90E-03	8	15	8,84E-03	12	23
PI	Nt=10	0,032	8	14	3,18E-02	11	20	3,18E-02	17	30
	Nt=20	1,74E-02	6	11	1,71E-02	8	17	1,71E-02	13	26
	Nt=40	9,15E-03	4	9	8,90E-03	6	13	8,84E-03	9	20
P-LSM1	Nt=10	0,032	4	10	3,18E-02	6	16	3,18E-02	12	26
	Nt=20	1,74E-02	2	7	1,71E-02	4	12	1,71E-02	7	20
	Nt=40	9,15E-03	1	5	8,90E-03	2	8	8,84E-03	4	13
P-LSM2	Nt=10	0,032	3	9	3,18E-02	5	13	3,18E-02	10	20
	Nt=20	1,74E-02	2	6	1,71E-02	3	9	1,71E-02	7	14
	Nt=40	9,15E-03	1	4	8,90E-03	1	6	8,84E-03	3	9

using additive methods for decomposing domains. It is also noteworthy that these directions of development (possibly in combination with approximation approaches) can be carried over to more general formulations of problems: in the presence of convection, nonlinear effects, etc.

5   Conclusion

The performed comparative analysis of iterative methods for solving algebraic systems with sparse matrices of high orders that arise in the implementation of implicit approximations of multidimensional initial-boundary value problems demonstrates the high efficiency of the algorithms while maintaining the absolute stability of numerical integration over time. The number of iterations at each time step is significantly reduced by choosing an initial approximation with the sequential use of already calculated solutions using the least squares method. The efficiency of the proposed approaches is illustrated by the results of experimental studies on a representative series of methodological problems using preconditioned iterative incomplete factorization processes in Krylov subspaces. The presented test results on accelerating computations of the proposed algorithms indicate their efficiency for supercomputers with distributed and hierarchical shared memory. The issues of transferring the proposed approaches to more general problem statements are discussed. A further increase in the performance of the algorithms is possible when using scalable parallelization based on additive methods for the decomposition of regions in Krylov subspaces. At the same time, an additional significant increase in the speed of computations can be achieved due to parallel methods of the decomposition of domains, as well as through the use of techniques for the multiple solution of SLAEs with sequentially determined right-hand sides.

References

1. Bychin, I.V., Gavrilenko, T.V., Galkin, V.A., et al.: Numerical modeling of 3D heat conduction problems with phase transitions on computing systems with distributed memory. Cybern. Herald **3**(19), 84–93 (2015)
2. Gander, M.J., Neumuller, M.: Analysis of a new space-time parallel multigrid algorithm for parabolic problems. SIAM J. Sci. Comput. **38**, A2173–A2208 (2016)
3. Gladkikh, V., Ilin, V.P., Petukhov, A.V., et al.: Numerical modeling of nonstationary heat problems in a two-phase medium. J. Phys. Conf. Ser. **1715**, 012002 (2020)
4. Gurieva, Y.L., Ilin, V.P.: Conjugate direction methods for multiple solution of slaes. J. Math. Sci. **255**, 231–241 (2021)
5. Ilin, V.P.: Finite element methods and technologies. ICMiMG SB RAS (2007)
6. Ilin, V.P.: Problems of parallel solution of large systems of linear algebraic equations. J. Math. Sci. **216**, 795–804 (2016)
7. Ilin, V.P.: Math modeling. Part 1 continuous and discrete models. Publisher SB RAS, p. 428 (2017)
8. Ilin, V.P.: Methods for solving ordinary differential equations. NSU Publishing House (2017)
9. Ilin, V.P.: Multi-preconditioned domain decomposition methods in the Krylov subspaces. In: Dimov, I., Faragó, I., Vulkov, L. (eds.) Numerical Analysis and Its Applications. LNCS, vol. 10187, pp. 95–106. Springer, Cham (2017). https://doi.org/10.1007/978-3-319-57099-0_9

10. Ilin, V.: High-performance computation of initial boundary value problems. In: Sokolinsky, L., Zymbler, M. (eds.) PCT 2018. CCIS, vol. 910, pp. 186–199. Springer, Cham (2018). https://doi.org/10.1007/978-3-319-99673-8_14
11. Roy, T., Jönsthövel, T.B., Lemon, C., et al.: A constrained pressure-temperature residual (CPTR) method for non-isothermal multiphase flow in porous media. SIAM J. Sci. Comput. **42**, B1014–B1040 (2020)
12. Saad, Y.: Iterative Methods for Sparse Linear Systems, 2nd edn. SIAM (2003). https://doi.org/10.1137/1.9780898718003
13. Vabishchevich, P.N., Samarsky, A.A.: Computational heat transfer. Editorial URSS (2003)
14. Vaganova, N.A., Filimonov, M.Y.: Simulation of cooling devices and effect for thermal stabilization of soil in a cryolithozone with anthropogenic impact. In: Dimov, I., Faragó, I., Vulkov, L. (eds.) FDM 2018. LNCS, vol. 11386, pp. 580–587. Springer, Cham (2019). https://doi.org/10.1007/978-3-030-11539-5_68
15. Vasiliev, V.I., Vasilieva, M.V., Grigoriev, A.V., et al.: Numerical modelling of heat and mass transfer processes in the permafrost zone. NEFU Publishing House, Yakutsk (2019)

Optimization of the Computational Process for Solving Grid Equations on a Heterogeneous Computing System

Alexander Sukhinov[1], Vladimir Litvinov[1,2(✉)] [iD], Alexander Chistyakov[1],
Alla Nikitina[1,3], Natalia Gracheva[2], and Nelli Rudenko[2]

[1] Don State Technical University, Rostov-on-Don, Russia
`litvinovvn@rambler.ru`
[2] Azov-Black Sea Engineering Institute of Don State Agrarian University,
Zernograd, Russia
[3] Southern Federal University, Rostov-on-Don, Russia

Abstract. To predict emergencies and the irreversible consequences of human activity, scientists widely use mathematical modeling. In the event of an emergency, it is important that the time for its elimination be the shortest. It is necessary to develop effective methods for solving systems of large-dimensional grid equations with a non-self-adjoint operator in the numerical solution of hydrophysics and biological kinetics problems. A large amount of processed information and the complexity of calculations lead to the need to use computing clusters, which include video adapters to increase the computing system performance and the data conversion rate. The research aim is to develop a software module that implements an algorithm for solving a system of linear algebraic equations (SLAE) of large dimensions by the modified alternately triangular iterative method (MATM), applicable in heterogeneous computing systems. The decomposition method of the computational domain in the three-dimensional case is described. A graph model for organizing a parallel pipeline computing process focused on heterogeneous computing systems is proposed. Based on the results of the research, a regression equation is obtained with a coefficient of determination equal to 0.86. The parameters of the obtained regression equation are the size of the CUDA computing block along the Oy axis and the size ratio along the Ox and Oz axes. The performed numerical experiments show that the minimum calculation time of one MATM step is achieved with the largest available value of the CUDA computing block size along the Ox axis.

Keywords: System of linear algebraic equations · Heterogeneous Computing System · Parallel algorithm

1 Introduction

The prediction of environmental risks allows one to reduce the damage from adverse situations and emergencies in nature, in particular, in the coastal water

The study was funded by the Russian Science Foundation (project No. 21-71-20050).

zone. Research in this area requires the construction of mathematical models and the study of the influence of various factors on the research object.

Currently, computer modeling is becoming more relevant, it replaces complex systems and physical models, as well as allows one to predict various phenomena and processes in nature. Computer modeling is usually based on mathematical models, the discretization of which leads to large-dimensional SLAEs with self-adjoint and non-self-adjoint operators. Solving such systems of grid equations requires a lot of computing capacity.

Both Russian and foreign researchers study the processes occurring in various reservoirs and water systems. Scientists of the Marchuk Institute of Computational Mathematics of the Russian Academy of Sciences and the Keldysh Institute of Applied Mathematics are engaged in the analysis and modeling of complex systems (in ecology, environment, etc.), modeling of hydrodynamic processes, and forecasting of climate changes in the world ocean. Studies on modeling hydrophysical processes are performed on the example of the Azov Sea under the leadership of G.G. Matishov. Mathematical models of sea level dynamics are described in the papers of A. Bonaduce, J. Staneva [1]. Scientists P. Marchesiello [2], A. Androsov [3], etc. are engaged in improving the ocean models. The existing standard software often includes simplified mathematical models that do not take into account the spatially inhomogeneous water transport, and have insufficient accuracy in modeling the vortex structures of water flow currents, shore and bottom topography [1–4]. The actual direction of improving software systems is the development of parallel algorithms executed on both the CPU (Central Processing Unit) and the GPU (Graphics Processing Unit). Scientists Weicheng Xue and Christopher J. Roy are engaged in research related to optimizing computing performance at solving fluid dynamics problems on multiple GPUs, improving the performance of multi-GPUs on structured grids. In their work, the use of GPUs improves the performance by 30–70 times [5,6]. Researchers Taku Nagatake and Tomoaki Kunugi analyze the possibility of using the GPU to accelerate the calculation of multiphase flows. They determine that the calculation time on the GPU (single GTX280) is about 4 times faster than the calculation time on the CPU (Xeon 5040, 4 parallelized threads) [7]. David J. Munk and Timoleon Kipouros describe the acceleration of the optimization process of multi-physical topology on the GPU architecture [8].

To increase the efficiency of using GPU computing resources, we propose an algorithm and a software module that implements it, which allows using functions from the NVIDIA CUDA library to select the optimal solution for a large-dimensional SLAE in the case of self-adjoint and non-self-adjoint operators. The developed software tools make it possible to more efficiently utilize the heterogeneous computing system resources used to computationally solve spatial and three-dimensional problems of hydrophysics.

2 Method for Solving Grid Equations

It becomes necessary to solve a high-dimensional SLAE in the mathematical modeling process of hydrodynamics and hydrobiology problems

$$Ax = f, \tag{1}$$

where A is the linear, positive definite operator $(A > 0)$ in the finite-dimensional Hilbert space H.

To solve SLAE (1) by iterative methods, the canonical form is used [9, 10]

$$B\frac{x^{m+1} - x^m}{\tau_{m+1}} + Ax^m = f, \tag{2}$$

where m is the iteration number, $\tau_{m+1} > 0$ is the iteration parameter, B is the preconditioner, which is formed as follows

$$B = (D + \omega R_1)\, D^{-1}\, (D + \omega R_2)\,, D = D^* > 0, \omega > 0, \tag{3}$$

where D is the diagonal operator, R_1, R_2 are the lower- and upper-triangular operators, respectively.

MATM calculation steps:

1. Calculation of the residual vector

$$r^m = Ax^m - f.$$

2. Calculation of the correction vector w^m

$$B(\omega_m)w^m = r^m.$$

3. Calculation of the convergence rate of the method

$$s_m^2 = 1 - \frac{(A_0 w^m, w^m)^2}{(B^{-1}A_0 w^m)\,(Bw^m, w^m)}.$$

4. Calculation of the ratio of the norm of the skew-symmetric part of the operator to the norm of the symmetric part

$$k_m^2 = \frac{\left(B^{-1}A_1 w^m, A_1 w^m\right)}{\left(B^{-1}A_0 w^m, A_0 w^m\right)},$$

5. Calculation of the coefficient θ_m

$$\theta_m = \frac{1 - \sqrt{\frac{s_m^2\, k_m^2}{(1+k_m^2)}}}{1 + k_m^2\,(1 - s_m^2)}.$$

6. Calculation of the iteration parameter

$$\tau_{m+1} = \theta_m \frac{(A_0 w^m, w^m)}{(B^{-1}A_0 w^m, A_0 w^m)}.$$

7. Recalculation of the vector x at the next iteration

$$x^{m+1} = x^m - \tau_{m+1} w^m.$$

8. Recalculation of the coefficient ω at the next iteration

$$\omega_{m+1} = \sqrt{\frac{(Dw^m, w^m)}{(D^{-1} R_2 w^m, R_2 w^m)}}.$$

3   Software Implementation of the Method for Solving Grid Equations

The software implementation of the MATM for solving high-dimensional SLAEs is based on the developed parallel algorithms that implement a pipeline computing process. The use of these algorithms allows one to fully utilize all available computing resources, including high-performance graphics accelerators. A distinctive feature of the proposed algorithms is the possibility of using calculators with different performance. This allows one to organize distributed computing using different models of central processing units (CPUs) on different nodes and even different video accelerators (GPUs) inside a separate compute node. The software implementation enables to indicate the number and technical characteristics of the CPU and GPU at the initial stage of the decomposition of the computational grid for each compute node of the cluster. For each CPU, the number of cores is set. For the GPU, the number of streaming multiprocessors is specified. Calculations are performed on the K60 hybrid supercomputer installed at the Supercomputer Centre of Collective Usage of KIAM RAS.

In the process of solving computational problems, it is necessary to dynamically distribute the computational load between dissimilar computers. Therefore, a class library is developed in C++, it allows describing the structure and hardware of a computing cluster. The class library contains the following classes:

- ComputingCluster, describes the structure of a computing cluster. Stores objects describing compute nodes in the std::map container. The class implements a number of auxiliary methods that allow one to manage the list of compute nodes, to determine the total performance of the cluster and display detailed information about it.
- ComputingNode, describes the structure and characteristics of a compute node. The methods of the class allow one to manage the list of computing devices, to determine the total performance and the size of the random access memory of the compute node.
- ComputingDevice is an abstract class that describes the general characteristics of computing devices located in a separate compute node of a cluster.
- ComputingDeviceCPU, a heir of the abstract ComputingDevice class, describing the characteristics of the CPU.
- ComputingDeviceGPU, a heir of the abstract ComputingDevice class, describing the characteristics of the GPU.

A multi-threaded computing process is controlled by an algorithm that allows each node to manage all available program threads (calculators) running on both the CPU and GPU. Each calculator handles only for its own fragment of the computational domain. For this, the computational domain is divided into subdomains assigned to individual compute nodes (Fig. 1). Next, each subdomain is divided into blocks assigned to each computing device (CPU or GPU). After that, each block is divided into fragments assigned to calculators (CPU cores and GPU streaming multiprocessors). Notations in Fig. 1: $Node1$, $Node2$, $Node3$ are compute nodes; $Device1$, $Device2$, $Device3$ are blocks of the computational domain calculated on separate computing devices of the node. $Thread1$, $Thread2$, $Thread3$, $Thread4$ are fragment arrays of the computational domain calculated by separate threads of the computing device.

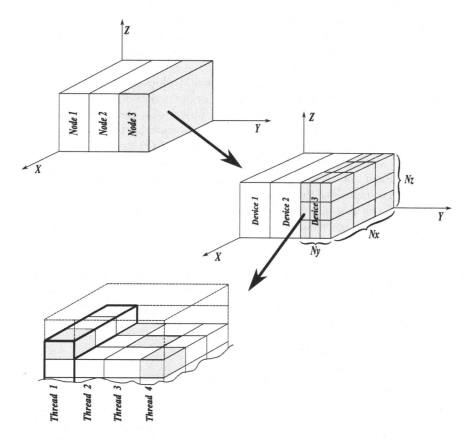

Fig. 1. Computational domain fragments distribution across the compute nodes, devices and threads

The subdivision of subdomains into fragments mapped to each calculator inside a separate compute node is performed as follows: the number of fragments of the computational domain along the Oz axis is selected as the smallest common multiple of the optimal dimensions of CUDA computing blocks for all video accelerators involved in the cluster (Fig. 2). In Fig. 2, Nv is the calculator index; Nx is the number of nodes of the computational domain on the Ox axis; Ny_0, Ny_1, Ny_2, Ny_3 is the number of nodes of the computational domain on the Oy axis for the calculator with indexes 0, 1, 2 and 3, respectively; z is the layer index on the Oz axis; s is the index of the pipeline calculation stage. The number of fragments of the computational domain on the Ox axis in the block (Nx) is selected in such a way that their number is greater than the number of calculators in the cluster, and they are the same. The number of fragments of the computational domain along the Oy axis in the block is selected so that the calculation time of each block by different calculators is approximately the same. For this, a series of experiments is preperformed to calculate the performance of calculators, which is the 95th percentile of the calculation time in terms of 1000 nodes of the computational grid.

The fragments of the computational domain processed in parallel are highlighted in gray. Note that the calculator index coincides with the fragment index of the computational domain on the Oy axis.

A graph model is used to describe the relationships between the adjacent fragments of the computational grid and the organization of a pipeline calculation process (Fig. 3). Each graph node is an object of a class that describes a fragment of the computational domain. This class contains the following fields: the dimensions of the fragment along the Ox, Oy, and Oz axes, the index of the zero node of the fragment in the global computational domain, pointers to the adjacent fragments of the computational grid, and pointers to the objects that describe the parameters of the calculators. The computational process is a graph traversal from the root node with a parallel launch of calculators that process the graph nodes in accordance with the value of the calculation step counter $s = ki + j$.

An algorithm and its program implementation in the CUDA C language are developed to improve the calculation efficiency of computational grid fragments assigned to graphics accelerators [12–16].

A fragment of the algorithm for solving a SLAE with a lower triangular matrix contains the following steps:

1. Computation of global thread indexes

$$tdX = bkDim.x \cdot bkIdx.x + tdIdx.x;$$

$$tdZ = bkDim.z \cdot bkIdx.z + tIdx.z.$$

2. Calculation of the indexes of the row, layer and initialization of the counter by the coordinate (variable) processed by the current thread

$$i = tdX + 1; k = tdZ + 1; j = 1.$$

3. Initialization of the loop parameter for calculating the residual vector:
   $s = 3$.

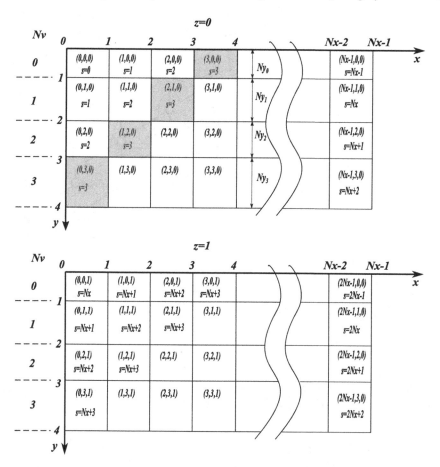

Fig. 2. Decomposition of the computational subdomain calculated by a separate compute node with the organization of a parallel pipeline computing process

4. Calculation of the indexes of the nodes of a seven-point grid pattern

$$mIdx_0 = i + (bkDim.x + 1) \cdot j + n_1 \cdot n_2 \cdot k;$$

$$mIdx_2 = mIdx_0 - 1;$$

$$mIdx_4 = mIdx_0 - n_1;$$

$$mIdx_6 = mIdx_0 - n_1 \cdot n_2.$$

5. Initialization of the residual vector value at the template point $mIdx_4 = 0$.
6. Checking the condition $(s > 3 + tdX + tdZ)$ for calculating the value of the residual vector at the template point $mIdx_4$. If the condition is met, then $rmIdx_4 = cmem[tdX][tdZ]$. Otherwise, $rmIdx_4 = r[mIdx_4]$.
7. Initialization of the residual vector value at the template point $mIdx_2 = 0$.

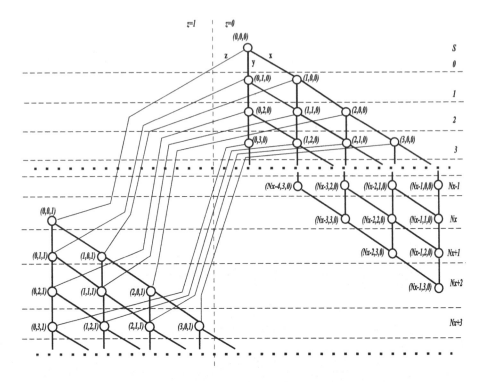

Fig. 3. Graph model that describes the relationships between the adjacent fragments of the computational grid and the process of pipeline calculation

8. Checking the condition $(tdX \neq 0) \wedge (s > 3+tdX+tdZ)$ for calculating the value of the residual vector at the template point $mIdx_2$. If the condition is met, then $rmIdx_2 = cmem[tdX-1][tdZ]$. Otherwise, $rmIdx_2 = r[mIdx_2]$.
9. Initialization of the residual vector value at the template point $mIdx_6 = 0$.
10. Checking the condition $(tdZ \neq 0) \wedge (s > 3+tdX+tdZ)$ for calculating the value of the residual vector at the template point $mIdx_6$. If the condition is met, then $rmIdx_6 = cmem[tdX][tdZ-1]$. Otherwise, $rmIdx_6 = r[mIdx_6]$.
11. Calculation of the value of the residual vector at the central point of the seven-point pattern $mIdx_0$

$$rmIdx_0 = (\omega \cdot (ksu_2[mIdx_0] \cdot rmIdx_2 + ksu_4[mIdx_0] \cdot rmIdx_4+$$

$$+ksu_6[m_0] \cdot rmIdx_6) + r[mIdx_0])/((0.5 \cdot \omega + 1) \cdot ksu_0[mIdx_0]);$$

$$cmem[tdX][tdZ] \leftarrow rmIdx_0;$$

$$r[mIdx_0] \leftarrow rmIdx_0.$$

12. Transition to the next node of the computational grid along the coordinate y: $j = j + 1$.

13. Assigning the loop parameter to the next value $s = s + 1$.
14. Checking the exit condition from the loop $s \leq n_1 + n_2 + n_3 - 3$. If the condition is true, then the transition to step 4 is performed; otherwise, the algorithm exits.

The conducted studies show a significant dependence of the algorithm implementation time for calculating the preconditioner on the ratio of threads in spatial coordinates.

The GeForce GTX 1650 video adapter is used in experimental studies. It has 4 GB of video memory, a core and memory clock frequency of 1485 MHz and 8000 MHz, respectively, and a video memory bus bit rate of 128 bits. The computing part consists of 56 texture processor clusters (TPC) with 2 multiprocessors (SM) in each. Each multiprocessor contains 8 streaming processors (SP) or CUDA cores. Therefore, the number of CUDA cores for the GeForce GTX 1650 video adapter is 896.

The purpose of the experiment is to determine the distribution of flows along the Ox and Oz axes of the computational grid at different values of its nodes along the Oy axis so that the implementation time on the GPU of one MATM step is minimal. Two values are taken as factors: $k = X/Z$ is the ratio of the number of threads on the Ox, (X) axis to the number of threads on the Oz, (Z) axis; Y is the number of threads on the Oy axis. Values of the objective function: T_{GPU} is the implementation time of one MATM step on the GPU in terms of 1000 nodes of the computational grid, ms. The multiply of threads X and Z must not exceed 640 – the number of threads in a single block. Therefore, the levels of variation of the values X and Z are chosen taking into account CUDA limitations. For example, the number of threads on the Oy axis varies in the range $[1000, 30000]$. Experimental data analysis for the factor values $X = 1$, $Z = 640$ and $X = 640$, $Z = 1$ shows that the allocated memory is not used when calculating the objective function at the specified points. Therefore, these points must be excluded from regression analysis.

The regression equation is obtained as a result of experimental data processing:

$$T_{GPU} = a - b \cdot Y - c \cdot ln(k) - d \cdot ln(Y), \qquad (4)$$

where T_{GPU} is the implementation time of one MATM step on the GPU in terms of 1000 nodes of the computational grid, ms. The determination coefficient is 0.86; $a = 0.026; b = 0.0000002; c = 0.00016; d = 0.00077$. The graph of the objective function is given in Fig. 4.

The analysis of the graph, constructed according to equation (6), shows a slowdown in the calculation speed at $k < 10$ and $Y < 1000$, which is explained in this case by the inefficient use of the distributed memory of the graphics accelerator (Fig. 4).

As a result of experimental data analysis, it is found that the shortest implementation time of one MATM step in terms of 1000 nodes of the computational grid on the GeForce GTX 1650 video adapter will be obtained with the largest number of threads along the Oy axis and the highest coefficient value k.

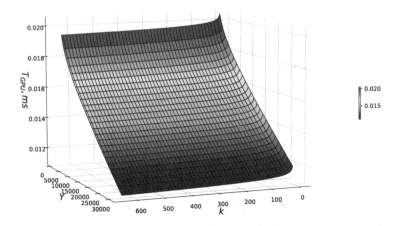

Fig. 4. Surface of the response function $T_{GPU} = f(k, Y)$

The implementation time of one MATM step in terms of 1000 nodes of the computational grid on the GeForce GTX 1650 video adapter is inversely proportional to the number of computational grid nodes on the Oz axis, i.e., with an increase in the number of nodes on the Oz axis, the calculation time decreases. The highest value of the coefficient k is achieved when the number of threads on the Ox axis increases, and the number of threads on the Oz axis decreases. Therefore, it is advisable to perform the decomposition of the computational domain in the form of parallelepipeds, in which the size on the Oz axis is minimal, and on the Ox axis is maximal. The choice of the decomposition method of the computational domain in the form of parallelepipeds must be made taking into account the architecture of the video adapter.

When developing a parallel algorithm that implements the pipeline process of computations, it is necessary to take into account the amount of data transmitted between compute nodes, i.e., the size of the transmitted plane (number of elements in the plane). To dynamically determine the size of the transmitted plane, it is necessary to determine the functional dependence of the time spent on transferring data between compute nodes on the size of the transmitted plane. The resulting dependence will make it possible to obtain such a decomposition of the computational domain that will reduce the execution time of the entire parallel algorithm.

The purpose of the experiment is to determine the functional dependence of the data transfer time between compute nodes on the number of elements in the transmitted plane. The number of elements in the plane is taken as a factor V. The value of the objective function $Time$, ms is the time of transmitting the number of elements V.

To determine the dependence of the time of data transmission between compute nodes on the number of transmitted elements, an algorithm and its software implementation in the C language are developed. The program considers three ranges of dimensions of the transmitted plane: $V \in [1; 100]$ with a step of 1,

$V \in [100; 10000]$ with a step of 100 elements, and $V \in [10000; 1000000]$ with a step of 10,000 elements.

The developed algorithm is tested on the main computing resource of the Keldysh Institute of Applied Mathematics, namely, the K-60 computing cluster. The specified cluster consists of two sections – one without graphics accelerators k60.kiam.ru, the other with graphics accelerators k60gpu.kiam.ru. The hardware of the GPU section consists of 10 compute nodes. Each node is a dual-processor server with the following characteristics: 2 x Intel Xeon Gold 6142 v4 processors (16 x cores), 4 x nVidia Volta GV100GL GPU, 768 GB RAM, 2 TB disk.

As a result of processing experimental data for the range of dimensions of the transmitted plane from 10,000 to 1,000,000 elements, a regression equation is obtained:

$$T = a + bV, \tag{5}$$

where T is the time of transmitting the number of V elements, ms. The determination coefficient is 0.995; $a = 278.72$; $b = 0.038$.

The resulting functional dependence is used by the decomposition algorithm to dynamically determine the dimensions of the plane transmitted between compute nodes.

4   Conclusions

As a result of the conducted research, an algorithm and a software module implementing it, designed to solve SLAEs that arise during the discretization of spatial-three-dimensional model problems of mathematical physics using the MATM, are developed.

A graph model that makes it possible to organize a parallel pipeline computing process on the GPU, designed to solve systems of large-dimensional grid equations, is proposed.

It is established that the shortest implementation time of one MATM step per 1000 nodes of the computational grid on the GeForce GTX 1650 video adapter will be obtained with the largest number of threads on the Oy axis and the highest value of the coefficient k, directly proportional to the number of threads, on the Ox axis. The optimal decomposition method for the three-dimensional computational grid with the number of nodes up to 10^{11} and the time layers number from 10^4 and more, if we focus on the limitations of computational stability and accuracy of discrete models, applicable to the GPU, is described.

References

1. Bonaduce, A., Staneva, J., Grayek, S., Bidlot, J.-R., Breivik, Ø.: Sea-state contributions to sea-level variability in the European Seas. Ocean Dyn. **70**(12), 1547–1569 (2020). https://doi.org/10.1007/s10236-020-01404-1
2. Marchesiello, P., Mc.Williams, J.C., Shchepetkin, A.: Open boundary conditions for long-term integration of regional oceanic models. Ocean. Model. **J.** 3, 1–20 (2001). https://doi.org/10.1016/S1463-5003(00)00013-5

3. Androsov, A.A., Wolzinger, N.E.: The Straits of the World Ocean: A General Approach to Modelling (In Russian). Nauka, Saint Petersburg (2005)
4. Westerweel, J.T.M., Boersma, B.J.J., Nieuwstadt, F.T.M.: Turbulence. Springer, Cham (2016). https://doi.org/10.1007/978-3-319-31599-7
5. Xue, W., Roy, C.J.: Multi-GPU performance optimization of a computational fluid dynamics code using OpenACC. Concurr. Comput. Pract. Exp. **33**, 1547–1569 (2021). https://doi.org/10.1002/cpe.6036
6. Xue, W., Jackson, C.W., Xue, W., Roy, C.J.: Multi-CPU/GPU parallelization, optimization and machine learning based autotuning of structured grid CFD codes. In: AIAA Aerospace Sciences Meeting, p. 0362 (2018)
7. Nagatake, T., Kunugi, T.: Application of GPU to computational multiphase fluid dynamics. In: IOP Conference Series: Materials Science and Engineering, vol. 10 (2010)
8. Munk, D.J., Kipouros, T., Vio, G.A.: Multi-physics bi-directional evolutionary topology optimization on GPU-architecture. Eng. Comput. **35**(3), 1059–1079 (2018). https://doi.org/10.1007/s00366-018-0651-1
9. Sukhinov, A.D., et al.: Data processing of field measurements of expedition research for mathematical modeling of hydrodynamic processes in the Azov Sea. Comput. Conti. Mech. **13**(2), 161–174 (2020). https://doi.org/10.7242/1999-6691/2020.13.2.13
10. Sukhinov, A., Litvinov, V., Chistyakov, A., Nikitina, A., Gracheva, N., Rudenko, N.: Computational aspects of solving grid equations in heterogeneous computing systems. In: Malyshkin, V. (ed.) PaCT 2021. LNCS, vol. 12942, pp. 166–177. Springer, Cham (2021). https://doi.org/10.1007/978-3-030-86359-3_13
11. Oyarzun, G., Borrell, R., Gorobets, A., Oliva, A.: MPI-CUDA sparse matrix-vector multiplication for the conjugate gradient method with an approximate inverse preconditioner. Comput. Fluids **92**, 244–252 (2014). https://doi.org/10.1016/j.compfluid.2013.10.035
12. Zheng, L., Gerya, T., Knepley, M., Yuen, D., Zhang, H., Shi, Y.: GPU implementation of multigrid solver for stokes equation with strongly variable viscosity. In: GPU Solutions to Multi-scale Problems in Science and Engineering, pp. 321-333. Springer, Heidelberg (2013). https://doi.org/10.1007/978-3-642-16405-7_21
13. Konovalov, A.: The steepest descent method with an adaptive alternating-triangular preconditioner. Diff. Equ. **40**, 1018–1028 (2004)
14. Sukhinov, A.I., et al.: Computational aspects of mathematical modeling of the shallow water hydrobiological processes. Num. Methods Program. **21**, 452–469 (2020). https://doi.org/10.26089/NumMet.v21r436
15. Samarskii, A.A., Vabishchevich, P.N.: Numerical Methods for Solving Convection-Diffusion Problems (In Russian). URSS, Moscow (2009)
16. Browning, J.B., Sutherland, B.: C++20 Recipes. A Problem-Solution Approach, p. 630. Apress, Berkeley (2020)

Parallel Methods for Solving Saddle Type Systems

V. P. Il'in[1] and D. I. Kozlov[1,2(✉)]

[1] Institute of Computational Mathematics and Mathematical Geophysics SB RAS,
Novosibirsk, Russia
{ilin,di_kozlov}@sscc.ru
[2] Novosibirsk State University, Novosibirsk, Russia

Abstract. Parallel methods for solving saddle-type algebraic systems that are relevant for modeling processes and phenomena in the problems of electromagnetism, hydro-gas dynamics, elastoplasticity, filtration and other applications are considered. Preconditioned iterative processes in the Krylov subspaces, including the efficient generalization of the Golub-Kahan-Arioli bidiagonalization method, are investigated as applied to large SLAEs with sparse matrices that arise when approximating multidimensional boundary value problems with a complex geometric configuration of computational domains and the contrasting material properties of various media on unstructured grids. It is supposed to store the matrices in compressed formats that require special technologies for working with big data. The parallelization of the proposed class of block algorithms is carried out by means of hybrid programming on supercomputers of a heterogeneous architecture with distributed and hierarchical shared memory, using the means of inter-node message transmission, multi-threaded computing, operation vectorization. A comparative analysis of various algorithmic approaches is carried out on the basis of the estimates of the performance and resource intensity of the corresponding software implementations.

Keywords: large sparse SLAEs · saddle matrices · iterative processes · algorithm parallelization · Krylov subspaces · computing performance

1 Introduction

Systems of linear algebraic equations (SLAEs) of the saddle type in their classical version are associated with second order block matrices having a zero lower-right block and written in the following form (we limit ourselves to a real case for simplicity):

$$Au \equiv \begin{bmatrix} D & C \\ C^\top & 0 \end{bmatrix} \begin{bmatrix} u_1 \\ u_2 \end{bmatrix} = \begin{bmatrix} f_1 \\ f_2 \end{bmatrix} \equiv f, \tag{1}$$

$$u, f \in \mathcal{R}^N; \quad u_1, f_1 \in \mathcal{R}^{N_1}; \quad u_2, f_2 \in \mathcal{R}^{N_2}; \quad N = N_1 + N_2,$$

$$D \in \mathcal{R}^{N_1, N_1}, \quad C \in \mathcal{R}^{N_1, N_2}, \quad A \in \mathcal{R}^{N, N}.$$

L. Sokolinsky and M. Zymbler (Eds.): PCT 2022, CCIS 1618, pp. 85–98, 2022.
https://doi.org/10.1007/978-3-031-11623-0_7

For a number of characteristic applications, the matrix A from (1) has the following property, see [1]–[2].

Property A. The matrix D is symmetric and positive definite (s.p.d.), the null spaces of the matrices D and $C^\top$ do not intersect, i.e., $ker(D) \cap ker(C^\top) = \{0\}$, which ensures the non-singularity of the matrix A.

The saddle-type matrices A from (1) are sometimes considered in a more general form

$$A = \begin{bmatrix} D & C_1 \\ C_2^\top & -\varepsilon H \end{bmatrix}, \quad \varepsilon > 0, \tag{2}$$

where $H \in \mathcal{R}^{N_2, N_2}$ is the positive-semi-definite matrix, in the sense of fulfilling the inequality $(Hv, v) \geq 0$ for $v \in \mathcal{R}^{N_2}$, introduced either by the conditions of the problem statement, or for the reasons of the regularization of original SLAEs (1). In addition, the matrices D, H, A can be asymmetric, i.e., $C_1 \neq C_2, D \neq D^\top, H \neq H^\top, A \neq A^\top$.

Note that without loss of generality, instead of (1), we can consider saddle SLAEs of the form

$$\begin{bmatrix} D & C \\ C^\top & 0 \end{bmatrix} \begin{bmatrix} u_1 \\ u_2 \end{bmatrix} = \begin{bmatrix} f_1 \\ 0 \end{bmatrix}. \tag{3}$$

Indeed, if we take any particular solution of the subsystem $C\hat{u}_1 = f_2$, the vector $u = \check{u} + \hat{u}$ is the solution of systems of linear algebraic equations (1), satisfying the system

$$\begin{bmatrix} D & C \\ C^\top & 0 \end{bmatrix} \begin{bmatrix} \check{u}_1 \\ u_2 \end{bmatrix} = \begin{bmatrix} f_1 - D\hat{u}_1 \\ 0 \end{bmatrix}.$$

Note also that any solution to SLAEs (1) simultaneously satisfies the system

$$\tilde{A}v = \tilde{A} \begin{bmatrix} u_1 \\ u_2 \end{bmatrix} \equiv \begin{bmatrix} \tilde{D} & C \\ C^\top & 0 \end{bmatrix} \begin{bmatrix} u_1 \\ u_2 \end{bmatrix} = \begin{bmatrix} f_1 \\ 0 \end{bmatrix} \equiv \tilde{f},$$
$$\tilde{D} = D + \gamma R, \quad R = CK^{-1}C^\top, \quad \gamma \geq 0, \tag{4}$$

where $v\tilde{f} \in \mathcal{R}^N$ and $K \in \mathcal{R}^{N_1, N_1}$ is an arbitrary non-degenerate matrix. Since the latter system is formally a regularization, or generalization, of SLAEs (1), we further focus on the algorithm for solving equation (4). The parameter γ is introduced for the convenience of varying the algorithm, in particular, $\gamma = 0$ means no regularization.

Note that the non-degenerate matrix of the form of (1) can have an alternating spectrum, which creates its own difficulties in the iterative solution of the corresponding algebraic system.

Without loss of generality, the studied SLAEs can be written down in the following form:

$$\tilde{A} \begin{bmatrix} u_1 \\ u_2 \end{bmatrix} \equiv \begin{bmatrix} \tilde{D} & C \\ C^\top & 0 \end{bmatrix} \begin{bmatrix} u_1 \\ u_2 \end{bmatrix} = \begin{bmatrix} 0 \\ g \end{bmatrix}, \quad \tilde{D} = D + \gamma CK^{-1}C^\top. \tag{5}$$

It is easy to check that if in (4), the vector u_1 is replaced by $u_1 + \tilde{D}^{-1}f_1$, then this system will take the form of (5) with the right hand side $g = -C^\top \tilde{D}^{-1}f_1$. It is assumed that in (5), $\tilde{D}$ and K are the s.p.d. matrices, and the inequality $N_1 \geq N_2$ also holds.

Algebraic systems of the form of (1), (2) are in demand in many topical problems of electromagnetism, hydro-gas dynamics, heat and mass transfer, elasticity, multiphase filtration in porous-fractured media and in other applications. In particular, they arise in mixed classical or generalized formulations for initial boundary value problems. A large number of papers are devoted to the study of the saddle SLAEs under consideration and methods for solving them, see [3–12] and an extensive list of literature given therein. In recent years, due to the increasing role of the predictive modeling of real processes and phenomena with big data, there has been a significant increase in the interest in high-performance methods and technologies for solving large SLAEs with sparse matrices arising from the approximations of multi-dimensional boundary value problems with complex configurations of computational domains and the contrasting material properties of different media using finite difference methods, finite volumes, finite elements and discontinuous Galerkin algorithms of various orders of accuracy on unstructured grids [13]. The resulting algebraic systems have $10^8 - 10^{10}$ sizes and are poorly conditioned (the conditioning numbers of matrices reach 10^{13} and greater), thus, their numerical solution in practice takes up to 80% of the total machine resources. Therefore, the main reserve for speeding up calculations is the scalable parallelization of algorithms by means of hybrid programming with the inter-node message transmission, multi-threaded messages and vectorization of operations (MPI, OpenMP, AVX systems, respectively) of heterogeneous architecture supercomputers with distributed and hierarchical shared memory, see [14–18]. It should be noted that due to the large-block structure of saddle matrices, two-level iterative algorithms with specific features of data organization and memory access methods are characteristic of solving the corresponding SLAEs, and optimization is critical for improving the performance of software implementations.

This paper is structured as follows. Section 2 discusses the main approaches to constructing preconditioned block iterative methods in the Krylov subspaces for the effective solution of the considered algebraic systems. Section 3 deals with the analysis of the performance of the scalable parallelization of the studied computational processes in the weak and strong senses. In conclusion, the problems of improving the performance of algorithms for solving saddle SLAEs are discussed in the light of the current trends in the development of supercomputer architectures.

2   Iterative Algorithms in the Krylov Subspaces for Solving Saddle SLAEs

In this section, we first characterize the general property of Krylov-type iterative processes and then focus on their features when solving SLAEs with saddle matrices.

2.1   General Scheme of the Krylov Approaches for Symmetric and Non-symmetric Algebraic Systems

For solving symmetric or non-symmetric SLAEs

$$Au = f, \quad A \in \mathcal{R}^{N,N}; \quad f \in \mathcal{R}^N \tag{6}$$

iterative methods in the Krylov subspaces can be written down as follows:

$$u^{n+1} = u^n + \alpha_n p^n = u^0 + \alpha_0 p^0 + ... + \alpha_n p^n,$$
$$r^{n+1} = r^n - \alpha_n A p^n = r^0 - \alpha_0 A p^0 - ... - \alpha^n A p^n, \tag{7}$$

Here u^0 is an arbitrary initial vector, $r^0 = f - Au^0$ is the corresponding residual, α_n and p^n are the iterative parameters and guiding vectors. In the absence of a precondition for system (6), $p^0 = r^0$ is conventionally assumed (to be used below), although formally the initial guiding vector can be arbitrary. Assume that the direction vectors are A^γ-orthogonal, i.e.,

$$(p^n, p^k)_\gamma = (A^\gamma p^n, p^k) = \rho_k^{(\gamma)} \delta_{n,k}, \quad \rho_k^{(\gamma)} = (A^\gamma p^k, p^k) = ||p^k||_\gamma^2, \tag{8}$$

where $\delta_{n,k}$ is the Kronecker symbol, and the exponents are equal to $\gamma = 0, 1, 2$. Then the residuals are r^n for the value of the parameters

$$\alpha_n = \sigma_n/\rho_n, \quad \sigma_n = (r^0, p^n)_{\gamma-1} = (r^n, p^n)_{\gamma-1} = ||r^n||_{\gamma-1}^2, \tag{9}$$

providing a minimum of the functional $\Phi_\gamma(r^n) = (A^{\gamma-2} r^n, r^n)$ in the Krylov subspaces

$$\mathcal{K}_n(r^0, A) = \mathrm{Span}(r^0, Ar^0, ..., A^{n-1} r^0). \tag{10}$$

If the matrix A is symmetric, then orthogonality conditions (8) are provided when determining the direction vectors p^n by the two-term recursive formulas

$$p^{n+1} = r^{n+1} + \beta_n p^n, \quad \beta_n = \sigma_{n+1}/\sigma_n. \tag{11}$$

For the case $\gamma = 0$, however, the calculation of α_n must be done in a different way. Since the exact solution of SLAEs can be represented as a basis decomposition

$$u = u^0 + \alpha_0 p^0 + ... + \alpha_{m-1} p^{m-1}, \quad m \leq N,$$

then the iterative vectors and the corresponding residual vectors are presented in the following form:

$$v^n = u - u^n = \alpha_n p^n + ... + \alpha_m p^m,$$
$$r^n = Av^n = \alpha_n A p^n + ... + \alpha_m A p^m. \tag{12}$$

Hence, using A^γ, the orthogonalization of the vectors p^k, we have

$$\alpha_n = (v^n, p^n)_\gamma/||p^n||_\gamma^2 = -\alpha_{n-1}(v^n, Ap^{n-1})/||p^n||_\gamma^2$$
$$= -\alpha_{n-1}(r^n, p^{n-1})_\gamma/||p^n||_\gamma^2. \tag{13}$$

Here the orthogonality of the vectors p^{n-2}, p^{n-1} and p^n is used. The calculation of the coefficient β_n in this case should be carried out according to formula (11).

These algorithms for $\gamma = 0, 1, 2$ have the names of the methods of minimal iterations, or errors [17], as well as conjugate gradients and conjugate residuals, respectively.

The described approaches allow for a simple generalization to SLAEs, preconditioned with the help of some s.p.d. matrices B. To preserve the symmetry of the systems, it is advisable to do this by two-way preconditioning using the formally introduced matrix $B^{1/2}$. As a result, system (1) takes the form

$$\bar{A}\bar{u} = \bar{f}, \quad \bar{A} = B^{-1/2}AB^{-1/2}, \bar{u} = B^{1/2}u, \quad \bar{f} = B^{-1/2}f. \tag{14}$$

A result of applying the conjugate direction formulas to SLAE (14), after certain transformations for $\gamma = 1, 2$, we obtain the following iterative process:

$$\hat{p}^0 = \hat{r}^0 = B^{-1}r^0 = B^{-1}(f - Au^0), \quad n = 0, 1, 2, ...;$$
$$u^{n+1} = u^n + \alpha_n \hat{p}^n, \quad \hat{r}^n = \hat{r}^n - \alpha_n A\hat{p}^n; \tag{15}$$
$$\hat{p}^{n+1} = \hat{r}^{n+1} + \beta_n \hat{p}^n, \quad \alpha_n = \sigma_n/\rho_n, \quad \beta_n = \sigma_{n+1}/\sigma_n;$$
$$\sigma_n = (A^{\gamma-1}\hat{r}^n, \hat{r}^n), \quad \rho_n = (B^{-1}A\hat{p}^n, A^{\gamma-1}\hat{p}^n),$$

where the new vectors are related to the previous relations $\hat{p}^n = B^{-1}p^n$, $\hat{r}^n = B^{-1}r^n$. In the method of minimum iterations with $\gamma = 0$, the calculation of the parameters α_n, β_n must be carried out according to formulas (9), (10), with the replacement values of $\bar{r}^n = B^{-1}r^n$, $\bar{p}^n = B^{-1}p^n$, respectively.

For non-symmetric algebraic systems, the methods of their solution become significantly more complicated. We briefly present a description of specific approaches for a fairly wide class of multi-preconditioned algorithms of semi-conjugate direction [18]. In general, these iterative processes in the block Krylov subspaces can be presented as follows:

$$r^0 = f - Au^0, \quad n = 0, ... : \quad u^{n+1} = u^n + P_n \bar{\alpha}_n,$$

$$P_n = (p_1^n, ..., p_{M_n}^n), \quad r^{n+1} = r^n - AP_n \bar{\alpha}_n, \quad \bar{\alpha}_n = (\alpha_{n,1}, ..., \alpha_{n,M_n})^{\top}.$$

Here $p_1^n, ..., p_{M_n}^n$ are the guiding vectors that make up the matrix P_n of the n-th iteration, and $\bar{\alpha}_n$ is the vector of the iterative parameters. With respect to the vectors p_k^n in the above relations, only orthogonality conditions are assumed to be fulfilled

$$(Ap_k^n, A^{\gamma}p_{k'}^{n'}) = \rho_{n,k}^{(\gamma)}\delta_{n,n'}^{k,k'}, \quad \rho_{n,k}^{(\gamma)} = (Ap_k^n, A^{\gamma}p_k^n),$$

$$\gamma = 0, 1, \quad n' = 0, 1, ..., n - 1, \quad k, k' = 1, 2, ..., M_n.$$

If, at the same time, the coefficients $\bar{\alpha}_n = \{\alpha_{n,l}\}$ are defined by the formulas

$$\alpha_{n,l} = \sigma_{n,l}/\rho_{n,n}^{(\gamma)}, \quad \sigma_{n,l} = (r^0, A^{\gamma}\bar{p}_l^n),$$

then the functional of the residual $\Phi_n^{(\gamma)}(r^{n+1}) \equiv (r^{n+1}, A^{\gamma-1}r^{n+1})$ reaches its minima in the Krylov block subspaces

$$\mathcal{K}_M = \mathrm{Span}\{p_1^0, ..., p_{M_0}^0, Ap_1^1, ..., Ap_{M_1}^1, ..., Ap_1^n, ..., Ap_{M_n}^n\},$$

$$M = M_0 + M_1 + \cdots + M_n,$$

for $\gamma = 1$, and in the case of symmetry of the matrix A and for $\gamma = 0$.

The orthogonality properties of the guiding vectors can be provided if they are determined using "multi-conditional" recurrence relations in which each vector p_l^{n+1} corresponds to "its" preconditioning matrix $B_{n+1,l}$:

$$p_l^0 = B_{0,l}^{-1}r^0, \quad p_l^{n+1} = B_{n+1,l}^{-1}r^{n+1} - \sum_{k=0}^{n}\sum_{l=1}^{M_k}\beta_{n,k,l}^{(\gamma)}p_l^k, \quad n = 0,1,...;$$

$$B_{n,l} \in \mathcal{R}^{N,N}, \quad i = 1,...,M_n; \ \gamma = 0,1,$$

$$\bar{\beta}_{n,k}^{(\gamma)} = \{\beta_{n,k,l}^{\gamma}\} = \left(\beta_{n,k,1}^{(\gamma)} \cdots \beta_{n,k,M_n}^{(\gamma)}\right)^{\top} \in \mathcal{R}^{M_n},$$

$$\beta_{n,k,l}^{(\gamma)} = -\left(A^\gamma p_l^k, AB_{n+1,l}^{-1}r^{n+1}\right)/\rho_{n,l}^\gamma, \quad n = 0,1,...;$$

$$k = 0,...,n; \quad l = 1,...,M_n.$$

The peculiarity of the algorithms under consideration when solving poorly conditioned asymmetric SLAEs is of a high resource intensity, in terms of both the amount of calculations and the required memory, when conducting a large number of iterations. The remedy for this disadvantage can be carried out in two ways by reducing the number of used and saved direction vectors. The first of them is to reduce the recursion taking into account only its last m vectors. The second way consists in periodic restarts when using a given number of m iterations, the residual vector being calculated from the recurrence formula, and the original equation being to zero as the iteration:

$$r^{n_t} = f - Au^{n_t}, \quad n_t = mt, \quad t = 0,1,...,$$

where t is the number for the restart. Further calculations up to $n = n_{t+1}$ are carried out according to usual recursions. Both of these approaches lead to a significant slowdown in the iterative process.

To eliminate such a stagnating effect, it is proposed to add the second level of iterations using the least squares method (LSM) [17]. Let the "restart" approximations $u^{n_0}, u^{n_1}, ..., u^{n_t}$, $n_0 = 0$ be known. Then to correct the iterative vector u^{n_t}, which is the initial one for the next restart period, we use the following linear combination:

$$\hat{u}^{n_t} = u^{n_t} + b_1v_1 + ... + b_tv_t = u^{n_t} + v^{n_t}, \quad v^{n_t} = V_t\bar{b}, \quad \bar{b} = (b_1,...,b_t)^{\top},$$

$$V_t = \{v_k = u^{n_k} - u^{n_{k-1}}, \ k = 1,...,t\} \in \mathcal{R}^{N,t},$$

the vector of the coefficients $\bar{b}$ of which is determined by the condition of the minimum norm of residuals $||r^{n_t}||$ from the generalized solution of the overdefined algebraic system

$$W_t^\top W_t \bar{b} = r^{n_t} \equiv a^{n_t}, \quad W_t = AV_t.$$

The solution to this problem can be obtained, for example, using the QR - or SVD - decomposition of the matrix W_t. The normal solution with the minimum norm $||\bar{b}||$ is determined after applying the left Gauss transformation:

$$W_t^\top W_t \bar{b} = W_t r^{n_t}.$$

A more lightweight SLAEs format, in the sense of reducing its condition number, follows after multiplying the system on the left by the matrix V_t:

$$C_t \bar{b} \equiv V_t^\top A V_t \bar{b} = V_t^\top r^{n_t}.$$

If the matrix V_t has a full rank, then the matrices A and C_t will be non-degenerate at the same time. In this case, for a correction vector we have $v^{n_t} = B_t r^{n_t} \equiv V_t (V_t^T A V_t)^{-1} V_t^T r^{n_t}$, where the matrix $B_t = V_t \hat{A}^{-1} V_t^T$, $\hat{A} = V_t^T A V$ is a low-rank approximation of the matrix A^{-1}. In the approach considered, all restart vectors are stored in the corrected form, and the corresponding residuals are calculated using the formula $r^{n_t} = f - A\hat{u}^{n_t}$.

If there is no inverse for some matrix under consideration, then a generalized inverse matrix is used. Numerous experiments using the LSM to speed up the Krylov processes with restarts show its high efficiency.

We also note the following possibility of improving the performance of the SCD (Semi-Conjugate Direction) methods with restarts: when iterating the first restart period, remember all the p^n direction vectors, as well as the Ap^n vectors, and when calculating subsequent restart periods, we do not consider new vectors p^n and Ap^k, but use the previous ones.

The described class of SCD-methods with dynamic multi-conditionality in terms of the rate of convergence of iterations is equivalent to other well-known algorithms for solving asymmetric SLAEs in the Krylov subspaces, among which the generalized minimum residuals method (GMRES) based on the Arnoldi orthogonalization and existing in various versions is the most popular. The research into iterative methods for solving algebraic systems with saddle-type matrices involves the use of a wide variety of block preconditioners. The starting point for their construction is the following formula for the factorization of the matrix $A = D + L + U$, where D is block-diagonal, and L, U are the strictly lower and upper triangular matrices:

$$A = (G + L)G^{-1}(G + U), \quad G = D - LG^{-1}U,$$

$$G_1 = D, \quad G_2 = -\varepsilon H - C_2^\top D^{-1} C_1.$$

In particular, if the matrix A has a block structure of the form of (2), then $G = block - diagonal\{G_1, G_2\}$ has non-zero diagonal blocks only

$$G_1 = D, \quad G_2 = -\varepsilon H - C_2^\top D^{-1} C_1.$$

Note that if the matrix A is symmetric, i.e., $C_1 = C_2$ and $L = U^\top$, D and R in (2) are s.p.d. matrices, the given factorization is a congruence transformation of the block-diagonal matrix G. Since it obviously has an alternating sign spectrum, the matrix A has the same property, which causes certain difficulties in constructing methods for solving the corresponding SLAEs. If the definition of the matrix G is replaced by some approximation that allows simple calculations, then we get a family of preconditioners $B \approx A$. This implies, in particular, an iterative method of the Uzava type (see [14–20]). Another promising way is to construct block-diagonal preconditioners of the form

$$
B = \begin{bmatrix} \tilde{D} + CK_1^{-1}C^\top & & 0 \\ & \ddots & \\ 0 & & K_2 \end{bmatrix},
$$

where K_1 and K_2 are some s.p.d. matrices, see [17,18].

2.2 Generalized G-K-A – Bidiagonalization Method

Next, we consider a family of iterative methods for solving saddle symmetric SLAEs with the matrix $\tilde{A}$ from (4), based on the efficient approach of the G-K – Golub-Kahan bidiagonalization, which was originally proposed for a singular decomposition of rectangular matrices, but then in the publications by M. Saunders, M. Arioli, C. Greif and some other authors was successfully used to solve algebraic systems, including those with allowance for a block saddle structure.

More specifically, we present a generalization of the Golub-Kahan-Arioli algorithm, which is published in [9] under the title <<generalized G-K–bidiagonalization method>>, based on the construction of $\tilde{D}$-orthogonal vectors v_k and P-orthogonal vectors q_k, which satisfy the conditions

$$
\begin{aligned}
CQ_n = \tilde{D}V_nB_n, \quad & V_n^\top \tilde{D}V_n = I_{N_1}, \\
C^\top V_n = PQ_nB_n^\top, \quad & Q_n^\top PQ_n = I_{N_2},
\end{aligned} \tag{16}
$$

where $V_n = [v_1, ..., v_n] \in \mathcal{R}^{N_1,n}$, $Q_n = [q_1, ..., q_n] \in \mathcal{R}^{N_2,n}, P \in \mathcal{R}^{N_2,N_2}$ – s.p.d. matrices and $B_n \in \mathcal{R}^{n,n}$ is the bidiagonal matrix

$$
B_n = \begin{bmatrix} \alpha_1 & \beta_2 & 0 & \cdots & 0 \\ 0 & \alpha_2 & \beta_3 & \ddots & 0 \\ \vdots & \ddots & \ddots & \ddots & \vdots \\ 0 & \cdots & 0 & \alpha_{n-1} & \beta_n \\ 0 & \ddots & 0 & 0 & \alpha_n \end{bmatrix}.
$$

Let us note that in [9] only the case of $K = P$ is considered, which is not is mandatory, see formula (5). Introducing new unknown vectors $\mu^n =$

$(\mu_1, ..., \mu_n)$, $\nu^n = (\nu_1, ..., \nu_n) \in \mathcal{R}^n$, substituting the expressions

$$u_1 = V_n \mu^n, \quad u_2 = Q_n \nu^n \tag{17}$$

in (5) and multiplying system (5) on the left by the block-diagonal matrix $block\text{-}diag(V^\top, Q^\top)$, we get

$$V_n^\top \tilde{D} V_n (\mu^n + B_n \nu^n) = 0, \quad Q_n^\top P Q_n B_n^\top \mu^n = Q_n^\top g. \tag{18}$$

Thus, SLAEs (18) are reduced to the form

$$\begin{bmatrix} I_n & B_n \\ B_n^\top & 0 \end{bmatrix} \begin{bmatrix} \mu^n \\ \nu^n \end{bmatrix} = \begin{bmatrix} 0 \\ Q^\top g \end{bmatrix}. \tag{19}$$

Assuming further $Q_n^\top g = e_1 \|g\|_{P^{-1}}$, $e_1 = (1, 0, ...)^\top$, we define the vector

$$q_1 = P^{-1} g / \|g\|_{P^{-1}}, \quad \|g\|_{P^{-1}} = (g, P^{-1} g)^{1/2}.$$

Let us find the initial vector v_1:

$$\alpha_1 \tilde{D}^{-1} v_1 = C q_1, \quad v_1 = w/\alpha_1, \quad \alpha_1 = \sqrt{w^\top C q_1}, \quad w = \tilde{D}^{-1} q_1. \tag{20}$$

Note that the vector $\mu = B_n^{-\top} Q_n^\top g$ is determined up to a constant by the first column of the matrix $B_n^{-1} = (B_n^\top)^{-1}$.

Further the vectors v_n, q_n and the matrix B entries α_n, β_n are calculated from the following recurrent relations, $n = 1, 2, ...$:

$$s = P^{-1}(C v_n - \alpha_n P q_n), \quad \beta_{n+1} = \sqrt{s^\top P s},$$
$$q_{n+1} = s/\beta_{n+1}, \quad w = \tilde{D}^{-1}(C^\top q_{n+1} - \beta_{n+1} \tilde{D} v_n), \tag{21}$$
$$\alpha_{n+1} = (w^\top \tilde{D} w)^{1/2}, \quad v_{n+1} = w/\alpha_{n+1}.$$

Successive approximations u^n, beginning with (17), (18), are determined by the first n columns of the matrix V, according to

$$u_1^{n+1} = \sum_{j=1}^n \mu_j v_j = u_1^n + \mu_n v_n, \tag{22}$$

where μ_j are the components of the vector μ^n from (19), calculated by the formulas

$$\mu_1 = \|g\|_{P^{-1}} / \alpha_1, \quad \mu_{j+1} = -\beta_{j+1} \mu_j / \alpha_{j+1} \quad j = 1, 2, ... \tag{23}$$

Omitting the details of the derivation of the formula (see [10]), we present the resulting recurrence relation for the iterative solution:

$$u_2^{n+1} = u_2^n - \nu_n d_{n+1}, \quad d_1 = q_1/\alpha_1, \quad d_{n+1} = (q_{n+1} - \beta_{n+1} \alpha_n)/\alpha_{n+1}, \tag{24}$$

where d_n is the n-th column $D = Q B^{-1}$. This approach is called the generalized G-K-A – bidiagonalization algorithm. At each step of such an iterative process, the error norm $\|u - u^n\|$ is minimized. As noted in [14], the two-level iterative method demonstrates high performance and convergence rate when solving saddle-type SLAEs obtained in grid approximations of the mixed formulations of multi-dimensional boundary value problems.

3   Scalable Parallelization of Iterative Methods

In general, the computational quality of the algorithm can be characterized by means of two different features. The first one is mathematical efficiency, which can be estimated by the total number of arithmetical operations. The second characteristic is more practical and is measured by the run time of the method implementation on a specific computer configuration. In other words, in this case we speak about the quality of mapping algorithms onto an architecture that usually has a heterogeneous structure with distributed and hierarchical shared memory. A significant complexity of the problem of studying the performance of an executable program code lies in the actual absence of a mathematical model of supercomputer calculations, and optimization attempts require some experience and skill gained in order to avoid repeated trials and errors. Scalable parallelization is conventionally understood in either a strong or weak sense. The first means a reduction in the calculation time of a fixed task with an increase in the number of computing devices, for example, cores. In the second case, a simultaneous proportional increase in the resource intensity of the problem (the number of degrees of freedom) and the number of arithmetic devices are considered (ideally, the estimated time remains approximately constant). The SLAEs of most interest to us have high orders and sparse matrices with large conditionality numbers and an irregular structure. This does not only lead to an increase in the number of iterations, but also forces one to work with distributed and/or hierarchical shared memory systems, and also significantly slows down the access to data. It should be said that the large-block structure of saddle matrices strongly affects the computational scheme of iterative algorithms and the ways of parallelizing them when changing the type of a preconditioner. In this section, we briefly focus on the general current problems of parallelization and in more detail on the proposed generalization of the G-K-A – bidiagonalization algorithm, as applied to the solution of saddle SLAEs obtained from a finite element approximation of the three-dimensional initial boundary value problem for the two-phase filtration proposed in [24]. In this case, the order of SLAEs (1)–(5) is equal to $N \cong 4h^{-3}$, where h is the characteristic element of the grid, and the dimensions of the diagonal blocks are equal to $N_1 \cong 3h^{-3}$ and $N_2 \cong h^{-3}$. In physical terms, the subvector $u_1 = \{u^x, u^y, u^z\}$ consists of components of the velocity vector along different axes of the Cartesian coordinate system referred to the midpoints of the faces of the cubic grid, and u_2 is a set of values of the scalar pressure function at the centers of the grid cells. The matrix D is block-diagonal, and its non-zero blocks are easily invertible s.p.d. tridiagonal matrices with a strict diagonal dominance. The off-diagonal matrix is represented as three block rows $C = (C_1^\top, C_2^\top, C_3^\top)$, and each C_k, $k = 1,2,3$, is a two-diagonal matrix. The parallelization of the G-K-A – bidiagonalization method, presented in Sect. 2.2., consists of the following main stages. The auxiliary orthogonal vectors v_n, q_n and the entries α_n, β_n of the matrix B by formulas (20), (21) are calculated. The tedious procedure of this stage essentially depends on the structure of the matrices $\tilde{D}$ and K introduced in (5), and the matrices of the form P of (16). We get a simple case at $\gamma = 0$ in (5), i.e., the matrix K

is missing, and P is a diagonal matrix. At the same time, the appeal $\tilde{D} = D$ is implemented by efficient iteration-free runs, which can be performed in parallel without any additional expenditure of machine resources. If $\gamma \neq 0$, then even with the diagonal character of K, the inversion of the matrix $\tilde{D}$ (more precisely, the solution of auxiliary SLAEs with such a matrix) requires the introduction of a two-level iterative process. The issue of optimizing these algorithm parameters, which can potentially significantly reduce the number of iterations, seems to be non-trivial and requires a special study.

We denote the possibilities of parallelization:

1. The parallelization of vector-matrix operations of the Krylov processes.
2. The calculation of two-term recursions for the vectors u_1^n, u_2^n is performed by formulas (24). These vector operations are naturally parallelized with a linear speedup.
3. The formation of data structures and buffers is based on the separation of computational vectors, which geometrically corresponds to the decomposition of computational and grid domains to subdomains. For big data tasks, reducing communications at each iteration is critical to scalable parallelization.

The performance of parallel computing is defined mainly by the speedup, which is determined by the formulas

$$S_p = T_1/T_p, \quad T_p = T^a + T^c. \tag{25}$$

Here, T_p means the run time of solving the task on p processors. This value consists of two parts: the times of data exchanges and the implementation of the arithmetic operations. The latter can be described approximately by the following relations:

$$T^a = \tau_a N_a, \quad T^c = N_t(\tau_0 + \tau_c N_c).$$

In these formulas, τ_a means the average run time of an arithmetic operation, N_a is their total number, N_t is the number of communications, τ_0 and τ_c are the memory system waiting time and the transfer duration of one value, and N_c is the average volume of one data exchange. Since the machine constants are satisfied to the conditions $\tau_0 \gg \tau_c \gg \tau_a$, we can propose the following recommendations for the algorithms being constructed: we should try to minimize the volume of communications, and the exchanges should be carried out not in small, but in large portions, i.e., if possible, to carry out the preliminary accumulation of data buffers. These conclusions are even true because interprocessor information transfers not only slow down the computing process, but are also the most energy-consuming operations, and this becomes a significant factor in the cost of operating a supercomputer.

One of the important practical problems of scalable parallelization is due to solving large SLAEs with sparse matrices that arise from the grid approximations of multi-dimensional boundary or initial-boundary value problems. Here, the main approaches are additive domain decomposition methods with two-level iterative processes and the use of hybrid programming tools. The top level iterations implemented over the subdomains are carried out by means of MPI (Massage Passing Interface) for communications between the contacting subdomains. The low level of the algorithm includes the simultaneous solution of algebraic subsystems in the corresponding subdomains. This stage is parallelized by multi-threaded computing (OpenMP). At each such iteration, the values of approximate solutions are exchanged on the interface boundary surfaces of the contacting subdomains. Naturally, all matrix and vector data for subsystems are performed in the process-distributed form. The solution to SLAEs in each of the subdomains is parallelized using multi-threaded computing (OpenMP-type systems) on multi-core processors with shared memory. Additional speedup here can be achieved by vectorizing operations (AVX-type command systems based on SIMD – Single Instruction Multi Data technologies), see reviews in [20–25]. Unfortunately, here we can state the absence of regular programming systems with the automatic parallelization of algorithms, so that the success in the scalability of speeding up calculations largely depends on the art and skill of a mathematician-programmer. One of the common modern supercomputer configurations is a network of multi-core servers, with a number of cores in several tens or hundreds, which have several memory levels with different information exchange rates. For quite understandable reasons, larger memory devices have a lower data transfer rate (the fastest are the registers of arithmetic units - AU). In this situation, communication channels between different levels of memory are represented as a bottleneck, the access to which dramatically degrades the performance of the computing process. The most successful algorithmic solutions are those that use a small-block structure of data with the maximum use of AU registers, as well as the features of implementing their communications with lower-level memory.

Strictly speaking, the main objective of code optimization is not parallelism, but high performance. A significant speedup of calculations can be attained using variable precision machine arithmetic. The conventional way to solve large SLAEs is to use standard double precision with a 64-bit floating-point representation length. Many years of numerical experience show that this accuracy is sufficient in practice. However, for some ill-conditioned algebraic problems, it is necessary to use quadruple precision (128 bits). On the other side, at many stages of the algorithms, it is enough to apply single (32 bits) and even half precision (16 bits) which can be performed much faster. Nevertheless, with this approach, it is necessary to check the stability of computations. Hopefully, such an intelligent problem will be solved in the near future. Another way to obtain high performance and code optimization can be achieved through the efficient use of reliable implemented numerical tools (from SPARSE BLAS, for example) that are adapted to various computer platforms.

4   Conclusion

Parallel iterative methods in the Krylov subspaces for solving large saddle-type SLAEs with various matrices, relevant in the problems of electromagnetism, strength, hydro-gas dynamics and other applications, are considered. The issues of constructing preconditioners for symmetric or non-symmetric systems using universal least squares algorithms to speed up the Krylov iterations are discussed. Approaches to the generalization of Golub-Kahan-Arioli bidiagonalization methods are described. Scalable distributed technologies in the strong and weak senses, focused on minimizing communication losses, based on the use of hybrid programming tools, namely, the transmission of inter-node messages, multi-threaded computing and the vectorization of operations (MPI, OpenMP, and AVX systems), on supercomputers of a heterogeneous architecture with distributed and hierarchical shared memory, are considered.

References

1. Benzi, M., Golub, G.H., Liesen, J.: Numerical Solution of Saddle Point Problems. Acta Numerica **14**, 1137 (2005). https://doi.org/10.1017/S0962492904000212
2. Brezzi, F.: Stability of saddle points in finite dimensions. In: Blowey, J.F., Craig, A.W., Shardlow, T. (Eds.) Frontiers in Numerical Analysis. Universitext, pp. 17–61. Springer, Berlin, Heidelberg (2013). https://doi.org/10.1007/978-3-642-55692-0_2
3. Vassilevski, P.S.: Preconditioning mixed finite element saddle - point elliptic problems. J. Numer. Linear Algebra App. **3**(1), 1–20 (1996). https://doi.org/10.1002/(SICI)1099-1506(199601/02)
4. Bychenkov, Y.V., Chizhonkov, E.V.: Iterative Methods for Solving Saddle Point Problems. Binom Publication, Moscow (2010). (in Russian)
5. Popov, P.E., Kalinkin, A.A.: The method of separation of variables in a problem with a saddle - point. Russian J. Numer. Anal. Math. Model. **23**(1), 97–106 (2008). https://doi.org/10.1515/rnam.2008.007
6. Mardal, K., Winther, R.: Preconditioning discretizations of systems of partial differential equations. Numer. Linear. Algebra Appl. **18**, 1–40 (2011). https://doi.org/10.1002/nla.716
7. Arioli, M., Manzini, M.: A network programming approach in solving Darcy's equations by mixed finite elements methods. Electron. Trans. Numer. Anal. **22**, 41–70 (2006)
8. Golub, G.H., Grief, C.: On solving block-structured indefinite linear systems. SIAM J. Sci. Comput. **24**, 2076–2092 (2003). https://doi.org/10.1137/S1064827500375096
9. Arioli, M.: Generalized Golub-Kahan bidiagonalization and stopping criteria. SIAM J. Matrix Anal. App. **34**, 571–592 (2013). https://doi.org/10.1137/120866543
10. Greif, C., Schotzau, D.: Preconditioners for saddle point linear systems with highly singular (1.1) blocks. Electron. Trans. Numer. Anal. **22**, 114–121 (2006). (Special Volume on Saddle Point Problems)
11. Arioli, M., Orban, D.: Iterative methods for symmetric quasi-definite linear systems Part I: Theory. Science & Tehnology, Facilities Council, RAL, Harwell Oxford, Technical report RAL-TR-2013-003 (2013)
12. Gould, N., Orban, D., Rees, T.: Projected Krylov methods for saddle-point systems. SIAM J. Matrix Anal. App. **35**(4), 329–343 (2014). https://doi.org/10.1137/130916394

13. Il'in, V.P.: Mathematical Modeling. Part I. Continuous and Discrete Models., SBRAS Publ., Novosibirsk (2017). (in Russian)

14. Greif, C., Wathen, M.: Conjugate gradient for nonsingular saddle-point systems with a maximally rank-deficient leading block. J. Comput. Appl. Math. **358**, 1–11 (2019). https://doi.org/10.1016/j.cam.2019.02.016

15. Estrin, R., Winther, R.: Preconditioning descretization of system of partial differential equations. Nuner. Linear. Algebra App. **18**, 1–40 (2011). https://doi.org/10.1002/nla.716

16. Estrin, R., Greif, C.: SPMR: a family of saddle-point minimum residual solvers. SIAM J. Sci. Comput. **40**(3), 1884–1914 (2018). https://doi.org/10.1137/16M1102410

17. Il'in, V.P., Kazantcev, G.Y.: Iterative solution of saddle-point systems of linear equations. J. Math. Sci. **249**(2), 199–208 (2020). https://doi.org/10.1007/s10958-020-04934-7

18. Notay, Y.: Convergence of some iterative methods for symmetric saddle point linear systems. SIAM J. Matrix Anal. Appl. **40**(1), 122–146 (2019). https://doi.org/10.1137/18M1208836

19. Il'in, V.P.: Two-level iterative methods for solving the saddle point problems. MSR 2020 J. Phys. Conf. Ser. **1715**, 012004 (2021). https://doi.org/10.1088/1742-6596/1715/1/012004

20. Ivanov, M.I., Kremer, I.A., Laevsky Yu.M.: On the streamline upwind scheme of solution to the filtration problem. Siberian Electron. Math. Rep. **16**, 757–776 (2019). (in Russian) https://doi.org/10.33048/semi.2019.16.051

21. Dongarra, J., et al.: Applied Mathematics Research for Exascale Computing. Technical report, Lawrence Livermore National Laboratory (LLNL), Livermore, CA (2014)

22. Kruse, C., Sosonkina, M., Arioli, M., Tardieu, N., Rude, U.: Parallel solution of saddle point systems with nested iterative solvers based on the Golub-Kahan bidiagonalization. Concurr. Comput. Pract. Exp. (2020). https://doi.org/10.1002/cpe.5914

23. Il'in, V.P.: Problems of parallel solution of large systems of linear algebraic equations. J. Math. Sci. **216**(6), 795–804 (2016). https://doi.org/10.1007/S10958-016-2945-4

24. Il'in, V.: Parallel intelligent computing in algebraic problems. In: Sokolinsky, L., Zymbler, M. (eds.) PCT 2021. CCIS, vol. 1437, pp. 108–117. Springer, Cham (2021). https://doi.org/10.1007/978-3-030-81691-9_8

25. Il'in, V.P.: Iterative preconditioned methods in Krylov spaces: trends of the 21st century. Comput. Math. Math. Phys. **61**(11), 1750–1775 (2021). https://doi.org/10.1134/S0965542521110099

Compact LRnLA Algorithms
for Flux-Based Numerical Schemes

Andrey Zakirov[1]([⊠])(ID), Boris Korneev[1,2](ID), Anastasia Perepelkina[2](ID),
and Vadim Levchenko[2](ID)

[1] Kintech Lab Ltd., 3rd Khoroshevskaya St. 12, Moscow, Russia
`zakirov@kintechlab.com`, `boris.korneev@phystech.edu`
[2] Keldysh Institute of Applied Mathematics RAS, Miusskaya sq. 4, Moscow, Russia
`mogmi@narod.ru`, `lev@keldysh.ru`

Abstract. Fluxes in computational fluid dynamics are often expressed through the variables defined in the neighboring cells of the spatial grid. The time required for a cell update is limited by the calculation performance, as well as by the bandwidth of the memory storage where the required and updated data is located. Thus, the data layout and the method of data access are important for the efficient parallel implementation. A new compact algorithm is proposed for numerical schemes on a cubic mesh that are defined through fluxes. It has a resemblance to Margolous neighborhood cellular automata and is inspired by the streaming patterns of the Lattice Boltzmann method. The data is stored in small groups of cells so that when each group is updated, there is no access to the neighboring cells. This results in the optimal use of memory bandwidth and in a high potential for parallelization.

Keywords: CFD · Fluxes · Margolous neighborhood · Roofline analysis · Parallel algorithms

1 Introduction

Computational Fluid Dynamics (CFD) [6] is a rapidly evolving field of study, and its new applications continue to be discovered [2,22]. Unfortunately, the scope of the problems that can be solved with CFD is limited not only by the imagination of scientists, but more so by the computing cost of the desired simulations [13].

To tackle new tasks, one can try to minimize the cost of the numerical scheme by inventing ways to perform simulations on a coarser grid with larger time steps. This is not what we consider in the current work. Computers currently available to researchers should be more than capable to deal with high-resolution problems.

Another way to make large-scale simulations feasible is to find ways to optimize the existing code for newer and more powerful computer hardware [1,5]. This is a crucial step, but the performance gain can be either relatively small, unless the unoptimized code is intentionally bad, or highly limited by legacy approaches to programming.

© The Author(s), under exclusive license to Springer Nature Switzerland AG 2022
L. Sokolinsky and M. Zymbler (Eds.): PCT 2022, CCIS 1618, pp. 99–115, 2022.
https://doi.org/10.1007/978-3-031-11623-0_8

This work deals with increasing the efficiency of CFD codes on modern hardware by developing advanced algorithms. The change in the algorithm can raise the peak performance towards which the code is optimized. It was done many times by the application of LRnLA (Locally Recursive non-Locally Asynchronous) algorithms [9,10,18]. Additionally, while the work on parallel code optimization for a specific system with specific programming tools may become obsolete with the advance of computer technologies, the algorithm construction theory is timeless. When properly parametrized, the theory can be applied to existing and theoretical processors, which are very unlike one another [11].

The basic issue that has to be solved with newer algorithms is the fact that, in the evolution of computers, the increase in memory bandwidth lags behind the increase in peak computer performance [3]. Since high-resolution CFD deals with big data problems, we need to optimize the data layout, methods of data access, and find ways to take advantage of all the complex inner architecture of the computer memory subsystem.

The current work is inspired by the success of the compact streaming scheme in Lattice Boltzmann Method (LBM) codes [20,30]. We anticipate that this success can be repeated for other numerical schemes for systems of conservation laws. The LBM implementation with a compact streaming pattern and LRnLA algorithms allows obtaining the fastest LBM code for the relevant vector CPU architectures with advanced memory hierarchy, since, with it, the computation can be localized in faster and smaller cache levels [20].

In the LBM [8,24], several floating point values are stored for each lattice site, and there is a streaming step, in which the values are transferred from one node to another. In the other steps, the data from the neighboring cells is often not required. Due to its transparency, the LBM has provided the base for the development of advanced temporal blocking algorithms [15,17,23,27]. It has been repeatedly proven that the data layout and the data access pattern have a great impact on the code performance. Thus, many variations of the streaming step were proposed [4,12,28]. In [20], a new compact streaming scheme was introduced, and it has been used with the recent advances of LRnLA algorithms in [19]. In the compact streaming in D-dimensions, to fully update all data in a group of 2^D cells, only the data in these 2^D cells is accessed. This is not the case in any other streaming scheme. For example, in the common 'pull' scheme [28], the data is collected from a cube of 3^D neighbors to update one cell. In higher dimensions, some cell is repeatedly accessed and loaded into higher levels of memory when its neighbors are updated. The issue is commonly mitigated by introducing an advanced data layout such as Morton Z-order [17] or Peano [14] space filling curves; or by spatial blocking [15], but with the compact streaming the issue does not appear.

In this paper, we propose a general method of compact scheme construction for numerical schemes for systems of conservation laws, which can be expressed with fluxes on a rectangular grid. The novel compact scheme for flux-based schemes is introduced in Sect. 2. A class of problems for which the current method is applicable and a basic scheme used for an illustration in the current paper are presented in Sect. 2.1. The target properties of the compact update are described in Sect. 2.2. The proposed compact update is presented in Sect. 2.3. The efficiency of the compact update is demonstrated with a sample implementation for CUDA GPU, which is described in Sect. 3. For a performance illustration, the scheme is implemented using modern temporal-blocking algorithms, and a significant increase in performance is obtained. The performance benchmark results are reported in Sect. 3.5.

2   Compact Streaming for Flux-Based Schemes

2.1   Problem Statement

A system of conservation laws in the differential form can be written as [26]:

$$\frac{\partial \mathbf{u}}{\partial t} + \frac{\partial \mathbf{F}(\mathbf{u})}{\partial x} + \frac{\partial \mathbf{G}(\mathbf{u})}{\partial y} + \frac{\partial \mathbf{H}(\mathbf{u})}{\partial z} = 0. \tag{1}$$

Here $\mathbf{u}$ is the set of conserved variables, and $\mathbf{F}, \mathbf{G}, \mathbf{H}$ are the flux vectors, which are some functions of $\mathbf{u}$. Numerical schemes differ in the manner of calculating fluxes and in the way of discretizing partial differentials.

Let us first consider a basic scheme with one conserved variable per cell with one stage per cell update, where only directly adjacent cells are to be read for the computation of fluxes.

For example, the advection equation can be discretized on a uniform rectangular grid in the following manner:

$$\begin{aligned}
u|_{x,y,z}^{t+1} = u|_{x,y,z}^{t} &- C_x \left(F_{x+\frac{1}{2},y,z}^{t+\frac{1}{2}} - F_{x-\frac{1}{2},y,z}^{t+\frac{1}{2}} \right) \\
&- C_y \left(F_{x,y+\frac{1}{2},z}^{t+\frac{1}{2}} - F_{x,y-\frac{1}{2},z}^{t+\frac{1}{2}} \right) - C_z \left(F_{x,y,z+\frac{1}{2}}^{t+\frac{1}{2}} - F_{x,y,z-\frac{1}{2}}^{t+\frac{1}{2}} \right),
\end{aligned} \tag{2}$$

where $u|_{x,y,z}^{t}$ is the variable of interest in the cubic cell at $\{x, y, z\}$ at time t, and F are the fluxes at the faces of this cell. We consider only fluxes that can be expressed as a function of values of u in the adjacent cells, i.e. $F_{x+1/2,y,z}^{t+1/2} = flux(u|_{x,y,z}^{t}, u|_{x+1,y,z}^{t})$. The coefficients C_x, C_y, C_z in (2) can be any functions of the local value of u, time or space.

For explicit scheme (2), the values C_x, C_y, C_z are limited by the Courant (CFL) condition:

$$|C_x| + |C_y| + |C_z| \leq 1. \tag{3}$$

For a simple flux computation, one can choose the second order Lax-Wendroff numerical scheme: $C_x flux(u_L, u_R) = \dfrac{\Delta t}{2\Delta x} V_x \left(u_L + u_R - \dfrac{\Delta t}{\Delta x} V_x (u_R - u_L) \right)$, for the *flux* through in the x axis direction. Here Δt is the time step, Δx is the space step for the x-axis, V_x is the x-component of the velocity vector. Similar equations can be written for the other directions.

For parabolic problems, the flux can be expressed as $C_x flux(u_L, u_R) = \dfrac{\Delta t}{\Delta x^2}(u_R - u_L)$, and it leads to the classical first-order explicit finite-difference numerical scheme for the heat equation.

2.2   Requirements for Compactness

The first requirement for the method is that the compact scheme is constructed without modifying the numerical expressions. It only deals with data structures and data access patterns.

Second, the data layout is Array of Structures (AoS). This way, all field and flux values of the cell are stored alongside each other, and the cell data is stored in memory linearly according to some space-filling curve.

Third, we require the compact property of data access: for the update of a group of 2^D cells only the data from these 2^D cells is accessed. For this purpose, we allow flexibility in data storage; the values or fluxes corresponding to the cell can be stored in its neighbors.

2.3   Compact Update

We propose the following method of data storage and update that satisfies the compact property. In the data structure, each cell contains one field for the value u and $D = 3$ fields for the fluxes in the x, y, z axis directions.

Let us take a group that is a cube of $2 \times 2 \times 2$ cells in 3D, or 2×2 cells for 2D illustrations. Please refer to Fig. 1, which illustrates three steps of the algorithm.

1. The fluxes through the inner cell faces of the cube, i.e. the fluxes between the cells of one group, are computed. There are 4 fluxes in 2D and 12 fluxes in 3D. The resulting flux through some cell interface is then stored in both cells that share this interface. Thus, the flux data is duplicated.
2. The cells are regrouped so that the new groups are shifted in the $(1, 1, 1)$ direction in relation to the previous configuration.
3. In each new group, the inner fluxes are computed, but they are not saved. Instead, the values of u are updated using the fluxes computed in step 1 and in the current step. The values of u are stored in the corresponding cells.

Immediately after the last step, the inner fluxes of the current groups can be computed, so the algorithm is repeated from step 1.

3   Implementation with LRnLA Algorithms

The compact update described in Sect. 2.3 can be implemented with any kind of traditional stepwise mesh traversal. In the stepwise compact update, there is an outer loop in time iterations, and the mesh update is the repetition (in a time loop) of the following steps: (1) perform step 1 for all mesh cells; (2) shift the point of reference; (3) perform step 3 for all mesh cells.

The memory bandwidth saturation is guaranteed here for any kind of mesh traversal, and communication for parallel computing is only required in the second step. However, it can be noted that the proposed compact scheme requires more data storage, and thus more memory transfers, than the traditional implementation.

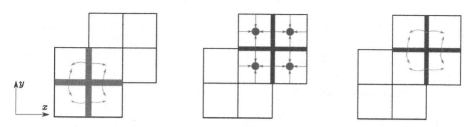

Fig. 1. Illustration for the compact scheme update in 2D. Left: the fluxes on the inner faces of the group (pink) are computed and stored in both cells that share the corresponding face. Center: the fluxes on the inner faces of the shifted group are computed, and the cell values are computed and stored. Right: the first step is repeated in the shifted group.

Let us compare the data requirements with the naive approach. A naive implementation of (2) would require either two data copies of the u value, or the storage of one copy of fluxes to exclude data race conditions. In the compact update, one copy of the field value u is required, and D fluxes per cell are stored between steps 1 and 3.

The drawback for the requirement of data storage can be crucial, since some modern hardware, like GPU, has very limited storage, and the resolution of simulation is limited by it.

This drawback, however, is erased with the use of the novel FArSh data structure for LRnLA algorithms [19, 21]. This method is used here. Below, we describe one sample implementation. Please refer to [10] for the details of LRnLA algorithm construction.

3.1   LRnLA Algorithm ConeTorre

In the ConeTorre Algorithm [10], unlike the traditional traversal, there is no outer loop in time steps. The dependency graph of the task is subdivided into prism-like shapes (subtasks), so that the dependencies between the subtasks are unilateral (Fig. 2). The order of execution is determined by the data dependencies. Asynchronous subtasks can be identified and processed in parallel. The whole mesh is updated to the same time step only once every N_T time step.

Here, one ConeTorre is a subtask of performing step 1 of the compact update for a cube of $N_B \times N_B \times N_B$ cells in $N_B^3/8$ groups, shifting the point of view in step 2, and performing step 3 for the cube shifted by $(1, 1, 1)$ (Fig. 3). Then the same cube undergoes step 1 of the compact update, so that steps 1,2,3 are repeated in the loop with N_T iterations on the cube, which shifts by (N_T, N_T, N_T) relative to its initial position.

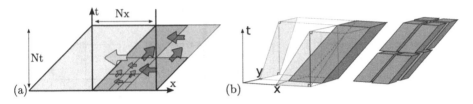

Fig. 2. (a) ConeTorre projection in 1D1T. The arrows show data dependencies. (b) ConeTorre and its decomposition projection in 2D1T.

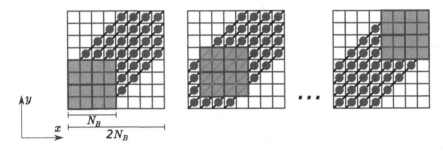

Fig. 3. ConeTorre kernel. For illustration purposes, $D = 2$, $N_B = N_T = 4$. Left: A `Tile` (green) is loaded into registers; the FArSh array is initialized in the shared memory (purple), and the FArSh lines are copied into it from the global FArSh array (red); step 1 of the compact update is processed. Center: the groups are shifted, the computed flux values to the bottom and left of the green tile are stored into the FArSh lines replacing the used values; step 2 of the compact scheme is processed. Right: final state of the ConeTorre; the FArSh lines are copied to the global FArSh array; the field values from the green cells are copied to the Tile array.

When the final or initial position is outside of the mesh domain, the update does not take place. ConeTorre subtasks are performed in the order determined by the dependencies between them. In a domain of $N_x + 1 \times N_y + 1 \times N_z + 1$ cells, the first one is performed for the cube that starts from $(N_x - N_B, N_y - N_B, N_z - N_B)$. The next three ConeTorres start from the cubes at $(N_x - 2N_B, N_y - N_B, N_z - N_B)$, $(N_x - N_B, N_y - 2N_B, N_Z - N_B)$, and $(N_x - N_B, N_y - N_B, N_z - 2N_B)$. These three are asynchronous and can be processed in parallel. The following ConeTorres are processed in the correct order until the cells in the whole domain are updated N_T times.

If $N_T = 1$, the traditional traversal with stepwise synchronization is realized. If N_T is higher, more floating point operations are possible with the data loaded to higher memory storage, so the increase in the efficiency of memory bandwidth utilization is even greater compared to the use of the compact scheme with the traditional traversal.

3.2   FArSh Data Structure

It is noteworthy that the flux data in the scheme computation is temporary and is only required for neighbor communication in the cell update.

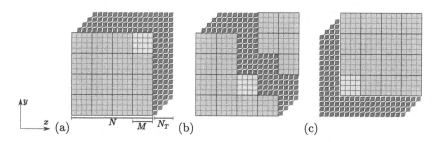

Fig. 4. Data structures in 2D projection. Yellow: tiles containing field values; red: cells containing fluxes; green: ConeTorre base, $M = N_B$. (a) Initial state; (b) state during the execution where the yellow data on the left of FArSh is on the step $t = 0$, and the data to the right of FArSh is on the step $t = N_T$, and the FArSH data is on all the intermediate time steps; (c) final step after the execution of the first N_T time steps in the whole domain.

A ConeTorre starts with a cube that requires only values of u and outputs the cube of u values from its top base. In its progression, the ConeTorre uses the flux data prepared by the previous ConeTorres and outputs the flux data to the ConeTorres on the same layer.

ConeTorres progress in a wavefront [29] manner across the domain. Thus, the FArSh data is required in a strip of N_T cells wide (Fig. 4). Moreover, the flux data in the ConeTorre is read and stored not in the order of a cardinal direction, but in the order of a diagonal $(1, 1, 1)$ direction.

Therefore, there are two types of data.

- The initial conditions and the data output contain the values of u. The data structure is organized for convenient visualization and input as common space-filling curves. For locality, it is preferable to organize cells into tiles of size $N_B \times N_B \times N_B$.
- Data communication between the ConeTorres is through the flux data. This data is stored in a manner convenient for reading and writing in ConeTorres as a set of diagonal lines of cells and cannot be output in a human-readable form without special conversion.

Thus, the flux data is not required in the whole domain. This approach was previously used in 'computational window' approaches in hydrodynamics and plasma physics [7], where the calculation of fluxes could be an expensive procedure. This flux storage reduces the overall number of flux calculations.

Since the flux data is stored only for a small portion of the domain, the increase in memory storage requirements for the compact scheme does not present a problem.

3.3 Sample Implementation in CUDA

We implemented the proposed scheme for the 3D advection equation with Lax-Wendroff fluxes on CUDA GPU [16]. Here we present some specifics of the implementation.

```
using ftype = float;
using ftype3 = float3;
struct Cell{
  ftype val;
  ftype3 fluxes
};
template<int NB> struct Tile {
  ftype val[NB*NB*NB];
};
```

Fig. 5. Data structure for the Cell and Tile data. Double or single precision can be used instead of ftype.

The CUDA GPU device has a global memory storage, which is used here as the main data storage site, shared memory for CUDA-thread communication, a register file for the localization of computations. To compute a ConeTorre, the data of a $N_B \times N_B \times N_B$ cube is loaded into the register file.

The cell and the tile are defined as a data structure (Fig. 5). The cell contains 4 values: the u value and the fluxes in three directions. Each flux can be on the right side or on the left side of the cell in its direction, depending on the stage of the algorithm and the cell position. The tile contains only the u field values in a cube of $N_B \times N_B \times N_B$ cells.

In the global device storage, there are two arrays:

– Main data, i.e. the u values on the mesh, organized in Tiles. Fluxes are not stored here. This data can be localized in CPU RAM or even on SSD, since the communication volume per time unit is minimal.
– FArSh data array that contains lines of N_B Cells, containing fluxes in addition to the u values. The FArSh line is a short array of N_T Cells. It should fit into the device memory [21].

The shared memory of the device is used for data exchange between groups in step 2 of the compact update (Sect. 2.3). An array of $2N_B \times 2N_B \times 2N_B$ Cells is initialized in the shared memory (Fig. 3).

One ConeTorre is a subtask that performs the following operations N_T/N_B times:

1. Load a cube of N_B^3 u values from the tiles in the main data array into the register file.
2. Load all data necessary for the current ConeTorre from the FArSh data array into the shared memory. This amounts to N_B lines of cells with 4 numbers in one cell.

3. Perform N_B time steps of the ConeTorre algorithm as described above. Here only the data from the shared memory and registers are used.
4. Transfer all necessary data from the shared memory to the FArSh array in the global memory (N_B lines of cells with 4 numbers in one cell);
5. Transfer one tile of the data values (N_B^3 field values) into the main storage.

This ConeTorre is implemented as a CUDA kernel (Fig. 6), where one thread is assigned to a cell, and it shifts to the next cell in the $(1, 1, 1)$ direction with each iteration of the compact update. This way, data load and store operations are coalesced. There are N_T such shifts total, that is why the introduced FArSh array of lines of N_B cells is convenient.

ConeTorres are assigned to asynchronous CUDA-blocks. The dependecies of ConeTorres in one time layer (from $t = 0$ to $t = N_T$) make up a dependency graph. There is an outer loop in the tiers of the graph; on each iteration the ConeTorres of one tier are performed in parallel by distributing them between asynchronous CUDA-blocks.

In the shared memory, FArSh is stored in a 3D array of cells, which is superfluous and has unused storage. However, the shared memory is a relatively fast storage, and the data is reused multiple times in the ConeTorre. Thus, we allow excessive memory usage here and leave this optimization for future studies.

In the global memory, the ability to cut storage costs by storing only the required cells is important. The minimal flux data, which is required in the introduced algorithm, is as follows. For each mesh cell, which is on the right boundary of the domain in x, y or z directions, a line of N_T cells in the $(1, 1, 1)$ direction should be initialized (see Fig. 4, left). The boundary is a 2D set, and the N_T span adds a third dimension, thus, the global FArSh array is 3D.

The correspondence of the 2D array to the 3D domain can be easily implemented in the following way. Let us rotate the domain so that the line in the $(1, 1, 1)$ direction is projected into a dot on the viewer plane (Fig. 8a). Each mesh cell, which is on the right boundary of the domain in x, y or z directions, has a unique projection on this plane in a hexagonal pattern. Any method of 2D indexing of a hexagonal mesh can be used here. For a demonstrative implementation, we chose to pad the domain to fill the rectangle. The overhead is $\sim 30\%$. For each cell of the 3D domain, the index of the corresponding FArSh line can be uniquely computed (Fig. 8b).

3.4 Performance and Data Sizes

In this work, the performance is measured in Gcells/sec: billions of cell updates per second for single precision (SP) and double precision (DP) implementations. According to the Roofline model, the chosen problem is memory-bound, so the peak performance can be evaluated as follows.

```
__global__ void compactStepSimpleConeTorre(int ix_base){
  const int ind1s = blockIdx.x%(Ny/NB+NT/NB)*NB;
  const int ind2s = blockIdx.x/(Ny/NB+NT/NB)*NB;
  const int ix0 = ix_base + ind1s + ind2s;
  const int iy0 = Ny-NB-ind1s;
  const int iz0 = Nz-NB-ind2s;
  if( ix0 < -NT || iy0 < -NT || iz0 < -NT ) return;
  if( ix0 >= Nx || iy0 >= Ny || iz0 > =Nz ) return;

  const int3 Lbase = make_int3(ix0,iy0,iz0); //bottom left of the ConeTorre
  const int3 Rbase = make_int3(ix0,iy0,iz0)+make_int3(NT); //top right

  extern __shared__ Cell c_sh[];
  const int thid = threadIdx.x + threadIdx.y*NB + threadIdx.z*NB*NB;

  // Load a tile from the global memory
  // isOut(..) checks if the coordinate is outside the domain
  if( !isOut(Lbase) ) load_tile (thid, Lbase, c_sh);

  for(int itn=0; itn<NT; itn+=NB ) {
    // Load lines of cells from the global FArSh. Every line is loaded by
    // successive threads so that data accesses are coalesced.
    load_farsh(thid, Lbase, c_sh, itn);
    __syncthreads();

    // NT steps of the ConeTorre algorithm
    CTloop(thid, make_int3(ix0,iy0,iz0), c_sh, itn);

    __syncthreads();
    // Store lines of cells in the global FArSh. Every line is loaded by
    // successive threads so that data accesses are coalesced.
    store_farsh(thid, Lbase, c_sh, itn);
  }
  const int shift = Nt;
  // Transfer the tile to store in the global memory
  if( !isOut(Rbase) ) store_tile (thid, Rbase, c_sh, shift);
}
```

Fig. 6. CUDA kernel for the ConeTorre implementing the compact update. The CTloop method is demonstrated in Fig. 7.

```
inline __device__ void CTloop(const int thid, const int3 crd0, Cell* csh, int it0) {
  for(int it=it0; it<it0+NB;) {
    calcFluxes(thid, make_int3(it), csh, crd0 ); //on the inner faces of groups
    __syncthreads();
    it++; //shift the cell groups
    updateVal(thid, make_int3(it), csh, crd0); //includes flux calculation
  }
}
```

Fig. 7. Compact update loop in the ConeTorre.

For the update of NB^4 cells, $3NB^2 - 3NB + 1$ lines of cells have to be loaded, and the same amount of data has to be written to the memory. Each line of cells has NB cells total. We can ignore the overhead of the load and store the data from the tiles at the start and finish of the ConeTorre, since these operations become neglectable as NT increases.

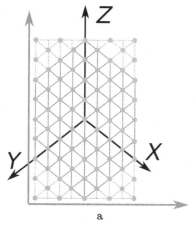

```
struct CellLine{
  static const int NT;
  Cell fval[NT];
};
struct Farsh{
  static const int LFX = (2*Ny/NB+1)*NB;
  static const int LFY = (4*Nz/NB+2)*NB;
  CellLine cl[LFX/2*LFY];
  int get_crd(const int3 crd) {
    int2 crd2d = make_int2(
      crd.x-crd.y,
      -crd.x-crd.y+2*crd.z);
    crd2d.x+= Nz;
    crd2d.y+= 2*Nz;
    return crd2d.x/2 + crd2d.y*(LFX/2);
  }
};
```

a   b

Fig. 8. FArSh indexing. For illustration purposes, the size of the whole simulation domain is sketched with $5 \times 5 \times 5$ mesh nodes. The size of the FArSh Array is $5 \times 9 \times N_T$ (a). Global FArSh array data structure and its indexing method (b).

The peak performance of the ConeTorre algorithm can be approximated by $\Theta L / sizeof(Cell)$, where L is the locality coefficient (ratio of the number of the updated cells to the number of cell load/store operations)

$$L = \frac{1}{2} \frac{NB^4}{(3NB^2 - 3NB + 1) \cdot NB}$$

and Θ is the GPU memory bandwidth. If $NB = 8$, $L = 1.515$.

The estimated memory bandwidth of RTX3090 is ~ 850 GBytes/sec. The cell size is 16B (single precision), thus, the peak performance has to be ~ 81 GCells/sec.

For the stepwise algorithm, the locality coefficient is $L = \frac{1}{2} \frac{NB^3}{(NB + 2)^3}$, and the size of the cell is 4B (fluxes are not stored). Thus, the peak performance on RTX 3090 is ~ 54 GCells/sec for $NB = 8$ or up to 106 GCells/sec if $NB \to \infty$.

3.5 Performance Benchmarks

We performed the comparative analysis of three implementations of the 3D advection equation with NVidia RTX3090 GPU. GPU-implemented LRnLA codes provide better performance [11], since the superior memory bandwidth of GPU devices is efficiently used.

In the 'Naive stepwise' implementation, only two copies of the u value are stored for each cell: old and new. Fluxes are not stored, and they are computed twice, for the update of the value in each of the interfacing cell. The excess computation is negligible, since the problem is memory-bound. For the same reason, the computation is faster without the flux storage, as no memory transfers for fluxes are performed.

In the 'Stepwise compact' algorithm, the compact scheme described in Sect. 2.3 is implemented without LRnLA algorithms and without the FArSh data structure. One u value and three fluxes are stored for each cell, and the cells are organized in a standard C 3-dimensional array in the AoS manner. The algorithm has global synchronization at each time step and consists of two sub-steps: (1) calculation of fluxes between 8 cells and (2) value updates of the 8 cells. There is a shift by one cell in each axis direction in between the substeps.

Finally, the 'Compact ConeTorre' implementation is described in Sect. 3.3.

In Fig. 9, the dependence of the performance on the block size is shown. For the ConeTorre algorithm, the block size is the size of the ConeTorre base in cells. For stepwise algorithms, it is the size of the tile of cells assigned to one CUDA-block. The performance of the compact stepwise implementation is lower than that of the naive stepwise implementation, since the compact scheme requires flux storage and memory transfers for fluxes, and the problem under study is memory-bound. In accordance with the LRnLA algorithm theory [10], the performance is higher with the larger block size. The code is optimized for $N_B = 8$.

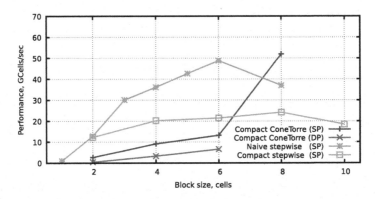

Fig. 9. Dependence on the block size N_B. Here the grid size is $N_x = N_y = N_z = 1080$ for the compact stepwise case and $N_x = N_y = N_z = 1440$ for other cases, $N_T = 16N_T$.

In Fig. 10, the dependence of the performance on the ConeTorre height N_T is shown for the compact ConeTorre algorithm. With higher N_T, memory transfers for the block bases become negligible, and most of the memory exchanges occur between FArSh structures. The implementation where the size of the problem does not fit the device memory and the Tile data is stored in CPU RAM is also studied here. With low N_T, data transfers between CPU and GPU significantly decrease the performance. In this case, the algorithm is closer to the stepwise algorithm, in which the GPU acceleration often becomes hidden by the cost of

CPU-GPU memory transfers, so that such storage is used only with temporal blocking approaches [23]. With higher N_T, memory transfers are concealed with computations, and the performance does not drop in comparison with runs where only the GPU device memory is used.

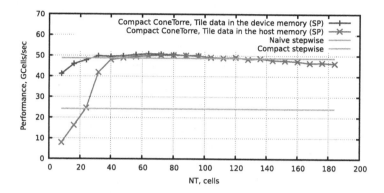

Fig. 10. Dependence on N_T. Here $N_B = 8$ for compact algorithms, $N_B = 6$ for the naive stepwise algorithm.

In Fig. 11, the dependence of the performance on the grid size is shown. The performance of the naive stepwise implementation is better than the performance of the compact stepwise code, since fluxes are not stored and thus fewer data loads and store operations are performed. When the temporal blocking is implemented with the ConeTorre algorithm, a significant increase in performance is evident. The performance of the compact ConeTorre implementation is superior to the naive approach for larger grid sizes. This is the common property of LRnLA algorithm implementations [10]. Furthermore, the expected drop in performance for the tasks that do not fit the GPU device memory is illustrated. It is important to emphasize that stepwise algorithms have no chance to overcome this limit if they are memory-bound. The implementation with the ConeTorre algorithm allows one to maintain the GPU device performance for larger problems, the data of which are stored in the host memory.

4   Results and Discussion

In this work, we introduced the construction of a compact update scheme for CFD numerical methods written in fluxes on a rectangular grid. Let us discuss the impact of this invention.

First, we note the simplicity and beauty of the scheme. Instead of partially referencing the data in the $3 \times 3 \times 3$ neighbourhood, we reference the data in the $2 \times 2 \times 2$ neighborhood in full. At the same time, the numerical expression is not changed, and the compact update can be similarly written for a large class of CFD methods.

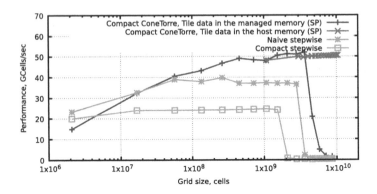

Fig. 11. Dependence on the grid size. The grid is cube-shaped for all cases, except for the Compact ConeTorre with the storage of the main data in the host memory. In this case, $N_y = N_z = 1440$, and N_x is variable.

In this fact, we see a resemblance with the Margolous neighborhood in block cellular automata [25]. First, all dependencies, the input and output of the update, are inside a group of 2^D cells, and the groups are shifted in even and odd steps. Second, the compact update is optimized for schemes in fluxes for conserved variables, and block cellular automata are also known for the value conservation properties.

From the computing point of view, such data access saturates memory bandwidth so that no data is accessed twice or more per time step update. This is guaranteed for any kind of data storage and any kind of mesh traversal. On the other hand, the implementation of the compact scheme shows lower performance. This is caused by the additional storage of fluxes and is remedied with the use of advanced temporal blocking algorithms. In the current performance study, the implementation of the FArSh data structure indeed added some complexity to the code. However, FArSh is a recent idea [19,21], so this complexity can only be due to the fact that this data structure is unfamiliar to programmers, but may become a new standard rather soon.

The idea seems promising for applying to state-of-the-art high-order numerical schemes, such as the Runge-Kutta discontinuous Galerkin method (RKDG), as well as actual physical models, e.g. multi-phase fluid dynamics, magneto-hydrodynamics, etc. In these applications, flux approximation plays the most significant part both in the sense of method accuracy and numerical complexity. The key feature of the proposed algorithm is that it is low-cost in terms of flux calculations, introducing as minimal flux calculations as possible by storing fluxes in a special way. Another useful feature is algorithm scalability in terms of the problem memory size, provided by FArSh. This is important, since the solution of problems with a large number of degrees of freedom using multistage high-order schemes can be very memory-consuming. In the future, it is possible to expand the approach to a wider range of numerical methods.

Acknowledgements. The work was supported by the Russian Science Foundation, grant #18-71-10004.

References

1. Borrell, R., et al.: Heterogeneous CPU/GPU co-execution of CFD simulations on the POWER9 architecture: application to airplane aerodynamics. Future Gener. Comput. Syst. **107**, 31–48 (2020). https://doi.org/10.1016/j.future.2020.01.045
2. Corson, D., Jaiman, R., Shakib, F.: Industrial application of RANS modelling: capabilities and needs. Int. J. Comput. Fluid Dyn. **23**(4), 337–347 (2009). https://doi.org/10.1080/10618560902776810
3. Endo, T., Midorikawa, H., Sato, Y.: Software technology that deals with deeper memory hierarchy in Post-petascale era. In: Sato, M. (ed.) Advanced Software Technologies for Post-Peta Scale Computing, pp. 227–248. Springer, Singapore (2019). https://doi.org/10.1007/978-981-13-1924-2_12
4. Geier, M., Schönherr, M.: Esoteric twist: an efficient in-place streaming algorithms for the lattice Boltzmann method on massively parallel hardware. Computation **5**(2), 19 (2017). https://doi.org/10.3390/computation5020019
5. Gorobets, A., Bakhvalov, P.: Heterogeneous CPU+GPU parallelization for high-accuracy scale-resolving simulations of compressible turbulent flows on hybrid supercomputers. Comput. Phys. Commun. **271**, 108, 231 (2022). https://doi.org/10.1016/j.cpc.2021.108231. URL https://www.sciencedirect.com/science/article/pii/S001046552100343X
6. Hirsch, C.: Numerical Computation of Internal And External Flows: The Fundamentals of Computational Fluid Dynamics. Elsevier, Amsterdam (2007)
7. Korneev, B., Levchenko, V.: DiamondTorre GPU implementation algorithm of the RKDG solver for fluid dynamics and its using for the numerical simulation of the bubble-shock interaction problem. Proc. Comput. Sci. **51**, 1292–1302 (2015). URL https://www.sciencedirect.com/science/article/pii/S1877050915011229
8. Krüger, T., Kusumaatmaja, H., Kuzmin, A., Shardt, O., Silva, G., Viggen, E.M.: The Lattice Boltzmann Method. GTP, Springer, Cham (2017). https://doi.org/10.1007/978-3-319-44649-3
9. Levchenko, V.: Asynchronous parallel algorithms as a way to archive effectiveness of computations (in Russian). J. Inf. Techn. Comp. Syst. **1**, 68–87 (2005)
10. Levchenko, V.D., Perepelkina, A.Y.: Locally recursive non-locally asynchronous algorithms for stencil computation. Lobachevskii J. Math. **39**(4), 552–561 (2018). https://doi.org/10.1134/S1995080218040108
11. Levchenko, V., Zakirov, A., Perepelkina, A.: LRnLA lattice Boltzmann method: a performance comparison of implementations on GPU and CPU. In: Sokolinsky, L., Zymbler, M. (eds.) PCT 2019. CCIS, vol. 1063, pp. 139–151. Springer, Cham (2019). https://doi.org/10.1007/978-3-030-28163-2_10
12. Mohrhard, M., Thäter, G., Bludau, J., Horvat, B., Krause, M.J.: Auto-vectorization friendly parallel lattice Boltzmann streaming scheme for direct addressing. Comput. Fluids **181**, 1–7 (2019). https://doi.org/10.1016/j.compfluid.2019.01.001. URL https://www.sciencedirect.com/science/article/pii/S0045793018308727
13. Moin, P., Mahesh, K.: Direct numerical simulation: a tool in turbulence research. Ann. Rev. Fluid Mechan. **30**(1), 539–578 (1998)

14. Neumann, P., Bungartz, H.J., Mehl, M., Neckel, T., Weinzierl, T.: A coupled approach for fluid dynamic problems using the PDE framework Peano. Commun. Comput. Phys. **12**(1), 65–84 (2012). https://doi.org/10.4208/cicp.210910.200611a

15. Nguyen, A., Satish, N., Chhugani, J., Kim, C., Dubey, P.: 3.5-D blocking optimization for stencil computations on modern CPUs and GPUs. In: SC 2010: Proceedings of the 2010 ACM/IEEE International Conference for High Performance Computing, Networking, Storage and Analysis, pp. 1–13. IEEE (2010)

16. NVIDIA Corporation: CUDA Toolkit Documentation, v11.5.1 edn. (2021). https://docs.nvidia.com/cuda/

17. Perepelkina, A., Levchenko, V.: LRnLA algorithm ConeFold with non-local vectorization for LBM implementation. In: Voevodin, V., Sobolev, S. (eds.) RuSCDays 2018. CCIS, vol. 965, pp. 101–113. Springer, Cham (2019). https://doi.org/10.1007/978-3-030-05807-4_9

18. Perepelkina, A., Levchenko, V.: Synchronous and asynchronous parallelism in the LRnLA algorithms. In: Sokolinsky, L., Zymbler, M. (eds.) PCT 2020. CCIS, vol. 1263, pp. 146–161. Springer, Cham (2020). https://doi.org/10.1007/978-3-030-55326-5_11

19. Perepelkina, A., Levchenko, V.D.: Functionally arranged data for algorithms with space-time wavefront. In: Sokolinsky, L., Zymbler, M. (eds.) PCT 2021. CCIS, vol. 1437, pp. 134–148. Springer, Cham (2021). https://doi.org/10.1007/978-3-030-81691-9_10

20. Perepelkina, A., Levchenko, V., Zakirov, A.: New compact streaming in LBM with ConeFold LRnLA algorithms. In: Voevodin, V., Sobolev, S. (eds.) RuSCDays 2020. CCIS, vol. 1331, pp. 50–62. Springer, Cham (2020). https://doi.org/10.1007/978-3-030-64616-5_5

21. Perepelkina, A., Levchenko, V., Zakirov, A.: Extending the problem data size for GPU simulation beyond the GPU memory storage with LRnLA algorithms. J. Phys. Confe. Ser. **1740**, 012,054 (2021). https://doi.org/10.1088/1742-6596/1740/1/012054

22. Sharma, K.V., Straka, R., Tavares, F.W.: Lattice Boltzmann methods for industrial applications. Indus. Eng. Chem. Res. **58**(36), 16205–16234 (2019). https://doi.org/10.1021/acs.iecr.9b02008

23. Shimokawabe, T., Endo, T., Onodera, N., Aoki, T.: A stencil framework to realize large-scale computations beyond device memory capacity on GPU supercomputers. In: Cluster Computing (CLUSTER), pp. 525–529. IEEE (2017). https://doi.org/10.1109/CLUSTER.2017.97

24. Succi, S.: The Lattice Boltzmann Equation: for Fluid Dynamics and Beyond. Oxford University Press, Oxford (2001)

25. Toffoli, T., Margolus, N.: II.12 The Margolus Neighborhood. Cellular Automata Machines: A New Environment for Modeling (1987)

26. Toro, E.F.: Riemann Solvers And Numerical Methods For Fluid Dynamics: A Practical Introduction. Springer Science & Business Media, Heidelberg (2013). https://doi.org/10.1007/b79761

27. Wellein, G., Hager, G., Zeiser, T., Wittmann, M., Fehske, H.: Efficient temporal blocking for stencil computations by multicore-aware wavefront parallelization. In: 2009 33rd Annual IEEE International Computer Software and Applications Conference, vol. 1, pp. 579–586. IEEE (2009)

28. Wittmann, M., Zeiser, T., Hager, G., Wellein, G.: Comparison of different propagation steps for lattice Boltzmann methods. Comput. Math. Appl. **65**(6), 924–935 (2013)

29. Wolfe, M.: Loops skewing: the wavefront method revisited. Int. J. Parallel Program. **15**(4), 279–293 (1986)

30. Zakirov, A., Perepelkina, A., Levchenko, V., Khilkov, S.: Streaming techniques: revealing the natural concurrency of the lattice Boltzmann method. J. Supercomput. **77**(10), 11911–11929 (2021). https://doi.org/10.1007/s11227-021-03762-z

Analysis of Block Stokes-Algebraic Multigrid Preconditioners on GPU Implementations

N. M. Evstigneev$^{(\boxtimes)}$ [iD]

Federal Research Center "Computer Science and Control"
of the Russian Academy of Sciences, Moscow, Russia
evstigneevnm@yandex.ru

Abstract. The Stokes and Oseen problems are saddle-point problems common to many methods aimed at the efficient solution of incompressible flows. There are basically two methods for solving saddle problems – coupled (solution of the whole system) and segregated (fractional step method). In this paper, we consider the first approach as the most efficient for steady state problems, in the form of block-triangular preconditioning and its variants. The most difficult part is the design of an efficient preconditioner for the saddle-point problem. Different variants of preconditioning and formulations of pressure Schur complement approximate matrices are considered. The main question is: Given that computations on Graphics Processing Units (GPUs) are cheaper and less energy demanding than computations only on Central Processing Units (CPUs), can an efficient preconditioner be implemented in GPU-only calculation mode? We apply these preconditioners with the most advanced Algebraic Multigrid methods (AMG) based on the AMGCL framework developed by D. Demidov. The AMGCL framework is extensively modified for the purpose of testing in GPU-only calculation modes. To formulate the Stokes problem, we use the classical MAC method on a staggered grid and consider different types of 3D problems. It is concluded that GPU-only computations can be approximately 3–4 times more efficient than CPU+GPU implementations and about 20 times more efficient than CPU-only implementations of the original AMGCL framework.

Keywords: Saddle-point problems · Stokes equations · Algebraic Multigrid methods · General Purpose GPU computations · Iterative methods · Pressure Schur complement

1 Introduction

The solution of Stokes-type linear systems is a problem that is considered complicated [3]. The original Stokes system is derived from the fluid dynamics of an incompressible viscous fluid when flow dynamics is such that the nonlinear

The study was funded by the Russian Foundation for Basic Research, project No. 20-07-00066.

L. Sokolinsky and M. Zymbler (Eds.): PCT 2022, CCIS 1618, pp. 116–130, 2022.
https://doi.org/10.1007/978-3-031-11623-0_9

effects of the advective terms can be neglected. In this case, the temporal scale becomes proportional to the scale of length squared, and the solution of the stationary problem is mainly of interest. The discretization of the problem can be formulated in two ways: without stabilization and with stabilization. In both cases, it is necessary to solve a saddle-point linear system in the form:

$$\mathcal{A}x = b \Leftrightarrow \begin{pmatrix} A & B^T \\ B & C \end{pmatrix} \begin{pmatrix} u \\ p \end{pmatrix} = \begin{pmatrix} f \\ g \end{pmatrix}. \tag{1}$$

In the first case, one arrives at the symmetric indefinite linear system that approximates the saddle-point problem where the approximation satisfies the Ladyzhenskaya–Babushka–Bretzi (LBB) or *inf-sup* condition, and $C = 0, g = 0$ in (1). In the case of finite differences (FDM) this is the well-known staggered grid [19], and in the case of finite elements (FEM) these are the unequal order finite element pairs [25] of different design. In the second case, one arrives at the indefinite problem with an arbitrary approximation and some way of stabilization, e.g. Rhie–Chow stabilization for FDM [24,28] or Brezzi–Pitkaranta stabilization for FEM [5], in this case $C \neq 0, g \neq 0$. There exist many different methods for solving the problem using different approaches. The resulting system can be factored to obtain the Schur complement matrix $S = C - BA^{-1}B^T$, which can be used to find the variable p. Depending on the way this system is solved, two approaches are possible:

- Segregated approach: 1. Solve for $p = \hat{S}^{-1}(g - BA^{-1}f)$, 2. solve for $u = A^{-1}(f - B^T p)$, each with the iterative method and an appropriate preconditioner, where $\hat{S}^{-1}$ is an approximation to the Schur complement inverse.
- Coupled approach: Solve the whole system $\mathcal{A}x = b$, usually with the Krylov-type method and an appropriate preconditioner for the saddle-point system.

The advantages and disadvantages of each approach are discussed in [3,13] in detail. In this research, we focus on the coupled system solution using different variants of preconditioners based on the Algebraic Multigrid Method (AMG). Such methods are efficient and, if correctly constructed, are close to optimal [12,18,21,27,29] in terms of the number of iterations and grid diameter independence. However, there is still no universal preconditioner that can solve a wide range of different problems, especially for parallel computational architectures. Such methods can be constructed in two different approaches: separate velocity and pressure preconditioning using the Schur complement matrix approximation [15,22] and Vanka-type preconditioning, which can be considered as a global symmetric block Gauss–Seidel iteration process over all discretization cells [26]. In this paper, we focus on the first approach, leaving the description of the Vanka smoother implementation elsewhere. In this case, the following system is solved:

$$\mathcal{P}^{-1}\mathcal{A}x = \mathcal{P}^{-1}b, \tag{2}$$

where $\mathcal{P}$ is the coupled left preconditioning operator. The formulation and inversion of this preconditioner can be done in different ways, including block pressure correction or bock triangular approaches. On each step, it is necessary to solve linear systems for the approximate matrix $\hat{S}$ and matrix A, which can be applied as exact or approximate factorization. In this study, we apply the AMG method.

The computational platform for the AMG method in this research is the AMGCL library developed by D.Demidov [8,9,11]. Our initial attempt to use the AMGX library failed [16], and the AMGCL framework was used instead. It is a header-only template library written in C++, which is very programmer-friendly and has many implemented features and methods, including GPU support. The library is also oriented on solving challenging linear systems, including Stokes-type systems, see [10]. The results obtained in the cited paper look promising. However, the idea of the AMGCL implementation is aimed at using a host-assembled matrix in the CPU memory. All methods constructing AMG hierarchies, prolongation and restriction operators are based on built-in matrix arrays that operate on CPU OpenMP or MPI parallel architectures. Hence, the framework cannot be used in GPU-only mode, where the system matrix $\mathcal{A}$ is stored in the device memory, without intermediate host-device memory transforms.

The analysis of different preconditioning strategies and approximate Schur complement matrices is performed. The main question is: Given that computations on Graphics Processing Units (GPUs) are cheaper and less energy demanding than computations only on Central Processing Units (CPUs), can an efficient preconditioner be implemented in GPU-only calculation mode? To achieve this goal, the AMGCL library is modified in order to execute the GPU-only mode when the matrix is formed in the device memory. The paper is laid out as follows. First, the problem formulation and different types of approximate Schur complement matrices are considered. Next, the AMG algorithm modifications of the GPU-only approach are described. Then, test problems and numerical experiments are conducted for different preconditioners and compared with each other and with the original AMGCL implementation.

2   Problem Formulation

2.1   Discretization and Formulation of Preconditioners

The nondimentionalized Stokes problem in the domain $\Omega \subset \mathbb{R}^3$ with the piecewise smooth Lipschiz boundary $\delta\Omega$ is described by the following system:

$$
\begin{aligned}
-\triangle\mathbf{v} + \nabla p &= \mathbf{f}, \\
\nabla \cdot \mathbf{v} &= 0, \\
\mathbf{v}|_{\delta\Omega_D} &= \mathbf{v_d}, \\
(\nabla\mathbf{v} - pI) \cdot \mathbf{n}|_{\delta\Omega_N} &= \mathbf{g}.
\end{aligned}
\tag{3}
$$

The vector function $\mathbf{v}$ is commonly referred to as the velocity, the scalar function p as the pressure, the known vector function in the right-hand side $\mathbf{f}$ as the source term, the subscripts D and N represent the Dirichlet and Neumann boundary conditions, respectively, and the vector $\mathbf{n}$ represents the outward normal vector on the boundary. This problem, despite being linear, is relatively computation-ally difficult. The solution pair $(\mathbf{v}, p)$ of (3) is not the minimizer of a quadratic functional, as it would be in the case of an elliptic-type Partial Differential Equation (PDE), but of a saddle point. The pressure function can be considered as the Lagrange multiplier for the original diffusive system being subject to the incompressibility constraint. Assuming that the functions under consideration are smooth, one can apply discretization to problem (3) to form discrete system (1). The main target of the research is the solution of linear system (2). The linear system is solved using the GMRES method, where the action of the preconditioner is supplied via the assembled hierarchies of AMG solvers. The first preconditioner tested is a block triangular preconditioner, which is applied as the following composition:

$$\mathcal{P}^{-1} = \begin{pmatrix} A & B^T \\ 0 & \hat{S} \end{pmatrix}^{-1} = \begin{pmatrix} A^{-1} & -A^{-1}B^T\hat{S}^{-1} \\ 0 & \hat{S}^{-1} \end{pmatrix} = \begin{pmatrix} A^{-1} & 0 \\ 0 & E \end{pmatrix} \begin{pmatrix} E & -B^T \\ 0 & E \end{pmatrix} \begin{pmatrix} E & 0 \\ 0 & \hat{S}^{-1} \end{pmatrix}.$$
(4)

Each element of the matrix composition is applied using an AMG solver sweep (single V or W-cycle). The second preconditioner is a variant of the Braess–Sarazin preconditioner [4], which is applied as the following application:

$$\mathcal{P}^{-1} = \begin{pmatrix} A & B^T \\ B & 0 \end{pmatrix}^{-1} = \begin{pmatrix} \left(A^{-1} - A^{-1}B^T\hat{S}^{-1}BA^{-1}\right) & \left(A^{-1}B^T\hat{S}^{-1}\right) \\ \left(\hat{S}^{-1}BA^{-1}\right) & \left(-\hat{S}^{-1}\right) \end{pmatrix}.$$
(5)

Having the residual vector of the coupled problem $r = (r_u, r_p)^T = \mathcal{A}x - b$, one usually applies the pressure solver first and then reuses the result in the velocity solver to minimize the number of solver applications in (5) as:

$$\begin{aligned} \hat{S}p &= BA^{-1}r_u - r_p \\ Au &= r_u - B^T p. \end{aligned}$$
(6)

In any case, both preconditioners allow one to apply pressure and velocity solvers separately. These approaches are implemented in the AMGCL Stokes preconditioner [10]. For each preconditioner it is necessary to define different forms of approximate A, $\hat{S}$ matrices. In this study, we use the following matrix approximations. The velocity matrix A is inverted via AMG sweeps using either V or W cycles.

The Schur complement pressure matrix in its exact form is prohibitively expensive both in terms of the computation time and device memory occupancy (due to the usage of the inverted velocity matrix). Instead, we apply two different strategies to construct the matrix. First, the approximation of Carriere and Jeandel [7] is used:

$$\hat{S} = B(\text{diag}(A))^{-1}B^T,$$
(7)

where $\text{diag}(A)$ is the diagonal of the velocity matrix A. The preconditioning with this matrix is applied through a single AMG sweep (V or W cycle) using the Sparse approximate inverse (SPAI0) [6] or Damped Jacobi smoother, which we call SIMPLE_amg. Another option is only a single application of the SPAI0 preconditioner formed from this matrix, which we call SIMPLE_spai0.

Another variant is the application of a weighted BFBt preconditioner of Elman [14] based on the concept of approximate commutators. In this case, the approximation to the inverse Schur complement is formulated as:

$$\hat{S}^{-1} = (\widetilde{B}\widetilde{B}^T + \widetilde{C})^{-1}\widetilde{B}\widetilde{A}\widetilde{B}^T(\widetilde{B}\widetilde{B}^T + \widetilde{C})^{-1}, \tag{8}$$

where the matrices with tilde are designated as weighted matrices, i.e. $\widetilde{C} = CM_d^{-1/2}$, $\widetilde{B} = BM_d^{-1/2}$, $\widetilde{A} = M_d^{-1/2}AM_d^{-1/2}$, and M_d is the diagonal of the velocity mass matrix for finite element discretization. In the case of finite difference discretization, non-scaled matrices are used [14], however, we apply block diagonal scaling as in [20]. According to our observations, such scaling slightly increased the convergence speed. The application of this approximate matrix can be performed in two different strategies. The first one is the application of a single sweep (V or W cycle) of the AMG preconditioner to each solution of the $\widetilde{B}\widetilde{B}^T$ equation, which we call BFBt_amg. The other option is the exact solution of this equation using the GMRES or CG method with the AMG preconditioner, which uses a single sweep with the SPAI0 smoother. We call this strategy BFBt_exact.

2.2   Discretization and Considered Problems

A simple staggered finite difference scheme discretization [19] is used in this study. Grid functions with indexes (j, k, l) in the (x, y, z) directions, respectively, are introduced and labeled identically to the continuous functions. Grid functions will be explicitly identified, if needed, to escape ambiguity. A single block of variables is formulated as $ux_{j-1/2,k,l}, uy_{j,k-1/2,l}, uz_{j,k,l-1/2}, p_{j,k,l}$. In this case, the formed matrix A is a 7-banded scalar matrix, and the matrices B and B^T each have 4 bands. In the case of boundary conditions, where interior walls present, the diffusion operator is discretized in such a way that the zero value is prescribed on the boundary of the wall. Inactive cells, where no flow occurs, are removed from the process of the matrix assembly.

This simple discretization is selected because it allows testing large matrices with a minimal number of nonzero elements. It is computationally convenient in a parallel processing and multigrid context since they hold an (almost) identical degree distribution for both the velocity and pressure and represent the lowest possible order approximation, which is LBB-stable. Several problems are formulated to verify the convergence of discrete system (3). Besides, the usage of some Finite Element discretization would require the application of block matrix operations, which are not yet implemented in our GPU AMG variant.

Problem 1. Stokes Lid Driven Cavity. The problem is formulated as a classical 3D lid driven cavity [1]. The aim of the test is to verify the convergence properties of the method for the problem with singularities in the corners, as well as a nontrivial kernel for the Schur complement matrix: $\ker(S) = \mathrm{span}(\mathbf{1})$. The domain is set to a unit cube $[0,1]^3$, zero Dirichlet boundary conditions are prescribed for the velocity on all plains, except one, where the unit tangential value is set.

Problem 2. Flow in a Channel with Obstacles. This problem poses some convergence complications. The part of the internal field (that corresponds to the internal walls) is excluded from the simulation. We also modify the aspect ratio of the domain in this problem. The boundary conditions are set as a unit streamwise pressure gradient and Neumann boundary conditions for the velocity vector. In other directions, the no-slip condition is set.

Problem 3. Flow in a Porous Medium. The last problem is taken from https://www.digitalrocksportal.org/projects/374/origin_data/1785/ as an example of a real world application. The problem is a unit cube $[0,1]^3$, the discretization of the original problem is 256 points in each direction, the porosity is 35%. This test verifies the performance and convergence of the method for a complex real world application. The boundary conditions are the same as for Problem 2.

3   AMGCL Framework Modifications

The process of the general preconditioned solution of the coupled Stokes system can be described by provided Algorithms 1, 2, which are implemented in AMGCL. The velocity solver is related to the preconditioner used to apply the system solve on A, and the pressure solver is related to the preconditioner used to apply the system solve on $\hat{S}$. In this implementation, the coupled system is solved using the GMRES method with a Krylov subspace size of 20 (parameter R in the SOLVE_SYSTEM call). In each iteration of the GMRES method, a preconditioner is called; it is applied by either process (4) or (6).

Algorithm 1. Setup phase

1: **function** SETUP_PRECONDITIONER($\mathcal{A}$, p_{ind})
2:    $\{A, B, B^T, C\} \leftarrow$ CUT_MATRICES($\mathcal{A}$, p_{ind});
3:    divn $\leftarrow$ FORM_VECTOR_DIVISION(p_{ind});
4:    U $\leftarrow$ FORM_VELOCITY_SOLVER(A);
5:    P $\leftarrow$ FORM_PRESSURE_SOLVER(A, B, B^T, C);
6:    $\mathcal{P} \leftarrow$ FORM_PRECONDITIONER($U, P, divn$);
7:    **return** ($\mathcal{P}$);

The implementation of these Algorithms is performed in original AMGCL. Methods based on (4), (6) and (7) are readily available in AMGCL. We implemented method (8) separately. However, setup phase Algorithm 1 uses CPU

Algorithm 2. Solve phase

1: **function** SOLVE_SYSTEM($\mathcal{A},\mathcal{P},b$, R)
2:     $x \leftarrow$ GMRES(R)($\mathcal{A}, \mathcal{P}, b$);
3:     **return** x;

---

matrices and performs a matrix copy to the host memory if the original matrix is located in the GPU device memory. All operations with the formulation of Schur complement approximates (7) are also performed using CPU matrices. The stages for building AMG hierarchies (if needed) in FORM_VELOCITY_SOLVER and FORM_PRESSURE_SOLVER require the utilization of significantly serial algorithms for AMGCL::COARSENING::PLAIN_AGGREGATES, which are used to construct operators on each level. In addition, some smoothers on the intermediate levels of AMG are also formed on the CPU only. As a result, according to Amdahl's law, the whole speedup is limited to these steps, and can only be speeded up partially using the OpenMP CPU implementation.

To circumvent this problem, it is necessary to reorganize the whole process of constructing AMG hierarchies, to specialize additional methods for CUDA_MATRIX classes and implement CUT_MATRICES and FORM_VECTOR_DIVISION methods on the GPU. Thus, CPU↔GPU memory copies are minimized, and the most time-consuming operations are executed on the GPU only.

To achieve the goal, we used CUDA C++ and templates extensively, since the original AMGCL framework heavily relies on template metaprogramming. The most time-consuming operations during the setup are the construction of additional matrices, the Schur complement approximation $\hat{S}$ and the formulation of pressure and velocity solvers. In turn, each solver can invoke the construction of AMG hierarchies, smoothers and prolongation/restriction operators on each level. The construction of additional matrices is replaced by direct CUDA kernel invokes, as well as by the process of constructing separate and joint residuals $r \leftrightarrow (r_u, r_p)^T$ using DIVN in Algorithm 1. The formulation of the preconditioning approximate matrix $\hat{S}$ is performed using the CUDA_MATRIX specialization for a sparse matrix product.

The construction of aggregates cannot be handled so easily. The serial version available in AMGCL::COARSENING::PLAIN_AGGREGATES cannot be implemented on the parallel architecture. Instead, an updated version of the Parallel Maximal Independent Set K (MIS(K)) is implemented, see [2,17]. An independent set is a set of nodes, in which no two of them are adjacent, and it is a maximal independent set (MIS) if it is not a subset of any other independent set. The generalization of MIS is MIS(K), in which the distance between any two independent nodes is greater than K, and for every other node there is at least one independent node that is within the distance less than or equal to K. Hence, the construction of interpolation operators and smoothing aggregation is performed on the GPU only using the obtained aggregates from the MIS(K) process. The whole redesign of the code resulted in a substantial modification of the original framework. The constructors had to be specified for the GPU-only operation through all classes. To obtain the maximum speedup on both the original and modified variants of the code, one needs to use the latest CUDA Developer Toolkit, version 11.5, where many functions from the CUSPARSE and CUSOLVER libraries are optimized. In addition, we used our own implementation of matrices and arrays, taking into account the optimization in terms of memory layout depending on the device, and the GPU-optimized sPECK library [23] to perform GEMM (sparse matrix – matrix product) operations. These modifications also boosted the original AMGCL implementation. However, the used sPECK library is not a header only, and it violates the philosophy of original AMGCL. Nevertheless, in this research, we are more interested in performance than in design features.

4   Numerical Results

In this section, we present the numerical results obtained by solving the problems listed above. The following hardware configuration is used: CPU – 2×Intel Xeon Gold 6248R, totally having 48 cores (96 threads) with 512 GB of ECC host memory, GPU – Nvidia Tesla V100 with 32 GB of ECC device memory. Double precision is used in all calculations, no mixed precision was used (which should boost GPU performance even further). All results presented in the research are obtained on the hardware listed above. Ten runs of each test configuration were performed, and mean values were used in all measured tests to obtain statistically justified results. For some problems, we estimate the mean residual reduction rate. The residual reduction rate on the n-th iteration is $\rho^n = \|r^{n+1}\|/\|r^n\|$, where $n \geq 1$, therefore, the initial residual is excluded. The mean residual reduction rate is the averaged value $\rho = \langle \rho^n \rangle$.

4.1   Unit Cube Problem

We used a set of matrices from [10] where the testing of the method with an analytical solution on a unit cube was performed. The target relative residual is set to $1.0 \cdot 10^{-8}$. The problem has a total dimension of $5.5E5$, $2.94E6$ and $4.38E6$ with $1.43E7$, $7.84E7$ and $1.17E8$ nonzero entries in the matrices, respectively. This test was chosen since it has a scalar structure, and block matrices are not yet implemented in our GPU variant. First, an analysis of the optimal number of OpenMP threads for the original implementation for the used hardware is carried out. The results are provided in Fig. 1 for the setup and solve phases of the original AMGCL implementations. These results are obtained for the Block Triangular preconditioner and the SIMPLE_spai0 Schur matrix, the other variants have the same time ratio distributions. One can observe that the speedup reverses from 32 to 64 threads, depending on the matrix size. For further tests, we shall use the best number of OpenMP threads without explicitly demonstrating this value.

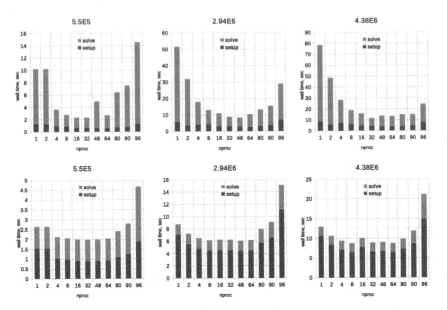

Fig. 1. Setup and solve wall times for the Unit cube problem for different vector sizes on the original AMGCL implementation depending on the number of OpenMP threads. Upper row - CPU, lower row - GPU.

One can also observe in Fig. 1, second row, an obvious bottleneck in the setup/solve phase ratio for the GPU implementation. This situation only confirms the need to implement a GPU-only variant with a full GPU setup phase.

In Fig. 2, upper row, we demonstrate the speedup obtained using the GPU-only variant of AMGCL compared to the original AMGCL GPU variant. It is shown that the setup phase was substantially speeded up. For a single core, we obtained a speedup of 8.29 on the biggest matrix and maximum speedup of 5.1 compared to the 64-core execution with the GPU. The solve phase either did not change or slightly decelerated with the worst value of 0.92 for the problem sized $2.94E6$ compared to the 64-core original implementation. This is because we used a smoothed aggregation based on the $MIS(K)$ algorithm instead of the original aggregation algorithm. As a result, the convergence of the problem to the preset relative tolerance required 1–2 more iterations. In the lower row in Fig. 2, we demonstrate the wall time of different preconditioners. It should be noted that BFBt preconditioners (8) are worse in this problem since the scaling was empirical as no mass matrices are available for this problem. In total, we obtained a speedup of about 2.6–2.9 for the largest matrix compared to the best (OpenMP GPU) original AMGCL implementation. For the pure single-threaded CPU implementation vs. the pure GPU implementation, we achieved a speedup of about 22.2 times on this problem against 7.08 times for the original AMGCL implementations.

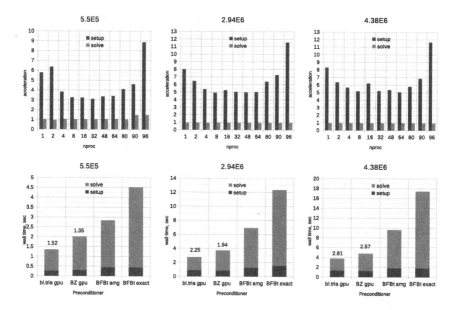

Fig. 2. Upper row: Setup and solve speedup using the new AMG GPU-only implementation vs. the original AMGCL implementation depending on the number of OpenMP threads. Lower row: Wall time for the new GPU-only speedup for different preconditioners. The numbers indicate the speedup vs. the best original implementation.

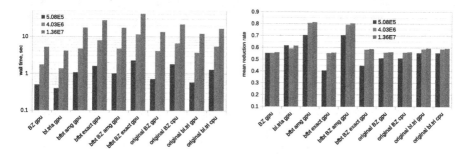

Fig. 3. Wall time in log scale (left) and mean residual reduction rate (right) for Problem 1: bl.tria is block triangular preconditioner (4) and BZ is Braess Sarazin preconditioner (5).

4.2   Stokes Lid Driven Cavity

We constructed three matrices corresponding to the problem domain sized 50^3, 100^3 and 150^3. The total problem sizes are $5.1E5$, $4.03E6$ and $1.35E7$, respectively. The numbers of nonzero elements in the matrices are $6.94E6$, $3.27E7$ and $1.11E8$, respectively. The target relative residual is set to $1.0 \cdot 10^{-8}$. The wall time execution and the mean residual reduction rate are presented in Fig. 3. In all variants, where applicable, we used the SIMPLE_spai0 approximate Schur matrix formulation as the fastest among those tested.

One can observe that the new GPU variant for both the block triangular and Braess Sarazin preconditioners is faster than the best variant of the original AMGCL implementation (GPU + 64 OpenMP threads) for these preconditioners. We obtained a speedup of 1.47, 1.49 for the smallest matrix and 2.92, 3.52 for the largest matrix, respectively. It can be seen that the performance of the preconditioners in terms of the residual reduction rate is different. The new variants of the BZ and bl.tria preconditioners based on the $MIS(K)$ aggregates are slightly worse. The BFBt preconditioner is worse in any variant. This is due to the nontrivial kernel for the Schur complement matrix. Possible remedies can be found in the literature and are beyond the scope of this paper, see [14]. The reduction rate in Fig. 3 on the right indicates that the grid independence was achieved for all preconditioners. For the GPU variant vs. the single-threaded CPU variant, we achieved a speedup of about 25.4 times against 8.1 times for the original AMGCL implementations.

4.3   Flow in a Channel with Obstacles

The problem of a channel with obstacles in different directions is presented with the domain sized 50^3, 100^3, 150^3 and 200^3. The obstacles are rotating planes in different directions that force the flow like a 3D heater, see Fig. 5, left, for the streamline visualization. The total problem sizes are $1.87E5, 1.84E6, 6.66E6$ and $1.62E7$, respectively. The numbers of nonzero elements in the matrices are $1.28E6$, $1.41E7$, $5.25E7$ and $1.29E8$, respectively. The target relative residual is set to $1.0 \cdot 10^{-8}$. The resulting wall time execution and the mean residual reduction rate are presented in Fig. 4.

We observe that only the BFBt-type approximation to the inverse of the Schur complement matrix is capable of correctly preconditioning the problem. Only 3 iterations were required for the smallest matrix in the case of the exact BFBt variant. The grid independence was achieved with a mean reduction rate of about 0.55–0.58 for the BFBt_amg variants. The other preconditioners were unable to converge for 300 iterations to the desired tolerance and were terminated. In this case, we can compare the original AMGCL implementation and the new one in terms of speedup for the same number of iterations. In this case, the GPU-only variant is about 1.3–2.0 times faster than the best AMGCL variant (GPU + 64 OpenMP threads) for the largest matrix. This is because more iterations were used where the difference in the implementations was not large. For the GPU variant vs. the single-threaded CPU variant, we achieved a speedup of about 32.18 times against 18.9 times for the original AMGCL implementations.

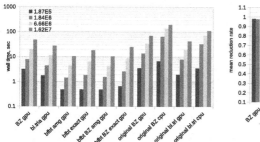
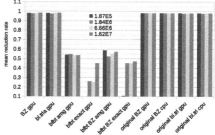

Fig. 4. Wall time in log scale (left) and mean residual reduction rate (right) for Problem 2: bl.tria is block triangular preconditioner (4) and BZ is Braess Sarazin preconditioner (5).

4.4   Flow in a Porous Medium

The total size of the problem is $1.96E7$, and the matrix has $1.54E8$ nonzero entries. The flow is visualized through the streamlines in Fig. 5, right. The target relative residual is set to $1.0 \cdot 10^{-8}$. The execution results are brought together in Table 1. The setup step was speeded up by 5.22 and 4.28 times for the GPU vs. CPU variants of the original implementation, respectively. The total speedup is about 1.6–1.8 times since more time was spent on iterations. Again, we can observe that for this type of problems and scalar matrices, the best variant is the BFBt_amg preconditioner. It can also be seen that since the original aggregation method is essentially serial, the speedup of the setup step in the original implementation is about 2.5 for 64 threads.

Table 1. Solution data for the problem of flow in a porous medium.

name	time_setup	time_solve	total_time	iterations	residual	$<\rho>$
BZ gpu	2.68	54.77	57.45	300	6.0E-7	0.97
bl.tria gpu	2.65	30.29	32.94	300	1.7E-6	0.97
bfbt amg gpu	3.46	10.08	13.54	30	7.7E-9	0.58
bfbt exact gpu	3.25	31.06	34.31	35	9.6E-9	0.71
bfbt BZ amg gpu	3.53	11.62	15.15	35	8.7E-9	0.60
bfbt BZ exact gpu	3.21	51.80	55.02	46	7.8E-9	0.76
original BZ gpu 64	13.97	69.46	83.43	300	5.4E-7	0.97
original BZ cpu 64	11.45	297.06	308.51	300	5.4E-7	0.97
original BZ cpu 1	28.22	1,586.05	1,614.27	300	5.4E-7	0.97
original bl.tri gpu 64	12.74	37.73	50.47	300	1.1E-6	0.97
original bl.tri cpu 64	11.34	160.72	172.06	300	1.1E-6	0.97
original bl.tri cpu 1	28.07	1,045.27	1,073.34	300	1.1E-6	0.97

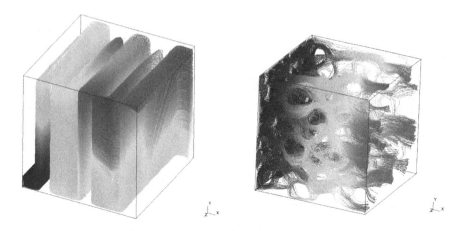

Fig. 5. Streamlines for Problem 2 (left) and Problem 3 (right).

5   Conclusion

We implemented the GPU-only variant of the aggregation AMG method based on the AMGCL implementation. To do it, we needed to change the aggregation algorithm on the parallel version (used $MIS(K)$) and redesign the whole library in such a way that no intermediate CPU calculations were required. We used CUDA C++ together with template programming to achieve this. We also suggested a scaled variant of the BFBt preconditioner implementation for the approximate Schur complement matrix inverse. The tests show that the suggested GPU-only variant can be approximately 3–4 times more efficient than CPU+GPU implementations and about 20–35 times more efficient than the CPU-only implementations of the original AMGCL framework. This speedup is obtained mostly due to the setup step, which is speeded up by about 5–7 times for large matrices compared to the best variant of the AMGCL configuration. The BFBt preconditioner shows efficient properties for the problems with obstacles. Support for block matrices and multiple GPUs is next to be implemented.

References

1. Albensoeder, S., Kuhlmann, H.: Accurate three-dimensional lid-driven cavity flow. J. Comput. Phys. **206**(2), 536–558 (2005). https://doi.org/10.1016/j.jcp.2004.12.024
2. Bell, N., Dalton, S., Olson, L.N.: Exposing fine-grained parallelism in algebraic multigrid methods. SIAM J. Sci. Comput. **34**(4), C123–C152 (2012). https://doi.org/10.1137/110838844
3. Benzi, M., Golub, G.H., Liesen, J.: Numerical solution of saddle point problems. Acta Numerica **14**, 1–137 (2005). https://doi.org/10.1017/s0962492904000212
4. Braess, D., Sarazin, R.: An efficient smoother for the stokes problem. Appl. Numer. Math. **23**(1), 3–19 (1997). https://doi.org/10.1016/s0168-9274(96)00059-1

5. Brezzi, F., Pitkäranta, J.: On the stabilization of finite element approximations of the stokes equations. In: Efficient Solutions of Elliptic Systems, pp. 11–19. Vieweg Teubner Verlag (1984). https://doi.org/10.1007/978-3-663-14169-3_2
6. Bröker, O.: Sparse approximate inverse smoothers for geometric and algebraic multigrid. Appl. Numer. Math. **41**(1), 61–80 (2002). https://doi.org/10.1016/s0168-9274(01)00110-6
7. Carriere, P., Jeandel, D.: A 3D finite element method for the simulation of thermo-convective flows and its performances on a vector-parallel computer. Int. J. Numer. Methods Fluids **12**(10), 929–946 (1991). https://doi.org/10.1002/fld.1650121003
8. Demidov, D.: AMGCL: an efficient, flexible, and extensible algebraic multigrid implementation. Lobachevskii J. Math. **40**(5), 535–546 (2019). https://doi.org/10.1134/S1995080219050056
9. Demidov, D.: AMGCL - A C++ library for efficient solution of large sparse linear systems. Softw. Impacts **6**, 100037 (2020). https://doi.org/10.1016/j.simpa.2020.100037
10. Demidov, D., Mu, L., Wang, B.: Accelerating linear solvers for stokes problems with C++ metaprogramming. J. Comput. Sci. **49**, 101285 (2021). https://doi.org/10.1016/j.jocs.2020.101285
11. Demidov, D., Shevchenko, D.: Modification of algebraic multigrid for effective GPGPU-based solution of nonstationary hydrodynamics problems. J. Comput. Sci. **3**(6), 460–462 (2012). https://doi.org/10.1016/j.jocs.2012.08.008
12. Elman, H.: Finite Elements and Fast Iterative Solvers: With Applications in Incompressible Fluid Dynamics. Oxford University Press, Oxford (2014)
13. Elman, H., Howle, V., Shadid, J., Shuttleworth, R., Tuminaro, R.: A taxonomy and comparison of parallel block multi-level preconditioners for the incompressible navier-stokes equations. J. Comput. Phys. **227**(3), 1790–1808 (2008). https://doi.org/10.1016/j.jcp.2007.09.026
14. Elman, H., Howle, V.E., Shadid, J., Shuttleworth, R., Tuminaro, R.: Block preconditioners based on approximate commutators. SIAM J. Sci. Comput. **27**(5), 1651–1668 (2006). https://doi.org/10.1137/040608817
15. Elman, H.C., Howle, V.E., Shadid, J.N., Tuminaro, R.S.: A parallel block multi-level preconditioner for the 3D incompressible navier-stokes equations. J. Comput. Phys. **187**(2), 504–523 (2003). https://doi.org/10.1016/s0021-9991(03)00121-9
16. Evstigneev, N.M., Ryabkov, O.I.: Application of the AmgX library to the discontinuous Galerkin methods for elliptic problems. In: Sokolinsky, L., Zymbler, M. (eds.) PCT 2021. CCIS, vol. 1437, pp. 178–193. Springer, Cham (2021). https://doi.org/10.1007/978-3-030-81691-9_13
17. Gandham, R., Esler, K., Zhang, Y.: A GPU accelerated aggregation algebraic multigrid method. Comput. Math. Appl. **68**(10), 1151–1160 (2014). https://doi.org/10.1016/j.camwa.2014.08.022
18. Gee, M.W., Küttler, U., Wall, W.A.: Truly monolithic algebraic multigrid for fluid-structure interaction. Int. J. Numer. Methods Eng. **85**(8), 987–1016 (2010). https://doi.org/10.1002/nme.3001
19. Harlow, F.H., Welch, J.E.: Numerical calculation of time-dependent viscous incompressible flow of fluid with free surface. Phys. Fluids **8**(12), 2182 (1965). https://doi.org/10.1063/1.1761178
20. May, D.A., Moresi, L.: Preconditioned iterative methods for stokes flow problems arising in computational geodynamics. Phys. Earth Planet. Inter. **171**(1–4), 33–47 (2008). https://doi.org/10.1016/j.pepi.2008.07.036
21. Notay, Y.: Algebraic multigrid for stokes equations. SIAM J. Sci. Comput. **39**(5), S88–S111 (2017). https://doi.org/10.1137/16m1071419

22. Olshanskii, M.A., Vassilevski, Y.V.: Pressure Schur complement preconditioners for the discrete Oseen problem. SIAM J. Sci. Comput. **29**(6), 2686–2704 (2007). https://doi.org/10.1137/070679776

23. Parger, M., Winter, M., Mlakar, D., Steinberger, M.: Speck: accelerating GPU sparse matrix-matrix multiplication through lightweight analysis. In: Proceedings of the 25th ACM SIGPLAN Symposium on Principles and Practice of Parallel Programming. ACM (2020). https://doi.org/10.1145/3332466.3374521

24. Rhie, C.M., Chow, W.L.: Numerical study of the turbulent flow past an airfoil with trailing edge separation. AIAA J. **21**(11), 1525–1532 (1983). https://doi.org/10.2514/3.8284

25. Temam, R.: Navier-Stokes Equations: Theory and Numerical Analysis. Elsevier Science, The Netherlands (1984)

26. Vanka, S.: Block-implicit multigrid solution of navier-stokes equations in primitive variables. J. Comput. Phys. **65**(1), 138–158 (1986). https://doi.org/10.1016/0021-9991(86)90008-2

27. Wabro, M.: Coupled algebraic multigrid methods for the Oseen problem. Comput. Vis. Sci. **7**(3–4), 141–151 (2004). https://doi.org/10.1007/s00791-004-0138-z

28. Zhang, S., Zhao, X., Bayyuk, S.: Generalized formulations for the Rhie-Chow interpolation. J. Comput. Phys. **258**, 880–914 (2014). https://doi.org/10.1016/j.jcp.2013.11.006

29. Zulehner, W.: A class of smoothers for saddle point problems. Computing **65**(3), 227–246 (2000). https://doi.org/10.1007/s006070070008

Implementation of the Algebraic Multigrid Solver Designed for Graphics Processing Units Based on the AMGCL Framework

O. I. Ryabkov[✉]

Federal Research Center "Computer Science and Control"
of the Russian Academy of Sciences, Moscow, Russia
roi-techsup@yandex.ru

Abstract. The implementation of the Algebraic Multigrid (AMG) solver designed specifically for Graphics Processing Units (GPUs) is presented. It is based on the well-known and highly efficient AMGCL header-only library designed and implemented by D. Demidov using C++. The original AMGCL approach for GPU speedup relies on the initialization (setup) phase performed purely on the CPU, while the solution (iteration process) is moved to the GPU. This approach works well for the case of transient solvers, when the system matrix does not change much during time-stepping. However, it does not fit for cases of highly nonlinear systems or stationary systems, especially when a linear system is formed in the device memory. For these systems it is better to use GPU-only solvers. To implement the GPU-oriented AMG solver, the design of the original framework had to be changed. The maximal independent set aggregation algorithm and derived smoothed aggregation operations are added to the framework. A number of smoothers on the intermediate levels are implemented with full support for GPUs. The full AMG hierarchy can now be constructed entirely on the GPU with no CPU invokes. The method is tested against the original AMGCL framework on matrices derived from elliptic and parabolic partial differential equations (PDEs). It is shown that the GPU-only approach can speed up the setup phase by up to 5-6 times compared to the original framework.

Keywords: Aggregation · Iterative methods · Algebraic Multigrid methods · Elliptic partial differential equations · General Purpose GPU computations

1 Introduction

There are few modern methods for solving large linear systems that can be considered mainstream. These include multigrid methods and domain decomposition methods. Among the former, Algebraic Multigrid (AMG) methods are one

The study was funded by the Russian Foundation for Basic Research, project No. 20-07-00066.

L. Sokolinsky and M. Zymbler (Eds.): PCT 2022, CCIS 1618, pp. 131–142, 2022.
https://doi.org/10.1007/978-3-031-11623-0_10

of the most popular choices. The methods (generally) require no additional information, however, the matrix itself is relatively memory thrifty and, if correctly constructed, can be as efficient as geometric multigrid (GMG) methods. All this makes AMG a very attractive "black box" solver for particular classes of problems (positive definite, semi-positive definite and M-matrices). Any multigrid solver has two stages: setup and solve. The setup stage performs the necessary computations and prepares operators for the solve phase. The solve phase actually solves a linear system. In AMG methods, the solve phase is a substantial and important part in both the convergence and wall time. We refer the reader to [6,8,11,16] for more detailed information on AMG methods. In this work, we mainly focus on the setup phase.

To construct matrices, smoothing, prolongation and restriction multigrid operators on all levels, one uses entries in the main system matrix, as well as, possibly, some external information. The resulting set of operators is called the AMG hierarchy. The classical AMG approach [11] constructs hierarchies by dividing matrix entries into coarse and fine ones so that the smoothed error slowly varies in the direction of large matrix coefficients. The coarse nodes are used to construct the lower level, and the prolongation operation is defined by interpolation. The restriction operation is usually defined by either the one-to-one restriction operation or the transpose of the prolongation operator. Smoothing operators are built based on the nodes on each levels. This approach often results in relatively good hierarchies that guarantee grid independent convergence. However, to achieve this quality, classical aggregation often leads to large coarse level matrices and requires a substantial amount of memory, see [10] for more information. In addition, the original classical aggregation algorithm is essentially serial. Other variants of the algorithm, such as PMIS, HMIS, CLJS, etc. (see [15]), do not produce hierarchies of such quality.

Another variant considered here is aggregation AMG methods [14]. These methods rely on grouping fine level nodes to form a coarse matrix on the lower level. Smoothing operations are also constructed on top of the formed matrices on each level. The restriction operation usually acts as an averaging of the variables inside each group, and the prolongation operator is a transposed restriction operator. Such an approach is much more economical in terms of memory consumption on the coarse levels, however, this approach is usually not applied since it cannot generally provide grid independent convergence rates [13]. To override this problem, smoothed aggregation was proposed [13,14]. However, smoothed aggregation AMG results in greater memory requirements, and grid independent convergence is still not guarantied for some classes of problems. For a comparison of different approaches see [12,15].

Having described one problem of selecting an appropriate setup procedure, one faces another problem, namely, how to speed up the setup phase. To speed up an aggregation-based algorithm, it is necessary to apply a parallel aggregation algorithm with all variants, including smoothed aggregation (since none of them can be universal). Modern high-performance computing architectures de facto must have Graphics Processing Units (GPUs). Such an architecture is efficient, if properly programmed, and more environmentally friendly. In addition, modern desktops can fit up to 4 (or 8) powerful GPUs capable of solving relatively large-scale problems. It would be unwise to deprive the users of these desktops from solving middle-sized problems of academic or engineering orientation. Hence, the implementation of the fully GPU-accelerated AMG solver is an important task.

We tried to utilize the AMGX solver for our problems on GPUs, but failed, see [5]. To verify our implementations of GPU-accelerated setup procedures, we used the AMGCL library [3] by D. Demidov. It is a C++ header-only library that heavily relies on template metaprogramming and has GPU support via CUDA and OpenCL. It is efficient and has been tested in many applications. However, the library is explicitly designed in such a way that the setup process is performed on CPUs only, accelerated by either OpenMP or MPI. GPU support is localized only in the solve stage. Besides, if the system matrix is formed on GPUs, then the library performs CPU↔GPU memcpy. The author's idea is that the setup is executed only a limited number of times, and the matrix of the linear system can be reused (by calling the rebuild process also performed on the CPU), if applied many times, say in Newton's method, see [4] for details. However, if the problem being solved is complicated, and the stationary point is not easily found (see, for example, [2]), then this strategy may lead to unsatisfactory results, e.g. substantially decrease the CFL number in implicit methods. In this paper, we would like to overcome this flaw. We apply the Parallel Maximal Independent Set K ($MIS(K)$) on the GPU, as described in [1,7], with modifications that form aggregates closer to the serial version. The method is implemented in CUDA C++ using templates.

The paper is laid out as follows. First, the aggregation method, the modified $MIS(K)$ method and its application in AMG during the setup are described. Next, the modifications introduced in the AMGCL library to implement this method in the GPU-only approach are outlined. Numerical experiments on several available and generated sparse matrices are also presented, and the performance and convergence of the modified and original AMGCL library are measured. The paper is finalized by a conclusion.

2 Aggregation AMG on the GPU

The initial approach adopted for the AMG hierarchy build process in AMGCL is based on constructing aggregates as noted in the introduction. Aggregates are unions of nodes (variables) on the fine level. After aggregation, each aggregate corresponds to one and only one node on the coarse level. Let n be the number of nodes on the current (fine) level. We can mathematically describe the aggregate structure by the array of numbers a_i, where $i \in \{0, ..., n-1\}$ and $a_i \in \{0, ..., n_c - 1\}$, and n_c is, in turn, the number of nodes on the next (coarse) level.

Transfer operators (prolongation and restriction) are fully determined by the aggregate structure. Regular (non-smoothed) aggregation builds the restriction operator (matrix) R in the following way:

$$R_{j,i} = \begin{cases} \frac{1}{|\{k|a_k=j\}|}, & \text{if } a_i = j \\ 0, & \text{otherwise} \end{cases}$$

The prolongation matrix is defined as a transposition of the restriction matrix: $P = R^T$. The coarse operator matrix is defined according to the Galerkin projection: $A_c = RAP$, where A is the fine level matrix. For smoothed aggregation, the restriction matrix is defined as a product of the restriction matrix defined above and the smoothing matrix $I + \omega A^F$. ω is the relaxation parameter, and A^F is a specially filtered version of the matrix A. Further levels are constructed in a recursive way.

One can see that in this formalism the overall aggregation algorithm is fully determined by the method of constructing aggregates. Regardless of the choice of a particular algorithm, a strong connections graph first needs to be constructed. There are several variations of strong connections criteria. The one used in AMGCL is described, for example, in [14]. We denote the strong connections graph incidence matrix by C, $C_{i,j} = 1$ means that the node with the number i is strongly connected to the node with the number j, while $C_{i,j} = 0$ means the absence of connection. Note that the matrix C is supposed to be symmetric in the algorithm mentioned below.

The initial algorithm in AMGCL (called plain aggregation) uses a substantially serial approach that exploits a given order of nodes for their grouping. On the other hand, our task was to implement the fully GPU workflow for the setup phase, thus the parallelizable algorithm had to be utilized. A common choice for constructing parallel aggregates is the Maximal Independent Set algorithm, see, for example, [1]. A parallel version of this algorithm uses random seeds to construct $\text{MIS}(K)$. $\text{MIS}(K)$ is the subset of fine level nodes, and the shortest path length between any two $\text{MIS}(K)$ nodes in the graph C is larger than K. "Maximal" means that adding any other node to $\text{MIS}(K)$ breaks this property. Usually $K = 2$ is used in the context of AMG.

Our version of the $\text{MIS}(K)$ algorithm for constructing aggregates is presented here as Algorithm 1. Note that there are two parts that differ from the original version of $\text{MIS}(K)$, highlighted in colour in the Algorithm. The first one is in the node weights (the second element of the tuples T_i). While originally only random numbers v_i were used for the weights, we added an extra term $n_i W_{nb}$. W_{nb} is the global algorithm parameter. $W_{nb} = 0$ falls back to the initial version, while $W_{nb} = 1$ or $W_{nb} = -1$ can be used to adjust the behavior of constructing aggregates. We noted that $W_{nb} = 0$ usually resulted in the lower aggregates number compared to the original AMGCL plain aggregation. This leads to a lower convergence rate, thus usually slowing down the solve phase. The $W_{nb} = -1$ choice enlarges the aggregates number, thereby partially fixing the convergence problem. However, for some matrices (not considered in the current paper), $W_{nb} = 1$ may be the best option, since the reduced number of variables on the coarse levels speeds up the computational wall time.

Algorithm 1. MIS(K) parallel, with modification outlined by colour.

```
1: function MISK_AGGREGATION(C, K, W_nb)
2:     I = {0, ..., n − 1};
3:     a ← −1; s ← 0; v ← random;                          ▷ init states and random vector
4:     while {i ∈ I : s_i = 0} ≠ ∅ do
5:         for i ∈ I do                                     ▷ for each node in parallel
6:             n_i ← #{j : C_{i,j} ≠ 0, s_j == 0};          ▷ number of neighbors
7:             T_i ← (s_i, v_i + n_i W_{nb}, i);             ▷ set tuple (state,value,index)
8:         for r = 1, ..., K do                             ▷ propagate distance K
9:             for i ∈ I do                                 ▷ for each node in parallel
10:                t ← T_i;
11:                for j : C_{i,j} ≠ 0 do
12:                    t ← max(t, T_j);                     ▷ maximal tuple among neighbors
13:                T̂ ← t;
14:            T = T̂;
15:        for i ∈ I do                                     ▷ for each node in parallel
16:            (s_max, v_max, i_max) ← T_i;
17:            if s_i == 0 then                             ▷ if unmarked...
18:                if i_max == i then                       ▷ if current is maximal...
19:                    s_i ← 1;                             ▷ mark as new aggregate
20:                    a_i ← i;
21:                else if s_max == 1 then
22:                    s_i ← −1;                            ▷ add to existing aggregate
23:                    a_i ← i_max;
24:    for i ∈ I do                                         ▷ for each node in parallel
25:        if s_i == −1 then                                ▷ not center of aggregate
26:            for j : C_{i,j} ≠ 0 do
27:                if s_j == 1 then                         ▷ neighbor is aggregate center...
28:                    a_i ← j;                             ▷ reconnect to neighbor
29:    return (a);                                          ▷ return list of MIS(K) aggregates
```

The second difference is in the post-processing part. One can consider it as a reconnection procedure. While the original plain aggregates implementation manually connects all closest strong neighbors to newly created aggregate centers, the MIS(K) algorithm can produce highly skewed aggregates. To overcome this problem, additional regrouping was added after the main iterations cycle. The point is to reconnect the nodes initially connected to the "far" aggregates center to the close ones, if any. Together, these two improvements reduce the convergence rate drop to an acceptable level of approximately 10% in the worst case among the systems under consideration. Moreover, the initial plain aggregates algorithm can produce different results depending on matrix ordering, while the randomized algorithm demonstrates robustness to this factor.

All other parts of the AMG hierarchy construction (transfer operators, Galerkin projections) are naturally parallelizable for both CPUs and GPUs.

The most time-consuming part is the sparse matrix-matrix product, and it will be addressed further in more detail.

3   Implementation

Algorithm 1 can be readily implemented on GPUs. Loops with the comment "for each node in parallel" turn into CUDA kernel calls, since there are no data dependencies inside them. There are some technical issues. First, it was not initially clear which data layout was the best for the tuples T. Experiments showed that the "structure of arrays" was still preferable, despite the fact that the size of one tuple is 16 bytes in our implementation. Second, tuples initialization and maximum tuple iterations loops were merged together using the CUB reduce_by_key algorithm, which resulted in better performance.

From the performance point of view, sparse matrix-matrix multiplication was found to be the bottleneck. We first used the legacy cusparseXcsrgemm2 operation from the cuSparse library of the CUDA toolkit, however, that already deprecated version performed badly. The new version introduced in the latest CUDA toolkit exposed a huge speedup of this operation, but failed in terms of extra memory consumption. Finally, we tried the SpECK library [9], which showed the best results in both memory consumption and performance. The only disadvantage of this library is the absence of support for Compute Capabilities lower than 6.1. The Legacy cuSparse implementation was left for the case of older hardware.

Another important aspect of the fully GPU AMG stack is a smoothers ("relaxation" in terms of AMGCL) implementation without any CPU invokes. We ported setups for three of them: spai0 (sparse approximate inversion), ilu0 (incomplete LU factorization) and damped Jacobi. Although in an algorithmic sense there are no problems with their implementation on the GPU, some problems arise with the AMGCL architecture. Initially it was not designed for such GPU-only usage, therefore, we needed to introduce a new setup constructor conveyor from the top make_solver class down to coarsening and smoothers initialization methods.

4   Numerical Experiments

All experiments are conducted on symmetric matrices. The following hardware is used in all experiments: CPU – 2×Intel Xeon Gold 6248R, totally having 48 cores (96 threads) with 512 GB of ECC host memory, GPU – Nvidia Tesla V100 with 32GB of ECC device memory. Double precision is used in all calculations. The AMGCL setup for all experiments is the same: the conjugate gradient method is used as the main solver, preconditioned by a single AMG V-cycle. The ilu0 smoother is used on each level of the multigrid, the exact solver is used in the lowest level. All problems are convergent, the target relative residual is set to $1.0 \cdot 10^{-14}$. All results are presented by three figures – wall time for the setup, solve phases and speedup. In addition, for each matrix, a table that contains the minimum wall time for all runs and for all implementations is presented. It should be noted once again that the original AMGCL implementation uses a multi-threaded CPU setup phase in both CPU and GPU implementations. Thus, the obtained speedup for the setup phase depends on the number of OpenMP threads for both implementations.

The first experiment is conducted with the matrix available in the AMGCL examples folder, i.e. a small matrix from the discretization of a Poisson equation called POISSON3DB. Its size is $8.56E4$, and the number of nonzero elements is $2.37E6$. The results are presented in Fig. 1 and Table 1.

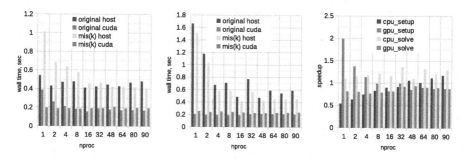

Fig. 1. Results for the POISSON3DB matrix depending on the number of OpenMP threads: setup phase - left, solve phase - center, speedup - right.

It is observed that for such matrix sizes, the speedup is negligible or even reversed. The setup of the AMG hierarchy using the $MIS(K)$ algorithm on the CPU is slower than the original algorithm. The GPU setup phase algorithm is faster than the single-threaded execution of the original algorithm. However, it is slower for 48, 64 and 80 threads. It is not recommended to use GPUs for small matrices.

The next experiment is taken from the sparse matrix market, the matrix is called PARABOLIC_FEM. Its size is $5.26E5$, and it has $3.67E6$ nonzero elements. The results are presented in Fig. 2 and Table 2.

Table 1. Minimum wall times, mean iterations and attained residuals for the POISSON3DB matrix.

name	time_setup	time_solve	total_time	iterations	residual
original host	0.409184	0.471179	0.892288	21	3.62E-16
original cuda	0.155554	0.189926	0.346058	21	5.55E-15
mis(k) host	0.409326	0.417123	0.847573	22	3.12E-15
mis(k) cuda	0.18529	0.225905	0.416847	23	9.47E-16

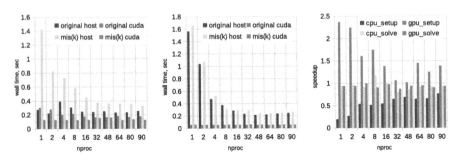

Fig. 2. Results for the PARABOLIC_FEM matrix: setup phase - left, solve phase - center, speedup - right.

Table 2. Minimum wall times, mean iterations and attained residuals for the PARABOLIC_FEM matrix.

name	time_setup	time_solve	total_time	iterations	residual
original host	0.221891	0.212528	0.453675	14	3.22E-15
original cuda	0.164093	0.055595	0.220113	14	3.22E-15
mis(k) host	0.334386	0.240353	0.597847	12	5.67E-15
mis(k) cuda	0.123283	0.05631	0.182331	11	1.17E-15

The results again indicate that the host variant of $MIK(K)$ is slower than the original variant in both the setup and solve phases. The GPU $MIS(K)$ setup phase is 2.4 times faster than the single-threaded original AMGCL implementation and about as fast as the 48-threaded version. The solve phase is slightly slower for the GPU implementation (0.96 times in average). The convergence is slower on 1–2 iterations. The results indicate that the CPU implementation can be used instead of the GPU implementation with a slight penalty on the wall time. These two matrices are small to be efficiently used on GPUs.

The next sparse market matrix is called THERMAL2, its size is $1.23E6$ with $8.58E6$ nonzero elements. The obtained speedup, presented in Fig. 3 and Table 3, shows that the CPU $MIS(K)$ version is slightly faster in the solve phase for 48 threads or more. However, it is almost twice slower for the setup phase.

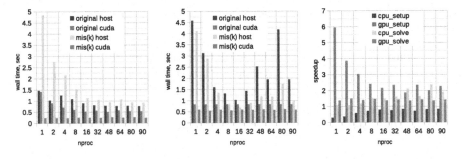

Fig. 3. Results for the THERMAL2 matrix: setup phase - left, solve phase - center, speedup - right.

Table 3. Minimum wall times, mean iterations and attained residuals for the THER-MAL2 matrix.

name	time_setup	time_solve	total_time	iterations	residual
original host	0.759762	1.030344	1.925627	13	6.70E-15
original cuda	0.511443	0.830287	1.342058	13	6.70E-15
mis(k) host	0.914104	0.691784	1.824731	11	4.82E-15
mis(k) cuda	0.233334	0.547645	0.780979	13	1.18E-15

The GPU MIS(K) variant is 6 times faster than the single-threaded setup phase of the original implementation. The minimum speedup of the GPU MIS(K) implementation compared to the best multi-threaded original GPU implementation is 1.85 times for the setup phase. The solve phase for the GPU MIS(K) implementation is about 1.5 times faster due to the difference in the obtained AMG hierarchy.

A set of parameterized matrices was generated to perform analysis in terms of matrix sizes. A finite difference 7-point 3D Laplace operator was generated and used for the Poisson equation with Neumann and a single Dirichlet boundary condition. The cubic domain was discretized with 50, 100, 150, 200 and 250 grid points in each direction, respectively. The results of the solution of this problem are presented in Fig. 4 and Table 4.

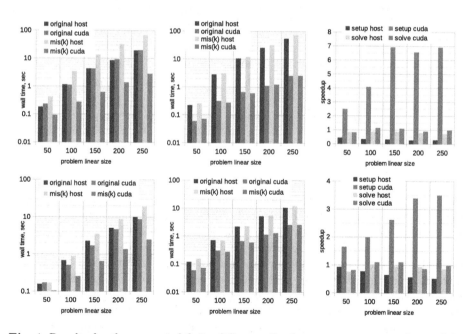

Fig. 4. Results for the generated finite difference Laplace operator: setup phase - left, solve phase - center, speedup - right, upper row - one thread, lower row - best times of all OpenMP threads.

First, we analyze the behavior for the case when a single thread is used in the original AMGCL implementation. The CPU variant of our implementation is clearly inferior compared to the original AMGCL implementation. The GPU variant, on the other hand, is efficient. For this case, we obtain a substantial speedup starting from a linear matrix size of 150. The maximum speedup in the setup phase of about 7 times is achieved for the largest matrix.

Next, we analyze the behavior for the best variant of the AMGCL multi-threaded GPU implementation. In this case, a speedup of about 3.51 times is achieved for the largest matrix in the setup phase. The solve phase is approximately the same for both implementations. The solve phase fluctuates around one, see Table 4.

Table 4. Minimum wall times for all generated Poisson problem matrices and all considered OpenMP threads.

lin.size	original host	original cuda	mis(k) host	mis(k) cuda
		setup		
50	0.160	0.167	0.146	0.094
100	0.694	0.508	0.854	0.250
150	2.239	1.554	3.401	0.607
200	4.943	4.449	8.844	1.375
250	9.754	8.253	16.345	2.346
		solve		
50	0.085	0.060	0.082	0.069
100	0.580	0.301	0.545	0.259
150	2.271	0.656	2.039	0.594
200	4.317	1.131	5.189	1.262
250	10.145	2.597	10.073	2.621

5   Conclusion

In this research, we presented the implementation of the AMG framework that targets GPUs. The AMGCL header-only library, designed and implemented by D. Demidov using C++, was used as a base framework, which was subject to deep modifications. The whole process (both setup and solve phases) was implemented and tested on multiple symmetric matrices, generated and real-world-alike. It is concluded that for small matrices, e.g. POISSON3DB, the usage of our implementation is not recommended. The GPU load is insufficient to deliver any speedup against modern CPUs. We also do not recommend using the CPU variant of MIS(K) aggregates since it is clearly inferior in all numerical experiments. On the other hand, we obtained a speedup of the setup phase for intermediate and large matrices (matrix size starting from $\sim 1E6$) by about 7 times against the AMGCL single-threaded GPU implementation and by about 3.5 times for the best multi-threaded variant. The speedup of the solve phase depends on the problem (since aggregates are generated differently for AMGCL and our implementation using $\mathrm{MIS}(K)$) and fluctuates between 0.95 and 1.15. The suggested GPU-only implementation can be recommended if matrices are generated on GPUs for stationary problems with a time-consuming setup phase, as well as for hard transient problems, when a matrix rebuild is required on each time step.

Variations of classical AMG aggregation algorithms, as well as support for multiple GPUs, are to be implemented for GPUs.

References

1. Bell, N., Dalton, S., Olson, L.N.: Exposing fine-grained parallelism in algebraic multigrid methods. SIAM J. Sci. Comput. **34**(4), C123–C152 (2012). https://doi.org/10.1137/110838844
2. Bocharov, A., Evstigneev, N., Petrovskiy, V., Ryabkov, O., Teplyakov, I.: Implicit method for the solution of supersonic and hypersonic 3D flow problems with lower-upper symmetric-gauss-seidel preconditioner on multiple graphics processing units. J. Comput. Phys. **406**, 109189 (2020). https://doi.org/10.1016/j.jcp.2019.109189
3. Demidov, D.: AMGCL - A C++ library for efficient solution of large sparse linear systems. Softw. Impacts **6**, 100037 (2020). https://doi.org/10.1016/j.simpa.2020.100037
4. Demidov, D.E.: Partial reuse AMG setup cost amortization strategy for the solution of non-steady state problems. Lobachevskii J. Math. **42**(11), 2530–2536 (2021). https://doi.org/10.1134/s1995080221110093
5. Evstigneev, N.M., Ryabkov, O.I.: Application of the AmgX library to the discontinuous Galerkin methods for elliptic problems. In: Sokolinsky, L., Zymbler, M. (eds.) PCT 2021. CCIS, vol. 1437, pp. 178–193. Springer, Cham (2021). https://doi.org/10.1007/978-3-030-81691-9_13
6. Falgout, R.: An introduction to algebraic multigrid. Comput. Sci. Eng. **8**(6), 24–33 (2006). https://doi.org/10.1109/mcse.2006.105
7. Gandham, R., Esler, K., Zhang, Y.: A GPU accelerated aggregation algebraic multigrid method. Comput. Math. Appl. **68**(10), 1151–1160 (2014). https://doi.org/10.1016/j.camwa.2014.08.022
8. McCormick, S.F.: Multigrid Methods. Society for Industrial and Applied Mathematics, Philadelphia (1987)
9. Parger, M., Winter, M., Mlakar, D., Steinberger, M.: Speck: accelerating GPU sparse matrix-matrix multiplication through lightweight analysis. In: Proceedings of the 25th ACM SIGPLAN Symposium on Principles and Practice of Parallel Programming. ACM (2020). https://doi.org/10.1145/3332466.3374521
10. Stüben, K.: Algebraic multigrid (AMG). An introduction with applications. Technical report (1999). http://publica.fraunhofer.de/documents/B-73234.html
11. Stüben, K.: A review of algebraic multigrid. In: Partial Differential Equations, pp. 281–309. Elsevier (2001). https://doi.org/10.1016/b978-0-444-50616-0.50012-9
12. Thomas, S.J., Ananthan, S., Yellapantula, S., Hu, J.J., Lawson, M., Sprague, M.A.: A comparison of classical and aggregation-based algebraic multigrid preconditioners for high-fidelity simulation of wind turbine incompressible flows. SIAM J. Sci. Comput. **41**(5), S196–S219 (2019). https://doi.org/10.1137/18m1179018

13. Vaněk, P., Brezina, M., Mandel, J.: Convergence of algebraic multigrid based on smoothed aggregation. Numerische Mathematik **88**(3), 559–579 (2001). https://doi.org/10.1007/s211-001-8015-y
14. Vaněk, P., Mandel, J., Brezina, M.: Algebraic multigrid by smoothed aggregation for second and fourth order elliptic problems. Computing **56**(3), 179–196 (1996). https://doi.org/10.1007/bf02238511
15. Yang, U.M.: Parallel algebraic multigrid methods – high performance preconditioners. In: Bruaset, A.M., Tveito, A. (eds.) Numerical Solution of Partial Differential Equations on Parallel Computers. LNCS, pp. 209–236. Springer, Heidelberg (2006). https://doi.org/10.1007/3-540-31619-1_6
16. Yavneh, I.: Why multigrid methods are so efficient. Comput. Sci. Eng. **8**(6), 12–22 (2006). https://doi.org/10.1109/mcse.2006.125

Measuring the Effectiveness of SAT-Based Guess-and-Determine Attacks in Algebraic Cryptanalysis

Andrey Gladush[1], Irina Gribanova[2], Viktor Kondratiev[3], Artem Pavlenko[3], and Alexander Semenov[3]([✉])

[1] Special Technological Center, St. Petersburg, Russia
[2] Matrosov Institute for System Dynamics and Control Theory, Irkutsk, Russia
[3] ITMO University, St. Petersburg, Russia
alex.a.semenov@itmo.ru

Abstract. This paper studies the problem of algebraic cryptanalysis where state-of-the-art SAT solvers are used to invert some cryptographic function. We define a new metric of the hardness of CNF formulas that encode the corresponding cryptanalysis problems. The introduced metric is similar to the well-known tree-like metrics used in the theory of propositional proofs. However, unlike the latter, the new metric can be effectively estimated in application to specific cryptographic functions. The corresponding approach combines the Monte Carlo method and metaheuristic black-box optimization algorithms. The proposed algorithms require a large amount of computational resources, and for their experimental evaluation we used a supercomputer. In the experiments, we applied the proposed metrics to construct estimations of guess-and-determine attacks on the compression function of the well-known MD4 cryptographic hash algorithm.

Keywords: Algebraic cryptanalysis · Boolean Satisfiability Problem (SAT) · SAT solvers · Guess-and-determine attacks · Inverse Backdoor Set (IBS)

1 Introduction

The present paper studies the application of parallel algorithms for solving the Boolean satisfiability problem (SAT) to the problems of algebraic cryptanalysis. In particular, we introduce new metrics that make it possible to estimate the complexity of SAT-based guess-and-determine cryptographic attacks [6]. The problem of constructing estimations of this kind is reduced to the optimization problem of the special fitness function, which is defined at the points of a Boolean hypercube. This fitness function is a black-box function whose values are calculated using the Monte Carlo method. To minimize this function, we use metaheuristic algorithms implemented in form of an MPI application. All computational experiments are carried out on a supercomputer.

© The Author(s), under exclusive license to Springer Nature Switzerland AG 2022
L. Sokolinsky and M. Zymbler (Eds.): PCT 2022, CCIS 1618, pp. 143–157, 2022.
https://doi.org/10.1007/978-3-031-11623-0_11

The Boolean satisfiability problem (SAT) is a combinatorial problem with an extremely wide range of practical applications. Like many other NP-hard problems, SAT is not always difficult in practice, and for many of its particular cases can be solved quite effectively using various additional techniques and heuristics. As said above, we use state-of-the-art SAT solving algorithms in application to algebraic cryptanalysis. In more detail, we construct the so-called guess-and-determine attacks on some cryptographic functions using SAT solvers. In this context, we follow [6] and many other works in which SAT solvers are applied to algebraic equations describing the calculation process of the considered cipher.

Roughly speaking, the idea of a guess-and-determine attack consists in choosing (guessing) bits from a certain set, the substitution of which greatly simplifies the original cryptanalysis problem. Such a set is called a *guessed bits set*. Various methods can be used to solve problems weakened by such substitutions. For example, a substitution of bits from some guessed bits set to the Multivariate Quadratic (MQ) system [22] may turn it into a linear system. However, examples of successful attacks of this kind are very rare (see, e.g., [4]). The approach with a wider area of applications implies a reduction of the considered cryptographic problem to some combinatorial problem, the algorithmic base of which is well developed. As G. Bard notices in [6], SAT is a good example of such a problem. In application to the SAT encodings of cryptanalysis problems, guess-and-determine strategies can also be defined quite naturally.

The main problem that arises when using SAT in cryptanalysis is that the runtime of a SAT solver on a specific formula is hard to predict [17]. There are a number of serious studies of possible measures that can be used to evaluate the hardness of concrete formulas w.r.t. concrete algorithms for solving SAT. Below we rely on the results of [5], in which various approaches to measuring tree-like metrics of the hardness of Boolean formulas are studied. Specifically, in this paper, several different tree-like metrics used in propositional proof complexity are unified. The most important result of [5] for our case is the conclusion about the relationship between the tree-like metric and the notion of a Backdoor set (concretely, we mean the Strong Backdoor Set), presented in [37]. This notion in the sense of the idea is very close to that of a guessed bits set. The Strong Backdoor Set (SBS) is a set of variables such that the substitution of any values to the corresponding variables in the original formula results in a formula for which SAT is solved by some polynomial algorithm A. As we will see below, only extremely small SBSs can give a gain in complexity, but such situations are very rare in practice.

The approach in which we do not require the algorithm A to have polynomial complexity turns out to be more practical. In such a case, A can be an arbitrary complete algorithm for solving some NP-hard problem, for example, a SAT solver. This is exactly the approach used in a number of works on the decomposition of hard SAT instances, including applications in cryptanalysis [31–33,38]. In fact, in these papers, it is shown that one can estimate the complexity of Boolean formulas using SBS generalizations for the case when A is a complete SAT solver. Specifically, in such cases, a special technique that combines the stochastic Monte Carlo method and metaheuristic optimization is used. In [34] there is presented a class of SAT-based cryptographic attacks that uses the so-called Inverse Backdoor Sets (IBS). For such backdoors, the complexity estimations of the corresponding attacks have convincing guarantees of accuracy. This allows one to compare the effectiveness of attacks based on an IBS with the effectiveness of other attacks, and in a number of cases, IBS-based attacks have the best-known effectiveness.

In the present paper, we combine ideas from [5] with ideas from [34] and propose new tree-like metrics of the hardness of SAT instances that encode the inversion problems of cryptographic functions. For these metrics, it is possible to construct estimations using probabilistic algorithms similar to those used in [34]. We construct such estimations for the functions considered in [18–20]. For this purpose, we use a metaheuristic optimization of a special fitness function calculated on a computing cluster.

As a result, we construct SAT-based guessed-and-determine attacks on reduced-round versions of the compression function of the well-known MD4 hashing algorithm. Namely, we mean the functions of the kind $MD4$-k, where k is the number of steps of the base algorithm ($MD4$-48 corresponds to the complete-round version of the considered function). In the computational part of our work, we present non-trivial attacks on the functions $MD4$-43, $MD4$-45 and $MD4$-47. The estimations of the hardness of these attacks are significantly smaller than those of brute-force attacks for these functions.

2   Preliminaries

All variables considered below are Boolean variables, i.e., they take values from $\{0, 1\}$. Assume that $X = \{x_1, \ldots, x_n\}$ is a set of Boolean variables. Then the Boolean formula F is an expression constructed with respect to special rules over the alphabet including X, brackets, and special symbols called logical connectives. The simplest Boolean formulas of the kind x or $\neg x$ are called *literals* (here $\neg$ is the negation connective). The Boolean Satisfiability Problem (SAT) is a problem that requires one to determine for an arbitrary Boolean formula F whether there exists such an assignment α of variables from X, the substitution of which [9] to F results in 1 (true). If such an α exists, then it is called a *satisfying assignment*, and the formula F is called *satisfiable*. Otherwise, F is called *unsatisfiable*. SAT is NP-complete [11, 25] in the decision variant and NP-hard in its search variant (where if the considered formula is satisfiable, it is required to find at least one satisfying assignment). Thus, SAT is most likely to be unsolvable in polynomial time in the general case. On the other hand, combinatorial problems from a wide variety of subject areas can be effectively reduced to SAT [8].

It is well known that the Tseitin transformations [35] can be used to transition from SAT for an arbitrary Boolean formula to SAT for a formula in the Conjunctive Normal Form (CNF). With respect to this, hereinafter we consider SAT for arbitrary CNFs. The CNF is a conjunction of elementary Boolean constraints called *clauses*. Each clause is a disjunction of different literals among which there are not complementary ones (remind that the literals x and $\neg x$ are called complementary). If x is an arbitrary Boolean variable, then the notation $x^\alpha, \alpha \in \{0,1\}$ means $\neg x$ if $\alpha = 0$ and x if $\alpha = 1$.

Let C be an arbitrary CNF over the set $X = \{0,1\}^n$. Consider an arbitrary subset $B \subseteq X$. Denote all possible assignments of variables from B as $\{0,1\}^{|B|}$. By $C[\beta/B]$ denote the CNF constructed from C by substituting an arbitrary assignment $\beta \in \{0,1\}^{|B|}$ to C. Let A be an arbitrary polynomial algorithm (subsolver in terms of [37]).

Definition 1. ([37]). *For a CNF C over the set of Boolean variables X, the set $B \subseteq X$ is a Strong Backdoor Set w.r.t. the polynomial subsolver A if for each $\beta \in \{0,1\}^{|B|}$, the algorithm A outputs the solution of SAT for $C[\beta/B]$.*

In [37] there is described an algorithm for solving SAT with complexity $O\left(p(|C|) \cdot \left(\dfrac{2^{|X|}}{\sqrt{|B|}}\right)^{|B|}\right)$ under the assumption that there exists an SBS B: $|B| \leq |X|/2$. However, this algorithm can be used in practice only if the considered formula has extremely small SBSs.

It is shown in [5] that the notion of SBS can be used to evaluate the hardness of Boolean formulas. In particular, the paper studies different approaches to estimating this hardness using tree-like metrics employed in propositional proof complexity. In addition, [5] demonstrates the relationship between these metrics and the so-called Backdoor hardness (the exact notion of Backdoor hardness is presented in [31]).

In [31], the following problem is considered: to construct such a set B, $B \subseteq X$ that the total time $\mu_{A,B}(C)$ of solving SAT for CNFs of the kind $C[\beta/B]$ over all possible $\beta \in \{0,1\}^{|B|}$ by some complete SAT solving algorithm A (which is not necessarily polynomial) is less than the runtime of A on the original CNF C. Following the terminology from [34], let us refer to such a set B as to a Non-deterministic Oracle Backdoor Set (NOBS). In [31], it is shown that one can estimate the value of $\mu_{A,B}(C)$ using Monte Carlo sampling. The problem of finding the NOBS with the smallest value of $\mu_{A,B}(C)$ can thus be viewed as the problem of minimizing a special pseudo-Boolean black-box fitness function [31–33,38].

Now consider the function

$$f : \{0,1\}^n \to \{0,1\}^m \tag{1}$$

defined by some cryptographic algorithm (cipher). This function is defined everywhere on $\{0,1\}^n$ (in the case of a stream cipher, it corresponds to the set of all possible secret keys). Denote the set of possible images of f as $Range f$, $Range f \subseteq \{0,1\}^n$. The main problem considered below is the problem of inversion (or of finding preimages) of the function f: given an arbitrary $\gamma \in Range f$ to find some $\alpha \in \{0,1\}^n$ such that $f(\alpha) = \gamma$. It is a well-known fact that such problems can be effectively reduced to SAT [6].

To reduce the problem of the inversion of a specific function to SAT, one can use a number of software tools: for example, the well-known CBMC tool for verifying C programs [10] or the TRANSALG translator specialized for cryptanalysis instances [29]. The advantage of TRANSALG consists in that it constructs the so-called template CNF C_f for the function f [23]. Essentially, the template CNF is a symbolic representation of the algorithm A_f that specifies the function f. An important fact is that one can model how A_f works on an arbitrary input $\alpha \in \{0,1\}^n$, $\alpha = (\alpha_1, \ldots, \alpha_n)$ by the iterative application of the Unit Propagation rule [27] to the CNF

$$x_1^{\alpha_1} \wedge \ldots \wedge x_n^{\alpha_n} \wedge C_f. \tag{2}$$

In (2), the variables $x_1, \ldots, x_n$ form a set, which we denote as X^{in}. These variables encode the input of the function f.

Our first goal is to use a SAT solver to construct an attack on the cryptographic function f: in particular, to learn how to effectively invert this function at least on some portion of its images. As mentioned above, we will construct SAT-based guess-and-determine attacks, i.e., search for such sets of guessed bits that make it possible to substantially simplify the solution of the inversion problem for f. It is quite clear that the notions of the guessed bits set and that of NOBS are very close in spirit. Unfortunately, as it follows from the results of [33,34], NOBSs do not suit well to constructing runtime estimations of guess-and-determine attacks due to the fact that in such estimations there is an unknown variance of some random variable.

To account for this, the notion of Inverse Backdoor Sets (IBS) is proposed in [34]. For IBS-based attacks, one can estimate their runtime with any predefined accuracy using the Monte Carlo scheme.

Briefly, the basic idea of IBS-based attacks proposed in [34] is as follows. Consider a template CNF C_f for the function f. Define a uniform distribution over $\{0,1\}^n$ and construct a random sample of inputs $\alpha^1, \ldots, \alpha^N$, $\alpha^j = \left(\alpha_1^j, \ldots, \alpha_n^j\right)$, $j \in \{1, \ldots, N\}$ for f. For each α^j, $j \in \{1, \ldots, N\}$ consider CNF (2). It is well-known [7] that one can derive from (2) the values of all variables in the CNF C_f using only the Unit Propagation rule. We will say that such values are induced by the input α^j of the considered function. In particular, during this process the values $y_1 = \gamma_1^j, \ldots, y_m = \gamma_m^j$, such that $f(\alpha^j) = \gamma^j$, $\gamma^j = \left(\gamma_1^j, \ldots, \gamma_m^j\right)$ will be obtained.

Assume that A is a SAT solving algorithm, $B \subseteq X$ is an arbitrary set of variables in C_f, $\alpha \in \{0,1\}^n$ is some input of f, and t is a positive constant that limits the runtime of A. Denote by $\beta(\alpha)$ the assignment of variables from B induced by the input α and by $\gamma(\alpha)$ the value of the function f on the input α. Associate with an arbitrary $\alpha \in \{0,1\}^n$ the value of the function $\xi : \{0,1\}^n \to \{0,1\}$ defined as follows: $\xi(\alpha) = 1$ if A in time $\leq t$ finds a satisfying assignment of the CNF $C_f(\beta(\alpha), \gamma(\alpha))$, which results from substituting the assignments $\beta(\alpha)$ and $\gamma(\alpha)$ to the template CNF C_f; otherwise $\xi(\alpha) = 0$.

Define a uniform distribution over $\{0,1\}^n$. Then the portion of vectors from $\{0,1\}^n$ on which the random variable ξ takes the value 1 is defined by the following probability:

$$\rho_{A,t}(B) = \frac{|\{\alpha \in \{0,1\}^n \mid \xi(\alpha) = 1\}|}{2^n} \tag{3}$$

Since ξ is a Bernoulli random variable, then $\rho_{A,t}(B) = E[\xi]$, and $E[\xi]$ can be estimated via the Monte Carlo method [28]. In particular, one can use the sample mean of the values of ξ observed in N independent experiments in the role of the estimation of $E[\xi]$. It is important to note that this estimation does not depend on the characteristics of the algorithm A (as in the case of the estimations for the NOBS in [31]) and can be made arbitrarily precise by increasing the number of observations N. In more detail, let $\xi^1, \ldots, \xi^N$ be independent observations of the variable ξ. Applying the Chebyshev inequality [16] (w.r.t. that ξ is a Bernoulli variable) to ξ, we conclude that the following holds:

$$Pr\left\{ \left| \rho_{A,t}(B) - \frac{1}{N} \sum_{j=1}^{N} \xi^j \right| \le \varepsilon \right\} \ge 1 - \frac{1}{4\varepsilon^2 N} \tag{4}$$

Definition 2 ([34]). *A non-empty set $B \subseteq X : |B| = s$ with the properties described above is called an Inverse Backdoor Set (IBS) with the parameters $(s, t, \rho_{A,t}(B))$ for C_f w.r.t. the algorithm A.*

In [34] there is described a general IBS-based guess-and-determine attack applicable to any function (1). This attack is applied to a set of outputs $\gamma^1, \ldots, \gamma^M$ of function (1). If we consider the probability of inverting at least one $\gamma^k, k \in \{1, \ldots, M\}$ to be $\ge 95\%$, then the runtime of this attack for some IBS B is:

$$Time_{A,t}(B) = 2^{|B|} \cdot t \cdot \frac{3}{\rho_{A,t}(B)} \tag{5}$$

As outlined in [34], it is possible to view the problem of constructing an effective guess-and-determine attack as a problem of finding a set B with the smallest value of (5). The latter problem can be considered as a problem of minimizing the following pseudo-Boolean fitness function:

$$\Phi_{A,t}(\theta_B) = 2^{|B|} \cdot t \cdot \frac{3N}{\sum_{j=1}^{N} \xi^j} \tag{6}$$

In (6), by θ_B we denote a Boolean vector of length $|X|$ where ones correspond to variables from X present in B, and zeroes correspond to variables from X absent from B. Probability (3) in (6) is replaced by its statistic estimation w.r.t. (4). To optimize functions (6), in [30,33,34] a computing cluster is used. In the role of optimization schemes the papers employ both local search algorithms and evolutionary algorithms.

3   Using Tree-Like Metrics to Estimate the Effectiveness of SAT-Based Guess-and-Determine Attacks

In this section, we introduce new metrics of effectiveness for IBS-based algebraic attacks. Our main motivation is inspired by the results of [5], where several different approaches to estimating the hardness of a Boolean formula via tree-like metrics are considered. For the measures studied in [5], it is possible to construct estimations of hardness for several infinite families of formulas (e.g., for pigeonhole principle formulas [12]). These estimations are constructed analytically, and it is completely unclear how one can obtain such estimations for arbitrary Boolean formulas. Below we introduce tree-like metrics of effectiveness for IBS-based guess-and-determine attacks. To solve SAT for CNFs of the kind $C_f(\beta, \gamma)$, we use modern complete SAT solvers based on the CDCL concept [27].

Let B, $|B| = s$ be an arbitrary IBS. The first observation consists in the fact that a Boolean hypercube $\{0,1\}^s$ can be represented by a complete binary tree $T_s(B)$ of the depth s: the arbitrary assignment β of variables from B corresponds to the path $\pi(\beta)$ in $T_s(B)$, which goes from a root to a leaf. We can establish some order over $B = \{x_1^B, \dots, x_s^B\}$ so that all paths in $T_s(B)$ are traversed in this order, e.g., $x_1^B < \dots < x_S^B$ (we assume that the variable x_1^B is associated with a root of $T_s(B)$).

Let f be function (1), C_f be a template CNF for f over a set X of Boolean variables, and B, $B \subseteq X$ be an arbitrary IBS. Assume that A is a complete deterministic SAT solving algorithm that traverses some tree or forest in the process of its work. Note that both DPLL and CDCL are examples of such algorithms. In particular, DPLL traverses a binary tree in which all paths follow some common order. On the other hand, CDCL works with a forest formed by different binary trees, and each tree corresponds to a specific restart. In general, different paths in such a forest have different variable orderings. If C is a fixed CNF, then by $F_A(C)$ denote the tree (in the case of DPLL) or forest (in the case of CDCL) traversed by the considered algorithm A in order to construct an unsatisfiability proof for C or its satisfying assignment. By $F_A(C, t)$ denote the part of $F_A(C)$ that contains the first t paths traversed by A.

Consider an arbitrary $\gamma \in Range f$. Let $\pi(\beta)$ be an arbitrary path in $T_s(B)$, and $l(\beta)$ be a leaf of this path. Let us connect $l(\beta)$ with the root or with the set of roots $F_A(C_f(\beta, \gamma), t)$ by a new edge or several edges. We do this for each $\beta \in \{0,1\}^{|B|}$ and for the corresponding path in $T_s(B)$. Denote the constructed tree as $T^*(C_f, A, B, \gamma, t)$. Let π^* be an arbitrary path in $T^*(C_f, A, B, \gamma, t)$. Taking into account the nature of the DPLL and CDCL algorithms, the path π^* corresponds to a sequence of decision levels [27] and literals derived via UP, which either ends in a conflict or in a derivation of an assignment that satisfies $C_f(\beta, \gamma)$.

Definition 3. *If the path π^* ends in a derivation of a satisfying assignment for $C_f(\beta, \gamma)$, then we refer to π^* as a positive path, otherwise, π^* is a negative path.*

Now let us establish the following fact.

Theorem 1. *Let α be an arbitrary input of f chosen from $\{0,1\}^n$ in accordance with a uniform distribution, and $\gamma = f(\alpha)$. Assume that B is an IBS with the parameters $(s, t, \rho_{A,t}(B))$ for C_f w.r.t. a SAT solving algorithm A. Then the probability that the tree $T^*(C_f, A, B, \gamma, t)$ contains a positive path is $\rho_{A,t}(B)$.*

Sketch Proof. As follows from the definition of $\rho_{A,t}(B)$, this is the probability of an event that consists in finding by the algorithm A a satisfying assignment for $C_f(\beta(\alpha), \gamma(\alpha))$ in time $\leq t$. It is supposed that α is chosen from $\{0,1\}^n$ w.r.t. the uniform distribution, and $\beta(\alpha)$, $\gamma(\alpha)$ are the assignments of variables from B and from the output of the function f, induced by α in the sense defined above. Denote the upper bound on the number of paths traversed by A in a tree or forest $F_A(C_f(\beta, \gamma))$ as t. Note that $T^*(C_f, A, B, \gamma, t)$ at the beginning is essentially a tree-like representation of the set $\{0,1\}^{|B|}$. However, in this case, the tree contains a path that starts from $\beta(\alpha)$, where α is the preimage of γ w.r.t. f. Denote this path as $\tilde{\pi}$. From (3) it follows that $\rho_{A,t}(B)$ is the probability that $\tilde{\pi}$ is positive. Thus, the theorem is proved.

If we construct trees of the kind $T^*(C_f, A, B, \gamma^k, t)$ for $k \in \{1, \ldots, M\}$, then from the proven theorem and the results of [34] it follows that for $M \geq 3/\rho_{A,t}(B)$, the probability that at least one of these trees has a positive path (which corresponds to the successful solution of the inversion problem for a specific γ^k) is at least 95%.

Definition 4. *We define the hardness of a guess-and-determine attack based on an IBS B in the context of the tree-like metric proposed above as the total number of paths in all trees $T^*(C_f, A, B, \gamma^k, t)$, $k \in \{1, \ldots, M\}$.*

Note that the approach from [34] that uses the statistic estimation of the hardness of IBS-based guess-and-determine attacks can be naturally transferred to the introduced tree-like metric. Thus, we can use the computational scheme of the Monte Carlo method in combination with metaheuristic optimization for this purpose.

4   Class of Considered Functions

In this section, we describe the functions for the inversion of which we run computational experiments on a supercomputer. These are the variants of the compression function of the well-known cryptographic MD4 hash function. The MD4 function is vulnerable to the so-called collision attack [36]. However, for its inversion problem, no attacks with realistic runtime are known so far. The best preimage attack known to the authors is the one described in [24]. The attack proposed in the paper has a complexity of 2^{96} calls of the MD4 compression function. It is noteworthy that the computational results of [24] are quite hard to reproduce.

Our goal is to construct an estimate of the hardness of the inversion problem of the MD4 compression function w.r.t. the tree-like metrics proposed above and compare it with the results of [24]. We would like to highlight that it is not hard to reproduce our results since for this purpose one can use publicly available software tools and a computer cluster.

In addition to the complete-round MD4 compression function, we will consider the inversion problems of the variants of this function, limited in the number of steps, for which we use the notation $f_{MD4\text{-}k}$, where k is the number of compression steps, $k \in \{1, \ldots, 48\}$, and the case $k = 48$ corresponds to the complete-round compression function.

In application to functions of the kind $f_{MD4\text{-}k}$, we use special techniques for weakening their inversion problems. The basic idea of such techniques goes back to H. Dobbertin [14] and consists in fixing the values of some chaining variables to a constant. This step leads to the derivation of the values of some other variables. The SAT variant of Dobbertin's attack is described in [13], and this attack turns out to be substantially more effective compared to the original one. In [18], it is suggested to use the automatic search of relaxation constraints a la Dobbertin by applying black-box optimization algorithms. As a result, new relaxation constraints are found, they give an attack that is significantly more effective than the attack from [13]. In particular, the attack from [18] allows inverting the $MD4$-39 function in less than 1 minute on randomly selected vectors from $\{0,1\}^{128}$ on a personal computer.

The key idea of the attacks from [18–20] is to reduce the inversion problem of functions of the kind

$$f_{MD4\text{-}k} : \{0,1\}^{512} \to \{0,1\}^{128}$$

to inverting functions of the kind

$$g^{\lambda_r}_{MD4\text{-}k} : \{0,1\}^{p_r} \to \{0,1\}^{128}, \tag{7}$$

where $p_r < 512$. Functions (7) are built using the vectors λ_r, which specify the sets of Dobbertin's relaxation constraints. Any λ_r is a Boolean vector of length 48: ones in it indicate at which step of the compression algorithm the corresponding chaining variable is replaced by the constant 0^{32}. So, for example, the vector λ_1 used in [18] (in the paper it appears as ρ_1) defines the function

$$g^{\lambda_1}_{MD4\text{-}k} : \{0,1\}^{128} \to \{0,1\}^{128}. \tag{8}$$

As shown in [19], function (8) is defined almost everywhere on $\{0,1\}^{128}$. At least half of the vectors from $\{0,1\}^{128}$ have $g^{\lambda_1}_{MD4\text{-}k}$-preimages (at least for $k \in \{39, \ldots, 45\}$). If for $\chi \in \{0,1\}^{128}$ there exists such $\alpha' \in \{0,1\}^{128}$ that $g^{\lambda_1}_{MD4\text{-}k}(\alpha') = \chi$, then from such α' we can effectively recover $\alpha \in \{0,1\}^{512}$ for which the following holds: $f_{MD4\text{-}k}(\alpha) = \chi$.

5   Computational Experiments

In this section, we provide a description of computational experiments in which SAT-based guess-and-determine attacks for functions of kind (8) are built.

In these experiments, at the stage of debugging and testing software applications, the "Akademik V.M. Matrosov" cluster of Irkutsk Supercomputer Center [2] is used. The main computational experiments are carried out on the cluster of Peter the Great St. Petersburg Polytechnic University [3].

5.1 General Scenario

Once again let us give a brief description of the computational problem, for the solution of which a supercomputer is used. We consider the inversion problems of a function of kind (8) for different k, $k \in \{40, \ldots, 48\}$ (for $k < 40$, the corresponding problems can be solved on a PC). For such functions, we build IBS-based guess-and-determine attacks. In the role of a SAT solving algorithm A, we use several state-of-the-art CDCL-based SAT solvers: MiniSat, Glucose, Cadical, MapleLCM.

Let us construct a template CNF $C_{g_{MD4\text{-}k}^{\lambda_1}}$ using the Transalg tool [29]. For each considered function of kind (8) we generate a sample on N random inputs $\alpha^1, \ldots, \alpha^N \in \{0,1\}^{128}$, and for each $j \in \{1, \ldots, N\}$ we generate the assignment of all variables in $C_{g_{MD4\text{-}k}^{\lambda_1}}$ by applying UP to CNFs of the kind $x_1^{\alpha_1^j} \wedge \ldots \wedge x_n^{\alpha_n^j} \wedge C_{g_{MD4\text{-}k}^{\lambda_1}}$. An arbitrary set $B \subseteq X$ is represented by a Boolean vector θ_B of length $|X|$. Let us define at an arbitrary point $\theta_B \in \{0,1\}^{|X|}$ the value of fitness function (6) as follows:

1. For a random sample $\alpha^1, \ldots, \alpha^N$ generate outputs $\gamma^1, \ldots, \gamma^N$ of the function $g_{MD4\text{-}k}^{\lambda_1}$ and assignments of variables from B: $\beta^1, \ldots, \beta^N$;
2. Consider CNF formulas $C_{g_{MD4\text{-}k}^{\lambda_1}}(\beta^j, \gamma^j)$, $j \in \{1, \ldots, N\}$ and apply the SAT solver A to each such a formula with a constraint on the number of conflicts $\leq t$ (the constant t is chosen during the experiments). If A has made more than t conflicts, the corresponding computation is interrupted;
3. With each run of A on the CNF $C_{g_{MD4\text{-}k}^{\lambda_1}}(\beta^j, \gamma^j)$ we associate the observed value ξ^j of the random variable ξ: if A managed to find a satisfying assignment for $C_{g_{MD4\text{-}k}^{\lambda_1}}(\beta^j, \gamma^j)$ using $\leq t$ conflicts, then $\xi^j = 1$, otherwise $\xi^j = 0$;
4. Calculate the value of the fitness function at the point θ_B according to formula (6);
5. Go to a new point θ_B using some metaheuristic strategy [26].

Note that a similar approach is used in several prior papers, e.g., [30,34]. However, in these papers, the runtime of the algorithm A is limited by a straightforward time limit in seconds, while in the present paper we impose a limit in the number of conflicts. In addition, the cited papers employ different algorithms to optimize the fitness function, in particular, [34] uses the tabu search algorithm, while [30] utilizes several variants of the (1+1) Evolutionary algorithm, as well as a special genetic algorithm (GA). It is the latter algorithm that we use in our experiments, however, for the purposes of the present paper it is reimplemented to fully work on clusters.

In this work, we use a version of the algorithm from [30] implemented as an MPI program, and thus one can run it on a computer cluster of any capacity. Specifically, the algorithm works with several points of the hypercube forming a population $\theta_{B_1}, \ldots, \theta_{B_Q}$. Let Π be an arbitrary population of the size Q. We associate the distribution $D_\Pi = \{p_1, \ldots, p_Q\}$ with it, defining the probabilities $p_l, l \in \{1, \ldots, Q\}$ as follows:

$$p_l = \frac{1/\Phi(\theta_{B_l})}{\sum_{i=1}^{Q} (1/\Phi(\theta_{B_i}))} \tag{9}$$

The transition from the current population Π towards the new population Π' is performed as follows. We select individuals from Π randomly w.r.t. the distribution D_Π and to each pair of selected individuals we apply the standard two-point crossover operator [26] in a combination of the FGA-mutation operator proposed in [15]. In such a way we construct G individuals of a new population. We also add to the new population H individuals from Π that have the best values of the fitness function (this step corresponds to the so-called elitism concept [26]). As a result, we ensure that the following holds: $G + H = Q$. In all computational experiments we use the following values of these parameters: $Q = 10$, $G = 8$, $H = 2$.

From the definition of the fitness function, it directly follows that this function is quite costly in a computational sense. Even with the use of a powerful supercomputer, optimizing such a function over the hypercube $\{0, 1\}^{|X|}$ would require colossal computational resources. That is why in our experiments we solve the optimization problems of functions (6) on some special subsets of X. As noted in [34], we can take as a started point of our optimization process some Strong Unit Propagation Backdoor Set (SUPBS). If B is a SUPBS, then the calculation of the value $\Phi(\theta_B)$ takes $t = 0$ conflicts. In our cases, a trivial SUPBS is formed by the input variables of the considered function, and we denote this set by X^{in}. For any function considered in this paper this set consists of 128 variables. In our experiments we optimize the functions of the kind $\Phi(\theta_B)$, namely, on $2^{X^{in}}$.

5.2   Implementation and Results

As said above, we conduct computational experiments on two supercomputers, the "Akademik V.M. Matrosov" cluster of Irkutsk Supercomputer center [2] and the computing cluster of St. Petersburg Polytechnic University (SPPU) [3]. Each compute node of the former is equipped with two 18-core processors Intel Xeon E5 2695 v4 and 128 GB DDR4-2400 RAM. In our experiments, we employ up to 10 nodes (180 cores) for up to one day. The nodes of the latter cluster are equipped with four 14-core processors Intel Xeon E5 2695 v3 and 64 GB DDR4-2400 RAM. In each experiment, we harness 25 nodes (1400 cores) and use the same duration (one day).

The "Akademik V.M. Matrosov" cluster is mainly used to debug and test the developed MPI program and the employed SAT solvers (see details further). The major part of the computational experiments is run on the SPPU cluster.

In our experiments, we consider the problems of inverting the functions $g^{\lambda_1}_{MD4\text{-}k}$, $k \in \{43, 45, 47, 48\}$ described above. To minimize the functions $\Phi(\theta_B)$, we employ the EvoGuess framework [1], specially developed for solving pseudo-Boolean optimization problems associated with SAT. This framework implements several evolutionary algorithms, however, we mainly use the implementation of the Genetic Algorithm described above. EvoGuess can be used as an MPI application and, thus, can harness any number of available cores. Actually, EvoGuess can be considered as an optimization wrap-around for the PySAT tool [21], which, in turn, is the environment for invoking SAT and MaxSAT solvers incrementally from Python. PySAT supports a number of modern SAT solvers (MiniSat, Glucose, Cadical, MapleLCMDist, etc.). On the testing stage, we check all of them, but for our class of instances the best results are obtained using MiniSat 2.2, thus in all experiments we use this solver.

The results of the computational experiments are presented in the following table.

Table 1. Results of the experiments. In each experiment, 1400 cores of the SPPU cluster are used (25 nodes) for 1 day (24 h). The SAT solver MiniSat 2.2 (embedded in the PySAT tool) is applied.

	$MD4$-43, (inverting $g^{\lambda_1}_{MD4\text{-}43}$)	$MD4$-45, (inverting $g^{\lambda_1}_{MD4\text{-}45}$)	$MD4$-47, (inverting $g^{\lambda_1}_{MD4\text{-}47}$)	$MD4$-48, (inverting $g^{\lambda_1}_{MD4\text{-}48}$)
Best value of $\Phi(\theta_B)$ in the proposed tree-like metric (estimation of guess-and-determine attack hardness)	2.489460e+13	1.770887e+21	2.415492e+28	8.222028e+36
Size of the best backdoor (w.r.t. the best value of $\Phi(\theta_B)$)	19	46	70	99
Number of visited points in the hypercube	54312	47840	42456	41984

Let us briefly discuss the obtained results. Recall that with respect to what is said above, we can consider one conflict as one elementary call of a special function (actually, a SAT solver), which is used to solve the corresponding cryptanalysis problem. On the other hand, in brute-force attacks on each of the considered functions we make $2^{128} \approx 3, 4e{+}38$ calls of the corresponding function in the worst case scenario and 2^{127} calls on average. Thus, we can conclude that the MD4 compression function has non-trivial SAT based guess-and-determine attacks for $k = 43, 45, 47$. For a complete-round version of this function, i.e., for $MD4$-48, the obtained attack is comparable to a brute-force attack, and thus the use of SAT solvers does not lead to any advantage in this case.

6   Conclusion

In this paper, we present new measures to estimate the hardness of algebraic attacks on cryptographic functions that use state-of-the-art SAT solvers. The proposed measures are tree-like. In fact, they are statistic estimations of the number of paths in some tree, which corresponds to the process of enumerating all possible assignments of variables in some guessed bits set. By estimating this number, we construct the estimation of the corresponding attack. The problem of constructing the best attack of this kind is viewed as a problem of minimizing some fitness function, the values of which are calculated probabilistically using the Monte Carlo method. To optimize such a function, we use a specially developed framework for solving black-box optimization problems associated with SAT, which is an MPI program that can work on a supercomputer. In our computational experiments, two clusters [2,3] are harnessed. As a result, we construct a non-trivial SAT based guess-and-determine attack on reduced-round versions of the compression function of the well-known MD4 hashing algorithm, namely, for $MD4$-43, $MD4$-45, $MD4$-47. Using the proposed tree-like metrics, it is shown that the constructed attacks are significantly more effective than brute-force attacks.

Acknowledgments. The research was supported by the Russian Science Foundation, project No. 22-21-00583.

References

1. Evoguess: Framework for hardness estimating of SAT instances by decomposition set searching. https://github.com/ctlab/evoguess. Accessed 11 Mar 2022
2. Irkutsk Supercomputer Center of the SB RAS. https://hpc.icc.ru/. Accessed 11 Mar 2022
3. Supercomputer center "Polytechnic". https://research.spbstu.ru/skc/. Accessed 11 Mar 2022
4. Anderson, R.: A5 (was: Hacking digital phones). Newsgroup Communication (1994)
5. Ansótegui, C., Bonet, M.L., Levy, J., Manyà, F.: Measuring the hardness of SAT instances. In: Proceedings of the 23rd National Conference on Artificial Intelligence - Volume 1, AAAI2008, pp. 222–228. AAAI Press (2008)
6. Bard, G.: Algebraic Cryptanalysis. Springer New York (2009). https://doi.org/10.1007/978-0-387-88757-9
7. Bessiere, C., Katsirelos, G., Narodytska, N., Walsh, T.: Circuit complexity and decompositions of global constraints. In: IJCAI, pp. 412–418. Morgan Kaufmann Publishers Inc., San Francisco (2009)
8. Biere, A., Heule, M., van Maaren, H., Walsh, T. (eds.): Handbook of Satisfiability, Frontiers in Artificial Intelligence and Applications, vol. 185. IOS Press, Amsterdam (2009)

9. Chin-Liang, C., Chang, C., Zhang, J., Lee, R., Coaut, C.: Symbolic logic and mechanical theorem proving. In: Computer Science and Applied Mathematics : A Series of Monographs and Textbooks. Elsevier Science (1973)

10. Clarke, E., Kroening, D., Lerda, F.: A tool for checking ANSI-C programs. In: Jensen, K., Podelski, A. (eds.) TACAS 2004. LNCS, vol. 2988, pp. 168–176. Springer, Heidelberg (2004). https://doi.org/10.1007/978-3-540-24730-2_15

11. Cook, S.A.: The complexity of theorem-proving procedures. In: Proceedings of the Third Annual ACM Symposium on Theory of Computing, STOC 1971, pp. 151–158. Association for Computing Machinery, New York, NY, USA (1971)

12. Cook, S.A., Reckhow, R.A.: The relative efficiency of propositional proof systems. J. Symb. Logic **44**(1), 36–50 (1979)

13. De, D., Kumarasubramanian, A., Venkatesan, R.: Inversion attacks on secure hash functions using SAT solvers. In: Marques-Silva, J., Sakallah, K.A. (eds.) SAT 2007. LNCS, vol. 4501, pp. 377–382. Springer, Heidelberg (2007). https://doi.org/10.1007/978-3-540-72788-0_36

14. Dobbertin, H.: The first two rounds of MD4 are not one-way. In: Vaudenay, S. (ed.) FSE 1998. LNCS, vol. 1372, pp. 284–292. Springer, Heidelberg (1998). https://doi.org/10.1007/3-540-69710-1_19

15. Doerr, B., Le, H.P., Makhmara, R., Nguyen, T.D.: Fast genetic algorithms. In: Proceedings of GECCO 2017, pp. 777–784 (2017)

16. Feller, W.: An Introduction to Probability Theory and Its Applications, vol. 1, 3rd edn. Wiley, New York (1968)

17. Gomes, C.P., Sabharwal, A.: Exploiting runtime variation in complete solvers. In: Biere, A., Heule, M., van Maaren, H., Walsh, T. (eds.) Handbook of Satisfiability, Amsterdam (2009)

18. Gribanova, I., Semenov, A.: Using automatic generation of relaxation constraints to improve the preimage attack on 39-step MD4. In: 2018 41st International Convention on Information and Communication Technology, Electronics and Microelectronics (MIPRO), pp. 1174–1179 (2018)

19. Gribanova, I., Semenov, A.: Parallel guess-and-determine preimage attack with realistic complexity estimation for MD4-40 cryptographic hash function. In: Proceedings of XIII Conference Parallel Computational Technologies (PaCT), pp. 8–18 (2019)

20. Gribanova, I., Semenov, A.: Constructing a set of weak values for full-round MD4 hash function. In: 2020 43rd International Convention on Information, Communication and Electronic Technology (MIPRO), pp. 1212–1217 (2020)

21. Ignatiev, A., Morgado, A., Marques-Silva, J.: PySAT: A Python toolkit for prototyping with SAT oracles. In: SAT, pp. 428–437 (2018)

22. Kipnis, A., Shamir, A.: Cryptanalysis of the HFE Public Key Cryptosystem by Relinearization. In: Wiener, M. (ed.) CRYPTO 1999. LNCS, vol. 1666, pp. 19–30. Springer, Heidelberg (1999). https://doi.org/10.1007/3-540-48405-1_2

23. Kochemazov, S., Zaikin, O., Gribanova, I., Otpuschennikov, I., Semenov, A.: Translation of algorithmic descriptions of discrete functions to SAT with applications to cryptanalysis problems. Log. Methods Comput. Sci. **16**, 1–42 (2020)

24. Leurent, G.: MD4 is not one-way. In: Nyberg, K. (ed.) FSE 2008. LNCS, vol. 5086, pp. 412–428. Springer, Heidelberg (2008). https://doi.org/10.1007/978-3-540-71039-4_26

25. Levin, L.A.: Universal Sequential Search Problems. Probl. Inf. Transm. **9**(3) (1973)

26. Luke, S.: Essentials of Metaheuristics, 2nd edn. Lulu, Raleigh (2013)

27. Marques-Silva, J., Lynce, I., Malik, S.: Conflict-driven clause learning SAT solvers. In: Biere, A., Heule, M., Van Maaren, H., Walsh, T. (eds.) Handbook of Satisfiability, Frontiers in Artificial Intelligence and Applications, pp. 133–182. IOS Press BV, Amsterdam (2009)

28. Metropolis, N., Ulam, S.: The Monte Carlo method. J. Am. Stat. Assoc. **44**(247), 335–341 (1949)

29. Otpuschennikov, I., Semenov, A., Gribanova, I., Zaikin, O., Kochemazov, S.: Encoding cryptographic functions to SAT using TRANSALG system. In: Proceedings of the Twenty-Second European Conference on Artificial Intelligence, ECAI 2016, pp. 1594–1595. IOS Press, NLD, Amsterdam (2016)

30. Pavlenko, A., Semenov, A., Ulyantsev, V.: Evolutionary computation techniques for constructing SAT-based attacks in algebraic cryptanalysis. In: Kaufmann, P., Castillo, P.A. (eds.) EvoApplications 2019. LNCS, vol. 11454, pp. 237–253. Springer, Cham (2019). https://doi.org/10.1007/978-3-030-16692-2_16

31. Semenov, A., Chivilikhin, D., Pavlenko, A., Otpuschennikov, I., Ulyantsev, V., Ignatiev, A.: Evaluating the hardness of SAT instances using evolutionary optimization algorithms. In: Michel, L.D. (ed.) 27th International Conference on Principles and Practice of Constraint Programming (CP 2021), Leibniz International Proceedings in Informatics (LIPIcs), vol. 210, pp. 47:1–47:18. Schloss Dagstuhl - Leibniz-Zentrum für Informatik, Dagstuhl, Germany (2021)

32. Semenov, A., Zaikin, O.: Algorithm for finding partitionings of hard variants of boolean satisfiability problem with application to inversion of some cryptographic functions. SpringerPlus **5**(1), 1–16 (2016). https://doi.org/10.1186/s40064-016-2187-4

33. Semenov, A., Zaikin, O., Kochemazov, S.: Finding effective SAT Partitionings Via black-box optimization. In: Pardalos, P.M., Rasskazova, V., Vrahatis, M.N. (eds.) Black Box Optimization, Machine Learning, and No-Free Lunch Theorems. SOIA, vol. 170, pp. 319–355. Springer, Cham (2021). https://doi.org/10.1007/978-3-030-66515-9_11

34. Semenov, A.A., Zaikin, O., Otpuschennikov, I.V., Kochemazov, S., Ignatiev, A.: On cryptographic attacks using backdoors for SAT. In: Thirty-Second AAAI Conference on Artificial Intelligence, pp. 6641–6648 (2018)

35. Tseitin, G.S.: On the complexity of derivation in propositional calculus. In: Studies in Constructive Mathematics and Mathematical Logic, Part II, Seminars in Mathematics, pp. 115–125 (1970)

36. Wang, X., Lai, X., Feng, D., Chen, H., Yu, X.: Cryptanalysis of the hash functions MD4 and RIPEMD. In: Cramer, R. (ed.) EUROCRYPT 2005. LNCS, vol. 3494, pp. 1–18. Springer, Heidelberg (2005). https://doi.org/10.1007/11426639_1

37. Williams, R., Gomes, C., Selman, B.: Backdoors to typical case complexity. In: International Joint Conference on Artificial Intelligence, pp. 1173–1178 (2003)

38. Zaikin, O.S., Kochemazov, S.E.: On black-box optimization in divide-and-conquer SAT solving. Optim. Methods Softw. **36**, 1–25 (2019)

Tuning of a Matrix-Matrix Multiplication Algorithm for Several GPUs Connected by Fast Communication Links

Yea Rem Choi[1]($\boxtimes$) (iD), Vsevolod Nikolskiy[1,2] (iD), and Vladimir Stegailov[1,2,3] (iD)

[1] HSE University, Moscow, Russia
echoj@hse.ru
[2] Joint Institute for High Temperatures of the RAS, Moscow, Russia
[3] Moscow Institute of Physics and Technology, Dolgoprudny, Russia

Abstract. The usage of one of the latest high-performance hardware types (nodes with several GPUs connected by high bandwidth and low latency communication links), requires algorithms where the CPU is used only to manage the program execution, and GPUs are used for computations. In this work, we study an original GPU-only parallel matrix-matrix multiplication algorithm ($C = \alpha A * B + \beta C$) for servers with multiple GPUs. The algorithm is implemented using CUDA. The performance of this multi-GPU GEMM algorithm and the method defining the optimal tile size using the hardware parameters and the matrix size are considered. The usability of the developed performance model by benchmarking two types of GPU servers is verified.

Keywords: Parallel computing · CUDA · GEMM · high-speed GPU interconnect · multi-GPU programming

1 Introduction

Today, accelerators, especially GPUs, have arisen as an important component of supercomputers. Therefore, many algorithms and programs have been modified accordingly: molecular dynamics codes such as GROMACS [1], particle-in-cell plasma simulation codes such as PICADOR [2], electronic structure calculation codes such as Quantum Espresso [3,4], or astrophysical hydrodynamics codes such as GPUPEGAS [5,6]. The main idea of these modifications is to offload some possible workload to be computed on GPUs. The strategy is to organize parallel computing across the nodes of a supercomputer using MPI and inside the node with GPUs using OpenCL/CUDA/HIP (see e.g. [7–9]). The common issue then is data transfer bandwidth, which restricts the GPU utilization rate [10,11], hence, there arises a need for very high-performance links such as NVlink or Infinity Fabric. Servers with GPU devices connected with such links generally show high efficiency, especially in the cases of GPU-only algorithms (e.g. [12–14]).

Many problems are based or rely on linear algebra, particularly, on matrix operations. Matrix multiplication is a more or less costly operation that might be appraised as a benchmark to study the performance of computers (e.g. [15–18]). While GPUs are used for such computations, we can distinguish cases when only GPUs are used for it or, otherwise, other types of computing units may participate in it. On the other hand, contemporary compute nodes have fast links (e.g. NVlink), such as those described earlier, between GPUs and slower links (e.g. PCIe) between the CPU and GPU. Thence, if we have to compute several consecutive mathematically heavy operations, it will be less costly to launch it on GPUs without giving requests to the host memory for data transfer. In addition, during multi-GPU computing, devices have to continuously send and receive data, therefore, the reuse of data on the units involved, if possible, will make the process faster and less complicated.

2   Related Work

Parallel matrix multiplication algorithms have a long history of development. For example, after the introduction of the MPI standard, a Scalable Universal Matrix Multiplication Algorithm (SUMMA) for parallel matrix multiplication was published [19]. Different parallel GEMM algorithm models and structures were under research [20,21]. There were attempts to redesign the core of the algorithm [22]. One of the recent works showing approximate peak performance is the Communication Optimal S-partition-based Matrix multiplication Algorithm (COSMA) [23]. Particular attention there is paid to the importance of I/O operations and communications management, which is the key to reach comparably fast performance in relation to the best existing solutions such as ScaLAPACK [23].

Analytical models help to find optimal parameters for GPU algorithms. Such a model for a single GPU is presented in Tran, Lee, and Choi [24].

Since we work with multiple GPUs, we also have to pay attention to the synchronization process between the devices [25].

The optimal partitioning of a computational domain over several heterogeneous processors, processor load balancing and the minimization of inter-processor communication costs are crucial for data-parallel dense linear algebra and other applications that have a similar communication pattern in modern hybrid servers. One of the most recent works in this field is devoted to the optimal partitioning of a square computational domain over three heterogeneous processors [26].

An algorithm showing high efficiency for hybrid platforms that have fast communication links installed between the CPU and GPU is built over the PaRSEC runtime system [27]. It stores data in the host memory, and GPUs are supplied with the necessary data chunks by the CPU-GPU interconnect.

In our previous work [28], we introduced a matrix multiplication algorithm for a multi-GPU node that uses only GPUs for data storage and computation. The algorithm is aimed for the use in nodes with a fast interconnect between GPUs. It was shown that the standard cuBLAS-XT function from Nvidia CUDA SDK provided suboptimal performance on a multi-GPU node. The asynchronous data transfer and compute organization in the algorithm allowed us to get much higher performance. In this work, we present an analytical model that estimates the time-to-solution for the proposed algorithm using basic hardware parameters. This analytical model can be used to optimize the algorithm verified in this work by benchmarking two different multi-GPU servers.

3   Testing Platforms

The results reported in this study are obtained on the K-type nodes of the cHARISMa supercomputer at HSE University [29,30]. The nodes are based on DELL PowerEdge C4140 servers with two Intel Xeon Gold 6152 CPUs, and four NVidia Tesla V100 GPUs (Fig. 1a). Each GPU has 32 GB of HBM2 memory, and the four GPUs are connected by NVLINK 2.0, forming a fully connected ('all-to-all') topology.

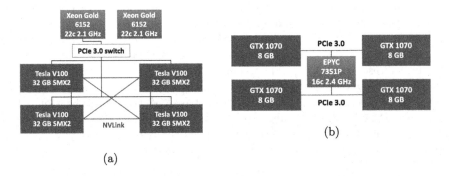

(a)

(b)

Fig. 1. Topology of the DELL PowerEdge C4140M node of the cHARISMa supercomputer with two CPUs and four Nvidia Tesla V100 GPUs connected by NVLINK 2.0 (a) and the TYAN B8021G88V2HR-2T server with one CPU and four Nvidia GTX1070 GPUs connected by PCIe 3.0 (b).

The benchmarking studies presented in this work are carried out using the standard HPC software stack based on CentOS Linux release 7.6.1810, GNU compilers 7.3, and CUDA Version 10.2.89 with driver ver. 440.33.01.

The second platform is the TYAN B8021G88V2HR-2T server at JIHT RAS. It has the EPYC 7351P CPU and four NVidia GeForce GTX1070 GPUs connected by PCIe 3.0 (Fig. 1b). Each GPU has 8 GB of GDDR5 memory.

4   Parallel Matrix-Matrix Multiplication Algorithm for Multiple GPUs

The studied algorithm is an improved version of the algorithm presented previously [28]. The research is based on the general matrix-matrix multiplication algorithm for the following matrix operation

$$C = \alpha A * B + \beta C.$$

The main idea of the process is to calculate the tiles of the resulting matrix C on each device with the reuse of possible data of the input matrix bands [28]. In the research, we observe a simpler case with 2 square matrices A and B, where $N * N$ elements are in both. Each matrix is divided into some number of equal-sized bands to share the computational load between different GPUs. Then, from the pairs of the bands from A and B, we calculate the appropriate tiles of the resulting matrix C.

The GEMM function from the cuBLAS library is used as the core of the proposed algorithm. It normally works with column-oriented matrices, but is also available for differently oriented matrices. In our case, if we perceive the column orientation as a default configuration, we store the data of the matrix A transposed. This simplifies the data transfer operation because we can just send one long data line from the source memory.

The algorithm is GPU-oriented, thus, the CPU gives only instructions. The source data are located in GPUs, and transfers are sent only between GPUs. For computation in devices, 2 bands are allocated for the same matrix.

The classical SUMMA algorithm [19] is developed using MPI for distributed memory systems. SUMMA does not use asynchronous data transfers, which could help overlapping computations and communications. The algorithm proposed here works with the "rows" of the matrix A and the "columns" of the matrix B. However, GPUs perform computational operations reasonably quickly. To supply data in time, high-speed communication links and data division into a sufficiently large number of chunks are required. To manage this issue, we organize asynchronous communications and computations. Then, we do not supply the original data of the matrix C, but we add βC due to the copy kernel of the results received in the final stage.

5   Theoretical Optimal Tile Size

For a better performance of the algorithm, we regulate the tile size one by one and find the best one. The performance time of the GEMM kernel can be approximated [31] as

$$T_{GEMM} = \max\left(T_{mem}, T_{math}, T_{instructions}\right), \qquad (1)$$

where T_{mem} is the data management time in the frame of a device, T_{math} is the time spent on mathematical operations, and $T_{instructions}$ is the time during which instructions are given by the CPU. In the basis of the algorithm, we assume in advance that $T_{instructions} \ll T_{math}$ since, otherwise, a multi-GPU implementation would slow down the execution by waiting for instructions. To satisfy this condition, the matrices involved in GEMM should not be too small. To understand if $T_{math} > T_{mem}$, we can find the arithmetic intensity [32] of

GEMM operations, which should be greater than the defined value for the devices involved, i.e., the math and memory bandwidth proportion. In the case of single precision (32-bit), it can be found by the proportion

$$Intensity = \frac{FLOPS}{bytes} = \frac{2MNK}{4(MN + NK + MK)} > BW_{math}/BW_{mem} = k_{BW},$$
(2)

where M, N, K are the numbers of elements in the columns or rows of the matrices A, B, C; BW is the processor math or memory bandwidth, appropriately. In our case, Eq. (2) becomes

$$Intensity = \frac{N_i^2 N}{2(N_i N + N_i N + N_i^2)} = \frac{N_i N}{4N + 2N_i} > k_{BW}.$$
(3)

After simple arithmetic we get $(N > 2k_{BW})$

$$N_i > 4k_{BW}N/(N - 2k_{BW}), \ T_{math} > T_{mem}.$$
(4)

For example, for single precision of the Nvidia V100 GPU ($k_{BW} = 16.6$) if $N = 2^{12}$, $N_i > 66.9$ needed to $T_{math} > T_{mem}$, if $N = 2^{13}$, then $N_i > 66.6$, if $N = 2^{14}$, then $N_i > 66.5$. Each time can be found by the equations

$$T_{math} = FLOPS/BW_{math}, \ T_{mem} = bytes/BW_{mem},$$
(5)

which for the algorithm transform into

$$T_{math} = 2N_i^2 N/BW_{math}, \ T_{mem} = (8NN_i + 4N_i^2)/BW_{mem}.$$
(6)

On the other hand, we have to keep data supply from memory storing original matrices simultaneously. The GPU device, where the original matrix is located, sends bands to the other GPUs, so $Num_{GPUs} - 1$ data transfer operations need be sent. If we are not dealing with a small number of tiles, the reuse of data in the model can approximate the time needed for one kernel launch (T_{kernel}) as follows:

$$T_{kernel} = \max(T_{GEMM}, (Num_{GPUs} - 1)T_{transfer}).$$
(7)

Otherwise, the transfer time ($T_{transfer}$) can increase by up to 3 times (3 matrices A, B, C). This effect is conspicuously demonstrated when we store all matrices in one device [28], where the transfer time influences the performance of the whole task and has decreased efficiency compared to the case with the spread store of the matrices.

Furthermore, if we suppose that we have reached a fully parallel model, then the full task performance time (T_{task}) will be approximately

$$T_{task} = 3T_{transfer} + N/(N_i Num_{GPUs})T_{kernel}.$$
(8)

Particularly, the data transfer time has a linear form [33]

$$T_{transfer} = bytes/BW_{transfer} + T_{latency}.$$
(9)

We work with sufficiently large matrices such that the term with transfer bandwidth between GPUs ($BW_{transfer}$) dominates [33]

$$bytes/BW_{transfer} \gg T_{latency}. \tag{10}$$

Accordingly, expression (9) together with condition (10) in single precision can be converted into

$$T_{transfer} = 4N_i N/BW_{transfer}. \tag{11}$$

Today, high-performance computing environments have exceptionally fast math bandwidth (BW_{math}) or in-device memory bandwidth (BW_{mem}) comparing with data transfer ($BW_{transfer}$) from another device. It means that we will slow down the execution of the task whenever we make GPUs wait for data supply. There are two possible situations, if $Intensity > k_{BW}$, we determine from Eqs. (1), (6), (7), (11)

$$T_{kernel} = T_{GEMM} = T_{math}, \quad N_i > 2(Num_{GPUs} - 1)BW_{math}/BW_{transfer}, \tag{12}$$

and if $Intensity < k_{BW}$,

$$T_{kernel} = T_{mem}, \quad N_i > N\left((Num_{GPUs} - 1)BW_{mem}/BW_{transfer} - 2\right). \tag{13}$$

Interesting remarks can be made here from conditions (12) and (13). If for some reason we have $BW_{transfer} \gg BW_{math \ or \ mem}$, we will also have $T_{kernel} = T_{GEMM}$ since N_i should be a natural number; but, probably, some reversed situation can be exposed for small N_i and will have a comparably fast $BW_{transfer}$.

We also minimize the performance time in Eq. (8) by regulating N_i. With (6), (11), (12), (13), we determine for $Intensity > k_{BW}$

$$T_{task}(N_i) = (3N/BW_{transfer} + 2N^2/(Num_{GPUs}BW_{math}))N_i, \tag{14}$$

otherwise

$$T_{task}(N_i) = (3N/BW_{transfer} + 4N/(Num_{GPUs}BW_{mem}))N_i \\ + 8N^2/(Num_{GPUs}BW_{mem}). \tag{15}$$

Expressions (14) and (15) show that the performance will be better for lower N_i. However, we still have to satisfy three conditions (12), (13), and (4) at once.

6   Tile Size Tuning for Different Platforms

To come up with the required tile size using the materials presented in Sect. 5, we have to pay attention to arithmetical intensity (4) and conditions (12) or (13). Importantly, we see that if the algorithm is math limited ($Intensity > k_{BW}$), then N_i is independent from N. In the work frame, we observe only matrices with $N \geq 8192$, and both N and N_i being some natural number power of 2.

6.1 Expected tile Size for Experimental Environments

The first computing system is composed by Nvidia V100 GPUs connected by NVLink 2.0. The V100 GPU single precision parameters are presented in Table 1. To find N_i, we use the maximal expected $BW_{math\ or\ mem}$, but for the transfer one, the rate is found by the bandwidth test. We have from (4) at least $N_i > 66$ to have a mathematical limited condition and from (12) $N_i > 616$ for 2 GPUs and $N_i > 1849$ for 4 GPUs. Thus, the optimal sizes are $N_i = 1024$ for 2 GPUs and $N_i = 2048$ for 4 GPUs.

The second system is Nvidia GeForce GTX 1070 GPUs connected by PCIe 3.0 (see Table 1). From the intensity condition we get $N_i > 90$, from (12) $N_i > 1352$ for 2 GPUs and $N_i > 4058$ for 4 GPUs. Thus, the optimal sizes are $N_i = 2048$ for 2 GPUs and $N_i = 4096$ for 4 GPUs.

Table 1. Test platform parameters and best predicted tile sizes

Hardware Parameters	Nvidia V100	Nvidia GTX1070
BW_{math} (Gflops/sec)	14899	5783
BW_{mem} (Gb/sec)	900	256
test $BW_{transfer}$ (Gb/sec)	48.33	8.55
ideal $BW_{transfer}$ (Gb/sec)	50	16
Algorithm Parameters	Nvidia V100	Nvidia GTX1070
N_i for 2 GPUs	1024	2048
N_i for 4 GPUs	2048	4096

6.2 Experimental Results

In this section, we would like to present the performance time and tile size dependence. For each test platform, we observed 2 cases of data store, when all square matrices with N^2 elements are located in the memory of one GPU, or the matrices A, B, C are located in 3 GPUs, one in each. We increased the testing data by 2, thus, N and N_i have the value being some power of 2. In addition, the size ranges are $N \geq 8192$ and $N_i \geq 512$. The matrix size is chosen consciously large to avoid the influence of minor parameters such as $T_{instructions}$ (Eq. (1)), and the tile size to show the behavior when it goes over the appointed value in Table 1. If we do not meet extra conditions to the tile size, the largest one we can deal with is $N_i = N/Num_{GPUs}$ due to equal task division between the implemented GPUs.

Each server we tested has 4 GPUs, which we could use when launching the program. For each, we analyzed the cases with 2 or 4 GPUs. In addition, we wanted to present some testing profiles to describe how GPU performance relates to the tile size (N_i). While working with CUDA, we got profiles using nvprof and visualized them by the Nvidia Visual Profiler. In Fig. 2, we can see the involved processor in the column on the left side and the type of operation described, such as instructions given on the CPU, data transfer, or kernel (GEMM) execution.

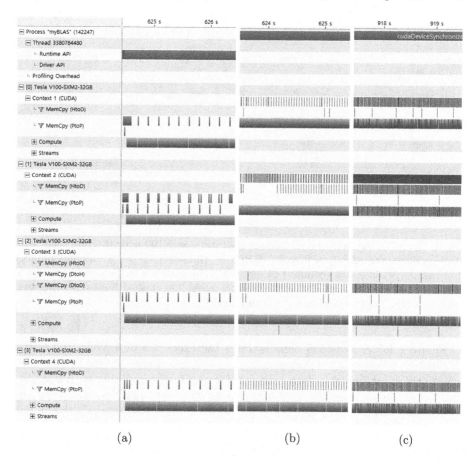

Fig. 2. Profile parts of the multi-GPU GEMM operation on V100 with the proposed algorithm performing on 4 GPUs. Number of elements ($N = 65536$) in a row (column) of matrices and different tile sizes ($N_i = 4096$ (a), $N_i = 2048$ (b), $N_i = 1024$ (c)). The matrices A, B, and C are stored in devices with id 0, 1, and 2.

Four V100 Connected by NVLink. The GPUs we worked with have 32 GB of in-device memory. For our experiments, the maximum matrices with $N = 32768$ fit in one device memory together and with $N = 65536$ separately. However, in the second case, we met the memory limit for allocating additional band matrices involved in the computing process, thus, the maximum tile size we could use was $N_i = 4096$. In Fig. 3, we can find the best performance with $N_i = 1024$ for 2 GPUs and $N_i = 2048$ for 4 GPUs. These numbers match with those defined in Sect. 6.1.

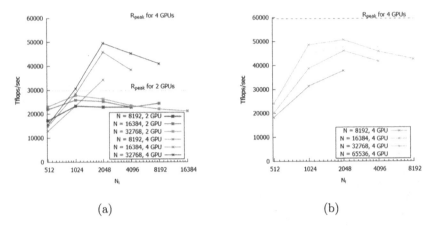

Fig. 3. Graph of the multi-GPU GEMM operation on V100 with the proposed algorithm performance speed on 2 and 4 GPUs by tile size (N_i) for a different number of elements (N) in a row (column) of matrices. The matrices A, B, and C are stored in device 0 (a) or in devices 0, 1, 2 (b), respectively. The dashed lines show the total single precision peak performance of 2 and 4 GPUs, respectively.

Figure 2 for $N = 65536$ demonstrates the execution of 4 Volta 100 GPUs for different tile sizes (N_i). When using the appointed size N_i (see Fig. 2b), we achieve the most frequent data transfer (for example, comparing with Fig. 2a), not taking longer than the kernel time (see Fig. 2c). This matches with the propositions given in Sect. 5. Therefore, the benchmark results verify the model.

Four GTX1070 Connected by PCIe 3.0. This testing platform has 8 GB of local memory in each GPU. We could perform benchmarks up to $N = 16384$ for a single device located case and $N = 32768$ and up to $N_i = 4096$ for a distributed storage case. The results are presented in Fig. 4.

The best performance with 2 GPUs is achieved with $N_i = 2048$ as proposed (Fig. 4a). For 4 GPUs, we have a lack of data due to the memory limit, however, the performance keeps growing to $N_i = 4096$, so we can expect it to be the best. Hence, the found tile size according to the arithmetical model matches for 2 GPUs, and, however, the tile size for 4 GPUs is shown to be the best only on one point due to the memory limit; the behavior of the graphs matches with the propositions given beforehand, that is why we can assume that the results fully comply with the mathematical algorithm.

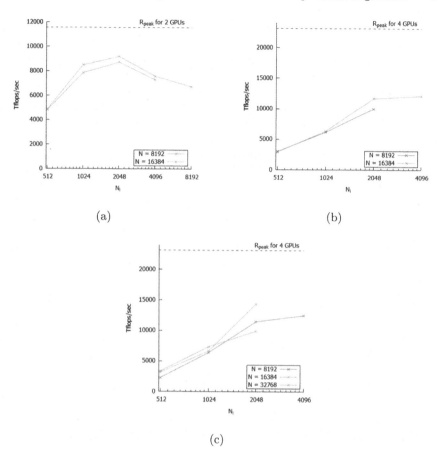

Fig. 4. Graph of the multi-GPU GEMM operation on GeForce GTX1070 with the proposed algorithm performance speed on 2 (a) and 4 GPUs (b,c) by tile size (N_i) for a different number of elements (N) in a row (column) of matrices. The matrices A, B, and C are stored in device 0 (a,b) or in devices 0, 1, 2 (c), respectively. The dashed lines show the total single precision peak performance of 2 and 4 GPUs, respectively.

7 Discussion

The performance of the proposed multi-GPU general matrix multiplication algorithm is dependent on the size of tile matrices. We determined tile size values for definite device and communication link properties, as well as the number of GPUs involved, to achieve the best performance in the tests. Then we performed experiments with large matrices to reach the performance limited by the computing ability of the GPU.

In the most general case, the computation of GEMM functions on a GPU can be limited by computational performance or memory bandwidth, depending on the matrix size. However, in our work, we observe only a computationally limited case. There are secondary, but still important conditions that affect the performance. The first is the initialization latency of kernels on the GPU called by the CPU, and the consumed time for it should be much less than the time of the actual workload. The second is the data transfer time, which should be less than the computing time to keep the continuous operation of multiple devices.

We propose a mathematical model to define the optimal tile size based on known hardware parameters. The model is based on some assumptions about the system. In particular, the system should include similar GPUs connected by links with the same and fairly stable throughput values. In practice, determining the real properties of communication networks may be a non-trivial task, in particular, the behavior of these links under a certain load may require additional tests and profiling.

The proposed algorithm with a high degree of probability will not be optimal for exotic and specific cases (see e.g. [34]). In this paper, more typical and common cases are considered. Further development of the algorithm may include increased flexibility and versatility to work effectively on a wide range of configurations.

8   Conclusion

An analytical model that takes into account the hardware parameters of the GPU server (data transfer bandwidth and GPU performance) and predicts the optimal tile size for the multi-GPU GEMM algorithm is developed. The benchmarks on two different GPU servers (one with V100 GPUs and NVlink and another with GTX1070 GPUs and PCIe links) confirm the applicability of the analytical model. The profiling of the algorithm execution on the GPU server with NVlink also verifies the model .

Acknowledgment. The article was prepared within the HSE University Basic Research Program. The research was partially supported by the resources of the supercomputer facilities provided by NRU HSE.

References

1. Abraham, M.J., et al.: GROMACS: high performance molecular simulations through multi-level parallelism from laptops to supercomputers. SoftwareX **1–2**, 19–25 (2015). https://doi.org/10.1016/j.softx.2015.06.001
2. Bastrakov, S., et al.: Particle-in-cell plasma simulation on heterogeneous cluster systems. J. Comput. Sci. **3**(6), 474–479 (2012). https://doi.org/10.1016/j.jocs.2012.08.012
3. Romero, J., Phillips, E., Ruetsch, G., Fatica, M., Spiga, F., Giannozzi, P.: A performance study of quantum ESPRESSO's PWscf code on multi-core and GPU systems. In: Jarvis, S., Wright, S., Hammond, S. (eds.) PMBS 2017. LNCS, vol. 10724, pp. 67–87. Springer, Cham (2018). https://doi.org/10.1007/978-3-319-72971-8_4

4. Spiga, F., Girotto, I.: phiGEMM: a CPU-GPU library for porting Quantum ESPRESSO on hybrid systems. In: 2012 20th Euromicro International Conference on Parallel, Distributed and Network-based Processing, pp. 368–375 (2012). https://doi.org/10.1109/PDP.2012.72

5. Akimova, E., Misilov, V., Kulikov, I., Chernykh, I.: Hydrodynamical simulation of astrophysical flows: high-performance GPU implementation. J. Phys. Conf. Ser. **1336**, 012014 (2019). https://doi.org/10.1088/1742-6596/1336/1/012014/meta

6. Kulikov, I.: GPUPEGAS: a new GPU-accelerated hydrodynamic code for numerical simulations of interacting galaxies. Astrophys. J. Suppl. Ser. **214**(1), 12 (2014). https://doi.org/10.1088/0067-0049/214/1/12

7. Nikolskiy, V.P., Stegailov, V.V.: GPU acceleration of four-site water models in LAMMPS. In: Advances in Parallel Computing, vol. 36: Parallel Computing: Technology Trends, Proceedings of PARCO-2019, pp. 565–573 (2019). https://doi.org/10.3233/APC200086

8. Stegailov, V., et al.: Angara interconnect makes GPU-based Desmos supercomputer an efficient tool for molecular dynamics calculations. Int. J. High Perform. Comput. Appl. **33**(3), 507–521 (2019). https://doi.org/10.1177/1094342019826667

9. Kondratyuk, N., Nikolskiy, V., Pavlov, D., Stegailov, V.: GPU-accelerated molecular dynamics: State-of-art software performance and porting from Nvidia CUDA to AMD HIP. Int. J. High Perform. Comput. Appl. **35**(4), 312–324 (2021). https://doi.org/10.1177/10943420211008288

10. Smirnov, G.S., Stegailov, V.V.: Efficiency of classical molecular dynamics algorithms on supercomputers. Math. Models Comput. Simul. **8**(6), 734–743 (2016). https://doi.org/10.1134/S2070048216060156

11. Morozov, I., Kazennov, A., Bystryi, R., Norman, G., Pisarev, V., Stegailov, V.: Molecular dynamics simulations of the relaxation processes in the condensed matter on GPUs. Comput. Phys. Commun. **182**(9), 1974–1978 (2011). https://doi.org/10.1016/j.cpc.2010.12.026

12. Anderson, J.A., Lorenz, C.D., Travesset, A.: General purpose molecular dynamics simulations fully implemented on graphics processing units. J. Comput. Phys. 227(10), 5342–5359 (2008). https://doi.org/10.1016/j.jcp.2008.01.047

13. Luehr, N., Ufimtsev, I.S., Martínez, T.J.: Dynamic precision for electron repulsion integral evaluation on graphical processing units (GPUs). J. Chem. Theory Comput. 7(4), 949–954 (2011). https://doi.org/10.1021/ct100701w

14. Rojek, K., Wyrzykowski, R., Kuczynski, L.: Systematic adaptation of stencil-based 3D MPDATA to GPU architectures. Concurr. Comput. **29**(9), e3970 (2017). https://doi.org/10.1002/cpe.3970

15. Dongarra, J., Pineau, J.F., Robert, Y., Vivien, F.: Matrix product on heterogeneous master-worker platforms. In: Proceedings of the 13th ACM SIGPLAN Symposium on Principles and Practice of Parallel Programming, pp. 53–62 (2008). https://doi.org/10.1145/1345206.1345217

16. DeFlumere, A., Lastovetsky, A.: Searching for the optimal data partitioning shape for parallel matrix matrix multiplication on 3 heterogeneous processors. In: 2014 IEEE International Parallel & Distributed Processing Symposium Workshops, pp. 17–28. IEEE (2014). https://doi.org/10.1109/IPDPSW.2014.8

17. Rohr, D., Lindenstruth, V.: A flexible and portable large-scale DGEMM library for Linpack on next-generation multi-GPU systems. In: 2015 23rd Euromicro International Conference on Parallel, Distributed, and Network-Based Processing, pp. 664–668. IEEE (2015). https://doi.org/10.1109/PDP.2015.89

18. Ryu, S., Kim, D.: Parallel huge matrix multiplication on a cluster with GPGPU accelerators. In: 2018 IEEE International Parallel and Distributed Processing Symposium Workshops (IPDPSW), pp. 877–882. IEEE (2018). https://doi.org/10.1109/IPDPSW.2018.00139

19. Van De Geijn, R.A., Watts, J.: SUMMA: scalable universal matrix multiplication algorithm. Concurr. Pract. Exp. **9**(4), 255–274 (1997). https://doi.org/10.1002/(SICI)1096-9128(199704)9:4⟨255::AID-CPE250⟩3.0.CO;2-2

20. Goto, K., Geijn, R.A.v.d.: Anatomy of high-performance matrix multiplication. ACM Trans. Math. Softw. **34**(3), 12–1 - 12–25 (2008). https://doi.org/10.1145/1356052.1356053

21. Kwasniewski, G., Kabić, M., Besta, M., VandeVondele, J., Solcà, R., Hoefler, T.: Red-blue pebbling revisited: near optimal parallel matrix-matrix multiplication. In: Proceedings of the International Conference for High Performance Computing, Networking, Storage and Analysis, SC 2019, pp. 24-1- -24-22. Association for Computing Machinery, New York, NY, USA (2019). https://doi.org/10.1145/3295500.3356181

22. Lai, P.W., Arafat, H., Elango, V., Sadayappan, P.: Accelerating Strassen-Winograd's matrix multiplication algorithm on GPUs. In: 20th Annual International Conference on High Performance Computing, pp. 139–148. IEEE (2013), https://doi.org/10.1109/HiPC.2013.6799109

23. Kwasniewski, G., Kabić, M., Besta, M., VandeVondele, J., Solcà, R., Hoefler, T.: Red-blue pebbling revisited: near optimal parallel matrix-matrix multiplication. In: Proceedings of the International Conference for High Performance Computing, Networking, Storage and Analysis, pp. 1–22 (2019). https://doi.org/10.1145/3295500.3356181

24. Tran, N.P., Lee, M., Choi, J.: Parameter based tuning model for optimizing performance on GPU. Cluster Comput. **20**(3), 2133–2142 (2017). https://doi.org/10.1007/s10586-017-1003-4

25. Zhang, L., Wahib, M., Zhang, H., Matsuoka, S.: A study of single and multi-device synchronization methods in Nvidia GPUs. In: 2020 IEEE International Parallel and Distributed Processing Symposium (IPDPS), pp. 483–493. IEEE (2020). https://doi.org/10.1109/IPDPS47924.2020.00057

26. Malik, T., Lastovetsky, A.: Towards optimal matrix partitioning for data parallel computing on a hybrid heterogeneous server. IEEE Access **9**, 17229–17244 (2021). https://doi.org/10.1109/ACCESS.2021.3052976

27. Herault, T., Robert, Y., Bosilca, G., Dongarra, J.: Generic matrix multiplication for multi-GPU accelerated distributed-memory platforms over parsec. In: 2019 IEEE/ACM 10th Workshop on Latest Advances in Scalable Algorithms for Large-Scale Systems (ScalA), pp. 33–41. IEEE (2019). https://doi.org/10.1109/ScalA49573.2019.00010

28. Choi, Y.R., Nikolskiy, V., Stegailov, V.: Matrix-matrix multiplication using multiple GPUs connected by Nvlink. In: 2020 Global Smart Industry Conference (GloSIC), pp. 354–361. IEEE (2020). https://doi.org/10.1109/GloSIC50886.2020.9267865

29. Kondratyuk, N., et al.: Performance and scalability of materials science and machine learning codes on the state-of-art hybrid supercomputer architecture. In: Voevodin, V., Sobolev, S. (eds.) Communications in Computer and Information Science. Supercomputing, pp. 597–609. Springer, Cham (2019), https://doi.org/10.1007/978-3-030-36592-9_49

30. Kostenetskiy, P.S., Chulkevich, R.A., Kozyrev, V.I.: HPC resources of the higher school of economics. J. Phys. Conf. Ser. **1740**, 012050 (2021). https://doi.org/10.1088/1742-6596/1740/1/012050

31. Kelefouras, V., Kritikakou, A., Mporas, I., Kolonias, V.: A high-performance matrix-matrix multiplication methodology for CPU and GPU architectures. J. Supercomput. **72**(3), 804–844 (2016). https://doi.org/10.1007/s11227-015-1613-7

32. Li, X., Liang, Y., Yan, S., Jia, L., Li, Y.: A coordinated tiling and batching framework for efficient GEMM on GPUs. In: Proceedings of the 24th Symposium on Principles and Practice of Parallel Programming, pp. 229–241 (2019). https://doi.org/10.1145/3293883.3295734

33. Boyer, M., Meng, J., Kumaran, K.: Improving GPU performance prediction with data transfer modeling. In: 2013 IEEE International Symposium on Parallel & Distributed Processing, Workshops and PhD Forum, pp. 1097–1106. IEEE (2013). https://doi.org/10.1109/IPDPSW.2013.236

34. Tang, H., Komatsu, K., Sato, M., Kobayashi, H.: Efficient mixed-precision tall-and-skinny matrix-matrix multiplication for GPUs. Int. J. Netw. Comput. **11**(2), 267–282 (2021). https://doi.org/10.15803/ijnc.11.2_267

Visualizing Multidimensional Linear Programming Problems

Nikolay A. Olkhovsky and Leonid B. Sokolinsky$^{(\boxtimes)}$ (ID)

South Ural State University (National Research University),
76, Lenin prospekt, Chelyabinsk 454080, Russia
{olkhovskiiNA,leonid.sokolinsky}@susu.ru

Abstract. The article proposes an n-dimensional mathematical model of the visual representation of a linear programming problem. This model makes it possible to use artificial neural networks to solve multidimensional linear optimization problems, the feasible region of which is a bounded non-empty set. To visualize a linear programming problem, an objective hyperplane is introduced, its orientation is determined by the gradient of the linear objective function: the gradient is the normal to the objective hyperplane. In the case of searching the maximum, the objective hyperplane is positioned in such a way that the value of the objective function at all its points exceeds the value of the objective function at all points of the feasible region, which is a bounded convex polytope. For an arbitrary point of the objective hyperplane, the objective projection onto the polytope is determined: the closer the objective projection point is to the objective hyperplane, the greater the value of the objective function at this point. Based on the objective hyperplane, a finite regular set of points, called the receptive field, is constructed. Using objective projections, an image of the polytope is constructed. This image includes the distances from the receptive points to the corresponding points of the polytope surface. Based on the proposed model, parallel algorithms for visualizing a linear programming problem are constructed. An analytical estimation of its scalability is performed. Information about the software implementation and the results of large-scale computational experiments confirming the efficiency of the proposed approaches are presented.

Keywords: Linear programming · Multydimensional visualization · Mathematical model · Parallel algorithm · BSF-skeleton

1 Introduction

The rapid development of Big Data technologies [11,12] has led to the emergence of mathematical optimization models in the form of large-scale linear programming (LP) problems [24]. Such problems arise in industry, economics, logistics, statistics, quantum physics, and other fields [3,4,8,22,25]. In many cases, the conventional software is not able to handle such large-scale LP problems in an

© The Author(s), under exclusive license to Springer Nature Switzerland AG 2022
L. Sokolinsky and M. Zymbler (Eds.): PCT 2022, CCIS 1618, pp. 172–196, 2022.
https://doi.org/10.1007/978-3-031-11623-0_13

acceptable time [2]. At the same time, in the nearest future, exascale supercomputers potentially capable of solving such problems will appear [6]. In accordance with this, the issue of developing new effective methods for solving large-scale LP problems using exascale supercomputing systems is urgent.

Until now, the class of algorithms proposed and developed by Dantzig on the basis of the simplex method [5] is one of the most common ways to solve LP problems. The simplex method is effective for solving a large class of LP problems. However, the simplex method has some fundamental features that limit its applicability to large LP problems. First, in the worst case, the simplex method traverses all the vertices of the simplex, which results in exponential time complexity [35]. Second, in most cases, the simplex method successfully solves LP problems containing up to 50,000 variables. However, a loss of precision is observed when the simplex method is used for solving large LP problems. Such a loss of precision cannot be compensated even by applying such computational intensive procedures as "affine scaling" or "iterative refinement" [34]. Third, the simplex method does not scale well on multiprocessor systems with distributed memory. Many attempts to parallelize the simplex method were made, but they all failed [19]. In [14], Karmarkar proposed the inner point method having polynomial time complexity in all cases. This method effectively solves problems with millions of variables and millions of constraints. Unlike the simplex method, the inner point method is self-correcting. Therefore, it is robust to the loss of precision in computations. The drawbacks of the interior point method are as follows. First, the interior point method requires the careful tuning of its parameters. Second, this method needs a known point that belongs to the feasible region of the LP problem to start calculations. Finding such an interior point can be reduced to solving an additional LP problem. An alternative is iterative projection-type methods [23, 26, 31], which are also self-correcting. Third, like the simplex method, the inner point method does not scale well on multiprocessor systems with distributed memory. Several attempts at effective parallelization for particular cases were made (see, for example, [10, 15]). However, it was not possible to make efficient parallelization for the general case. In accordance with this, research directions related to the development of new scalable methods for solving LP problems are urgent.

A possible efficient alternative to the conventional methods of LP is optimization methods based on neural network models. Artificial neural networks [20, 21] are one of the most promising and rapidly developing areas of modern information technology. Neural networks are a universal tool capable of solving problems in almost all areas. The most impressive success was achieved in image recognition and analysis using convolutional neural networks [18]. However, in scientific periodicals, there are almost no works devoted to the use of convolutional neural networks for solving linear optimization problems [17]. The reason is that convolutional neural networks focus on image processing, but there are no works on the visual representation of multidimensional linear programming problems in the scientific literature. Thus, the issue of developing new neural network models and methods focused on linear optimization remains open.

In this paper, we try to develop an n-dimensional mathematical model of the visual representation of the LP problem. This model allows one to employ

the technique of artificial neural networks to solve multidimensional linear optimization problems, the feasible region of which is a bounded non-empty set.
The visualization method based on the described model has high computational
complexity. For this reason, we propose its implementation as a parallel algorithm designed for cluster computing systems. The rest of the paper is organized
as follows. Section 2 is devoted to the design of the mathematical model of the
visual representation of multidimensional LP problems. Section 3 describes the
implementation of the proposed visualization method as a parallel algorithm and
provides an analytical estimation of its scalability. Section 4 presents information about the software implementation of the described parallel algorithm and
discusses the results of large-scale computational experiments on a cluster computing system. Section 5 summarizes the obtained results and provides directions
for further research.

2   Mathematical Model of the LP Visual Representation

The linear optimization problem can be stated as follows

$$\bar{x} = \arg\max\left\{ \langle c, x \rangle \mid Ax \leqslant b, x \in \mathbb{R}^n \right\}, \tag{1}$$

where $c, b \in \mathbb{R}^n$, $A \in \mathbb{R}^{m \times n}$, and $c \neq \mathbf{0}$. Here and below, $\langle \cdot, \cdot \rangle$ stands for the dot
product of vectors. We assume that the constraint $x \geqslant \mathbf{0}$ is also included in the
system $Ax \leqslant b$ in the form of the following inequalities:

$$
\begin{array}{rcccccccc}
-x_1 & + & 0 & + & \cdots\cdots\cdots & + & 0 & \leqslant & 0; \\
0 & - & x_2 & + & 0 & + & \cdots & + & 0 & \leqslant & 0; \\
\cdots & \cdots\cdots\cdots\cdots\cdots\cdots\cdots\cdots\cdots\cdots\cdots \\
0 & + & \cdots\cdots\cdots & + & 0 & - & x_n & \leqslant & 0.
\end{array}
$$

The vector c is the gradient of the linear objective function

$$f(x) = c_1 x_1 + \ldots + c_n x_n. \tag{2}$$

Let M denote the feasible region of problem (1):

$$M = \{ x \in \mathbb{R}^n \mid Ax \leqslant b \}. \tag{3}$$

We assume from now on that M is a non-empty bounded set. This means that
M is a convex closed polytope in the space $\mathbb{R}^n$, and the solution set of problem
(1) is not empty.

Let $\tilde{a}_i \in \mathbb{R}^n$ be a vector formed by the elements of the ith row of the matrix A.
Then, the matrix inequality $Ax \leqslant b$ is represented as a system of inequalities

$$\langle \tilde{a}_i, x \rangle \leqslant b_i, i = 1, \ldots, m. \tag{4}$$

We assume from now on that

$$\tilde{a}_i \neq \mathbf{0}. \tag{5}$$

for all $i = 1, \ldots, m$. Let us denote by H_i the hyperplane defined by the equation

$$\langle \tilde{a}_i, x \rangle = b_i \ (1 \leqslant i \leqslant m). \tag{6}$$

Thus,

$$H_i = \{x \in \mathbb{R}^n | \langle \tilde{a}_i, x \rangle = b_i\}. \tag{7}$$

Definition 1. *The half-space H_i^+ generated by the hyperplane H_i is the half-space defined by the equation*

$$H_i^+ = \{x \in \mathbb{R}^n | \langle \tilde{a}_i, x \rangle \leqslant b_i\}. \tag{8}$$

From now on, we assume that problem (1) is non-degenerate, i.e.,

$$\forall i \neq j : H_i \neq H_j \ (i, j \in \{1, \ldots, m\}). \tag{9}$$

Definition 2. *The half-space H_i^+ generated by the hyperplane H_i is recessive with respect to the vector c if*

$$\forall x \in H_i, \forall \lambda \in \mathbb{R}_{>0} : x - \lambda c \in H_i^+ \wedge x - \lambda c \notin H_i. \tag{10}$$

In other words, the ray coming from the hyperplane H_i in the direction opposite to the vector c lies completely in H_i^+, but not in H_i.

Proposition 1. *The necessary and sufficient condition for the recessivity of the half-space H_i^+ with respect to the vector c is the condition*

$$\langle \tilde{a}_i, c \rangle > 0. \tag{11}$$

Proof. Let us prove the necessity first. Let condition (10) hold. Equation (7) implies

$$x = \frac{b_i \tilde{a}_i}{\|\tilde{a}_i\|^2} \in H_i. \tag{12}$$

By virtue of (5),

$$\lambda = \frac{1}{\|\tilde{a}_i\|^2} \in \mathbb{R}_{>0}. \tag{13}$$

Comparing (10) with (12) and (13), we obtain

$$\frac{b_i \tilde{a}_i}{\|\tilde{a}_i\|^2} - \frac{1}{\|\tilde{a}_i\|^2} c \in H_i^+;$$
$$\frac{b_i \tilde{a}_i}{\|\tilde{a}_i\|^2} - \frac{1}{\|\tilde{a}_i\|^2} c \notin H_i.$$

In view of (7) and (8), this implies

$$\left\langle \tilde{a}_i, \frac{b_i \tilde{a}_i}{\|\tilde{a}_i\|^2} - \frac{1}{\|\tilde{a}_i\|^2} c \right\rangle < b_i. \tag{14}$$

Using simple algebraic transformations of inequality (14), we obtain (11). Thus, the necessity is proved.

Let us prove the sufficiency by contradiction. Assume that (11) holds, and there are $x \in H_i$ and $\lambda > 0$ such that

$$x - \lambda c \notin H_i^+ \vee x - \lambda c \in H_i.$$

In accordance with (7) and (8), this implies

$$\langle \tilde{a}_i, x - \lambda c \rangle \geqslant b_i$$

that is equivalent to

$$\langle \tilde{a}_i, x \rangle - \lambda \langle \tilde{a}_i, c \rangle \geqslant b_i.$$

Since $\lambda > 0$, it follows from (11) that

$$\langle \tilde{a}_i, x \rangle > b_i,$$

but this contradicts our assumption that $x \in H_i$. □

Definition 3. *Fix a point $z \in \mathbb{R}^n$ such that the half-space*

$$H_c^+ = \{x \in \mathbb{R}^n | \langle c, x - z \rangle \leqslant 0\} \tag{15}$$

includes the polytope M:

$$M \subset H_c^+.$$

In this case, we call the half-space H_c^+ the objective half-space, and the hyperplane H_c, defined by the equation

$$H_c = \{x \in \mathbb{R}^n | \langle c, x - z \rangle = 0\}, \tag{16}$$

the objective hyperplane.

Denote by $\pi_c(x)$ the *orthogonal projection* of the point x onto the objective hyperplane H_c:

$$\pi_c(x) = x - \frac{\langle c, x - z \rangle}{\|c\|^2} c. \tag{17}$$

Here, $\| \cdot \|$ stands for the Euclidean norm. Define the *distance* $\rho_c(x)$ from $x \in H_c^+$ to the objective hyperplane H_c as follows:

$$\rho_c(x) = \|\pi_c(x) - x\|. \tag{18}$$

Comparing (15), (17) and (18), we find that, in this case, the distance $\rho_c(x)$ can be calculated as follows:

$$\rho_c(x) = \frac{\langle c, z - x \rangle}{\|c\|}. \tag{19}$$

The following Proposition 2 holds.

Proposition 2. *For all* $x, y \in H_c^+$,

$$\rho_c(x) \leqslant \rho_c(y) \Leftrightarrow \langle c, x \rangle \geqslant \langle c, y \rangle.$$

Proof. Equation (19) implies that

$$\rho_c(x) \leqslant \rho_c(y) \Leftrightarrow \frac{\langle c, z - x \rangle}{\|c\|} \leqslant \frac{\langle c, z - y \rangle}{\|c\|}$$
$$\Leftrightarrow \langle c, z - x \rangle \leqslant \langle c, z - y \rangle$$
$$\Leftrightarrow \langle c, z \rangle + \langle c, -x \rangle \leqslant \langle c, z \rangle + \langle c, -y \rangle$$
$$\Leftrightarrow \langle c, -x \rangle \leqslant \langle c, -y \rangle$$
$$\Leftrightarrow \langle c, x \rangle \geqslant \langle c, y \rangle.$$

$\square$

Proposition 2 says that problem (1) is equivalent to the following problem:

$$\bar{x} = \arg\min \left\{ \rho_c(x) \mid x \in M \right\}. \tag{20}$$

Definition 4. *Let the half-space* H_i^+ *be recessive with respect to the vector* c. *The objective projection* $\gamma_i(x)$ *of the point* $x \in \mathbb{R}^n$ *onto the recessive half-space* H_i^+ *is a point defined by the equation*

$$\gamma_i(x) = x - \sigma_i(x)c, \tag{21}$$

where

$$\sigma_i(x) = \min \left\{ \sigma \in \mathbb{R}_{\geqslant 0} \mid x - \sigma c \in H_i^+ \right\}.$$

Examples of objective projections in $\mathbb{R}^2$ are shown in Fig. 1.

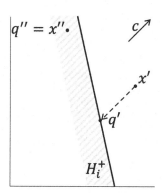

Fig. 1. Objective projections in the space $\mathbb{R}^2$: $\gamma_i(x') = q'$; $\gamma_i(x'') = q'' = x''$.

The following Proposition 3 provides an equation for calculating the objective projection onto a half-space that is recessive with respect to the vector c.

Proposition 3. *Let the half-space* H_i^+ *defined by the inequality*

$$\langle \tilde{a}_i, x \rangle \leqslant b_i \tag{22}$$

be recessive with respect to the vector c. Let

$$g \notin H_i^+. \tag{23}$$

Then,

$$\gamma_i(g) = g - \frac{\langle \tilde{a}_i, g \rangle - b_i}{\langle \tilde{a}_i, c \rangle} c. \tag{24}$$

Proof. According to Definition 4, we have

$$\gamma_i(g) = g - \sigma_i(g)c,$$

where

$$\sigma_i(x) = \min \left\{ \sigma \in \mathbb{R}_{\geqslant 0} \mid x - \sigma c \in H_i^+ \right\}.$$

Thus, we need to prove that

$$\frac{\langle \tilde{a}_i, g \rangle - b_i}{\langle \tilde{a}_i, c \rangle} = \min \left\{ \sigma \in \mathbb{R}_{\geqslant 0} \mid x - \sigma c \in H_i^+ \right\}. \tag{25}$$

Consider the strait line L defined by the parametric equation

$$L = \{ g + \tau c \mid \tau \in \mathbb{R} \}.$$

Let the point q be the intersection of the line L with the hyperplane H_i:

$$q = L \cap H_i. \tag{26}$$

Then, q must satisfy the equation

$$q = g + \tau' c \tag{27}$$

for some $\tau' \in \mathbb{R}$. Substitute the right side of Eq. (27) into Eq. (6) instead of x:

$$\langle \tilde{a}_i, g + \tau' c \rangle = b_i.$$

It follows that

$$\langle \tilde{a}_i, g \rangle + \tau' \langle \tilde{a}_i, c \rangle = b_i,$$
$$\tau' = \frac{b_i - \langle \tilde{a}_i, g \rangle}{\langle \tilde{a}_i, c \rangle}. \tag{28}$$

Substituting the right side of Eq. (28) into Eq. (27) instead of τ', we obtain

$$q = g + \frac{b_i - \langle \tilde{a}_i, g \rangle}{\langle \tilde{a}_i, c \rangle} c,$$

which is equivalent to

$$q = g - \frac{\langle \tilde{a}_i, g \rangle - b_i}{\langle \tilde{a}_i, c \rangle} c. \tag{29}$$

Since, according to (26), $q \in H_i$, Eq. (25) will hold if

$$\forall \sigma \in \mathbb{R}_{>0} : \sigma < \frac{\langle \tilde{a}_i, g \rangle - b_i}{\langle \tilde{a}_i, c \rangle} \Rightarrow g - \sigma c \notin H_i^+ \tag{30}$$

holds. Assume the opposite, i.e., there exist $\sigma' > 0$ such that

$$\sigma' < \frac{\langle \tilde{a}_i, g \rangle - b_i}{\langle \tilde{a}_i, c \rangle} \tag{31}$$

and

$$g - \sigma' c \in H_i^+. \tag{32}$$

Then, it follows from (22) and (32) that

$$\langle \tilde{a}_i, g - \sigma' c \rangle \leqslant b_i.$$

This is equivalent to

$$\langle \tilde{a}_i, g \rangle - b_i \leqslant \sigma' \langle \tilde{a}_i, c \rangle. \tag{33}$$

Proposition 1 implies that $\langle \tilde{a}_i, c \rangle > 0$. Hence, Eq. (33) is equivalent to

$$\sigma' \geqslant \frac{\langle \tilde{a}_i, g \rangle - b_i}{\langle \tilde{a}_i, c \rangle}.$$

Thus, we have a contradiction with (31). □

Definition 5. *Let $g \in H_c$. The objective projection $\gamma_M(g)$ of the point g onto the polytope M is a point defined by the following equation:*

$$\gamma_M(g) = g - \sigma_M(g)c, \tag{34}$$

where

$$\sigma_M(g) = \min \{\sigma \in \mathbb{R}_{\geqslant 0} | g - \sigma c \in M\}.$$

If

$$\neg \exists \, \sigma \in \mathbb{R}_{\geqslant 0} : g - \sigma c \in M,$$

then we set $\gamma_M(g) = \tilde{\infty}$, where $\tilde{\infty}$ stands for a point that is infinitely far from the polytope M.

Examples of objective projections onto the polytope M in $\mathbb{R}^2$ are shown in Fig. 2.

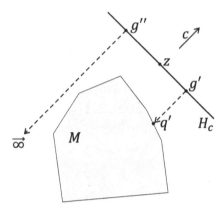

Fig. 2. Objective projections onto the polytope M in $\mathbb{R}^2$: $\gamma_M(g') = q'$; $\gamma_M(g'') = \vec{\infty}$.

Definition 6. *The receptive field $\mathfrak{G}(z, \eta, \delta) \subset H_c$ of the density $\delta \in \mathbb{R}_{>0}$ with the center $z \in H_c$ and the rank $\eta \in \mathbb{N}$ is a finite ordered set of points satisfying the following conditions:*

$$z \in \mathfrak{G}(z, \eta, \delta); \tag{35}$$

$$\forall g \in \mathfrak{G}(z, \eta, \delta) : \|g - z\| \leqslant \eta \delta \sqrt{n}; \tag{36}$$

$$\forall g', g'' \in \mathfrak{G}(z, \eta, \delta) : g' \neq g'' \Rightarrow \|g' - g''\| \geqslant \delta; \tag{37}$$

$$\forall g' \in \mathfrak{G}(z, \eta, \delta) \,\exists g'' \in \mathfrak{G}(z, \eta, \delta) : \|g' - g''\| = \delta; \tag{38}$$

$$\forall x \in \mathrm{Co}(\mathfrak{G}(z, \eta, \delta)) \,\exists g \in \mathfrak{G}(z, \eta, \delta) : \|g - x\| \leqslant \tfrac{1}{2}\delta\sqrt{n}. \tag{39}$$

The points of the receptive field will be called receptive points.

Here, $\mathrm{Co}(X)$ stands for the convex hull of a finite point set $X = \{x^{(1)}, \ldots, x^{(K)}\} \subset \mathbb{R}^n$:

$$Co(X) = \left\{ \sum_{i=1}^{K} \lambda_i x^{(i)} \,\middle|\, \lambda_i \in \mathbb{R}_{\geqslant 0}, \sum_{i=1}^{K} \lambda_i = 1 \right\}.$$

In Definition 6, condition (35) means that the center of the receptive field belongs to this field. Condition (36) implies that the distance from the central point z to each point g of the receptive field does not exceed $\eta\delta\sqrt{n}$. According to (37), for any two different points $g' \neq g''$ of the receptive field, the distance between them cannot be less than δ. Condition (38) says that for any point g' of the receptive field, there is a point g'' in this field such that the distance between g' and g'' is equal to δ. Condition (39) implies that for any point x belonging to the convex hull of the receptive field, there is a point g in this field such that the distance between x and g does not exceed $\tfrac{1}{2}\delta\sqrt{n}$. An example of the receptive field in the space $\mathbb{R}^3$ is presented in Fig. 3.

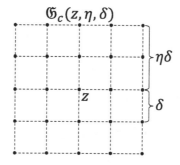

Fig. 3. Receptive field in the space $\mathbb{R}^3$.

Let us describe a constructive method for building a receptive field. Without loss of generality, we assume that $c_n \neq 0$. Consider the following set of vectors:

$$c^{(0)} = c = (c_1, c_2, c_3, c_4, \ldots, c_{n-1}, c_n);$$

$$c^{(1)} = \begin{cases} \left(-\frac{1}{c_1}\sum_{i=2}^{n} c_i^2, c_2, c_3, c_4, \ldots, c_{n-1}, c_n\right), & \text{if } c_1 \neq 0; \\ (1, 0, \ldots, 0), & \text{if } c_1 = 0; \end{cases}$$

$$c^{(2)} = \begin{cases} \left(0, -\frac{1}{c_2}\sum_{i=3}^{n} c_i^2, c_3, c_4, \ldots, c_{n-1}, c_n\right), & \text{if } c_2 \neq 0; \\ (0, 1, 0, \ldots, 0), & \text{if } c_2 = 0; \end{cases}$$

$$c^{(3)} = \begin{cases} \left(0, 0, -\frac{1}{c_3}\sum_{i=4}^{n} c_i^2, c_4, \ldots, c_{n-1}, c_n\right), & \text{if } c_3 \neq 0; \\ (0, 0, 1, 0, \ldots, 0), & \text{if } c_3 = 0; \end{cases}$$

$$\cdots\cdots\cdots\cdots\cdots\cdots\cdots\cdots\cdots\cdots\cdots\cdots\cdots\cdots\cdots\cdots$$

$$c^{(n-2)} = \begin{cases} \left(0, \ldots, 0, -\frac{1}{c_{n-2}}\sum_{i=n-1}^{n} c_i^2, c_{n-1}, c_n\right), & \text{if } c_{n-2} \neq 0; \\ (0, \ldots, 0, 1, 0, 0), & \text{if } c_{n-2} = 0; \end{cases}$$

$$c^{(n-1)} = \begin{cases} \left(0, \ldots, 0, -\frac{c_n^2}{c_{n-1}}, c_n\right), & \text{if } c_{n-1} \neq 0; \\ (0, \ldots, 0, 0, 1, 0), & \text{if } c_{n-1} = 0. \end{cases}$$

It is easy to see that

$$\forall i, j \in \{0, 1, \ldots, n-1\}, i \neq j : \left\langle c^{(i)}, c^{(j)} \right\rangle = 0.$$

This means that $c_0, \ldots, c_{n-1}$ is an orthogonal basis in $\mathbb{R}^n$. In particular,

$$\forall i = 1, \ldots, n-1 : \left\langle c, c^{(i)} \right\rangle = 0. \tag{40}$$

The following Proposition 4 shows that the linear subspace of the dimension $(n-1)$ generated by the orthogonal vectors $c_1, \ldots, c_{n-1}$ is a hyperplane parallel to the hyperplane H_c.

Proposition 4. *Define the following linear subspace S_c of the dimension $(n-1)$ in $\mathbb{R}^n$:*

$$S_c = \left\{ \sum_{i=1}^{n-1} \lambda_i c^{(i)} \,\middle|\, \lambda_i \in \mathbb{R} \right\}. \tag{41}$$

Then,

$$\forall s \in S_c : s + z \in H_c. \tag{42}$$

Proof. Let $s \in S_c$, i.e.,

$$s = \lambda_1 c^{(1)} + \ldots + \lambda_{n-1} c^{(n-1)}.$$

Then,

$$\langle c, (s+z) - z \rangle = \lambda_1 \left\langle c, c^{(1)} \right\rangle + \ldots + \lambda_{n-1} \left\langle c, c^{(n-1)} \right\rangle.$$

In view of (40), this implies

$$\langle c, (s+z) - z \rangle = 0.$$

Comparing this with (16), we obtain $s + z \in H_c$.   □

Define the following set of vectors:

$$e^{(i)} = \frac{c^{(i)}}{\|c^{(i)}\|} \quad (i = 1, \ldots, n-1). \tag{43}$$

It is easy to see that the set $\{e_1, \ldots, e_{n-1}\}$ is an orthonormal basis of the subspace S_c.

The procedure for constructing a receptive field is presented as Algorithm 1. This algorithm constructs a receptive field $\mathfrak{G}(z, \eta, \delta)$ consisting of

$$K_{\mathfrak{G}} = (2\eta + 1)^{n-1} \tag{44}$$

points. These points are arranged at the nodes of a regular lattice having the form of a hypersquare (a hypercube of the dimension $n-1$) with the edge length equal to $2\eta\delta$. The edge length of the unit cell is δ. According to Step 13 of Algorithm 1 and Proposition 4, this hypersquare lies in the hyperplane H_c and has the center at the point z. The drawback of Algorithm 1 is that the number of nested **for** loops depends on the dimension of the space. This issue can be solved using the function G, which calculates a point of the receptive field by its ordinal number (numbering starts from zero; the order is determined by Algorithm 1). The implementation of the function G is represented as Algorithm 2. The following Proposition 5 provides an estimation of the time complexity of Algorithm 2.

Proposition 5. *Algorithm 2 enables an implementation that has time complexity*[1]

$$c_G = 4n^2 + 5n - 9, \tag{45}$$

where n is the space dimension.

---

[1] Here, time complexity refers to the number of arithmetic and comparison operations required to execute the algorithm.

Algorithm 1. Building a receptive field $\mathfrak{G}(z, \eta, \delta)$

Require: $z \in H_c$, $\eta \in \mathbb{N}$, $\delta \in \mathbb{R}_{>0}$
1: $\mathfrak{G} := \emptyset$
2: **for** $i_{n-1} = 0 \ldots 2\eta$ **do**
3: $\quad s_{n-1} := i_{n-1}\delta - \eta\delta$
4: $\quad$ **for** $i_{n-2} = 0 \ldots 2\eta$ **do**
5: $\quad\quad s_{n-2} := i_{n-2}\delta - \eta\delta$
6: $\quad\quad \ldots$
7: $\quad\quad$ **for** $i_1 = 0 \ldots 2\eta$ **do**
8: $\quad\quad\quad s_1 := i_1\delta - \eta\delta$
9: $\quad\quad\quad s := \mathbf{0}$
10: $\quad\quad\quad$ **for** $j = 1 \ldots n - 1$ **do**
11: $\quad\quad\quad\quad s := s + s_j e^{(j)}$
12: $\quad\quad\quad$ **end for**
13: $\quad\quad\quad \mathfrak{G} := \mathfrak{G} \cup \{s + z\}$
14: $\quad\quad$ **end for**
15: $\quad$ **end for**
16: **end for**

Proof. Consider Algorithm 3 representing a low-level implementation of Algorithm 2. The values calculated in Steps 1–2 of Algorithm 3 do not depend on the receptive point number k and therefore can be considered constants. In Steps 3–8, the **repeat/until** loop runs $(n-1)$ times and requires $c_{3:8} = 5(n-1)$ operations. In steps 13–16, the nested **repeat/until** loop runs n times and requires $c_{13:16} = 4n$ operations. In steps 10–18, the external **repeat/until** loop runs $(n-1)$ times and requires $c_{10:18} = (4 + c_{13-16})(n-1) = 4(n^2 - 1)$ operations. In total, we obtain

$$c_G = c_{3:8} + c_{10:18} = 4n^2 + 5n - 9.$$

□

Corollary 1. *The time complexity of Algorithm 2 can be estimated as $O(n^2)$.*

Definition 7. *Let $z \in H_c$. Fix $\eta \in \mathbb{N}$, $\delta \in \mathbb{R}_{>0}$. The image $\mathfrak{I}(z, \eta, \delta)$ generated by the receptive field $\mathfrak{G}(z, \eta, \delta)$ is an ordered set of real numbers defined by the equation*

$$\mathfrak{I}(z, \eta, \delta) = \{\rho_c(\gamma_M(g))| \, g \in \mathfrak{G}(z, \eta, \delta)\}. \tag{46}$$

The order of the real numbers in the image is determined by the order of the respective receptive points.

Algorithm 2. The function G calculates a receptive point by its number k

---

Require: $z \in H_c$, $\eta \in \mathbb{N}$, $\delta \in \mathbb{R}_{>0}$
1: **function** $G(k, n, z, \eta, \delta)$
2:     **for** $j = (n-1) \ldots 1$ **do**
3:         $i_j := \lfloor k/(2\eta+1)^{j-1} \rfloor$
4:         $k := k \mod (2\eta+1)^{j-1}$
5:     **end for**
6:     $g := z$
7:     **for** $j = 1 \ldots (n-1)$ **do**
8:         $g := g + (i_j\delta - \eta\delta)e^{(j)}$
9:     **end for**
10:     $G := g$
11: **end function**

The following Algorithm 4 implements the function $\mathfrak{I}(z, \eta, \delta)$ building an image as a list of real numbers.

Algorithm 3. Low-level implementation of Algorithm 2

1: $p := 2\eta + 1$; $r := \eta\delta$; $h := p^{n-2}$; $g := z$
2: $j := n - 1$
3: **repeat**
4:     $l_j := \lfloor k/h \rfloor$
5:     $k := k \mod h$
6:     $h := h/p$
7:     $j := j - 1$
8: **until** $j = 0$
9: $j := 1$
10: **repeat**
11:     $w_j := l_j\delta - r$
12:     $i := 1$
13:     **repeat**
14:         $g_i := g_i + w_j e_i^{(j)}$
15:         $i := i + 1$
16:     **until** $i > n$
17:     $j := j + 1$
18: **until** $j = n$

Here, $[]$ stands for the empty list, and $+\!\!+$ stands for the operation of list concatenation.

Let $\langle \tilde{a}_i, c \rangle > 0$. This means that the half-space H_i^+ is recessive with respect to the vector c (see Proposition 1). Let there be a point $u \in H_i \cap M$. Assume that we managed to create an artificial neural network DNN, which receives the image $\Im(\pi_c(u), \eta, \delta)$ as an input and outputs the point u' such that

$$u' = \arg\min \{\rho_c(x)|\, x \in H_i \cap M\}.$$

Then, we can build the following Algorithm 5 solving linear programming problem (20) using the DNN.

Algorithm 4. Building an image $\Im(z, \eta, \delta)$

Require: $z \in H_c$, $\eta \in \mathbb{N}$, $\delta \in \mathbb{R}_{>0}$
1: **function** $\Im(z, \eta, \delta)$
2:     $\Im := [\,]$
3:     **for** $k = 0 \ldots ((2\eta + 1)^{n-1} - 1)$ **do**
4:         $g_k := G(k, n, z, \eta, \delta)$
5:         $\Im := \Im + [\rho_c(\gamma_M(g_k))]$
6:     **end for**
7: **end function**

Algorithm 5. Linear programming using a DNN

Require: $u^{(1)} \in H_i \cap M$, $\langle \tilde{a}_i, c \rangle > 0$, $z \in H_c$; $\eta \in \mathbb{N}$, $\delta \in \mathbb{R}_{>0}$
1: $k := 1$
2: **repeat**
3:     $\mathcal{I} := \Im(u^{(k)}, \eta, \delta)$
4:     $u^{(k+1)} := \text{DNN}(\mathcal{I})$
5:     $k := k + 1$
6: **until** $u^{(k)} \neq u^{(k-1)}$
7: $\bar{x} := u^{(k)}$
8: **stop**

Only an outline of the forthcoming algorithm is presented here, it needs further formalization, detalization and refinement.

3 Parallel Algorithm for Building an LP Problem Image

When solving LP problems of large dimension with a large number of constraints, Algorithm 4 of building an LP problem image can incur significant runtime overhead. This section presents a parallel version of Algorithm 4, which significantly reduces the runtime overhead of building the image of a large-scale LP problem. The parallel implementation of Algorithm 4 is based on the BSF parallel computation model [27,28]. The BSF model is intended for a cluster computing system, uses the master/worker paradigm and requires the representation of the algorithm in the form of operations on lists using higher-order functions *Map* and *Reduce* defined in the Bird–Meertens formalism [1]. The BSF model also provides a cost metric for the analytical evaluation of the scalability of a parallel algorithm that meets the specified requirements. Examples of the BSF model application can be found in [7,30–33].

Let us represent Algorithm 4 in the form of operations on lists using higher-order functions *Map* and *Reduce*. We use the list of ordinal numbers of inequalities of system (4) as a list, which is the second parameter of the higher-order function *Map*:

$$\mathcal{L}_{map} = [1,\ldots,m]. \tag{47}$$

Designate $\mathbb{R}_\infty = \mathbb{R} \cup \{\infty\}$. We define a parameterized function

$$F_k : \{1,\ldots,m\} \to \mathbb{R}_\infty,$$

which is the first parameter of the higher-order function *Map*, as follows:

$$F_k(i) = \begin{cases} \rho_c\left(\gamma_i(g_k)\right), & \text{if } \langle \tilde{a}_i, c\rangle > 0 \text{ and } \gamma_i(g_k) \in M; \\ \infty, & \text{if } \langle \tilde{a}_i, c\rangle \leqslant 0 \text{ or } \gamma_i(g_k) \notin M. \end{cases} \tag{48}$$

where $g_k = G(k,n,z,\eta,\delta)$ (see Algorithm 2), and $\gamma_i(g_k)$ is calculated by Eq. (24). Informally, the function F_k maps the ordinal number of the half-space H_i^+ to the distance from the objective projection to the objective hyperplane if H_i^+ is recessive with respect to c (see Proposition 1), and the objective projection belongs to M. Otherwise, F_k returns the special value ∞.

The higher-order function *Map* transforms the list $\mathcal{L}_{map}$ into the list $\mathcal{L}_{reduce}$ by applying the function F_k to each element of the list $\mathcal{L}_{map}$:

$$\mathcal{L}_{reduce} = \text{Map}\left(F_k, \mathcal{L}_{map}\right) = [F_k(1),\ldots,F_k(m)] = [\rho_1,\ldots,\rho_m].$$

Define the associative binary operation $\bigcirc : \mathbb{R}_\infty \to \mathbb{R}_\infty$ as follows:

$$\infty \bigcirc \infty = \infty;$$
$$\forall \alpha \in \mathbb{R} : \alpha \bigcirc \infty = \alpha;$$
$$\forall \alpha,\beta \in \mathbb{R} : \alpha \bigcirc \beta = \min(\alpha,\beta).$$

Informally, the operation $\bigcirc$ calculates the minimum of two numbers.

The higher-order function *Reduce* folds the list $\mathcal{L}_{reduce}$ to the single value $\rho \in \mathbb{R}_\infty$ by sequentially applying the operation $\bigcirc$ to the entire list:

$$\text{Reduce}(\bigcirc, \mathcal{L}_{reduce}) = \rho_1 \bigcirc \rho_2 \bigcirc \ldots \bigcirc \rho_m = \rho.$$

Algorithm 6. Building an image $\mathfrak{I}$ by *Map* and *Reduce*

Require: $z \in H_c$, $\eta \in \mathbb{N}$, $\delta \in \mathbb{R}_{>0}$
1: **input** $n, m, A, b, c, z, \eta, \delta$
2: $\mathfrak{I} := [\ ]$
3: $\mathcal{L}_{map} := [1, \ldots, m]$
4: **for** $k = 0 \ldots ((2\eta + 1)^{n-1} - 1)$ **do**
5:    $\mathcal{L}_{reduce} := \text{Map}(\text{F}_k, \mathcal{L}_{map})$
6:    $\rho := \text{Reduce}(\textcircled{1}, \mathcal{L}_{reduce})$
7:    $\mathfrak{I} := \mathfrak{I} + [\rho]$
8: **end for**
9: **output** $\mathfrak{I}$
10: **stop**

Algorithm 6 builds the image $\mathfrak{I}$ of the LP problem using higher-order functions *Map* and *Reduce*. The parallel version of Algorithm 6 is based on algorithmic template 2 in [28]. The result is presented as Algorithm 7.

Algorithm 7. Parallel algorithm of building the image $\mathfrak{I}$

Master	lth Worker (l=0,...,L-1)
1: **input** n	1: **input** $n, m, A, b, c, z, \eta, \delta$
2: $\mathfrak{I} := [\ ]$	2: $L := \text{NumberOfWorkers}$
3: $k := 0$	3: $\mathcal{L}_{map(l)} := [lm/L, \ldots, ((l+1)m/L) - 1]$
4: **repeat**	4: **repeat**
5: **SendToWorkers** k	5: **RecvFromMaster** k
6:	6: $\mathcal{L}_{reduce(l)} := \text{Map}\left(\text{F}_k, \mathcal{L}_{map(l)}\right)$
7:	7: $\rho_l := \text{Reduce}\left(\textcircled{1}, \mathcal{L}_{reduce(l)}\right)$
8: **RecvFromWorkers** $[\rho_0, \ldots, \rho_{L-1}]$	8: **SendToMaster** ρ_l
9: $\rho := \text{Reduce}\left(\textcircled{1}, [\rho_0, \ldots, \rho_{L-1}]\right)$	9:
10: $\mathfrak{I} := \mathfrak{I} + [\rho]$	10:
11: $k := k + 1$	11:
12: $exit := \left(k \geqslant (2\eta + 1)^{n-1}\right)$	12:
13: **SendToWorkers** $exit$	13: **RecvFromMaster** $exit$
14: **until** $exit$	14: **until** $exit$
15: **output** $\mathfrak{I}$	15:
16: **stop**	16: **stop**

Let us explain the steps of Algorithm 7. For simplicity, we assume that the number of constraints m is a multiple of the number of workers L. We also assume that the numbering of inequalities starts from zero. The parallel algorithm includes $L + 1$ processes: one master process and L worker processes.

The master manages the computations. In Step 1, the master reads the space dimension n. In Step 2 of the master, the image variable $\Im$ is initialized to the empty list. Step 3 of the master assigns zero to the iteration counter k. At Steps 4–14, the master organizes the **repeat/until** loop, in which the image $\Im$ of the LP problem is built. In Step 5, the master sends the receptive point number g_k to all workers. In Step 8, the master expects particular results from all workers. These particular results are folded to a single value, which is added to the image $\Im$ (Steps 9–10 of the master). Step 11 of the master increases the iteration counter k by 1. Step 12 of the master assigns the logical value $\left(k \geqslant (2\eta + 1)^{n-1}\right)$ to the Boolean variable *exit*. In Step 13, the master sends the value of the Boolean variable *exit* to all workers. According to (44), *exit* = *false* means that not all the points of the receptive field are processed. In this case, the control is passed to the next iteration of the external **repeat/until** loop (Step 14 of the master). After exiting the **repeat/until** loop, the master outputs the constructed image $\Im$ (Step 15) and terminates its work (Step 16).

All workers execute the same program codes, but with different data. In Step 3, the lth worker defines its own sublist. In Step 4, the worker enters the **repeat/until** loop. In Step 5, it receives the number k of the next receptive point. In Step 6, the worker processes its sublist $\mathcal{L}_{map(l)}$ using the higher-order function *Map*, which applies the parameterized function F_k, defined by (48), to each element of the sublist. The result is the sublist $\mathcal{L}_{reduce(l)}$, which includes the distances $F_k(i)$ from the objective hyperplane H_c to the objective projections of the receptive point g_k onto the hyperplanes H_i for all i from the sublist $\mathcal{L}_{map(l)}$. In Step 7, the worker uses the higher-order function *Reduce* to fold the sublist $\mathcal{L}_{reduce(l)}$ to the single value of ρ_l, using the associative binary operation $\oslash$, which calculates the minimum distance. The computed particular result is sent to the master (Step 8 of the worker). In Step 13, the worker waits for the master to send the value of the Boolean variable *exit*. If the received value is false, the worker continues executing the **repeat/until** loop (Step 14 of the worker). Otherwise, the worker process is terminated in Step 16.

Let us obtain an analytical estimation of the *scalability bound* of parallel Algorithm 7 using the cost metric of the BSF parallel computation model [28]. Here, the scalability bound means the number of workers at which the maximum speedup is achieved. The cost metric of the BSF model includes the following cost parameters for the **repeat/until** loop (Steps 4–14) of parallel Algorithm 7:

m : length of the list $\mathcal{L}_{map}$;

D : latency (time taken by the master to send one byte message to a single worker);

t_c : time taken by the master to send the coordinates of the receptive point to a single worker and receive the computed value from it (including latency);

t_{Map} : time taken by a single worker to process the higher-order function *Map* for the entire list $\mathcal{L}_{map}$;

t_a : time taken by computing the binary operation $\oslash$.

According to Eq. (14) from [28], the scalability bound of Algorithm 7 can be estimated as follows:

$$L_{max} = \frac{1}{2} \sqrt{\left(\frac{t_c}{t_a \ln 2}\right)^2 + \frac{t_{Map}}{t_a} + 4m} - \frac{t_c}{t_a \ln 2}. \tag{49}$$

Calculate estimations for the time parameters of Eq. (49). To do this, we introduce the following notation for a single iteration of the **repeat/until** loop (Steps 4–14) of Algorithm 7:

c_c : quantity of numbers sent from the master to the worker and back within one iteration;

c_{Map} : quantity of arithmetic and comparison operations computed in Step 5 of serial algorithm 6;

c_a : quantity of arithmetic and comparison operations required to compute the binary operation $\textcircled{\downarrow}$.

At the beginning of every iteration, the master sends each worker the receptive point number k. In response, the worker sends the distance from the receptive point g_k to its objective projection. Therefore,

$$c_c = 2. \tag{50}$$

In the context of Algorithm 6

$$c_{Map} = (c_G + c_{F_k}) m, \tag{51}$$

where c_G is the number of operations taken to compute the coordinates of the point g_k, and c_{F_k} is the number of operations required to calculate the value of $F_k(i)$, assuming that the coordinates of the point g_k have already been calculated. The estimation of c_G is provided by Proposition 5. Let us estimate c_{F_k}. According to (24), calculating the objective projection $\gamma_i(g)$ takes $(6n-2)$ arithmetic operations. It follows from (19) that the calculation of $\rho_c(x)$ takes $(5n-1)$ arithmetic operations. Inequalities (4) imply that checking the condition $x \in M$ takes $m(2n-1)$ arithmetic operations and m comparison operations. Hence, $F_k(i)$ takes a total of $(2mn + 11n - 3)$ operations. Thus,

$$c_{F_k} = 2mn + 11n - 3. \tag{52}$$

Substituting the right-hand sides of Eqs. (45) and (52) in (51), we obtain

$$c_{Map} = 4n^2 m + 2m^2 n + 16nm - 12m. \tag{53}$$

To perform the binary operation $\textcircled{\downarrow}$, one comparison operation must be executed:

$$c_a = 1. \tag{54}$$

Let τ_{op} stand for the average execution time of arithmetic and comparison operations, and let τ_{tr} stand for the average time of sending a single real number (excluding latency). Then, using Eqs. (50), (53), and (54) we obtain

$$t_c = c_c \tau_{tr} + 2D = 2(\tau_{tr} + D); \tag{55}$$

$$t_{Map} = c_{Map} \tau_{op} = (4n^2m + 2m^2n + 16nm - 12m)\tau_{op}; \tag{56}$$

$$t_a = c_a \tau_{op} = \tau_{op}. \tag{57}$$

Substituting the right-hand sides of Eqs. (55)–(57) in (49), we obtain the following estimations of the scalability bound of Algorithm 7:

$$L_{max} = \frac{1}{2}\sqrt{\left(\frac{2(\tau_{tr} + D)}{\tau_{op}\ln 2}\right)^2 + 4n^2m + 2m^2n + 16nm - 12m} - \frac{2(\tau_{tr} + D)}{\tau_{op}\ln 2}.$$

where n is the space dimension, m is the number of constraints, D is the latency. For large values of m and n, this is equivalent to

$$L_{max} \approx O(\sqrt{2n^2m + m^2n + 8nm - 6m}). \tag{58}$$

If we assume that $m = O(n)$, then it follows from (58) that

$$L_{max} \approx O(n\sqrt{n}), \tag{59}$$

where n is the space dimension. Estimation (59) allows us to conclude that Algorithm 7 scales very well[2]. In the following section, we verify analytical estimation (59) by conducting large-scale computational experiments on a real cluster computing system.

4   Computational Experiments

We performed a parallel implementation of Algorithm 7 in the form of the ViLiPP (Visualization of Linear Programming Problem) program in C++ using a BSF-skeleton [29]. The BSF-skeleton based on the BSF parallel computation model encapsulates all aspects related to the parallelization of the program using the MPI [9] library and the OpenMP [13] programming interface. The source code of the ViLiPP program is freely available on the Internet at https://github.com/nikolay-olkhovsky/LP-visualization-MPI. Using the ViLiPP parallel program, we conducted experiments to evaluate the scalability of Algorithm 7 on the "Tornado SUSU" cluster computing system [16], the characteristics of which are presented in Table 1.

To conduct computational experiments, we constructed three random LP problems using the FRaGenLP problem generator [32]. The parameters of these

---

[2] Let $L_{max} = O(n^\alpha)$. We say: the algorithm *scales perfectly* if $\alpha > 1$; the algorithm *scales well* if $\alpha = 1$; the algorithm demonstrates *limited scalability* if $0 < \alpha < 1$; the algorithm does *not scale* if $\alpha = 0$.

Table 1. Specifications of the "Tornado SUSU" computing cluster

Parameter	Value
Number of processor nodes	480
Processor	Intel Xeon X5680 (6 cores, 3.33 GHz)
Processors per node	2
Memory per node	24 GB DDR3
Interconnect	InfiniBand QDR (40 Gbit/s)
Operating system	Linux CentOS

Table 2. Parameters of test LP problems

Problem ID	Dimension	Number of constraints	Non-zero values in A	Receptive field cardinality
LP7	7	4 016	100%	15 625
LP6	6	4 014	100%	3 125
LP5	5	4 012	100%	625

problems are given in Table 2. In all cases, the number of non-zero values of the matrix A of problem (1) was 100%. For all problems, the rank η of the receptive field was assumed to be equal to 2. In accordance with Eq. (44), the receptive field cardinality demonstrated an exponential growth with an increase in the space dimension.

The results of the computational experiments are presented in Table 3 and in Fig. 4. In all runs, a separate processor node was allocated for each worker. One more separate processor node was allocated for the master. The computational experiments show that the ViLiPP program scalability bound increases with an increase in the problem dimension. For LP5, the maximum of the speedup curve is reached around 190 nodes. For LP6, the maximum is located around 260 nodes. For LP7, the scalability bound is approximately equal to 326 nodes. At the same time, there is an exponential increase in the runtime of building the LP problem image. Building the LP5 problem image takes 10 s on 11 processor nodes. Building the LP7 problem image takes 5 min on the same number of nodes. An additional computational experiment shows that building an image of the problem with $n = 9$ takes 1.5 h on 11 processor nodes.

The conducted experiments show that on the current development level of high-performance computing, the proposed method is applicable to solving LP problems that include up to 100 variables and up to 100 000 constraints.

Table 3. Runtime of building an LP problem image (sec.)

Number of processor nodes	LP5	LP6	LP7
11	9.81	54.45	303.78
56	1.93	10.02	59.43
101	1.55	6.29	33.82
146	1.39	4.84	24.73
191	1.35	4.20	21.10
236	1.38	3.98	19.20
281	1.45	3.98	18.47
326	1.55	4.14	18.30

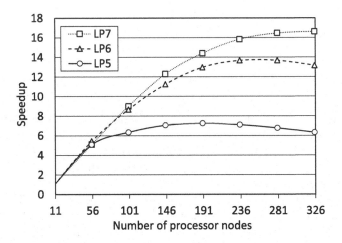

Fig. 4. ViLiPP parallel program speedup for LP problems of various sizes.

5 Conclusion

The main contribution of this work is a mathematical model of the visual representation of a multidimensional linear programming problem of finding the maximum of a linear objective function in a feasible region. The central element of the model is the receptive field, which is a finite set of points located at the nodes of a square lattice constructed inside a hypercube. All points of the receptive field lie in the objective hyperplane orthogonal to the vector $c = (c_1, \ldots, c_n)$, which is composed of the coefficients of the linear objective function. The target hyperplane is placed so that for any point x from the feasible region and any point z of the objective hyperplane, the inequality $\langle c, x \rangle < \langle c, z \rangle$ holds. We can say that the receptive field is a multidimensional abstraction of the digital camera image sensor. From each point of the receptive field, we construct a ray parallel to the vector c and directed to the side of the feasible region. The point at which the ray hits the feasible region is called the objective projection. The image of the linear programming problem is a matrix of the dimension $(n-1)$, in which each element is the distance from the point of the receptive field to the corresponding point of the objective projection.

The algorithm for calculating the coordinates of a receptive field point by its ordinal number is described. It is shown that the time complexity of this algorithm can be estimated as $O(n^2)$, where n is the space dimension. An outline of the algorithm for solving the linear programming problem by an artificial neural network using the constructed images is presented. A parallel algorithm for constructing the image of a linear programming problem on computing clusters is proposed. This algorithm is based on the BSF parallel computation model, which uses the master/workers paradigm and assumes a representation of the algorithm in the form of operations on lists using higher-order functions *Map* and *Reduce*. It is shown that the scalability bound of the parallel algorithm admits the estimation of $O(n\sqrt{n})$. This means that the algorithm demonstrates good scalability.

The parallel algorithm for constructing the multidimensional image of a linear programming problem is implemented in C++ using the BSF–skeleton that encapsulates all aspects related to parallelization by the MPI library and the OpenMP API. Using this software implementation, we conducted large-scale computational experiments on constructing images for random multidimensional linear programming problems with a large number of constraints on the "Tornado SUSU" computing cluster. The conducted experiments confirm the validity and efficiency of the proposed approaches. At the same time, it should be noted that the time of image construction increases exponentially with an increase in the space dimension. Therefore, the proposed method is applicable to problems with the number of variables not exceeding 100. However, the number of constraints can theoretically be unbounded.

Future research directions are as follows.

1. Develop a method for solving linear programming problems based on the analysis of their images and prove its convergence.
2. Develop and implement a method for training data set generation to create a neural network that solves linear programming problems by analyzing their images.
3. Develop and train an artificial neural network solving multidimensional linear programming problems.
4. Develop and implement a parallel program on a computing cluster that constructs multidimensional images of a linear programming problem and calculates its solution using an artificial neural network.

Funding Information. The study was partially funded by the Russian Foundation for Basic Research (project No. 20-07-00092-a) and the Ministry of Science and Higher Education of the Russian Federation (government order FENU-2020-0022).

References

1. Bird, R.S.: Lectures on constructive functional programming. In: Broy, M. (ed.) Constructive Methods in Computing Science. NATO ASI Series, vol. 55, pp. 151–216. Springer, Heidelberg (1988). https://doi.org/10.1007/978-3-642-74884-4_5
2. Bixby, R.: Solving real-world linear programs: a decade and more of progress. Oper. Res. **50**(1), 3–15 (2002). https://doi.org/10.1287/opre.50.1.3.17780
3. Brogaard, J., Hendershott, T., Riordan, R.: High-frequency trading and price discovery. Rev. Financ. Stud. **27**(8), 2267–2306 (2014). https://doi.org/10.1093/rfs/hhu032
4. Chung, W.: Applying large-scale linear programming in business analytics. In: 2015 IEEE International Conference on Industrial Engineering and Engineering Management (IEEM), pp. 1860–1864. IEEE (2015). https://doi.org/10.1109/IEEM.2015.7385970
5. Dantzig, G.: Linear Programming and Extensions. Princeton University Press, Princeton (1998)
6. Dongarra, J., Gottlieb, S., Kramer, W.: Race to exascale. Comput. Sci. Eng. **21**(1), 4–5 (2019). https://doi.org/10.1109/MCSE.2018.2882574
7. Ezhova, N.A., Sokolinsky, L.B.: Scalability evaluation of iterative algorithms used for supercomputer simulation of physical processes. In: Proceedings - 2018 Global Smart Industry Conference, GloSIC 2018, Art. No. 8570131, p. 10. IEEE (2018). https://doi.org/10.1109/GloSIC.2018.8570131
8. Gondzio, J., Gruca, J.A., Hall, J., Laskowski, W., Zukowski, M.: Solving large-scale optimization problems related to Bell's Theorem. J. Comput. Appl. Math. **263**, 392–404 (2014). https://doi.org/10.1016/j.cam.2013.12.003
9. Gropp, W.: MPI 3 and beyond: why MPI is successful and what challenges it faces. In: Träff, J.L., Benkner, S., Dongarra, J.J. (eds.) EuroMPI 2012. LNCS, vol. 7490, pp. 1–9. Springer, Heidelberg (2012). https://doi.org/10.1007/978-3-642-33518-1_1
10. Hafsteinsson, H., Levkovitz, R., Mitra, G.: Solving large scale linear programming problems using an interior point method on a massively parallel SIMD computer. Parallel Algorithms Appl. **4**(3–4), 301–316 (1994). https://doi.org/10.1080/10637199408915470
11. Hartung, T.: Making big sense from big data. Front. Big Data **1**, 5 (2018). https://doi.org/10.3389/fdata.2018.00005
12. Jagadish, H.V., et al.: Big data and its technical challenges. Commun. ACM **57**(7), 86–94 (2014). https://doi.org/10.1145/2611567
13. Kale, V.: Shared-memory parallel programming with OpenMP. In: Parallel Computing Architectures and APIs, chap. 14, pp. 213–222. Chapman and Hall/CRC, Boca Raton (2019). https://doi.org/10.1201/9781351029223-18/SHARED-MEMORY-PARALLEL-PROGRAMMING-OPENMP-VIVEK-KALE
14. Karmarkar, N.: A new polynomial-time algorithm for linear programming. Combinatorica **4**(4), 373–395 (1984). https://doi.org/10.1007/BF02579150
15. Karypis, G., Gupta, A., Kumar, V.: A parallel formulation of interior point algorithms. In: Proceedings of the 1994 ACM/IEEE Conference on Supercomputing (Supercomputing 1994), Los Alamitos, CA, USA, pp. 204–213. IEEE Computer Society Press (1994). https://doi.org/10.1109/SUPERC.1994.344280
16. Kostenetskiy, P., Semenikhina, P.: SUSU supercomputer resources for industry and fundamental science. In: Proceedings - 2018 Global Smart Industry Conference, GloSIC 2018, Art. No. 8570068, p. 7. IEEE (2018). https://doi.org/10.1109/GloSIC.2018.8570068

17. Lachhwani, K.: Application of neural network models for mathematical programming problems: a state of art review. Arch. Comput. Methods Eng. **27**(1), 171–182 (2019). https://doi.org/10.1007/s11831-018-09309-5

18. LeCun, Y., Bengio, Y., Hinton, G.: Deep learning. Nature **521**(7553), 436–444 (2015). https://doi.org/10.1038/nature14539

19. Mamalis, B., Pantziou, G.: Advances in the parallelization of the simplex method. In: Zaroliagis, C., Pantziou, G., Kontogiannis, S. (eds.) Algorithms, Probability, Networks, and Games. LNCS, vol. 9295, pp. 281–307. Springer, Cham (2015). https://doi.org/10.1007/978-3-319-24024-4_17

20. Prieto, A., et al.: Neural networks: an overview of early research, current frameworks and new challenges. Neurocomputing **214**, 242–268 (2016). https://doi.org/10.1016/j.neucom.2016.06.014

21. Schmidhuber, J.: Deep learning in neural networks: an overview. Neural Netw. **61**, 85–117 (2015). https://doi.org/10.1016/j.neunet.2014.09.003

22. Sodhi, M.: LP modeling for asset-liability management: a survey of choices and simplifications. Oper. Res. **53**(2), 181–196 (2005). https://doi.org/10.1287/opre.1040.0185

23. Sokolinskaya, I.: Parallel method of pseudoprojection for linear inequalities. In: Sokolinsky, L., Zymbler, M. (eds.) PCT 2018. CCIS, vol. 910, pp. 216–231. Springer, Cham (2018). https://doi.org/10.1007/978-3-319-99673-8_16

24. Sokolinskaya, I., Sokolinsky, L.B.: On the solution of linear programming problems in the age of big data. In: Sokolinsky, L., Zymbler, M. (eds.) PCT 2017. CCIS, vol. 753, pp. 86–100. Springer, Cham (2017). https://doi.org/10.1007/978-3-319-67035-5_7

25. Sokolinskaya, I., Sokolinsky, L.B.: Scalability evaluation of NSLP algorithm for solving non-stationary linear programming problems on cluster computing systems. In: Voevodin, V., Sobolev, S. (eds.) RuSCDays 2017. Communications in Computer and Information Science, vol. 793, pp. 40–53. Springer, Cham (2017). https://doi.org/10.1007/978-3-319-71255-0_4

26. Sokolinskaya, I.M., Sokolinsky, L.B.: Scalability evaluation of cimmino algorithm for solving linear inequality systems on multiprocessors with distributed memory. Supercomput. Front. Innov. **5**(2), 11–22 (2018). https://doi.org/10.14529/jsfi180202

27. Sokolinsky, L.B.: Analytical estimation of the scalability of iterative numerical algorithms on distributed memory multiprocessors. Lobachevskii J. Math. **39**(4), 571–575 (2018). https://doi.org/10.1134/S1995080218040121

28. Sokolinsky, L.B.: BSF: a parallel computation model for scalability estimation of iterative numerical algorithms on cluster computing systems. J. Parallel Distrib. Comput. **149**, 193–206 (2021). https://doi.org/10.1016/j.jpdc.2020.12.009

29. Sokolinsky, L.B.: BSF-skeleton: a template for parallelization of iterative numerical algorithms on cluster computing systems. MethodsX **8**, Article Number 101,437 (2021). https://doi.org/10.1016/j.mex.2021.101437

30. Sokolinsky, L.B., Sokolinskaya, I.M.: Scalable method for linear optimization of industrial processes. In: Proceedings - 2020 Global Smart Industry Conference, GloSIC 2020, pp. 20–26. Article Number 9267,854. IEEE (2020). https://doi.org/10.1109/GloSIC50886.2020.9267854

31. Sokolinsky, L.B., Sokolinskaya, I.M.: Scalable parallel algorithm for solving non-stationary systems of linear inequalities. Lobachevskii J. Math. **41**(8), 1571–1580 (2020). https://doi.org/10.1134/S1995080220080181

32. Sokolinsky, L.B., Sokolinskaya, I.M.: FRaGenLP: a generator of random linear programming problems for cluster computing systems. In: Sokolinsky, L., Zymbler, M. (eds.) PCT 2021. CCIS, vol. 1437, pp. 164–177. Springer, Cham (2021). https://doi.org/10.1007/978-3-030-81691-9_12

33. Sokolinsky, L.B., Sokolinskaya, I.M.: VaLiPro: linear programming validator for cluster computing systems. Supercomput. Front. Innov. **8**(3), 51–61 (2021). https://doi.org/10.14529/js210303

34. Tolla, P.: A survey of some linear programming methods. In: Paschos, V.T. (ed.) Concepts of Combinatorial Optimization, 2 edn, chap. 7, pp. 157–188. Wiley, Hoboken (2014). https://doi.org/10.1002/9781119005216.ch7

35. Zadeh, N.: A bad network problem for the simplex method and other minimum cost flow algorithms. Math. Program. **5**(1), 255–266 (1973). https://doi.org/10.1007/BF01580132

Supercomputer Simulation

Quantum-Chemical Calculations of the Enthalpy of Formation of Some Tetrazine Derivatives

Vadim Volokhov[1] , Elena Amosova[1]([✉]) , Alexander Volokhov[1] ,
David Lempert[1] , Vladimir Parakhin[2] , and Tatiana Zyubina[1]

[1] Institute of Problems of Chemical Physics, Chernogolovka, Russian Federation
{vvm,aes,vav,lempert,zyubin}@icp.ac.ru
[2] N.D. Zelinsky Institute of Organic Chemistry, Moscow, Russian Federation
parakhin@ioc.ac.ru

Abstract. The paper addresses to the study of the physicochemical properties of new high-energy substances: nitro derivatives of various kinds of nitrogenous heterocyclic nuclei. The enthalpy of formation of the molecules in the gas phase is obtained using quantum-chemical calculations (Gaussian 09). Various methods for solving the stationary Schrödinger equation are used: G4MP2, G4, CBS-4M, CBS-QB3, ωB97XD/aug-cc-pVTZ, B3LYP/6-311+G(2d,p), M062X/6-311+G(2d,p). The results of calculations obtained by the atomization method and the method of isogyric reactions are comparatively assessed. Various calculation methods are compared in terms of accuracy and time costs.

Keywords: Enthalpy of formation · Quantum-chemical calculations · High-energy materials · Calculation efficiency

1 Introduction

One of the fundamental problems in the field of energy-intensive compounds is the search for new high-energy density materials (HEDMs) and the study of their properties. Most of the suggested new HEDMs are nitro derivatives of various nitrogenous heterocyclic nuclei. For example, several first representatives of a series of high-energy 5/6/5 tricyclic derivatives of 1,2,3,4-tetrazines have been recently proposed in [1–3] and reported to possess a number of attractive physicochemical and energetic properties. The high-energy potential of these compounds is determined by the fact that the presence of nitro groups in their structure provides an acceptable oxygen balance, and a large number of $C - N$, $N - N$ and N=N bonds of the heterocyclic system sets a high level of the enthalpy of formation. The first of these derivatives to be synthesized was 2,9-dinitrobis([1,2,4]triazolo)[1,5-d:5',1'-f][1,2,3,4]tetrazine (**1**) [1], the structure of which combines 1,2,3,4-tetrazine and two nitro-1,2,4-triazoles annelated with it. A preliminary assessment of the properties of this compound shows that it is not

L. Sokolinsky and M. Zymbler (Eds.): PCT 2022, CCIS 1618, pp. 199–209, 2022.
https://doi.org/10.1007/978-3-031-11623-0_14

only characterized by a relatively high density, but is also comparable to HMX in terms of detonation characteristics; however, at the same time it has a noticeably lower sensitivity than both HMX and RDX. The above mentioned advantages of compound 1 make the entire range of energy-intensive 5/6/5 tricyclic derivatives of 1,2,3,4-tetrazines annelated with triazoles attractive for the search for new HEDMs. In addition, since the disadvantage of compound **1** is its relatively low thermal stability, it might be interesting to study the isomeric analogs of 5/6/5 tricyclic derivatives of unsymmetrical 1,2,3,4-tetrazine based on symmetric 1,2,4,5-tetrazine, as they can potentially provide greater thermal stability.

It should be noted that the key parameter that defines the energy capabilities of the HEDM is the enthalpy of formation, and the reliability of the results of calculating the energy characteristics of the compound depends on the accuracy of its value. Therefore, the purpose of this work was to determine the enthalpy of formation for 5/6/5 tricyclic derivatives of tetrazines annelated with nitrotriazoles (Table 1) $C_4N_{10}O_4$: 2,9-dinitrobis([1,2,4]triazolo)[1,5-d:5',1'-f][1,2,3,4]tetrazine (structure **1**), 2,7-dinitrobis([1,2,4]triazolo)[1,5-b:5',1'-f][1,2,4,5]tetrazine (structure **2**), 3,8-dinitrobis([1,2,4]triazolo)[4,3-d:3',4'-f][1,2,3,4]tetrazine (structure **3**), 1,8-dinitrobis([1,2,4]triazolo)[4,3-b:3',4'-f][1,2,4,5]tetrazine (structure **4**), 1,10-dinitrobis([1,2,3]triazolo)[1,5-d:5',1'-f][1,2,3,4]tetrazine (structure **5**) and 3,6-dinitrobis([1,2,3]triazolo)[1,5-b:5',1'-f][1,2,4,5]tetrazine (structure **6**) and in the gas phase at a temperature of 298 K and pressure p = 1 atm $(\Delta H_{f(g)}^{298})$ using various quantum-chemical methods and reveal regularities in the dependence of the value of ΔH_f on the structure of nitrotriazole isomers.

2   Calculation Method

At present, quantum-chemical calculations along with experimental measurement methods have become widespread as a means of determining the enthalpy of formation. The time-consuming synthetic production of the compounds under consideration is not required for such calculations, which advantages them greatly. Quantum-chemical calculations based on ab initio approaches (along with experimental data) enable the most accurate determination of the enthalpy of formation. The accuracy of such calculations by the G4 method of the Gaussian quantum-chemical package is assessed by Curtiss and his coauthors [4]. They use a test set of 454 substances to calculate thermochemical properties and compare the results with experimental data. A detailed analysis shows that the deviation of the calculation results from experimental data is less than 1 kcal/mol averagely (the deviation is less than 1% for high-enthalpy substances). Another noteworthy advantage of quantum-chemical methods is the possibility of designing molecules of new compounds that have not been yet synthesized, but look very promising. Their physicochemical characteristics (thermochemical properties, in particular) can be determined with high accuracy, and structural factors affecting such properties can be discovered.

Table 1. Molecules under consideration.

Formula	α^a	N%[b]	№	Structural formula	№	Structural formula
$C_4N_{10}O_4$	0.500	55.56	1	O$_2$N, N, N, NO$_2$ / N–N, N–N / N=N	2	O$_2$N, N, N, NO$_2$ / N–N–N / N= , =N / N=N
$C_4N_{10}O_4$	0.500	55.56	3	N, N, N, N / N, N / O$_2$N, N=N, NO$_2$	4	NO$_2$ O$_2$N / N, N–N, N / N= , =N / N=N
$C_4N_{10}O_4$	0.500	55.56	5	NO$_2$ O$_2$N / N, N, N, N / N–N, N–N / N=N	6	N=, N, N, =N / N–N / O$_2$N, N=N, NO$_2$

^{a} - oxygen saturation coefficient of the $C_xH_yN_wO_z$ molecule, $\alpha = 2z/(4x + y)$;
^{b} - mass content of nitrogen.

The enthalpy of formation can be calculated by examining reactions in which the test substance serves as a reagent or a product [5]. The standard enthalpy of formation of a substance can be determined by considering the energy balance equations of such reactions. This paper compares two approaches to evaluating the enthalpy of formation: 1) analysis of the atomization reaction of a substance (similar to our previous works [6–11]) and 2) analysis of the reaction of the substance formation from simple substances in standard states.

3 Results and Discussion

3.1 Enthalpy of Formation

The structures and the most significant geometric parameters of the molecules under consideration are calculated at the B3LYP/6-311+G(2d,p) level and shown in Fig. 1. The calculated values of the enthalpy of formation of the molecules in the gas phase, determined using various calculation methods (G4MP2, G4, ωB97XD/aug-cc-pVTZ, CBS-4M, CBS-QB3, B3LYP/6-311+G(2d,p), M062X/6-311+G(2d,p)), are presented in Table 2.

The enthalpy of formation of various isomers of the $C_4N_{10}O_4$ molecule are calculated by two approaches: $\Delta H_f(\text{I})$ represents a calculation based on the change in the enthalpy for the reaction $4C(g) + 10N(g) + 4O(g) = C_4N_{10}O_4(g)$, and $\Delta H_f(\text{II})$ represents a calculation based on the change in the enthalpy for the reaction $4C(g) + 5N_2(g) + 2O_2(g) = C_4N_{10}O_4(g)$. A comparison of the two calculation approaches shows that for all levels of calculation, the values of $\Delta H_f(\text{I})$ are greater than the values of $\Delta H_f(\text{II})$ by 7-101 kJ/mol, with the exception of the most accurate G4 method, for which the values of $\Delta H_f(\text{II})$

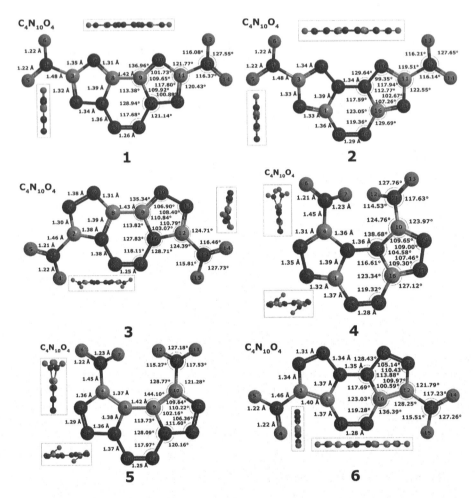

Fig. 1. Structures (in different angles) and most significant geometric parameters (in Å and °) of the calculated molecules (calculation level B3LYP/6-311+G(2d,p)).

are greater than the values of $\Delta H_f(\mathrm{I})$ by 3 kJ/mol. The more accurate the calculation is, the smaller is the difference between the $\Delta H_f(\mathrm{I})$ and $\Delta H_f(\mathrm{II})$ values, thus, for the CBS-4M method this difference is 101 kJ/mol, and for G4MP2 it is 7 kJ/mol.

All the considered $C_4N_{10}O_4(g)$ isomers (structures **1-6**) show similar tendencies of change in the values of the enthalpy of formation along the isomer series (Table 2). The enthalpy-of-formation values obtained at different levels of calculation increase in the following sequence CBS-4M < ωB97XD/aug-cc-pVTZ < CBS-QB3 < CBS-APNO < G4 < G4MP2 < M062X/6-311+G(2d,p) < B3LYP/6-311+G(2d,p), changing from structure **1** to structure **6** by approximately the same value 171-175 kJ/mol. Table 2 shows that the enthalpy of formation of various isomers increases from 867.5 kJ/mol to 1066.8 kJ/mol (G4).

The most important issue for the development of new high-energy materials is to establish the relationship between the value of the enthalpy of formation and the molecule structure. Let us consider the sequence of isomers based on 1,2,3,4-tetrazine: structures **1, 3, 5**. The isomer with structure **5**, which contains a chain of eight nitrogen atoms, is characterized by the highest enthalpy of formation (1012.8 kJ/mol), The enthalpy of formation is 41 kJ/mol lower (867.5 kJ/mol) for structure **3** with a chain of four nitrogen atoms in the tetrazine ring and two chains of two nitrogen atoms in the triazole rings. The lowest enthalpy of formation (867.5 kJ/mol) is that of structure **1** with a chain of six nitrogen atoms and two separate nitrogen atoms in the triazole rings.

In the case of isomers based on 1,2,4,5-tetrazine with two oppositely located pairs of nitrogen atoms (structures **2, 4, 6**), the enthalpy of formation increases by 43 kJ/mol (structure **2** as compared to structure **1**), 37 kJ/mol (structures **3-4**), and 54 kJ/mol (structures **5-6**). However, as mentioned above, the structure with a chain of six nitrogen atoms (**6**) has the highest value of the enthalpy of formation (1066.8 kJ/mol)). The enthalpy of formation of structure **4** with two pairs of nitrogen atoms is 58 kJ/mol lower than that of structure **6**, and the lowest value is that of structure **2** with two isolated nitrogen atoms (910.8 kJ/mol).

Thus, it can be assumed that if all other structural parameters are equal:

1) the presence in the tetrazine ring of two oppositely located pairs of nitrogen atoms is preferable to their sequential arrangement in the form of a chain;
2) lengthening the chain of nitrogen atoms by triazole rings has a positive effect on the value of the enthalpy of formation;
3) the presence of pairs of nitrogen atoms in the triazole rings is preferable to single atoms.

3.2   IR Spectra and Frequency Analysis

Figures 2 and 3 show the IR absorption spectra and atom displacements for the most intense vibrations of the molecules under consideration, calculated at the B3LYP/6-311+G(2d,p) level.

Table 2. Enthalpies of formation of the molecules in the gas phase, calculated at different levels.

Formula		$C_4N_{10}O_4$					
Structure		1	2	3	4	5	6
CBS-4M	kcal/mol	202.67^a	211.79^a	230.38^a	239.19^a	237.19^a	249.76^a
		178.45^b	187.57^b	206.16^b	214.98^b	212.98^b	225.55^b
	kJ/mol	847.95^a	886.12^a	963.89^a	1000.78^a	992.41^a	1045.01^a
		746.64^b	784.81^b	862.58^b	899.47^b	891.09^b	943.70^b
ωB97XD/ aug-cc-pVTZ	kcal/mol	208.26^a	218.05^a	234.31^a	244.39^a	244.69^a	256.53^a
		196.32^b	206.11^b	222.37^b	232.45^b	232.75^b	244.59^b
	kJ/mol	871.37^a	912.32^a	980.36^a	1022.52^a	1023.79^a	1073.34^a
		821.41^b	862.36^b	930.38^b	972.55^b	973.83^b	1023.38^b
CBS-QB3	kcal/mol	201.37^a	211.36^a	226.69^a	2336.02^a	235.66^a	248.11^a
		198.56^b	208.55^b	223.88^b	233.21^b	232.85^b	245.29^b
	kJ/mol	842.53^a	884.35^a	948.48^a	987.52^a	986.02^a	1038.08^a
		830.76^b	872.58^b	936.71^b	975.75^b	974.25^b	1026.31^b
CBS-APNO	kcal/mol	209.00^a	218.89^a	234.67^a	242.89^a	243.45^a	256.40^a
		203.51	213.40^b	229.18^b	237.40^b	237.96^b	250.91^b
	kJ/mol	874.45^a	915.85^a	981.85^a	1016.27^a	1018.60^a	1072.77^a
		851.47^b	892.87^b	958.87^b	993.29^b	995.61^b	1049.79^b
G4	kcal/mol	$\mathbf{206.64^a}$	$\mathbf{216.99^a}$	$\mathbf{231.58^a}$	$\mathbf{240.39^a}$	$\mathbf{241.37^a}$	$\mathbf{254.28^a}$
		$\mathbf{207.34^b}$	$\mathbf{217.69^b}$	$\mathbf{232.28^b}$	$\mathbf{241.09^b}$	$\mathbf{242.07^b}$	$\mathbf{254.98^b}$
	kJ/mol	$\mathbf{864.57^a}$	$\mathbf{907.88^a}$	$\mathbf{968.92^a}$	$\mathbf{1005.80^a}$	$\mathbf{1009.89^a}$	$\mathbf{1063.89^a}$
		$\mathbf{867.50^b}$	$\mathbf{910.81^b}$	$\mathbf{971.85^b}$	$\mathbf{1008.73^b}$	$\mathbf{1012.82^b}$	$\mathbf{1066.82^b}$
G4MP2	kcal/mol	211.34^a	222.02^a	236.37^a	245.90^a	245.94^a	258.84^a
		209.74^b	220.42^b	234.76^b	244.30^b	244.34^b	257.23^b
	kJ/mol	884.27^a	928.94^a	988.96^a	1028.85^a	1029.01^a	1082.97^a
		877.56^b	922.24^b	982.26^b	1022.15^b	1022.31^b	1076.27^b
M062X/ 6-311+ G(2d,p)	kcal/mol	231.79^a	241.11^a	258.09^a	266.42^a	270.16^a	281.44^a
		210.16^b	219.48^b	236.46^b	244.80^b	248.53^b	259.82^b
	kJ/mol	969.81^a	1008.80^a	1079.84^a	1114.72^a	1130.34^a	1177.56^a
		879.33^b	918.32^b	989.36^b	1024.24^b	1039.85^b	1087.08^b
B3LYP/ 6-311+ G(2d,p)	kcal/mol	224.04^a	232.87^a	249.20^a	259.62^a	260.33^a	270.28^a
		220.29^b	229.12^b	245.45^b	255.87^b	256.58^b	266.53^b
	kJ/mol	937.37^a	974.32^a	1042.64^a	1086.24^a	1089.22^a	1130.85^a
		921.69^b	958.64^b	1026.97^b	1070.56^b	1073.54^b	1115.17^b

$^a \Delta H_f(\text{I})$
$^b \Delta H_f(\text{II})$

According to Fig. 2 and 3, structure **1** is characterized by angular vibrations of the $N - O$ bonds of the nitro group NO_2 in the region of 841 cm^{-1}, vibrations of the $N - N$ bonds in the tetrazine ring in the region of 1220–1262 cm^{-1}, vibrations of the $N - N$ bonds in the triazole rings in the region 1317 cm^{-1}, vibrations of the $C - N$ bonds in the region of 1337–1377 cm^{-1}, and the vibrations of the $N - O$ bonds of the nitro group correspond to a peak in the region of 1620 cm^{-1}. Structure **2** is characterized by angular vibrations of the $N - O$ bonds of NO_2 fragments in the region of 845 cm^{-1}, vibrations of the $C - N$ bonds in the

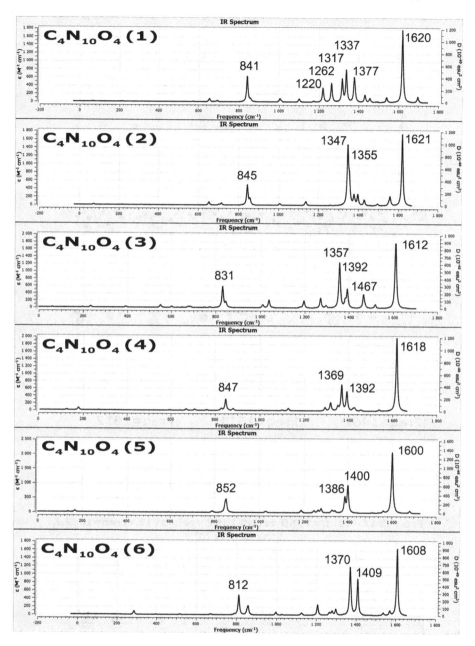

Fig. 2. IR absorption spectra.

region of 1347–1355 cm^{-1}, and vibrations of the $N - O$ bonds in the region of 1621 cm^{-1}. For structure **3**, the peak at 831 cm^{-1} corresponds to angular vibrations of the $N - O$ bonds of the nitro groups NO_2, the vibrations in the region

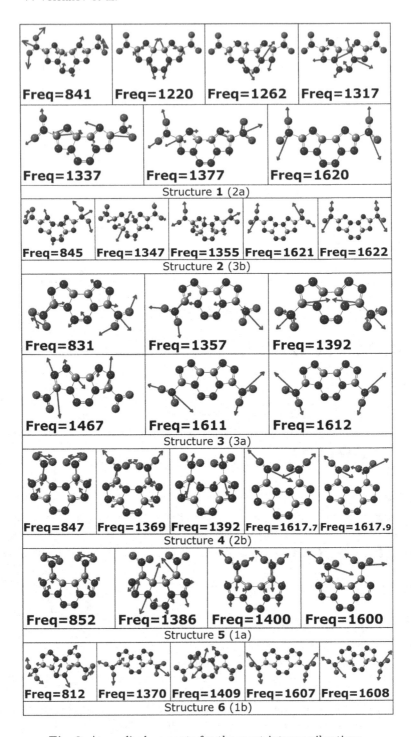

Fig. 3. Atom displacements for the most intense vibrations.

of 1357–1467 cm^{-1} correspond to vibrations of the $C - N$ bonds, and the peak at 1612 cm^{-1} corresponds to vibrations of the $N - O$ bonds in the nitro groups. Structure **4** is characterized by angular vibrations of the $N - O$ bonds in the region of 847 cm^{-1}, vibrations of the $C - N$ bonds in the region of 1369–1392 cm^{-1}, and vibrations of the $N - O$ bonds in the region of 1618 cm^{-1}. For structures **5** and **6**, the peaks at 852 cm^{-1} and 812 cm^{-1}, respectively, correspond to angular vibrations in the nitro groups, and the peaks at 1600 cm^{-1} and 1608 cm^{-1} for vibrations of the $N - O$ bonds. The vibrations of the $C - N$ bonds on the crosslinking of the tetrazine and triazole rings correspond to peaks at 1386 cm^{-1} (for structure **5**) and 1409 cm^{-1} (for structure **6**), and the vibrations of the $C - N$ bonds of the nitro groups correspond to 1400 cm^{-1} (structure **5**) and 1370 cm^{-1} (structure **6**).

4 Computational Details

The Lomonosov-2 compute node with the following configuration: Intel(R) Xeon(R) Gold 6140 CPU @ 2.30 GHz, RAM 259 GB, 20 Tb disk space, was used for calculations.

In regard to the parallelization degree of the executed calculations, it should be noted that the Gaussian package uses its own Linda software for parallelization. Some observations concerning the efficiency of calculations were made. While running a number of test tasks, a stable acceleration on pools up to 8 cores was noted, but further the acceleration effect decreased (Fig. 4). Thus, we used 8 cores per task in our calculations. The calculation speed also depends

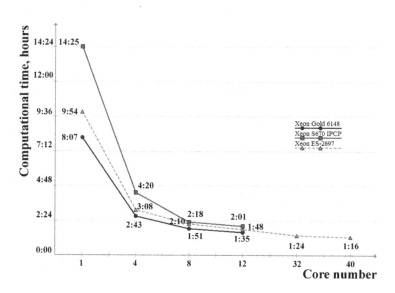

Fig. 4. Comparison of the computational time for the standard task in the Gaussian package on various computational configurations.

on processors' support of the avx2 and sse42 instructions, the former one, in particular, can profit by 8–10 times on some tasks using processors with a close clock rate [12]. In the calculation process, the Gaussian package creates enormous intermediate files, which size up to 2TB. It can take up to 35–50 min to write them to an SSD disk and noticeably longer to SATA arrays. Thereby, SSD disks or high-speed SAS disks with a large amount of allocated disk memory are very advisable for calculations.

The calculation time by the given conditions for the structures under consideration varied from 300–600 core-hours (1–3 days) for the CBS-4M and M062X/6-311+G(2d,p) methods to 3000–6000 core-hours (17–33 days) for the most time-consuming G4 and CBS-APNO methods.

5   Conclusions

The study of quantum-chemical methods for calculating the enthalpy of formation of dinitrobistriazoletetrazines made it possible for this group of compounds to determine the isomeric series of the increasing enthalpy of formation and reveal structural factors affecting the value of their ΔH_f, such as the structure of the nitrotriazole fragment (1,2,4-triazoles or 1,2,3-triazole) and the type of tetrazine nucleus (1,2,3,4- or 1,2,4,5-tetrazine). The highest value in the series of considered isomers differs from the lowest one by 199 kJ/mol (calculation by the G4 method). Calculations were carried out by methods of varying complexity and by two different approaches for establishing the enthalpy of formation. The results of calculation by two approaches differ by 3–101 kJ/mol, and the observation has been made that the more accurate the calculation is, the smaller is this difference. Analysis of IR absorption spectra and atom displacements for the most intense vibration has been made.

Acknowledgements. The equipment of the Center for Collective Use of Super High-Performance Computing Resources of Lomonosov Moscow State University [13,14] (projects Enthalpy-2065 and Enthalpy-2219) and the computational resources of IPCP RAS were used in this work.

V. Volokhov, E. Amosova and A. Volokhov conducted quantum-chemical research in accordance with the State task, state registration No. AAAA-A19-119120690042-9. Calculations by resource-intensive methods were performed with the support of the RFBR, project No. 20-07-00319. D. Lempert assessed the energy potential in accordance with the State task, state registration No. AAAA-A19-119101690058-9. T. Zyubina carried out the calculation and analysis of the IR spectra and atom displacements in accordance with the State task, state registration No. AAAA-A19-119061890019-5.

References

1. Chavez, D.E., Bottaro, J.C., Petrie, M., Parrish, D.A.: Synthesis and thermal behavior of a fused, tricyclic 1,2,3,4-tetrazine ring system. Angew. Chem. Int. Ed. **54**, 12973–12975 (2015). https://doi.org/10.1002/anie.201506744

2. Tang, Y., Kumar, D., Shreeve, J.M.: Balancing excellent performance and high thermal stability in a dinitropyrazole fused 1,2,3,4-tetrazine. J. Am. Chem. Soc. 139, 13684–13687 (2017) https://doi.org/10.1021/jacs.7b08789

3. Tang, Y., He, C., Yin, P., Imler, G.H., Parrish, D.A., Shreeve, J.M.: Energetic functionalized Azido/Nitro imidazole fused 1,2,3,4-Tetrazine. Eur. J. Org. Chem. **19**, 2273–2276 (2018). https://doi.org/10.1002/ejoc.201800347

4. Curtiss, L.A., Redfern, P.C., Raghavachari, K.: Gaussian-4 theory. J. Chem. Phys. **126**(8), 084108 (2007). https://doi.org/10.1063/1.2436888

5. Irikura, K.K., Frurip, D.J.: Computational thermochemistry. In: ACS Symposium Series 667. American Chemical Society, Washington (1998)

6. Volokhov, V.M., Zyubina, T.S., Volokhov, A.V., Amosova, E.S., Varlamov, D.A., Lempert, D.B., Yanovskiy, L.S.: Computer design of hydrocarbon compounds with high enthalpy of formation. In: Sokolinsky, L., Zymbler, M. (eds.) PCT 2020. CCIS, vol. 1263, pp. 291–304. Springer, Cham (2020). https://doi.org/10.1007/978-3-030-55326-5_21

7. Volokhov, V., Zyubina, T., Volokhov, A., Amosova, E., Varlamov, D., Lempert, D., Yanovskiy, L.: Predictive quantum-chemical design of molecules of high-energy heterocyclic compounds. In: Voevodin, V., Sobolev, S. (eds.) RuSCDays 2020. CCIS, vol. 1331, pp. 310–319. Springer, Cham (2020). https://doi.org/10.1007/978-3-030-64616-5_27

8. Lempert, D.B., et al.: Regularities in the dependence of the enthalpies of formation of certain conjugated polynitrogen heterocyclic compounds on their structure. Russian J. Appl. Chem. **93**(12), 1852–1867 (2020). https://doi.org/10.1134/S1070427220120071

9. Volokhov, V.M., et al.: Computer design of structure of molecules of high-energy tetrazines. Calculation of thermochemical properties. Supercomput. Front. Innov. **7**(4), 68–79. (2020). https://doi.org/10.14529/jsfi200406

10. Volokhov, V.M., et al.: Quantum chemical simulation of hydrocarbon compounds with high enthalpy. Russian J. Phys. Chemi. B **15**(1), 12–24 (2021). https://doi.org/10.1134/S1990793121010127

11. Volokhov, V.M., et al.: Predictive Modeling of Molecules of High-Energy Heterocyclic Compounds. Russian J. Inorg. Chem. **66**(1), 78–88 (2021). https://doi.org/10.1134/S0036023621010113

12. Grigorenko, B., Mironov, V., Polyakov, I., Nemukhin, A.: Benchmarking quantum chemistry methods in calculations of electronic excitations. Supercomput. Front. Innov. **5**(4), 62–66 (2019). https://doi.org/10.14529/jsfi180405

13. Voevodin Vl, V., Antonov, A.S., Nikitenko, D.A., et al.: Supercomputer Lomonosov-2: largescale, deep monitoring and fine analytics for the user community. Supercomput. Front. Innov. **6**(2), 4–11 (2019). https://doi.org/10.14529/jsfi190201

14. Nikitenko, D.A., Voevodin, V.V., Zhumatiy, S.A.: Deep analysis of job state statisticson "Lomonosov-2" supercomputer. Supercomput. Front. Innov. **5**(2), 4–10 (2019). https://doi.org/10.14529/jsfi180201

A New Approach to the Supercomputer Simulation of Carbon Burning Sub-grid Physics in Ia Type Supernovae Explosion

Igor Kulikov$^{(\boxtimes)}$ ⓘ, Igor Chernykh, Dmitry Karavaev, Vladimir Prigarin,
Anna Sapetina, Ivan Ulyanichev, and Oleg Zavyalov

Institute of Computational Mathematics and Mathematical Geophysics SB RAS,
Novosibirsk, Russia
kulikov@ssd.sscc.ru, chernykh@parbz.sscc.ru, kda@opg.sscc.ru

Abstract. Supernovae are the major sources of elements in the periodic table, planets, and life. Type Ia supernovae (SNeIa) are not only sources of elements, but also "standard candles" to measure distances in the Universe. We propose a mechanism of carbon burning that causes non-standard Type Ia supernova explosions. The mechanism is based on intensity variations in the incomplete nuclear burning of carbon. In this case, the explosion energy can vary significantly due to the presence of different regimes of carbon burning during the development of turbulence in the burning zone. The energy released during burning, sufficient for the explosion of a white dwarf (as a type Ia supernova), can be achieved with a smaller Chandrasekhar mass. In addition, the explosion energy of a white dwarf with a Chandrasekhar mass can differ considerably. Such a conclusion can be made from modern observations of incomplete burning and chemistry of burning, which determine the explosion energy. In the present paper, a software tool is proposed to demonstrate a significant difference in the values of the explosion energy obtained with different parameterizations of subgrid carbon burning. For computational experiments, we use a code developed by the authors, which is extended using an adaptive nested grid approach to achieve a more accurate reproduction of turbulent burning.

Keywords: Computational Astrophysics · Numerical Methods · High-Performance Computing

1 Introduction

Supernovas are the major sources of "life" elements—from carbon to iron. Type Ia supernovas are very bright and, therefore, are used as "standard candles" to determine distances to galaxies and the expansion rate of the Universe. The mathematical simulation of supernova explosions is the major tool for studying their dynamics and formation. The formation of complex flows in supernova explosions imposes rigid requirements on the spatial resolution of the simulation.

L. Sokolinsky and M. Zymbler (Eds.): PCT 2022, CCIS 1618, pp. 210–232, 2022.
https://doi.org/10.1007/978-3-031-11623-0_15

The major scenario [17] of supernova explosion is based on the merging of two degenerate white dwarfs with the subsequent collapse of a new star when it reaches the Chandrasekhar mass, ignition of the carbon burning process, and type Ia supernova explosion.

The realistic computer simulation of SNeIa remains an unsolved problem. However, there exist some approaches to solving this problem. These are the collision of white dwarfs [28,37,38], violent merger [34,40], spiral instability [18,19], and tidal heating [8], D6 [13,34,41]. In the present paper, no review of possible scenarios is made: it is also too early to compare our preliminary results with those of other authors; it is planned to do this in the forthcoming paper. Here the process of the noncentral ignition of a white dwarf in a merging close pair, first studied in [16], is considered. This model will be extended with modern computational tools enabling a more detailed description of the process of nuclear carbon burning. The model demonstrates that tidal heating shifts the maximum temperature point in a degenerate dwarf from the center to the mantle.

Noncentral explosions should be studied for the following reason: the observed "dipole" character of SNeIa explosions is typically explained by the presence of a close satellite of a degenerate dwarf [5], although it may be a result of a noncentral explosion. Both scenarios are considered in the present paper. Double detonation, which can cause a noncentral explosion, is due to other chemistry and other masses of the explosion point [12]. Tidal heating is also studied in [8]. It should be noted that the noncentral location of the explosion point can be caused by other reasons: helium layer detonation, magnetic field, jet formation, etc. Therefore, a comprehensive study of possible noncentral explosions is of great interest.

The goal of this paper is to determine the role of the ignition point in nuclear fuel burning and in the dynamics of the remnants of a degenerate dwarf explosion. For this, the nuclear burning of carbon in the development of supersonic turbulence will be simulated directly, not as a subgrid process. The computational model is implemented by using distributed computing: the hydrodynamic evolution of white dwarfs is simulated on nested meshes (basic calculation). As the temperature and density reach some critical values, a new task is started on a distributed memory architecture to simulate the development of hydrodynamic turbulence leading to supersonic nuclear carbon burning (satellite calculation).

The present paper is devoted to the study of the pattern of 3D gas dynamical explosions of carbon dwarfs. The main parameter of the problem is the intensity of the nuclear burning of carbon in the explosion zone. In this case, the explosion energy can vary considerably due to the variable carbon burning regime during the development of turbulence in the burning region. The goal of this study is to assess the impact of some so far undetermined parameters and factors on the observed manifestations of explosions and on the limits to what extent SNeIa can be considered "standard".

In the second section, a numerical model of white dwarfs is formulated. The third section describes the parallel and distributed organization of calculations for a detailed description of turbulent carbon burning and explosion hydrodynamics. The fourth section is devoted to the results of computational experiments. In the fifth section, we will discuss some important issues. The sixth section provides conclusions to the paper.

2   Numerical Model

2.1   Hydrodynamic Equations

Consider an overdetermined conservative form of the equations of gravitational gas dynamics: the law of conservation of mass

$$\frac{\partial \rho}{\partial t} + \nabla \cdot (\rho \mathbf{u}) = 0, \tag{1}$$

the law of conservation of momentum

$$\frac{\partial \rho \mathbf{u}}{\partial t} + \nabla \cdot (\rho \mathbf{u} \mathbf{u}) = -\nabla p - \rho \nabla \Phi, \tag{2}$$

the law of conservation of total mechanical energy

$$\frac{\partial}{\partial t} \left[E + \rho \frac{\mathbf{u}^2}{2} \right] + \nabla \cdot \left(\left[E + \rho \frac{\mathbf{u}^2}{2} \right] \mathbf{u} \right) = -\nabla \cdot (p\mathbf{u}) - (\rho \nabla \Phi, \mathbf{u}) + Q, \tag{3}$$

and the equation for entropy S

$$\frac{\partial \rho S}{\partial t} + \nabla \cdot (\rho S \mathbf{u}) = \frac{2Q}{3\rho^{2/3}}, \tag{4}$$

supplemented by the Poisson equation for the gravitational potential

$$\Delta \Phi = 4\pi G \rho, \tag{5}$$

where ρ is the density, $\mathbf{u}$ is the velocity, p is the pressure, Φ is the gravitational potential, E is the internal energy of the gas, G is the gravitational constant, and Q is the energy source due to nuclear reactions.

2.2   Stellar Equation of State

The stellar equation of state consists of the pressure of a nondegenerate hot gas, the pressure due to radiation, and a degenerate gas [42]. In the case of a degenerate gas, relativistic and nonrelativistic regimes are considered. In the equation of state $p = (\rho, T)$, p will be sought for as the sum of four components:

$$p = p_{rad} + p_{ion} + p_{deg,nrel} + p_{deg,rel}, \tag{6}$$

where T is the temperature, p_{rad} is the radiation pressure, p_{ion} is the pressure of a nondegenerate hot gas (ions), $p_{deg,nrel}$ is the pressure of a degenerate non-relativistic gas, and $p_{deg,rel}$ is the pressure of a degenerate relativistic gas. Let us present formulas for each pressure type:

$$p_{rad} = \frac{4\sigma T^4}{3c}, \tag{7}$$

where c is the speed of light, and σ is the Stefan-Boltzmann constant. Let us write the pressure of a cold gas in terms of an entropy function:

$$p_{ion} = \frac{k}{\mu}T\rho = S\rho^{5/3}, \tag{8}$$

where k is the Boltzmann constant, and μ is the chemical potential,

$$p_{deg,nrel} = \begin{cases} \rho_0 K_{deg,nrel} \left(\frac{\rho}{\rho_0 \mu_e}\right)^{5/3}, \rho < \rho_0 \\ 0, \rho > \rho_0 \end{cases}, \tag{9}$$

where $K_{deg,nrel} = 10^{13}$ Erg/g, μ_e is the number of nucleons per electron, and $\rho_0 = 10^6$ g/cm^3,

$$p_{deg,rel} = \begin{cases} \rho_0 K_{deg,rel} \left(\frac{\rho}{\rho_0 \mu_e}\right)^{4/3}, \rho > \rho_0 \\ 0, \rho < \rho_0 \end{cases}, \tag{10}$$

where $K_{deg,rel} = 10^{15}$ Erg/g. In this case, the internal energy is written as

$$E = E_{rad} + E_{ion} + E_{deg,nrel} + E_{deg,rel} \tag{11}$$

$$= 3p_{rad} + \frac{3}{2}p_{ion} + \frac{3}{2}p_{deg,nrel} + 3p_{deg,rel}.$$

The formulation of pressure and internal energy in terms of the entropy function makes it possible to calculate temperature variations without solving a nonlinear equation.

2.3   Initial Profile

To specify the equilibrium initial data, we fix the initial temperature T and the characteristic density. The latter is important for determining the adiabatic index of a degenerate gas. Assume that the adiabatic index γ is determined as a constant K at the exponential function for the pressure of a degenerate gas (9) or (10). Let us present the balance of pressure and gravity forces in Eq. (2) and Poisson Eq. (5) in spherical one-dimensional coordinates using ordinary differential equations:

$$-\frac{dp}{dr} = \rho\frac{d\Phi}{dr}, \quad \frac{d}{dr}\left(r^2\frac{d\Phi}{dr}\right) = 4\pi Gr^2\rho,$$

where r is the spherical radius. With the fixed parameters, we obtain an equation of the Emden type:

$$-\frac{d}{dr}\left(\frac{r^2}{\rho}\frac{d}{dr}\left[\frac{4\sigma}{3c}T^4 + \frac{k}{\mu}T\rho + K\rho^\gamma\right]\right) = 4\pi Gr^2\rho.$$

It is evident that the radiation term $\frac{4\sigma}{3c}T^4$ does not depend on the radius r. Therefore, the equation for the equilibrium density profile can be written as

$$-\frac{d}{dr}\left(\frac{r^2}{\rho}\frac{d}{dr}\left[\frac{k}{\mu}T\rho + K\rho^\gamma\right]\right) = 4\pi Gr^2\rho. \tag{12}$$

Equation (12) can be solved numerically [43]. To speed up the iterative process, one can linearize the equation and use the solution to the linearized problem as an initial temperature approximation.

2.4   Carbon Burning

When burning carbon in white dwarfs, the main way to obtain heavy elements (such as nickel and iron) is to pass the α-network [39]. Since we are primarily interested in the explosion energy, we will consider a chain of reactions of the form $14 \times^{12}C \rightarrow 3^{56}Ni$. Let X_C be the abundance of carbon. Carbon burning may be written as [11]

$$\frac{dX_c}{dt} = -\frac{7}{36} \times \rho \times N_A \times \lambda \times X_c^2, \tag{13}$$

where ρ is the density, N_A is the Avogadro number, and λ is the reaction rate, which can be written as

$$\lambda = \frac{1.26 \times 10^{27} \times T_{9a}^{\frac{5}{6}} \times T_9^{-\frac{3}{2}} \times exp\left(-84.165 \times T_{9a}^{-\frac{1}{3}}\right)}{N_A \times \left(exp\left(-0.01 \times T_{9a}^4\right) + exp\left(1.685 \times T_{9a}^{\frac{2}{3}}\right)\right)}, \tag{14}$$

where T_9 is a temperature of 10^9 K, $T_{9a} = T_9/(1 + 0.067 \times T_9)$. The energy release is determined as follows:

$$Q = -\rho \times \varepsilon \times \frac{dX_c}{dt} = \frac{7 \times \varepsilon}{36} \times \rho \times N_A \times \lambda \times X_c^2, \tag{15}$$

where $\varepsilon = 7 \times 10^7$ Erg/g [20].

The burning rate in the above equation cannot be found with the IEEE 754 standard. Therefore, we use the following method:

$$10^{27} \times exp\left(-84.165 \times T_{9a}^{-\frac{1}{3}}\right) = exp\left(27 \times ln10 - 84.165 \times T_{9a}^{-\frac{1}{3}}\right).$$

This expression can be represented in the IEEE 754 floating point standard and used in calculations.

3   Parallel & Distributed Code

To simulate the evolution of white dwarfs, supernova explosions, and turbulent carbon burning, we will use a modification of our code published in [22,23,25]. Figure 1 shows a schematic diagram of the calculations. Nested grids are used

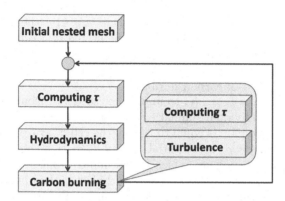

Fig. 1. Schematic diagram of Parallel & Distributed computing on nested grids (blue color) and regular grids (red color). (Color figure online)

to simulate the basic process of the evolution of white dwarfs. In the subgrid carbon burning process, the evolution of a cell where carbon burning takes place is simulated on regular grids. Note that the simulations on the nested and regular grids are performed with all MPI processes being used. The calculation algorithm is as follows:

1. Construct a workable nested grid configuration to simulate the hydrodynamics of a single dwarf or a system of white dwarfs. For this, a simulation corresponding to the simple analytics described in Sect. 2.4 can be performed on regular grids using subgrid carbon burning. This configuration is used to minimize the reconstruction of nested grids. The nested grid configuration turns out to be appropriate, and the Increase/Decrease operations with the nested grids do not require additional balancing of data loading.
2. Balance the loading of calculations on the nested grids between the MPI processes (see Sect. 3.2 for a detailed description of the balancing).
3. Determine a single time step τ_{WD} in solving the hydrodynamic equations to describe the evolution of white dwarfs on nested grids. For this, the maximum velocity v_{max} and the sound speed c_{max} are determined for all cells of the nested grids. For definiteness, let h_{min} be the minimum cell size of the nested grids, and let CFL be the Courant number. In this case, the time step is calculated from the condition

$$\frac{(v_{max} + c_{max})\,\tau_{WD}}{h_{min}} = CFL. \tag{16}$$

This method of determining the time step provides the uniqueness of the numerical solution on nested grids, since in this case the characteristics obtained from the Riemann problems on the nested grid cells do not intersect. Note that this calculation method allows using nested grids with any ratio of the neighboring cells (not only 1:2, as described in [4]).

4. Calculate the hydrodynamics of the evolution of white dwarfs in time τ_{WD} on nested grids (see Sect. 3.2 for a detailed description of the calculation).

5. Define nested grid cells (i, j, k, l, m, n), where (i, j, k) is the number of a root grid cell, and (l, m, n) is the number of the nested grid cell (i, j, k); in these cells there is a carbon burning trigger $T = 10^9$ K, and a density $\rho = 10^7$ g cm^{-3}. Form a list of cells R_n, $n = 1, \ldots, K$, where K is the number of cells with the real trigger of carbon burning.

6. For all cells R_n, $n = 1, \ldots, K$, to implement subgrid turbulent carbon burning, perform an individual simulation of hydrodynamic turbulence. The size of the simulated domain is equal to that of the cell h_n, τ_{WD} is the turbulence simulation time, $\rho_0 = \rho_n$ is the initial density, $T_0 = T_n$ is the temperature, and σ_n^2 is the velocity dispersion, which is determined from the neighboring cells (see Sect. 3.1 for a detailed deception of turbulent carbon burning). All problems of turbulent burning are simulated sequentially on a regular grid using all MPI processes. The percentage of burned carbon and the released energy are returned to the corresponding cell of the nested grids (i, j, k, l, m, n). The calculation of the hydrodynamic equations on regular grids is described in detail in [25].

Such an organization of calculations naturally requires great computational costs, since a single problem of hydrodynamic turbulence is calculated in a large number of cells. Note that the calculation time needed for turbulence problems is two orders of magnitude greater than that for the hydrodynamics of the evolution of white dwarfs. Therefore, the speedup and scalability of Parallel & Distributed computing are determined by the source code and coincide with those obtained in [25]. Section 3.3 presents the estimates of the efficiency of a code modification for the calculation on nested grids.

3.1   Turbulence Model of Carbon Burning

When the temperature in the cell reaches a critical value, $T = 10^9$ K, and the density $\rho = 10^7$ g cm^{-3}, distributed calculations of the hydrodynamic turbulence of carbon burning are launched on a regular mesh, and the results are returned to the main calculation of hydrodynamics. Carbon burning during the development of turbulence [7] and in the process of a collapse [27] are considered by many authors. We propose a method when turbulent carbon burning takes place "on the fly" when calculating the basic hydrodynamics of the process. In [26], we study in detail the development of hydrodynamic turbulence with and without self-gravity forces. In the present paper, gravitation is neglected, since the characteristic time of the process is much less than the free fall time. However, if necessary, we can take into account the collapse process (as in [27]) or self-gravity forces in the development of hydrodynamic turbulence [26].

The critical density $\rho = 10^7$ g cm^{-3} of the transition from deflagration to detonation is taken as a characteristic density value, and the temperature $T = 10^9$ K. The initial velocity perturbation at a known turbulence energy, σ^2, is taken from [1]. Let us describe this procedure in detail. Consider the energy spectrum $E(k) = A \times k^{-5/3}$ with the known turbulence energy, σ^2. Then the coefficient A can be found from the equation

$$\int_{k_{min}}^{k_{max}} E(k)dk = \sigma^2, \qquad (17)$$

where k_{min} and k_{max} are the minimum and maximum wave numbers, respectively. The turbulent pulsation field $\mathbf{u}(x)$, where x is a space point, is given by the equation

$$\mathbf{u}(x) = \frac{3\sigma}{\sqrt{2N}} \sum_{n=1}^{N} \mathbf{u}_n(x), \qquad (18)$$

where N is the number of harmonics. Each of the harmonics is given by the equation

$$\mathbf{u}_n(x) = Q(w^n)\left[\xi^n sin(k_n(w^n, x)) + \eta^n cos(k_n(w^n, x))\right], \qquad (19)$$

where $w^n = (w_1^n, w_2^n, w_3^n)$ is the unit vector uniformly distributed over the sphere to provide $\nabla \cdot \mathbf{u} = 0$, $Q(w^n)$ is a random matrix with elements $q_{ij}^n = \delta_{ij} - w_i^n \times w_j^n$, δ_{ij} is the Kronecker symbol, the coefficients ξ^n and η^n have the standard Gaussian distribution $N(0,1)$. The wave numbers k_n are distributed with the density $\rho(k) = E(k)/\sigma^2$.

The model of subgrid carbon burning based on turbulent burning being used exactly corresponds to the model described in [10]. The main difference is as follows: the process of subgrid turbulence starts when the critical temperature of carbon burning is reached. This is primarily due to computational aspects. In the present paper, the critical temperature is used to start the burning process, and the "turbulization" of the medium increases the efficiency of burning. In [10], a temperature starting from $T = 10^8$ K is considered, and the use of such an initial temperature is mainly motivated by the reproduction of the initial burning front. In our study, we use the energy component where the kinetic energy of turbulence transforms to the internal energy and becomes an additional trigger for carbon burning intensification and, hence, for obtaining more explosion energy with less fuel consumption. In this way we demonstrate a possible SNeIa explosion scenario at masses smaller than the Chandrasekhar mass.

3.2 Nested Grid

To discretize with nested grids, we introduce, in a three-dimensional solution domain, a uniform cubic root grid with the coordinates of the centers of cells $x_i = i \times h - h/2$, $i = 1, .., I_{max}$, $y_k = k \times h - h/2$, $k = 1, .., K_{max}$, $z_l = l \times h - h/2$, $l = 1, .., L_{max}$, where h is the root grid spacing, $I_{max}, K_{max}, L_{max}$ is the number of cells in the x, y, z directions, respectively. In this implementation, for the convenience of organizing calculations and without loss of generality of the code, we use $I_{max} = K_{max} = L_{max} = N$. In a cell (i, k, l), we introduce a nested cubic grid with the coordinates of the centers of cells $x_{i,nested} = i \times h_{nested} - h_{nested}/2$, $i = 1, .., M$, $y_{k,nested} = k \times h_{nested} - h_{nested}/2$, $k = 1, .., M$, $z_{l,nested} = l \times h_{nested} - h_{nested}/2$, $l = 1, .., M$, where h_{nested} is the nested grid spacing, and M is the number of nested grid cells in the x, y, z directions. The hydrodynamic equations will be calculated for quantities in the cells of the root and nested grids. A detailed arrangement of the hydrodynamic quantities in the calculations is shown in Fig. 2. Solving the equations of hydrodynamics (finding solutions to the Riemann problems) consists of the following two steps:

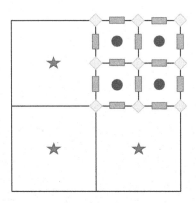

Fig. 2. Arrangement of hydrodynamic quantities on the root and nested grids: the hydrodynamic parameters on the root grid (blue asterisks), the hydrodynamic parameters on the nested grid (red circles), nested grid nodes (yellow rhombuses), the Riemann problem solution at the interfaces between the internal cells of the nested grid, the intraboundary cells of the nested grid, and the cells of the neighboring root cell (green rectangles). (Color figure online)

1. solving the Riemann problems at all nested grid boundaries,
2. solving the Riemann problems at all internal nested grid interfaces.

Whereas the second step of finding solutions to the Riemann problems is trivial, the first step requires a specific method of calculations depending on the cell sizes of two neighboring nested grids. Only three types of arrangement of the cells of neighboring grids are possible (see Fig. 3). If the cell sizes are equal (Fig. 3 (middle)), the solution of the Riemann problem is similar to that of the Riemann problems at the internal interfaces of the nested grid, and is trivial. If the cell of the neighboring nested grid is larger than the one being considered (Fig. 3 (left)), it is assumed that the quantities in the blue cell have a uniform distribution,

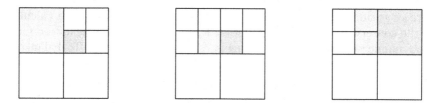

Fig. 3. Three types of arrangement of the cells of neighboring nested grids: a cell for which the Riemann problem is solved (pink color), and a cell of the neighboring nested grid (blue color) (Color figure online)

and the Riemann problem is solved at the interface between the decreased blue cell and the pink cell. If the pink cell borders on several cells of the neighboring nested grid (Fig. 3 (right)), a uniform distribution of the hydrodynamic quantities in the pink cell is assumed, the Riemann problems are solved at all interfaces, and then the fluxes are averaged. The grid is restructured according to the root cell mass. The size of the nested grid is calculated from the condition

$$M = 2^{\mathcal{C}_1 \lfloor log(\rho) \rfloor + \mathcal{C}_2}, \tag{20}$$

where $\mathcal{C}_{1,2}$ are the scaling constants chosen according to the requirements of the characteristic density and the minimum resolution of the problem. We use $\mathcal{C}_1 = 1$ and $\mathcal{C}_2 = 5$ as characteristic parameters in this work, i.e., at the characteristic carbon combustion density $\rho = 10^7$ g cm^{-3}, a grid with an effective resolution of 4096^3 is used. At each time step, it is checked whether the grid needs to be restructured. Therefore, the grid is changed not more than by a factor of two. The grid restructuring scheme is shown in Fig. 4. Figure 4 illustrates the projections of the conservative quantities (density, angular momentum, entropy density, and total energy). Once the grid is restructured, the nonconservative

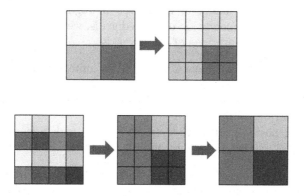

Fig. 4. Refinement (top) and coarsening (bottom) of the nested grid

quantities (primitive in the case of relativistic hydrodynamics) are calculated from the conservative variables. A detailed description of the calculation for the hydrodynamic equations in nested grids can be found in [24]. To balance the load between the processes, we use the following algorithm performed by all MPI processes (P processes in total) located on individual nodes:

1. Calculate the number of nested grid cells in each slice (YZ plane) of the root grid W_i, where $i = 1, \ldots, N$ and N is the number of root grid cells in the X-direction.
2. Determine the average number of cells in the slice for the entire root grid $M = \sum W_i/P$, and distribute this value as evenly as possible between the processes.
3. Set $k = 1$, where k is the number of the process for which the slice thickness is formed.
4. Set $i = 1$, where $1 \le i \le N$ is the number of the slice.
5. Set $N_k = 0$, where N_k is the slice thickness of the kth process.
6. If $N_k + W_i > M$, N_k is the final slice thickness for the processor k. Increase k by unity and go to step 5. Otherwise, go to step 7.
7. Increase the slice thickness N_k by W_i, increase the number of the slice i by unity and go to step 6.

As a result, the slice thicknesses between the processes differ by no more than unity. To perform the boundary layer exchange between the overlapping nested grids, a plan of overlapping YZ planes for nested grids is formed.

3.3 Performance

To perform calculations and computational experiments, we use a hybrid super-computer, NKS-1P of the Siberian Supercomputer Center at ICM & MG SB RAS (16 nodes, RSC Tornado Phi architecture: Intel Xeon Phi 7290 1.5 GHz, 72 cores, 16 GB MCDRAM; 96 GB DDR4 DRAM; Intel Omni Path 100 Gb/s interconnect). The performance of the solver on regular grids is estimated in [25]. In the parallel implementation on nested grids, we use a 128^3 root grid and the following three configurations of nested grids:

1. Config 1: All nested grids have a size of 4^3 (a uniform grid with an effective resolution of 512^3).
2. Config 2: 75% of nested grids have a size of 2^3, and 25% have a size of 8^3 (the effective resolution is 1024^3).
3. Config 3: 75% nested grids have a size of 2^3, 15% have a size of 8^3, and 10% have a size of 32^3 (the effective resolution is 4096^3).

The code speedup for some nested grid configurations is presented in Table 1. At a uniform distribution of calculations, we have a 38-fold code speedup; less uniform calculations drop the speedup to 34-fold, which is achieved with fewer

Table 1. Speedup.

Threads	Config 1	Config 2	Config 3
1	1.0	1.0	1.0
2	1.9	1.9	1.9
4	3.9	3.9	3.8
8	7.9	7.9	7.8
12	11.6	11.6	11.8
16	15.7	15.5	15.7
24	21.2	22.9	22.3
32	25.4	28.0	25.6
48	30.7	37.6	34.9
64	33.1	32.5	33.6
96	38.2	27.1	32.3
128	33.6	26.2	31.1

threads. In a study of scalability when the grid configuration is doubled for a given number of processes, it is found that the scalability corresponds to the source code one and is about 96% with 16 Intel Xeon Phi 7290 accelerators.

4   Numerical Simulation of SNeIa Explosion

Here we consider two components of the problem of type Ia supernova explosion: turbulent carbon burning and an experimental study of the energy released at various perturbations, and the hydrodynamics of SNeIa explosion.

4.1   Turbulence Carbon Burning

To study various regimes of turbulent carbon burning, we will consider a $100\,\mathrm{km}^3$ domain with the density $\rho = 10^7$ g cm^{-3} and the temperature $T = 10^9$ K with a normal velocity distribution and a Mach number of the root-mean-square deviation $\mathcal{M}_{RMS}$. The characteristic density corresponding to the density of the transition from deflagration to detonation in carbon burning is taken according to [14, 30, 45]. Figure 5 presents the results of simulation: the relative increase in the explosion energy versus the Mach number of the root-mean-square deviation $\mathcal{M}_{RMS}$. One can see in Fig. 5 that in considerable supersonic turbulence, the explosion energy can have a relative increase of more than three times. In the present paper, the question of whether such a turbulence regime can be achieved in the merging of white dwarfs is not considered. In what follows, we will study how the explosion energy affects the explosion hydrodynamics pattern. This issue has been actively studied recently, for instance, in [2, 29]. The simulation with all the resources of the Siberian Supercomputer Center (16 Intel Xeon Phi 7290 and 72 physical cores in an accelerator on a regular 256^3 calculation grid) is about 10 min.

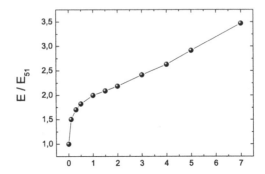

Fig. 5. Relative increase in the explosion energy versus Mach number of the root-mean-square deviation $\mathcal{M}_{RMS}$. The basic explosion energy corresponds to an energy release of 10^{51} Erg.

When simulating an SNeIa explosion on the basis of the merging of white dwarfs and the asymmetric explosion of a single dwarf, the typical time step, τ_{WD}, is 10 ms. Thus, the typical calculation time of the next two problems using the approach with the direct simulation of turbulent carbon burning is about one week. As mentioned earlier, the major computational load is the reproduction of turbulent carbon burning as an individual problem. In a series of experiments, we consider the turbulent combustion of carbon at various perturbation velocity dispersions. The kinetic energy obtained from the nonzero dispersion of perturbation velocities is converted into the internal energy and, as a result, into a more intense mode of carbon combustion, which gives a greater energy yield compared to static combustion used in classical methods for specifying subgrid processes. In further calculations, we use this problem as a component for describing the subgrid process of carbon combustion.

4.2   Hydrodynamics of SNeIa Explosion

We identified 11 possible scenarios (see Fig. 6) of a supernova explosion, which differ in the hydrodynamics of the process:

1. The merger of white dwarfs [15] is the classical scenario of a merger of two white dwarfs with the achievement of a mass greater than the mass of Chandrasekhar and the subsequent explosion of a type Ia supernova (see Fig. 6I).
2. The off-center collision of white dwarfs [37] is a collision of two white dwarfs of arbitrary masses moving in parabolic orbits. The high kinetic energy and, therefore, the interaction energy lead to the launch of the nuclear combustion of the material of white dwarfs, followed by a type Ia supernova explosion (see Fig. 6II).
3. The central collision of white dwarfs [38] is a degenerate scenario of a high-velocity collision of two white dwarfs, followed by a type Ia supernova explosion (see Fig. 6III).

4. The close passage of white dwarfs [28] is a motion of white dwarfs along parabolic trajectories without collision. The high speed of movement prevents the dwarfs from entering the merge mode (see Fig. 6IV).

5. The forced fusion of white dwarfs of equal [34] and different masses [40] is a merger of white dwarfs forced out of equilibrium due to a mass difference of 20% or the slowing down of the dwarf's velocity in a tight binary pair. Both scenarios result in dwarf fusion and Chandrasekhar mass excess, leading to a Type Ia supernova explosion (see Fig. 6V).

6. The supernova explosion based on the development of spiral instability [18, 19] is a type Ia supernova explosion based on the development of turbulence in spirals in merging white dwarfs. The development of turbulence in high-density islands that are in spirals is the main explosion mechanism [10]. A feature of such turbulent combustion can be the occurrence of any scenario of the nuclear combustion of the material: detonation model [3], deflagration model [32], delayed detonation model [21] (see Fig. 6VI).

7. Tidal heating [8] is a scenario of the explosion of a new super or new type Ia based on a combination of tidal heating, accretion heating and material nuclear burning. The location of ignition due to tidal heating is a feature of this scenario. In the case of a surface explosion, the white dwarf degenerates into a new star. When the detonation point is deep enough, an off-center explosion of a type Ia supernova occurs (see Fig. 6VII).

8. The dynamic double detonation of double degenerate dwarfs of a pre-Chandrasekhar mass or D6 [13] is a scenario of a merging of two degenerate dwarfs, one of which receives a shear momentum of the base relative to the nucleus. As a result, an instability of the Kelvin-Helmholtz type develops at the boundary between the nucleus and the shell of one of the dwarfs. Primary detonation occurs in dense waves of an unstable flow. The shock waves from waves come on the shell surface. At this moment, a second detonation, sufficient for the formation of a type Ia supernova, occurs (see Fig. 6VIII).

9. The tidal detonation of a white dwarf during the close passage of a black hole [41] is a scenario of a shell detonation of a white dwarf of an arbitrary mass and an explosion in the form of a type Ia supernova due to tidal heating caused by the close passage of a black hole. A preliminary analysis of such scenarios shows that a medium-mass black hole is sufficient (see Fig. 6IX).

10. The merger of a white dwarf with a star of main sequence [44] is another classical scenario of the merging of a white dwarf with a star of main sequence with achieving a mass greater than the Chandrasekhar mass, followed by a type Ia supernova explosion (see Fig. 6X).

11. The collision of a white dwarf type with a terrestrial planet is a hypothetical scenario of a collision of a white dwarf with a planet from the terrestrial type to a gas giant. The achieved Chandrasekhar mass and, in addition, the kinetic impulse obtained from the planet lead to a type Ia supernova explosion (see Fig. 6XI).

The consideration of these possible scenarios from the point of view of the hydrodynamics of the process can be reduced to three fundamentally different scenarios:

1. "Merger" is a scenario of stars interaction, among which three variants can also be distinguished: evolutionary merging, central and off-center collisions of stars.
2. "Gravity Shock" is a scenario with an explosion of a static or moving point of detonation. The movement of the detonation point is associated with the direction of the influence of the gravitational impact.
3. "Bubbles" is a multiple detonation when the number of detonation points can reach hundreds [9].

Next, we will demonstrate computational experiments to study these scenarios.

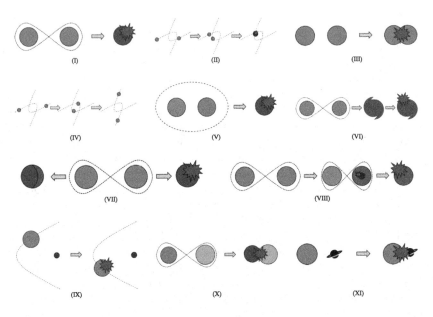

Fig. 6. SNeIa Explosion Scenarios

SNeIa Explosion Scenario Based on White Dwarf Merger. We will simulate two white dwarfs with solar masses and the temperature $T = 10^9$ K. The angular velocity of white dwarfs, v, is obtained from an analytical solution based on the following equality of the centripetal force and the force of gravity:

$$\frac{v^2}{r} = G\frac{M_\odot}{r^2},$$

where v is the equilibrium angular velocity, $M_\odot$ is the mass of dwarfs, and r is the distance between the dwarfs. The rotation speed of one of the dwarfs is decreased by 20%. This results in the merger of the white dwarfs. Figure 7 presents the simulation results: the initial state of the dwarfs, the beginning of the merging of the dwarfs, the state of the merging at the time of the explosion, and an asymmetric supernova Ia explosion. To simulate nuclear carbon burning, we use the perturbation rate obtained by simulating the hydrodynamics of the merging

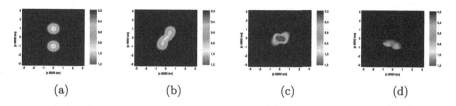

Fig. 7. Relative density distribution in the equatorial plane during the merger of white dwarfs and the subsequent type Ia supernova explosion at 0 s (a), 40 s (b), 60 s (c), and 70 s (d).

of the dwarfs. The simulation results (7) show that critical densities for starting detonation carbon burning are reached in the merger. The explosion dynamics is subsequently determined by the results of the non-center white dwarf explosion.

SNeIa Explosion Scenario Based on White Dwarf Central Collision.
We will simulate two white dwarfs with solar masses and the temperature $T = 10^9$ K. The velocity of the central collision is equal to $1000 \, \text{km s}^{-1}$. Figure 8 presents the simulation results: the initial state of the dwarfs, the beginning of the collision of the dwarfs, the late state of the collision, and an supernova Ia explosion. To simulate nuclear carbon burning, we use the perturbation rate obtained by simulating the hydrodynamics of the merging of the dwarfs. It can

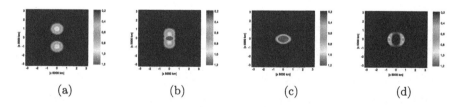

Fig. 8. Relative density distribution in the equatorial plane during the central collision of white dwarfs and the subsequent type Ia supernova explosion at 0 s (a), 20 s (b), 40 s (c), and 45 s (d).

be seen from the simulation results that after the explosion, two diverging shock fronts, similar to jets, are formed. The whole simulation in general repeats the previous scenario.

SNeIa Explosion Scenario Based on White Dwarf Non Central Collision. We will simulate two white dwarfs with solar masses and the temperature $T = 10^9$ K. The velocity of the non-central collision is equal to 1000 km s^{-1}. Figure 9 presents the simulation results: the initial state of the dwarfs, the beginning of the collision of the dwarfs, the late state of the collision, and an supernova Ia explosion. To simulate nuclear carbon burning, we use the perturbation rate obtained by simulating the hydrodynamics of the merging of the dwarfs. The whole simulation in general repeats the previous scenarios.

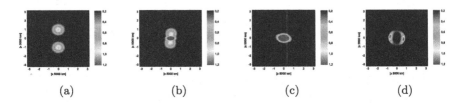

(a)   (b)   (c)   (d)

Fig. 9. Relative density distribution in the equatorial plane during the non-central collision of white dwarfs and the subsequent type Ia supernova explosion at 0 s (a), 20 s (b), 40 s (c), and 45 s (d).

Asymmetric Explosions of White Dwarfs. Let us simulate a single white dwarf with two solar masses and the temperature $T = 10^9$ K. The explosion zone is specified at a distance of 20% of the radius from the center. The explosion energy is specified with the values obtained in the previous subsection. Figure 10 presents the simulation results: the density distribution at the time when the explosion takes place in most of the star at various explosion energies. The simulation results (10) show that when the explosion force is considerable,

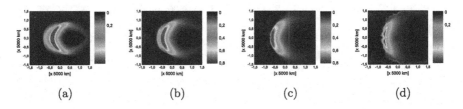

(a)   (b)   (c)   (d)

Fig. 10. Relative density distribution in the equatorial plane at explosion energy values of $1/2 \times E_0$ (a), E_0 (b), $2 \times E_0$ (c), $4 \times E_0$ (d).

the star collapses, and a thin shock wave from the supernova is formed. As the explosion energy decreases, the wave dissipates over a sufficiently large distance. It is obvious that in this case, the brightness of the supernova changes considerably depending on the carbon burning mode and the subsequent explosion energy. Increasing the explosion energy produces a hydrodynamic instability due to the presence of a small perturbation in the white dwarf density (see Fig. 10 for relative densities at one second after the explosion).

Multiply Explosions of White Dwarfs. Finally, let us simulate a single white dwarf with two solar masses and the temperature $T = 10^9$ K. The explosion zones are specified at a distance of 20% of the radius from the center and in the center. The explosion energy is specified with the values obtained in the previous subsection. Figure 11 presents the simulation results. Thanks to the numerical

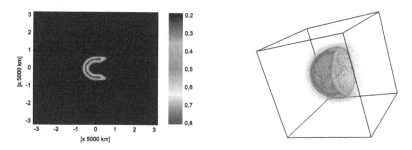

Fig. 11. Isolines (left) and isosurface (right) of the relative density distribution in 5 s.

simulation, we can see the result of the supernovae Ia explosion in the form of a "horseshoe" image.

5 Discussion

1. We do not deny the concept of "standard candles" for measuring distances in the Universe. Let us only pay attention to the fact that the energy behavior of the process of the explosion of white dwarfs in the form of supernovae with the incomplete combustion of the material is non-standard. We offer only one scenario that reveals the ambiguity of the burning process.
2. The computational model has a simple adiabatic form of the stellar equation of state. Although numerous studies of the stellar equation of state are available, we have not found any convincing arguments in favor of using more complicated coefficients of the adiabatic density function when considering the energy behavior. Maybe the model should be complicated considering the concentration distributions of the elements.
3. In our model of burning, we use the alpha process of carbon burning up to iron and nickel. The concentration distributions of the elements in supernova explosions are not considered. The major attention is given to the explosion energy with incomplete carbon burning and the non-standard character of this process.

4. To describe subgrid carbon burning, the model considered in detail in [39] is used. The advantage of this model is that it has an analytical solution for determining the energy released as a result of carbon burning. In the present paper, the chemical composition of the remnant is not considered. The chemical composition of the remnant is described in [6, 31, 33, 35, 36].

5. The main calculation time in our model of the evolution of white dwarfs and the explosion of type Ia supernovae is spent on modeling the subgrid process of carbon combustion in white dwarfs. We start such turbulent combustion at each time step in each computational cell of nested grids used to simulate the hydrodynamics of white dwarfs, provided that the required values of temperature and density in the cells are reached. In fact, at each time step, we run a fairly large number of full-fledged hydrodynamic calculations using a regular grid on the time step of white dwarf hydrodynamics. For the calculation, we use the already developed parallel code computing infrastructure from [25]. The calculations of the hydrodynamics of white dwarfs take negligible time and are reduced by the use of nested grids. In connection with this way of organizing calculations, we do not consider scalability studies on regular grids (they are described in detail in [25]), but we present scalability results only for nested grids.

6. It is known that the classical SNeIa supernova scenario is based on the merger of white dwarfs, reaching the mass of Chandrasekhar, the start of the thermonuclear combustion of carbon, and the subsequent supernova explosion with the almost complete combustion of the material. Professor A.V. Tutukov proposed a hypothesis about the possibility of an explosion of SNeIa during the combustion of a mass smaller than the mass of Chandrasekhar, which led to the formation of many scenarios described in this article. The key point, in our opinion, is related to the more intense combustion of the white dwarf material. To describe such combustion, we propose the subgrid carbon combustion apparatus in the form of an independent hydrodynamic problem of turbulence development.

6   Conclusions

In this paper, a non-standard mechanism of carbon burning in type Ia supernova explosions is proposed. The mechanism is based on intensity variations in the nuclear burning of carbon during its incomplete combustion. In this case, the explosion energy can vary significantly due to the presence of different regimes of carbon burning during the development of turbulence in the burning zone. The energy released during burning, sufficient for the explosion of a white dwarf (as a type Ia supernova), can be achieved with a mass smaller than the Chandrasekhar mass. In addition, the explosion energy of a white dwarf with a Chandrasekhar mass can differ considerably.

Acknowledgements. This work was supported by the Russian Science Foundation (project 18-11-00044) https://rscf.ru/project/18-11-00044/.

References

1. Alexandrov, A.V., Dorodnicyn, L.W., Duben, A.P.: Generation of three-dimensional homogeneous isotropic turbulent velocity fields using the randomized spectral method. Math. Models Comput. Simul. **12**(3), 388–396 (2020). https://doi.org/10.1134/S2070048220030047

2. Antoniadis, J., Chanlaridis, S., Graefener, G., Langer, N.: Type Ia supernovae from non-accreting progenitors. Astron. Astrophys. **635**, Article Number A72 (2020). https://doi.org/10.1051/0004-6361/201936991

3. Arnett, W.: A possible model of supernovae: detonation of ^{12}C. Astrophys. Space Sci. **5**, 180–212 (1969). https://doi.org/10.1007/BF00650291

4. Berger, M.J., Colella, P.: Local adaptive mesh refinement for shock hydrodynamics. J. Comput. Phys. **82**, 64–84 (1989). https://doi.org/10.1016/0021-9991(89)90035-1

5. Bulla, M., Liu, Z.W., Roepke, F.K., et al.: White dwarf deflagrations for Type Iax supernovae: polarisation signatures from the explosion and companion interaction. Astron. Astrophys. **635**, Article Number A179 (2020). https://doi.org/10.1051/0004-6361/201937245

6. Calder, A.C., Krueger, B.K., Jackson, A.P., Townsley, D.M.: The influence of chemical composition on models of Type Ia supernovae. Front. Phys. **8**, 168–188 (2013). https://doi.org/10.1007/s11467-013-0301-4

7. Cristini, A., Meakin, C., Hirschi, R., et al.: 3D hydrodynamic simulations of carbon burning in massive stars. Mon. Not. R. Astron. Soc. **471**, 279–300 (2017). https://doi.org/10.1093/mnras/stx1535

8. Fenn, D., Plewa, T., Gawryszczak, A.: No double detonations but core carbon ignitions in high-resolution, grid-based simulations of binary white dwarf mergers. Mon. Not. R. Astron. Soc. **462**, 2486–2505 (2016). https://doi.org/10.1093/mnras/stw1831

9. Ferrand, G., Warren, D., Ono, M., et al.: From supernova to supernova remnant: comparison of thermonuclear explosion models. Astrophys. J. **906**, Article Number 93 (2021). https://doi.org/10.3847/1538-4357/abc951

10. Fisher, R., Mozumdar, P., Casabona, G.: Carbon detonation initiation in turbulent electron-degenerate matter. Astrophys. J. **876**, Article Number 64 (2019). https://doi.org/10.3847/1538-4357/ab15d8

11. Fowler, W.A., Caughlan, G.R., Zimmermann, B.A.: Thermonuclear reaction rates, II. Ann. Rev. Astron. Astrophys. **13**, 69–112 (1975). https://doi.org/10.1146/annurev.aa.13.090175.000441

12. Gronow, S., Collins, C., Ohlmann, S.T., et al.: SNe Ia from double detonations: impact of core-shell mixing on the carbon ignition mechanism. Astron. Astrophys. **635**, Article Number A169 (2020). https://doi.org/10.1051/0004-6361/201936494

13. Guillochon, J., Dan, M., Ramirez-Ruiz, E., Rosswog, S.: Surface detonations in double degenerate binary systems triggered by accretion stream instabilities. Astrophys. J. Lett. **709**, L64–L69 (2010). https://doi.org/10.1088/2041-8205/709/1/L64
14. Golombek, I., Niemeyer, J.: A model for multidimensional delayed detonations in SN Ia explosions. Astron. Astrophys. **438**, 611–616 (2005). https://doi.org/10.1051/0004-6361:20042402
15. Iben, I., Jr., Tutukov, A.: Supernovae of type I as end products of the evolution of binaries with components of moderate initial mass ($M \leq M_\odot$). Astrophys. J. Suppl. Ser. **54**, 335–372 (1984). https://doi.org/10.1086/190932
16. Iben, I., Jr., Tutukov, A., Fedorova, A.: On the luminosity of white dwarfs in close binaries merging under the influence of gravitational wave radiation. Astrophys. J. **503**, 344–349 (1998). https://doi.org/10.1086/305972
17. Iben, I., Tutukov, A.: On the evolution of close triple stars that produce type Ia supernovae. Astrophys. J. **511**, 324–334 (1999). https://doi.org/10.1086/306672
18. Kashyap, R., Fisher, R., Garcia-Berro, E., et al.: Spiral instability can drive thermonuclear explosions in binary white dwarf mergers. Astrophys. J. Lett. **800**, Article Number L7 (2015). https://doi.org/10.1088/2041-8205/800/1/L7
19. Kashyap, R., Fisher, R., Garcia-Berro, E., et al.: One-armed spiral instability in double-degenerate post-merger accretion disks. Astrophys. J. **840**, Article Number 16 (2017). https://doi.org/10.3847/1538-4357/aa6afb
20. Khokhlov, A.: Thermonuclear burning and the explosion of degenerate matter in supernovae. Soviet Scientific Reviews. Section E, Astrophysics and Space Physics Reviews, vol. 8, pp. 1–75 (1989)
21. Khokhlov, A.M.: The structure of detonation waves in supernovae. Mon. Not. R. Astron. Soc. **239**, 785–808 (1989). https://doi.org/10.1093/mnras/239.3.785
22. Kulikov, I., Chernykh, I., Karavaev, D., Berendeev, E., Protasov, V.: HydroBox3D: parallel & distributed hydrodynamical code for numerical simulation of supernova Ia. In: Malyshkin, V. (ed.) PaCT 2019. LNCS, vol. 11657, pp. 187–198. Springer, Cham (2019). https://doi.org/10.1007/978-3-030-25636-4_15
23. Kulikov, I.M., et al.: Using adaptive nested mesh code HydroBox3D for numerical simulation of type Ia supernovae: merger of carbon-oxygen white dwarf stars, collapse, and non-central explosion. In: 2018 Ivannikov ISPRAS Open Conference (ISPRAS), Moscow, Russia, 2018, pp. 77–81 (2019). https://doi.org/10.1109/ISPRAS.2018.00018
24. Kulikov, I.: The numerical modeling of the collapse of molecular cloud on adaptive nested mesh. J. Phys. Conf. Ser. **1103**, Article Number 012011 (2018). https://doi.org/10.1088/1742-6596/1103/1/012011
25. Kulikov, I., Chernykh, I., Tutukov, A.: A New hydrodynamic code with explicit vectorization instructions optimizations that is dedicated to the numerical simulation of astrophysical gas flow. I. Numerical method, tests, and model problems. Astrophys. J. Suppl. Ser. **243**, Article Number 4 (2019). https://doi.org/10.3847/1538-4365/ab2237
26. Kulikov, I., et al.: Numerical modeling of hydrodynamic turbulence with self-gravity on Intel Xeon Phi KNL. In: Sokolinsky, L., Zymbler, M. (eds.) PCT 2019. CCIS, vol. 1063, pp. 309–322. Springer, Cham (2019). https://doi.org/10.1007/978-3-030-28163-2_22

27. Kushnir, D., Katz, B.: An accurate and efficient numerical calculation of detonation waves in multidimensional supernova simulations using a burning limiter and adaptive quasi-statistical equilibrium. Mon. Not. R. Astron. Soc. **493**, 5413–5433 (2020). https://doi.org/10.1093/mnras/staa594

28. Loren-Aguilar, P., Isern, J., Garcia-Berro, E.: Smoothed particle hydrodynamics simulations of white dwarf collisions and close encounters. Mon. Not. R. Astron. Soc. **406**, 2749–2763 (2010). https://doi.org/10.1111/j.1365-2966.2010.16878.x

29. Magee, M.R., Maguire, K., Kotak, R., Sim, S.A.: Exploring the diversity of double-detonation explosions for Type Ia supernovae: effects of the post-explosion helium shell composition. Mon. Not. R. Astron. Soc. **502**, 3533–3553 (2021). https://doi.org/10.1093/mnras/stab201

30. Niemeyer, J.: Can deflagration-detonation transitions occur in type Ia supernovae? Astrophys. J. **523**, L57–L60 (1999). https://doi.org/10.1086/312253

31. Niemeyer, J.C., Hillebrandt, W.: Turbulent nuclear flames in type Ia supernovae. Astrophys. J. **452**, 769–778 (1995). https://doi.org/10.1086/176345

32. Nomoto, K., Sugimoto, D., Neo, S.: Carbon deflagration supernova, an alternative to carbon detonation. Astrophys. Space Sci. **39**, L37–L42 (1976). https://doi.org/10.1007/BF00648354

33. Nouri, A.G., Givi, P., Livescu, D.: Modeling and simulation of turbulent nuclear flames in Type Ia supernovae. Prog. Aerosp. Sci. **108**, 156–179 (2019). https://doi.org/10.1016/j.paerosci.2019.04.004

34. Pakmor, R., Kromer, M., Roepke, F.K., et al.: Sub-luminous type Ia supernovae from the mergers of equal-mass white dwarfs with mass $\approx 0.9 M_\odot$. Nature **463**, 61–64 (2010). https://doi.org/10.1038/nature08642

35. Pfannes, J.M.M., Niemeyer, J.C., Schmidt, W., Klingenberg, C.: Thermonuclear explosions of rapidly rotating white dwarfs. I. Deflagrations. Astron. Astrophys. **509**, Article Number A74 (2010). https://doi.org/10.1051/0004-6361/200912032

36. Pfannes, J.M.M., Niemeyer, J.C., Schmidt, W.: Thermonuclear explosions of rapidly rotating white dwarfs. II. Detonations. Astron. Astrophys. **509**, Article Number A75 (2010). https://doi.org/10.1051/0004-6361/200912033

37. Raskin, C., Timmes, F.X., Scannapieco, E., Diehl, S., Fryer, C.: On Type Ia supernovae from the collisions of two white dwarfs. Mon. Not. R. Astron. Soc. **399**, L156–L159 (2009). https://doi.org/10.1111/j.1745-3933.2009.00743.x

38. Rosswog, S., Kasen, D., Guillochon, J., Ramirez-Ruiz, E.: Collisions of white dwarfs as a new progenitor channel for type Ia supernovae. Astrophys. J. **705**, L128–L132 (2009). https://doi.org/10.1088/0004-637X/705/2/L128

39. Steinmetz, M., Muller, E., Hillebrandt, W.: Carbon detonations in rapidly rotating white dwarfs. Astron. Astrophys. **254**, 177–190 (1992)

40. Tanikawa, A., Nakasato, N., Sato, Y., Nomoto, K., Maeda, K., Hachisu, I.: Hydrodynamical evolution of merging carbon-oxygen white dwarfs: their pre-supernova structure and observational counterparts. Astrophys. J. **807**, Article Number 40 (2015). https://doi.org/10.1088/0004-637X/807/1/40

41. Tanikawa, A.: High-resolution hydrodynamic simulation of tidal detonation of a helium white dwarf by an intermediate mass black hole. Astrophys. J. **858**, Article Number 26 (2018). https://doi.org/10.3847/1538-4357/aaba79

42. Timmes, F.X., Arnett, D.: The accuracy, consistency, and speed of five equations of state for stellar hydrodynamics. Astrophys. J. Suppl. Ser. **125**, 277–294 (1999). https://doi.org/10.1086/313271

43. Vshivkov, V., Lazareva, G., Snytnikov, A., Kulikov, I., Tutukov, A.: Hydrody-
    namical code for numerical simulation of the gas components of colliding galaxies.
    Astrophys. J. Suppl. Ser. **194**, Article Number 47 (2011). https://doi.org/10.1088/
    0067-0049/194/2/47
44. Whelan, J., Iben, I.: Binaries and Supernovae of Type I. Astrophys. J. **186**, 1007–
    1014 (1973)
45. Willcox, D., Townsley, D., Calder, A., Denissenkov, P., Herwig, F.: Type Ia super-
    nova explosions from hybrid carbon - oxygen - neon white dwarf progenitors. Astro-
    phys. J. **832**, Article Number 13 (2016). https://doi.org/10.3847/0004-637X/832/
    1/13

Parallel Simulations of Dynamic Interaction Between Train Pantographs and an Overhead Catenary Line

Evgeny Kudryashov[1]([⊠]) and Natalia Melnikova[2]([⊠])

[1] Universal Catenary Systems, St. Petersburg, Russia
kev@uks.ru
[2] Peter the Great St. Petersburg Polytechnic University, Saint Petersburg, Russia
naunat@mail.ru

Abstract. The paper describes a computational model and an original software system, UKS-Dynamic, for the analysis of dynamic interaction between train pantographs and an overhead catenary system at high-speed railway lines. The study focuses on the problem of reducing non-physical high-frequency oscillations arising in dynamic simulations due to the spatial discretization of flexible wires of the catenary. A number of model problems are solved both analytically and numerically, and the quality of high-frequency mode suppression is studied for several suppression techniques, including specific time integrators (beta-Newmark and generalized-alpha methods) and Rayleigh damping. The model is validated against the solutions of etalon problems given by the EN 50318:2018 standard for alternating and direct current catenary lines at a train speed of 320 km/h. Code parallelization employs the OpenMP library; the code profiling results are presented for both serial and parallel implementations.

Keywords: Overhead catenary line · Dynamic simulation · High-frequency oscillation suppression

1 Introduction

In the design of overhead contact lines for high-speed railway tracks, it is important to ensure a high quality of electric current collection. The analysis of the current collection quality requires a realistic simulation of the dynamic contact between train pantographs and contact wires. These contact interactions are influenced by the elastic waves propagating in the catenary system. At train speed values of 350–400 km/h, high-frequency oscillations can physically emerge in the catenary. On the other hand, the finite element models of catenaries also spawn non-physical high-frequency oscillation modes that occur due to the space discretization of continuous elastic wires. These non-physical high-frequency modes can be withdrawn from the solution using different suppression techniques, such as specific time integrators (beta-Newmark and generalized-alpha methods), Rayleigh damping and output filtering.

L. Sokolinsky and M. Zymbler (Eds.): PCT 2022, CCIS 1618, pp. 233–247, 2022.
https://doi.org/10.1007/978-3-031-11623-0_16

The goals of this study are: (a) to analyze dynamic processes occurring in the catenary system by solving a number of analytical model problems; (b) to test the quality of numerical time integrators on model problems; (c) to examine high-frequency suppression techniques for the degree of dissipation. After considering the model problems, we switch to real-life catenaries and demonstrate the validation of the presented computational model against the etalon problem solution from [1].

The UKS computational system for the design of railway overhead catenary lines (OHL) has been being developed by the team of Universal Catenary Systems Co. and researchers from St. Petersburg Polytechnic University over the past twenty years [2,3]. Computational models involved in OHL dynamics simulations are constantly upgraded in accordance with the international standards developed by the European Committee for Electrotechnical Standardization [1]. To the authors' knowledge, the described computational package is the only domestic professional software used at the industrial level and supporting all stages of the OCL design, from the initial scratch to the final technical documentation albums for railway construction and maintenance staff.

The functionality of the software system includes:

- UKS-Static module for the non-linear static finite element analyses of catenary lines, trusses and frames with large nodal displacements;
- UKS-Dynamic module for the linear dynamic finite element analyses of catenary lines, including near real-time simulations of contact interaction between pantographs and the catenary;
- statistical analysis of the simulation output (mean value, standard deviation calculation);
- spectral analysis of the simulation output;
- output signal filtering;
- GUI pre- and post-processing modules: integration with AutoCAD, production of design documentation, visualization of simulation results.

The presented computational system was successfully applied for designing overhead catenary lines at high-speed railway lines, including the Moscow—St. Petersburg 250 km/h line (currently in operation), the Moscow—St. Petersburg 400 km/h line (under construction) and the Moscow—Kazan 400 km/h line (design stage competed, construction suspended).

The rest of the paper is organized as follows: Sect. 2 describes the mathematical models employed in the design of catenary lines; in Sect. 3, model problems are stated; Sect. 4 describes the numerical time integration schemes employed in the analyses (namely, beta-Newmark and generalized alpha method families); Sect. 5 outlines the features of the numerical implementation; in Sect. 6, the simulation results are presented, and the quality of high-frequency suppression is analyzed both for model problems and one etalon problem from the EN 50318:2018 standard [1] for a train speed of 320 km/h; Sect. 7 describes the OpenMP parallelization of the code and presents the code profiling results.

2   Mathematical Models

2.1   Catenary Line Model

A schematic view of a section of the overhead catenary line is shown in Fig. 1:
the messenger wire and the contact wire are supported by cantilevers, which
are, in turn, mounted to supports. The contact wire is fixed by the cantilevers'
steady arms and droppers mounted between the contact wire and the messenger
wire.

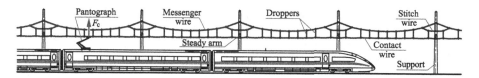

Fig. 1. Catenary line with supporting elements (supports, cantilevers and fixation
arms)

In the presented model, catenary wires (contact and messenger wires and
droppers) are simulated as ideally flexible threads using finite elements of "link"
type with the account for unloading (folding) under a negative axial force.
Supporting constructions (rotating cantilevers and fixation arms) are modeled
as truss elements connected to catenary wires. Supporting constructions are
included in the model to take into account their response (for example, at rotation) on the position and tension of catenary wires.

2.2   Non-linear Static Analysis

The wires of the catenary line are modeled as elastic, pre-tensioned, ideally flexible threads. At the first simulation stage, the static configuration of the catenary
line under the action of gravity, pre-tension and static pressure from pantographs
is determined. Static analysis takes into account the actual configuration of the
catenary under the acting loads ("large displacements" analysis). The 3D displacement field of each wire in the catenary is described in the local coordinate
system (which is attached to the reference configuration of the wire) by the
following equations:

$$\begin{cases} H(u', v', w')\frac{d^2v'}{dx'^2} + q'(x') = 0 \\ H(u', v', w')\frac{d^2w'}{dx'^2} + p'(x') = 0 \\ ES\frac{d^2u'}{dx'^2} + \tau'(x') = 0, \end{cases} \tag{1}$$

where x' is the axial coordinate in the local basis, $v(x')$, $w(x')$ are the transversal
displacements, $u(x')$ is the axial displacement, ES is the axial stiffness of the
wire, $H(x')$ is the axial force, $q'(x')$, $p'(x')$ are the transversal distributed loads,
$\tau'(x')$ is the axial distributed load.

After the finite element discretization of 1 and the transformation of element matrices to the global coordinates, the resulting system of nonlinear algebraic equations is written as:

$$K(U)U = F_{\text{ext}}, \tag{2}$$

where U is the vector of nodal displacements measured from the reference (unloaded) configuration, $K(U)$ is the stiffness matrix and F_{ext} is the vector of external nodal loads.

System 2 is solved using the fixed-point iteration method with the relaxation factor $r \in (0; 1]$. The ith iteration of the method is written as follows:

$$K(U_{i-1})\Delta U_i = r(F_{\text{ext}} - K(U_{i-1})U_{i-1}), \quad U_i = U_{i-1} + \Delta U_i.$$

2.3 Dynamic Analysis

In dynamic analysis, small oscillations of the wires around their static configuration are considered. In the local coordinate system, the oscillations of each wire are modeled with the following equations:

$$\begin{cases} m\frac{\partial^2 v'}{\partial t^2} + 2D\frac{\partial v'}{\partial t} - H_{\text{static}}(x')\frac{\partial^2 v'}{\partial x'^2} = q'(x', t') \\ m\frac{\partial^2 w'}{\partial t^2} + 2D\frac{\partial w'}{\partial t} - H_{\text{static}}(x')\frac{\partial^2 w'}{\partial x'^2} = p'(x', t') \\ m\frac{\partial^2 u'}{\partial t^2} + 2D\frac{\partial u'}{\partial t} - ES\frac{\partial^2 u'}{\partial x'^2} = \tau'(x', t), \end{cases} \tag{3}$$

where m is the mass per unit length, g is the gravity acceleration, $H_{\text{static}}(x)$ is the axial tension force obtained from static analysis, D is the viscous damping coefficient.

In the finite element formulation, a linear ODE system is solved:

$$M\ddot{U} + B\dot{U} + KU = F_{\text{ext}}(t). \tag{4}$$

Here M is the mass matrix, B is the damping matrix. The constant stiffness matrix K is computed in the reference configuration obtained from static analysis 2.

During time integration, the tensions in the droppers are checked; in the case of dropper unloading, the stiffness matrix is corrected, and the time step is repeated until the stiffness matrix is stabilized (see [2] for more details).

Supporting elements (such as fixation arms or cantilevers) are modeled as visco-elastic nodal supports at this stage.

The EN 50318:2018 standard [1] does not require using any specific structural damping model; the standard requires that the damping of the overhead contact line is adjusted to a non-dimensional damping rate (ratio of damping vs. critical damping) of 0.1% to 0.15% for the overhead contact line. The standard recommends using Rayleigh damping in the discretized (finite element) model:

$$B = \alpha M + \beta K, \quad \alpha = 1.25 \cdot 10^2 \text{ s}^{-1}, \quad \beta = 10^{-4} \text{ s}. \tag{5}$$

The Rayleigh damping model [4] was originally proposed to the mimic internal damping of materials in structures. However, it does not agree with nature experiments [5]: material damping does not tend to depend on the frequency [5]. Nevertheless, the Rayleigh damping model can be useful for suppressing artificial high-frequency oscillations arising in the numerical solution due to the distortion of the frequency characteristics of a continuous elastic body after spatial discretization.

In the Rayleigh model, the damping ratio ζ depends on the mode frequency ω as follows [4]:

$$\zeta = \frac{n}{\omega} = \frac{1}{2}\left(\frac{\alpha}{\omega} + \beta\omega\right),$$ (6)

where n is the decay ratio. The first natural frequency of the catenary line is typically 1 Hz. The substitution of $\omega = 2\pi \times 1$ Hz and 5 into 6 gives the damping ratio $\zeta = 0.0013$.

2.4 Pantograph Model. Contact Interaction Between Pantographs and the Contact Wire

Pantographs are modeled as discrete systems containing two or three lumped masses connected with elastic springs, dry friction elements and viscous dampers as shown in Fig. 2.

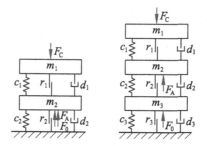

Fig. 2. Two-mass and three-mass pantograph models

In Fig. 2, the vectors F_A and F_0 are the aerodynamic lift force and static push force, correspondingly, and the vector F_C is the force of contact interaction between the contact wire and the pantograph.

Contact interaction between the pantograph and the contact wire is modeled with the penalty method [6]: a restoring force proportional to the value of the mutual penetration of the pantograph and the CW is applied to the contact wire in order to eliminate the penetration of the contacting parts. More details on applying the method to the UKS-dynamic model can be found in [2].

3   Model Problems Setup

In the model problems, small transversal oscillations of an ideally flexible pre-tensioned wire are modeled using Eqs. 3–4. In problems 1 and 2, the oscillations are free (the only load is gravity). In the 3rd problem, the oscillations are driven by the moving force of the constant magnitude. The pretension value and all characteristics of the wire (see Table 1) represent a real-life contact wire. The length of the wire $L = 50$ m is a typical railway span length.

Table 1. Parameters of the model problems

Parameter	Value
Span length L	50 m
Pretension T	20 kN
Mass per unit length m	1 kg/m
Viscous damping coefficient $2D/m$	0.010185342 s^{-1}
Disturbing force F in problem 1	10 N
Impact impulse S in problem 2	25 kg · m/s
Moving force F magnitude in problem 3	110 N
Moving force velocity V in problem 3	135 m/s

Due to the lack of space, we omit the expressions for analytical and semi-analytical solutions of the model problems; however, the curves representing these solutions are presented in the Results section.

3.1 Problems 1,2: Free Oscillations Excited Statically and Dynamically (by Impact Interaction)

In problem 1, free oscillations of the wire are excited in a static way: at $x = L/2$, a lumped force is applied (quasi-statically) and then released at $t = 0$ s. In problem 2, free oscillations are excited by impact interaction: at $x = L/2$, the impulse $s = M \cdot V_0$ is applied at $t = 0$ s.

3.2 Problem 3: Oscillations Driven by a Constant Push Force Moving Along the Span

In problem 3, driven oscillations of the wire are excited by the vertical force F moving with the constant speed V along the span. In this case, the critical (resonance) speed of the load V_{cr} equals to the speed of the wave propagation c along the span: $V_{cr} = c$, where $c = \sqrt{\frac{T}{m}} = 141$ m/s.

4 Numerical Time-Integration Methods

The time-integration schemes implemented and tested in the current study include Newmark-beta schemes [8] and the generalized alpha-method [9]. All used methods are absolutely stable, implicit and have the 2nd order of precision except for the 1st order Newmark-beta scheme with $\beta = 0.3025$, $\gamma = 0.6$.

Designed for Hamiltonian systems, the methods significantly differ in computational complexity, internal dissipation and wave dispersion. We performed a comparative study of these methods to estimate the quality of numerical solutions in catenary line dynamics simulations.

The generalized alpha-method for numerical time integration [9] was proposed for suppressing non-physical high-frequency oscillations occurring in numerical solutions due to spatial discretization. The method is described with the following formulas:

$$\begin{cases} (1 - \alpha_m)MA_{n+1} + \alpha_m MA_n = \alpha_f F_n + (1 - \alpha_f)F_{n+1} \\ \frac{U_{n+1}-U_n}{\tau} = V_n + \tau(\frac{1}{2} - \beta)A_n + \tau\beta A_{n+1} \\ \frac{V_{n+1}-V_n}{\tau} = (1 - \gamma)A_n + \gamma A_{n+1}, \end{cases} \qquad (7)$$

where $n + 1$ is the current time layer number, τ is the time integration step, U, V, A are the arrays of nodal displacements, velocities and accelerations, correspondingly, and α_m, α_f, β, γ are the parameters of the method. The parameters α_m, α_f were calculated depending on the desired dissipation of high frequencies using the formula proposed in [9]:

$$\alpha_m = \frac{2\rho_\infty - 1}{\rho_\infty + 1}, \quad \alpha_f = \frac{\rho_\infty}{\rho_\infty + 1}, \quad \beta = \frac{1}{4}(\gamma + \frac{1}{2})^2, \quad \gamma = \frac{1}{2} + \alpha_f - \alpha_m, \qquad (8)$$

where $\rho_\infty = \lim_{\omega \to \infty} \rho$, ρ is the spectral radius of the transfer matrix of the method.

The generalized alpha methods defined by formulae 7–8 are absolutely stable and have the second order of precision [9]. The values $\rho_\infty = 0$ and $\rho_\infty = 0$ correspond to the total and zero dissipation of the method at high frequencies, correspondingly. Imposing $\alpha_m = \alpha_f = 0$ in 7 produces the family of beta-Newmark methods. In this study, the absolutely stable implicit first order beta-Newmark scheme with $\beta = 0.3025$, $\gamma = 0.6$ and the second order trapezoidal rule with $\beta = 0.25$, $\gamma = 0.5$ were tested. In all time integration schemes, the time step was chosen so that the Courant number [10] equaled 0.5. The maximal finite element length varied between 10 cm and 25 cm.

5   Software Implementation

The software system basically consists of two modules, UKS-Static and UKS-Dynamic, aimed for the static and dynamic analyses of mechanical interactions between train pantographs and an overhead catenary line. The computational core of the system is implemented in Fortran 2018 and parallelized with the OpenMP library [11]. The core employs the classical mathematical libraries LAPACK and BLAS [12] for solving systems of linear algebraic equations. The system is closely integrated with the AutoCAD software [13]: the AutoCAD system is used for the pre- and post-processing of simulations, as well as for the production of design documentation. Integration with AutoCAD is performed via AutoLISP scripts. The post-processing utilities of the system also employ the GTK library for creating animations.

The workflow of the UKS-Dynamic computational module is presented in Fig. 3, with the external libraries (BLAS/LAPACK and GTK) shown as blue rectangles. The main submodules of UKS-Dynamic are listed below:

- Dat, DataFileRes—submodules defining initial data: basic global constants, variables and data structures;
- ConvCalcVal—converts data types and performs geometric calculations;
- ToSurface—produces the graphical output using the GTK Cairo library;
- OutDataRes—sets scale factors for graphs, colors for suspension elements and graphs;
- ToAutoCAD—translates graphical data into AutoCAD;
- MfCacl—simulates interaction between pantographs and the catenary line;
- Pantograph2, Pantograph3—calculate two-mass and three-mass pantograph configurations;
- WithoutPantograph—simulates the dynamics of the catenary line in the absence of pantographs;
- WithPantograph—simulates the dynamics of interaction between pantographs and the catenary line within one tensioning section;
- Overlap—simulates the dynamics of interaction between pantographs and the catenary line within two tensioning sections, taking into account the overlap zone;
- LibFS—low-level C language library for file I/O, interacts with a Windows API;
- FSWrappers, FortranFSWrappers—Fortran wrappers for C functions and interfaces for lower-level functions from FSWrappers and LibFS modules, correspondingly;
- Drawing15b, Drawing15bACAD—export catenary line views and data graphs to PNG files and AutoCAD;
- UKSDynamic—program entry point.

6   Results

6.1   Model Problems: Free Oscillations

In model problems simulations, the finite element length was 25 cm, and the time step value was 1 ms. In Fig. 4 and 5, the analytical solutions are shown by red lines. The green lines correspond to the generalized alpha-method with $\rho_\infty = 0.1$, the blue and violet lines correspond to the beta-Newmark method with $\beta = 0.3025$, $\gamma = 0.6$ and the beta-Newmark trapezoidal rule $\beta = 0.25$, $\gamma = 0.5$, correspondingly.

Figure 4 shows the simulation results of problem 1 (free oscillations of the wire excited by a static force) for a viscous damping model (with the diagonal damping matrix B) and a Rayleigh damping model. The displacement dynamics

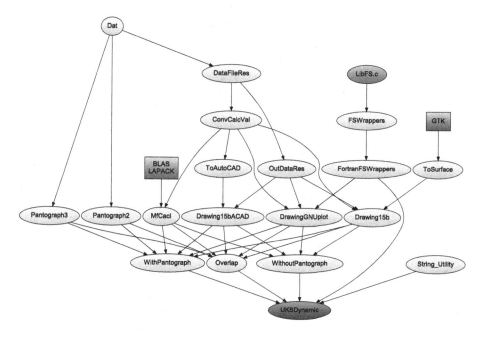

Fig. 3. Workflow of the UKS-Dynamic computational module

is well mimicked by all methods, independently of the damping model (Fig. 4a, c). In the absence of Rayleigh damping, the velocity dynamics graph (Fig. 4b) shows intensive non-physical oscillations for all methods except beta-Newmark $\beta = 0.3025$, $\gamma = 0.6$. The latter has a very strong internal dissipation (which is expressed in a higher oscillation decay compared to the analytical solution). Since this beta-Newmark scheme has only the first order of precision, the accuracy of the solution should be controlled with a sufficiently small time step.

Together with Rayleigh damping (Fig. 4c, d), all schemes show satisfactory results, although beta-Newmark $\beta = 0.3025$, $\gamma = 0.6$ tends to overdamp the solution.

Figure 5 shows the simulation results of problem 2 (free oscillations of the wire excited by impact interaction). In the absence of Rayleigh damping, the displacements (Fig. 5a) oscillate heavily in all methods except beta-Newmark $\beta = 0.3025$, $\gamma = 0.6$. In Fig. 5b, the wave shape is shown at the time moment $t = 0.1$ s (the wave crosses the span in about 0.3 s); the shape is distorted in all time integration schemes (however, it should be noted, that all non-physical oscillations and distortions shown in Fig. 4 and 5 tend to decay with a decrease in the finite element size).

Together with Rayleigh damping (Fig. 4 and 5c, d), all schemes show satisfactory results, with some overdamping in beta-Newmark $\beta = 0.3025$, $\gamma = 0.6$.

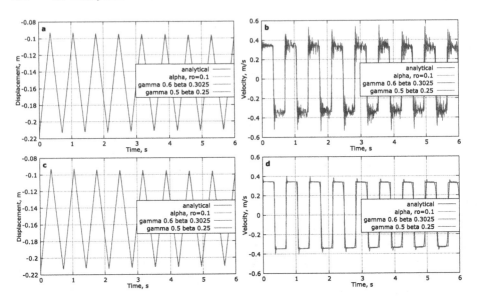

Fig. 4. Model problem 1: free oscillations of the wire excited by a lumped force. Displacement and velocity in the middle of the span, viscous damping (a, b) and Rayleigh damping (c, d)

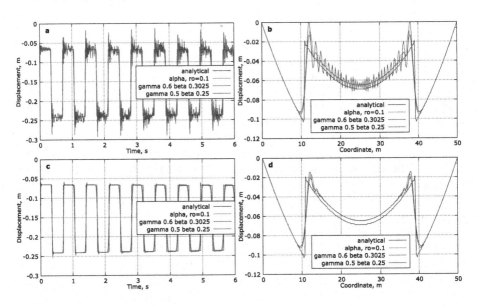

Fig. 5. Model problem 2: free oscillations of the wire excited by impact interaction. Displacements in the mid-span and wave shape at $t = 0.1$ s, viscous damping (a, b) and Rayleigh damping (c, d)

6.2   Model Problem: Driven Oscillations

In the problem of driven oscillations, only the subcritical load velocity value (135 m/s) is considered; supercritical train speeds are prohibited by design standards. According to the analytical solution, the critical load speed equals to the wave propagation speed, which is 141 m/s for the considered wire. When the load speed is under the critical value, the maximal displacement occurs in the point of force application. The distribution of displacements at the moment when the load is at the middle of the span is shown in Fig. 6. The beta-Newmark scheme $\beta = 0.3025$, $\gamma = 0.6$ shows the smoothest results.

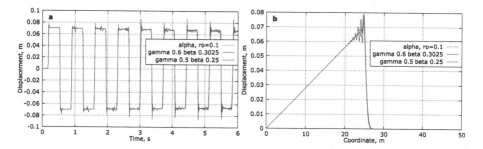

Fig. 6. Model problem 3: driven oscillations, load speed 135 m/s (486 km/h). Wave shape at the moment when the force is in the middle of the span

6.3   Validation of the Model Against the Etalon Problem from EN 50318:2018

The described computational model was successfully validated against etalon problems and experimental data for real existing overhead contact line sections of high speed railway lines (Annex A, B of EN 50318:2018, [1]). Figure 7 presents simulation results for the etalon problem of a catenary line containing a messenger wire, one contact wire, two pantographs located at a 200 m distance (the three lumped masses model of the pantograph is used according to [1]). The messenger wire is connected to fixed points via spring-damping elements. The contact wire is connected to fixed points via supporting elements, i.e. steady arms. The finite element model contains 22 spans, 10 of them are reference spans (according to [1]). Pantographs start moving at the beginning of the section. Ten referent spans are located in the middle of the section, between supports 7 and 17. The time integration step is 0.5 ms. The maximal finite element length is 0.1 m. The contact stiffness in the penalty method is 50 000 N/m, in accordance with the recommendations of EN 50318:2002. The sampling 200 Hz (the sampling interval is 5 ms) is decoupled from the time integration step. The output signal is filtered by band filters with bandwidths 0–20 Hz, 0–5 Hz and 5–20 Hz according to [1].

The initial configuration of the catenary and pantographs is shown in Fig. 7a. The dynamics of the vertical elevations of two contacts along the train trajectory is presented in Fig. 7b. Figure 7c, d shows the statistical distribution of the contact force values. The variation of the contact force along the track after filtering with a bandwidth of 0–20 Hz is presented in Fig. 7e, f. The simulated parameters, which are the most important for the current collection quality, are listed in the tables in Fig. 7.

All simulation results for the etalon model fit into the reference ranges given in [1].

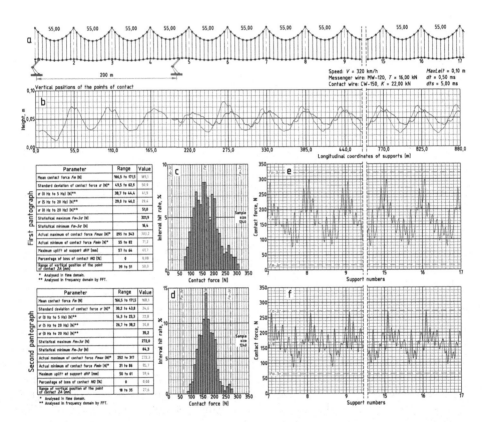

Fig. 7. Etalon problem solution, train speed of 320 km/h: (a) initial configuration of the catenary and pantographs, (b) vertical positions of two contact points along the train trajectory, (c, d) statistical distribution of the contact force values, (e, f) variation of the contact force along the track

7 OpenMP Parallelization and Code Performance

To identify the bottlenecks of the UKS-Dynamics program, the profiling of the serial version was performed using the gprof profiler. The profiling showed that the main bottleneck was the matrix multiplication procedure: it took about 54% of the elapsed time. In the second place, it was the linear algebraic equations system solution in the LAPACK dpbtrs package (19%), wherein the factorization itself did not take up significant resources (taking into account the fact that it is taken out of the time integration loop). Parallelization was performed using the OpenMP library. The loops containing matrix multiplications and the procedures for simulation output filtering were parallelized. Additionally, a number of loops were rewritten to enable automatic parallelization by the compiler.

The computational time spent on solving the etalon problem from EN 50318:2018 for a train speed of 320 km/h with a finite element length of 0.1 m and a time step of 0.5 ms is shown in Fig. 9. The results are obtained at the optimization level of the compiler -O2 on an Intel Core i5-3450 3.5 GHz computer with two physical and four logical cores. A relatively modest speed-up is due to the usage of an algorithmically sequential Holecky solver for the SLAE (system of linear algebraic equations) solution. However, iterative SLAE solvers are less preferable here due to small problem sizes ($\approx 10^4 - 10^5$ degrees of freedom) (Fig. 8).

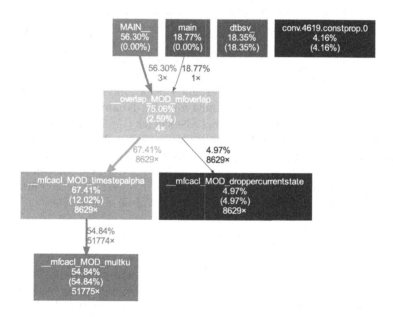

Fig. 8. Serial mode: code profiling results

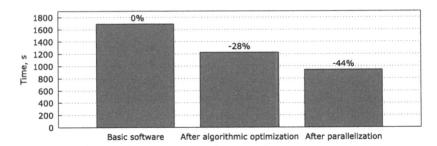

Fig. 9. Computational time spent on the etalon problem solution in serial and parallel modes on an Intel Core i5-3450 3.5 GHz standalone computer

8   Conclusions

Several techniques of high-frequency oscillation suppression were tested and applied to the problem of modeling the dynamics of interaction between train pantographs and a catenary line. The techniques include three special time integration schemes (generalized-alpha with $\rho_\infty = 0.1$, beta-Newmark $\beta = 0.3025$, $\gamma = 0.6$ and beta-Newmark trapezoidal rule $\beta = 0.25$, $\gamma = 0.5$) and Rayleigh damping. The simulation results indicate that Rayleigh damping alone is not sufficient in high-frequency suppression. Qualitatively, beta-Newmark $\beta = 0.3025$, $\gamma = 0.6$ is the best high-frequency suppression scheme in all computational tests, despite the first order of precision. Quantitatively, beta-Newmark $\beta = 0.3025$, $\gamma = 0.6$ in combination with Rayleigh damping tends to overdamp the problem due to the lower accuracy of the scheme; appropriate time stepping should be used. Another advantage of this scheme is lower computational costs compared to generalized-alpha methods. The trapezoidal rule produced intensive non-physical oscillations and cannot be recommended for wire dynamics modeling.

For the etalon problem solution, beta-Newmark $\beta = 0.3025$, $\gamma = 0.6$ was chosen as the fastest and most robust integration scheme. All simulation results for the etalon model fit into the reference ranges given in [1]. The serial optimization and OpenMP parallelization of the program were performed; the computational time spent on the etalon problem solution was reduced by 44%. Further work on improving the performance of the program will be continued.

References

1. EN 50318:2018. Railway applications – Current collection systems – Validation of simulation of the dynamic interaction between pantograph and overhead contact line. European Committee for Electrotechnical Standardization. CEN-CENELEC Management Centre: Rue de la Science 23, B-1040 Brussels (2018)
2. Grigoryev, B., Golovin, O., Viktorov, E., Kudryashov, E.: Matematicheskoe modelirovanie mehanicheskogo vzaimodeystviya tokopriemnikov i kontaktnoy podveski dlya-skorostnyh electrificirovannih zheleznih dorog. Nauchno-Tehnicheskiye Vedomosti SPbSTU **4**, 155–162 (2012). (in Russian)

3. Kudryashov, E.: Sovershenstvovaniye mehanicheskih raschetov kontaktnih pod-vesok na osnove staticheskih konechno-elementnih modeley. Ph.D. thesis, Saint-Petersburg (2010). (in Russian)

4. Wilson, E.: Static and Dynamic Analysis of Structures, 4th edn. Computers and Structures, Inc., Berkeley (2004)

5. Nakamura, N.: Extended Rayleigh damping model. Front. Built Environ. (2016). https://doi.org/10.3389/fbuil.2016.00014

6. Collina, A., Bruni, S.: Numerical simulation of pantograph-overhead equipment interaction. Veh. Syst. Dyn. **38**(4), 261–291 (2002)

7. Miano, G., Maffucci, A.: Transmission Lines and Lumped Circuits, p. 130. Academic Press (2001). ISBN 0-12-189710-9

8. Newmark, N.: A method of computation for structural dynamics. ASCE J. Eng. Mech. Div. **85**, 67–94 (1959)

9. Chung, J., Hulbert, G.: A time integration algorithm for structural dynamics with improved numerical dissipation: the generalized-alpha method. ASME J. Appl. Mech. **60**, 371–375 (1993)

10. Courant, R., Friedrichs, K., Lewy, H.: On the partial difference equations of mathematical physics. IBM J. Res. Dev. **11**(2), 215–234 (1967)

11. OpenMP Homepage. http://www.openmp.org

12. LAPACK and BLAS Homepage. http://www.netlib.org

13. AutoCAD Homepage. http://www.autocad.com

Construction of a Parallel Algorithm for the Numerical Modeling of Coke Sediments Burning from the Spherical Catalyst Grain

Olga Yazovtseva[1]($\boxtimes$), Olga Grishaeva[1], Irek Gubaydullin[2], and Elizaveta Peskova[1]

[1] National Research Mordovia State University, 68, Bolshevistskaya Street, Saransk 430005, Russia
kurinaos@gmail.com
[2] Institute of Petrochemistry and Catalysis of the Russian Academy of Sciences, 141, pr. Oktyabria, Ufa 430005, Russia

Abstract. The article presents a parallel algorithm for the numerical modeling of coke sediments burning from the catalyst grain. Coke sediments burning from the catalyst grain is also called oxidative regeneration. It is one of the simplest and most effective methods for restoring the activity of a coked catalyst. The mathematical model of this process is a system of non-linear partial differential equations. It includes equations for describing the material and heat balance, kinetic equations for describing chemical transformations. The model under study is developed on the basis of a previously known model with changes in terms of kinetic equations. The article considers a difference scheme that approximates the obtained initial-boundary value problem for a system of partial differential equations using the integro-interpolation method. The temperature and concentrations of mixture components are considered as integral averages in grid cells. Time derivatives are approximated by forward differences with the first order of accuracy, and space derivatives are approximated by central differences with the second order of accuracy. A well-known problem of the numerical modeling of processes that combine diffusion and chemical processes is the high level of system stiffness. An effective method for reducing stiffness is the transition to dimensionless quantities and variables. The applied dimensionless technique significantly reduces the computational complexity of the developed numerical algorithm. The need to decrease the time spent on calculations determines the use of a parallel algorithm. The developed numerical algorithm is implemented using OpenMP technology. The paper presents the results of a numerical experiment and the evaluation of the algorithm's efficiency.

Keywords: oxidative regeneration · nonlinear model · chemical kinetics · stiff systems · parallel algorithm

The work was partially supported by the Russian Science Foundation (project no. 21-71-20047).

1   Introduction

At present, catalytic processes form the main part of the chemical industry. The catalyst is inevitably covered with a layer of coke sediments during reactions. The composition of sediments varies depending on the composition of reactants, reaction conditions, type of catalyst, and other factors. Most often, coke is a hydrocarbon compound. Therefore, an effective method for removing coke sediments is to burn them with oxygen-containing gas from the catalyst grain. It is convenient to take air as the reaction mixture, since this avoids additional costs. This method of restoring catalytic activity is called oxidative catalyst regeneration [1,2].

An intractable task is to determine the technological conditions of regeneration, which simultaneously provide a high burnout rate of coke sediments and the safety of the catalyst layer. The greatest threat to the efficiency of the catalyst lies in the high probability of the occurrence of "hot spots" [3,4]. This phenomenon is explained by the ability of coal to adsorb flammable oxygen during low-temperature combustion [5]. The burnout temperature of coke sediments must be constantly monitored to prevent the occurrence of hot spots.

Many tasks arise during regeneration: it is necessary to remove as much coke as possible in the shortest possible time, while maintaining the efficiency of the catalyst. As known, the velocities of chemical reactions directly depend on the temperature of their carrying out, however, it is necessary to take into account the possibility of the occurrence of hot spots, i.e. coke combustion zones, leading to the irreversible deterioration of the catalyst. Full-scale experiments that make it possible to predict the current of regeneration under various conditions are expensive and unsafe; it is proposed to solve the emerging problems using mathematical modeling [3].

Formally, oxidative regeneration is low-temperature carbon combustion, therefore, the regularities accompanying such processes are valid for it. The need to take into account many conditions affecting the process leads to complex mathematical models described by partial differential equations, the analytical solution of which is impossible. In addition, the resulting models are stiff and require calculations with a small time step due to a combination of factors of different nature [6]. An effective method to reduce the time spent on such calculations is to use parallel technologies [7].

The main physicochemical regularities of the coke burning process for various types of catalysts are given in [2]. The problem of the dynamic control of oxidative regeneration is introduced in [3]. The article [8] discusses an averaged model of oxidative catalyst regeneration.

The article [9] investigates the regeneration of a diesel fraction hydrotreating catalyst based on the analysis of circulating regeneration gases.

The article [10] analyzes the regeneration modes of platinum catalysts for gasoline reforming and the dehydrogenation of higher paraffins.

The work [11] is devoted to the study of the deactivation and oxidative regeneration of modern catalysts for deep diesel fuel hydrotreating, and the activity of regenerated catalysts is compared with new samples.

The investigation of nickel and vanadium catalysts and the conditions for reducing the regeneration time are obtained in [12,13].

Currently, the investigation on the regeneration of a commercial zeolite catalyst by burning coke using ozone is underway [14,15].

An analysis of the qualitative change in the catalyst coked due to the catalytic pyrolysis of plastics is given in [16]. The process of coke formation is described in detail, as well as irreversible changes in the catalyst, to which it leads. The process of oxidative regeneration is modeled in terms of kinetics, taking into account sorption processes.

Various modeling approaches are outlined in [17]. The oxidative regeneration process is presented as part of a continuous production cycle. The article considers a function of catalyst activity, which depends on time and is related to the reaction rate. The kinetics of coke formation is revised in accordance with new experimental data. The production process is optimized based on the developed models.

The regeneration of a vanadium catalyst with an oxygen-nitrogen mixture is studied in [18]. The process is analyzed taking into account ionic interactions.

The oxidative regeneration of coked modified metal chloride catalysts as part of the catalytic cracking process is described in [19]. On the basis of a full-scale experiment, graphs describing the process are constructed. A conclusion about the effectiveness of several approaches to the restoration of catalytic activity is made. The regeneration of the flow in the helium flow with subsequent calcination is recognized as the most effective.

The article [20] is devoted to the investigation of the effect of oxidative regeneration on the activity of a catalyst. It is made of the activation energy of the destruction of surface coke-containing products on the catalyst grain. It is found that the long stay of the catalyst under regeneration conditions reduces the activation energy.

The above works on the investigation of oxidative regeneration do not take into account the distribution of coke over the catalyst grain and, as a result, the diffusion of reagents in grain pores. This article is a development of [2,3]. The kinetic models given in them are modified in terms of the departure from the quasi-stationarity principle, and an alternative method of non-dimensionalization of the model is also used to more effectively reduce the stiffness. To investigate the obtained model, a parallel algorithm is constructed and implemented for the numerical modeling of coke sediments burning from the spherical catalyst grain, using which the patterns of the distribution of reagents and coke components over the catalyst grain are obtained.

2   Mathematical Model of Coke Burning

The burning of coke sediments from the catalyst grain is a complex heterogeneous sorption process, for the correct description of which it is necessary to take into account the material and heat balances [21,24].

There are a scheme of chemical transformations of burning out coke sediments and kinetic equations [3]:

$$
\begin{aligned}
2\Theta_C + O_2 &\longrightarrow 2\Theta_{CO}, & W_1 &= k_1(T)\,\Theta_3^2\,y_1; \\
\Theta_{CO} + O_2 &\longrightarrow \Theta_{CO} + CO_2, & W_2 &= k_2(T)\,\Theta_2\,y_1; \\
\Theta_{CO} &\longrightarrow \Theta_C + CO, & W_3 &= k_3(T)\,\Theta_2; \\
\Theta_{CH_2} + O_2 &\longrightarrow \Theta_{CO} + H_2O, & W_4 &= k_4(T)\,\Theta_1\,y_1; \\
\Theta_{CO} + \Theta_{CO} &\longrightarrow 2\Theta_C + CO_2, & W_5 &= k_5(T)\,\Theta_2^2; \\
\Theta_{CH_2} &\rightleftarrows \Theta_C + Z_{H_2}, & W_6 &= k_6(T)\,\frac{\rho_C}{R_C}(\Theta_1^* - z_1); \\
\Theta_{CO} &\rightleftarrows \Theta_C + Z_O, & W_7 &= k_7(T)\,\frac{\rho_C}{R_C}(\Theta_2^* - z_2).
\end{aligned}
\tag{1}
$$

Here W_i, $i = \overline{1,7}$, are the velocities of chemical interaction stages, the dimension W_r, $r = \overline{1,5}$ – mole/(l·sec^2), W_6 and W_7 – g/(m^2·sec); $k_j(T)$, $j = \overline{1,7}$, are the constants of the velocities of chemical interaction stages, the dimension k_j corresponds to ω_j; Θ_l, $l = \overline{1,3}$, is the degree of coverage of the coke surface with various carbon complexes (Θ_1 – hydrogen-carbon complex, Θ_2 – oxygen-carbon complex, Θ_3 – free carbon surface); y_1 is the concentration of oxygen in the gas phase in mole fractions; z_1 and z_2 are the concentrations of hydrogen and oxygen in the coke layer in mass fractions; $\Theta_1^* = \dfrac{\Theta_1}{6}$ and $\Theta_2^* = \dfrac{4\Theta_2}{3}$ are the amount of hydrogen and oxygen adsorbed by coke in relation to the current state of the coke sediment surface; ρ_C and R_C are the density (g/m^3) and average radius of coke granules (m). Besides,

$$
\Theta_1 + \Theta_2 + \Theta_3 = 0.
$$

The method for modeling the process of oxidative regeneration is given in [2]. Regeneration requires a description of the material and heat balance like any catalytic process. Material balance equations are compiled taking into account the diffusion and Stefan flows, as well as the source member, which includes the kinetics of the process. The heat balance equation reflects the heat transfer in the grain and its heating due to exothermic chemical reactions. A feature of this model is the inclusion of the Stefan flow velocity, which is required to fulfill the mass conservation law in the model. The equation for calculating the Stefan flow velocity is obtained from the condition that it is equal to zero at the grain boundary. The use of spherical coordinates to describe the model is due to the assumption of a quasi-homogeneous structure of the grain and its shape [2].

The kinetic equations included in the model reflect changes in the composition of coke sediments, sorption processes, and changes in the total mass fraction of coke in the catalyst grain. In [2] it is proposed to use the principle of quasi-stationarity to find the mass fractions of the constituents of coke sediments. This assumption is due to the need to reduce the computational complexity of the numerical algorithm, since the replacement of two differential equations by algebraic ones, firstly, simplifies the difference analog of the system under study, and secondly, reduces its stiffness. The authors refuse to use the principle of quasi-stationarity for the sake of completeness and apply an alternative variant of non-dimensionalization of the new model.

The mathematical model for burning out coke sediments from the catalyst grain in a dimensionless form is a nonlinear system of partial differential equations:

$$
\begin{cases}
\dfrac{\partial \Theta}{\partial \tau} = \dfrac{D^* \tau_k}{R_z^2} \dfrac{1}{\rho^2} \dfrac{\partial}{\partial \rho}\left(\rho^2 \dfrac{\partial \Theta}{\partial \rho}\right) + \dfrac{\hat{S} c_0}{T_{op} c} \sum_{j=1}^{5} Q_j \omega_j, \\[2ex]
\dfrac{\partial y_i}{\partial \tau} = \dfrac{D^* \tau_k}{R_z^2 \varepsilon} \dfrac{1}{\rho^2} \dfrac{\partial}{\partial \rho}\left(\rho^2 \dfrac{\partial y_i}{\partial \rho} - \rho^2 \hat{\mu} y_i\right) + \dfrac{\hat{S}}{\varepsilon} \sum_{j=1}^{5} \nu_{ij} \omega_j, \\[2ex]
\dfrac{\partial}{\partial \rho}\left(\rho^2 \hat{\mu}\right) = \rho^2 \dfrac{R_z^2 c_0 \hat{S}}{D^* \tau_k \gamma}(-\omega_1 + \omega_3 + \omega_5), \\[2ex]
\dfrac{\partial q_c}{\partial \tau} = -\dfrac{M_C c_0}{\gamma} \hat{S}(\omega_2 + \omega_3 + \omega_5), \\[2ex]
\dfrac{\partial z_1}{\partial \tau} = \dfrac{c_0}{\gamma q_c} \hat{S}(\omega_6 + z_1 M_C(\omega_2 + \omega_3 + \omega_5)), \\[2ex]
\dfrac{\partial z_2}{\partial \tau} = \dfrac{c_0}{\gamma q_c} \hat{S}(\omega_7 + z_2 M_C(\omega_2 + \omega_3 + \omega_5)), \\[2ex]
\dfrac{\partial \theta_1}{\partial \tau} = -\hat{S}\left(\omega_4 + \dfrac{c_0}{\gamma} \omega_6\right), \\[2ex]
\dfrac{\partial \theta_2}{\partial \tau} = \hat{S}\left(2\omega_1 - \omega_3 + \omega_4 - 2\omega_5 - \dfrac{c_0}{\gamma} \omega_7\right).
\end{cases}
\tag{2}
$$

Here ρ is the dimensionless catalyst grain radius, $\rho \in [0,1]$ (independent spatial variable); τ is the dimensionless time, $\tau \in [0, +\infty)$ (independent time variable); $\Theta(\rho, \tau)$ is the dimensionless catalyst grain temperature; $y_i(\rho, \tau)$, $i = \overline{1,4}$ is the mole fraction of components in the gas phase of the reaction (index 1 corresponds to oxygen, 2 to carbon monoxide, 3 to carbon dioxide, 4 to water); $\hat{\mu}(\rho, \tau)$ is the dimensionless velocity of the Stefan flow; $q_c(\rho, \tau)$ is the mass fraction of coke on the catalyst grain; $z_1(\rho, \tau)$ and $z_2(\rho, \tau)$ are the mass fractions of hydrogen and oxygen in coke sediments; $\theta_1(\rho, \tau)$ and $\theta_2(\rho, \tau)$ are the fractions of hydrogen-carbon and oxygen-carbon complexes on the coke granule surface; $\hat{S}(\rho, \tau)$ is the dimensionless area of coke granules; $\omega_j(\rho, \tau)$, $j = \overline{1,5}$ are the dimensionless rates of quasi-homogeneous reactions taken from the kinetic scheme; $\omega_j(\rho, \tau)$, $j = \overline{6,7}$ are the rates of heterogeneous reactions taken from the kinetic scheme, g/mol; D^* is the effective diffusion coefficient, m^2/sec; τ_k is the contact time, sec; R_z is the catalyst grain radius, m; ε is the catalyst grain porosity; ν_{ij}, $i = \overline{1,4}$ are the stoichiometric coefficients from the reaction scheme; c_0 is the gas molar density, mol/m^3; $T_{op} = 520°$ is the temperature at which the reaction rate constants are experimentally determined, K; c is the volumetric heat capacity of the catalyst, J/(m$^3 \cdot$ K); Q_j, $j = \overline{1,5}$, are the thermal effects of chemical reactions, J/mol; γ is the catalyst bulk density, g/m^3; M_C is the molecular weight of coke, g/mol.

It should be noted that there is a decrease in the volume of coke sediments over time. This fact is taken into account in the (2) model as a decrease in the reaction surface area $\hat{S}(\rho,\tau) = \left(\dfrac{q_c(\rho,\tau)}{q_c(\rho,0)}\right)^{\frac{2}{3}}$, while the catalyst grain size remains unchanged.

The (2) system is supplemented with boundary and initial conditions chosen on the basis of experimental conditions:

$$\rho = 0: \ \hat{\mu} = 0, \ \frac{\partial y_i}{\partial \rho} = 0, \ \frac{\partial \Theta}{\partial \rho} = 0;$$

$$\rho = 1: \ \frac{\partial y_i}{\partial \rho} = 0, \ \frac{\partial \Theta}{\partial \rho} = \beta_0 \left(\frac{T_0}{T_{op}} - \Theta\right); \tag{3}$$

$$\tau = 0: \ q_c = q_C^0, \ z_1 = z_1^0, \ z_2 = 0, \ \theta_1 = \theta_1^0, \ \theta_2 = 0,$$

$$\Theta = \frac{T_0}{T_{op}}, \ y_1 = 1, \ y_i = 0, i = \overline{2,4},$$

where T_0 is the initial temperature of the catalyst grain, K.

3   Constructing a Parallel Algorithm and Efficiency

The difference approximation for the initial-boundary value problem (2), (3) is performed using the Euler scheme in time. Since the model includes one spatial coordinate, i.e. the dimensionless radius, the computational domain is the segment $[0,1]$. The temperature and concentration of mixture components are considered as integral averages in grid cells. Time derivatives are approximated by forward differences with the first order of accuracy, and space derivatives are approximated by central differences with the second order of accuracy.

The developed algorithm is implemented in the $C++$ language using OpenMP parallel programming technology. The choice of OpenMP technology is dictated by a relatively small number of computational cells, which is an indisputable advantage of the dimensionless model. It is inappropriate to use systems with distributed memory in this case, since interprocessor exchange will require enormous time costs. In the future, MPI technology will be used to model the catalyst layer, since the size of the computational domain will be set on the basis of experimental problems.

The issue of convergence is resolved in the formulation of refining grids due to the lack of an exact solution to the problem. The calculations are carried out for a different number of cells in space with the preservation of the Courant number. The convergence is preserved when the computational grid is refined.

The system of difference equations approximating the initial-boundary value problem (2), (3) has the following form:

$$
\begin{cases}
\Theta_k^{n+1} = \Theta_k^n + \Delta t \left(\dfrac{1}{\varphi} \dfrac{1}{r_k^2 h_r} \left(r_{k+1/2}^2 \dfrac{\Theta_{k+1}^n - \Theta_k^n}{h_r} - r_{k-1/2}^2 \dfrac{\Theta_k^n - \Theta_{k-1}^n}{h_r} \right) \right. \\
\hspace{6cm} \left. + \left(\dfrac{\hat{S} c_0}{T_{op} c} \sum_{j=1}^{5} Q_j \omega_j \right) \right)_k^n, \\[4mm]
(y_i)_k^{n+1} = (y_i)_k^n \\
+ \Delta t \left(\dfrac{1}{\varphi \varepsilon} \dfrac{1}{r_k^2 h_r} \left(\left(r_{k+1/2}^2 \dfrac{(y_i)_{k+1}^n - (y_i)_k^n}{h_r} - r_{k+1/2}^2 \hat{\mu}_{k+1/2} \dfrac{(y_i)_{k+1}^n + (y_i)_k^n}{2} \right) \right. \right. \\
\hspace{2cm} \left. - \left(r_{k-1/2}^2 \dfrac{(y_i)_k^n - (y_i)_{k-1}^n}{h_r} - r_{k-1/2}^2 \hat{\mu}_{k-1/2} \dfrac{(y_i)_k^n + (y_i)_{k-1}^n}{2} \right) \right) \\
\hspace{6cm} \left. + \left(\dfrac{\hat{S}}{\varepsilon} \sum_{j=1}^{7} \nu_{ij} \omega_j \right) \right)_k^n, \\[4mm]
\hat{\mu}_{k+1/2} = \dfrac{1}{r_{k+1/2}^2} \left(r_{k-1/2}^2 \hat{\mu}_{k-1/2} + h_r r_k^2 \left(\dfrac{\varphi c_0 \hat{S}}{\gamma} \sum_{j=1}^{7} (-\omega_1 + \omega_3 + \omega_5) \right) \right)_k, \\[4mm]
(q_c)_k^{n+1} = (q_c)_k^n + \Delta t \left(-\dfrac{M_C c_0}{\gamma} \hat{S}(\omega_2 + \omega_3 + \omega_5) \right)_k^n, \\[4mm]
(z_1)_k^{n+1} = (z_1)_k^n + \Delta t \left(\dfrac{c_0}{\gamma q_c} \hat{S}(\omega_6 + z_1 M_C(\omega_2 + \omega_3 + \omega_5)) \right)_k^n, \\[4mm]
(z_2)_k^{n+1} = (z_2)_k^n + \Delta t \left(\dfrac{c_0}{\gamma q_c} \hat{S}(\omega_7 + z_2 M_C(\omega_2 + \omega_3 + \omega_5)) \right)_k^n, \\[4mm]
(\theta_1)_k^{n+1} = (\theta_1)_k^n + \Delta t \left(\omega_4 + \dfrac{c_0}{\gamma} \omega_6 \right)_k^n, \\[4mm]
(\theta_2)_k^{n+1} = (\theta_2)_k^n + \Delta t \left(\hat{S} \left(2\omega_1 - \omega_3 + \omega_4 - 2\omega_5 - \dfrac{c_0}{\gamma} \omega_7 \right) \right)_k^n.
\end{cases}
$$

$$(4)$$

Here Δt is the time step, h_r is the space step, $r_k = k\, h_r$.

The software package includes several modules corresponding to the parts of the block diagram. The main procedures and functions are placed in a separate file to optimize the execution time of the program. The calculations of the source terms, the Stefan flow velocity, the diffusion part and the resulting flow are implemented using parallel computations. The distribution of streams is carried out by the standard *Omp parallel for* directive. The computational algorithm can be represented as a block diagram (Fig. 1).

The capacity of the software package that implements the developed parallel algorithm for the model (2) is estimated as follows. The calculations are performed using a different number of threads for a given number of computational cells (10, 100, 1000), acceleration (ratio of the computation time for several threads to the computation time for one) and efficiency (ratio of acceleration to the number of threads) are calculated. The calculation time (in seconds) is shown in Table 1.

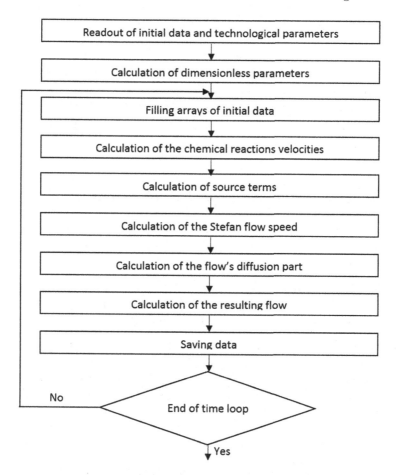

Fig. 1. Block diagram of the software

Table 1. Calculation time for a different number of cells

	10 cells	100 cells	1000 cells
1 processor	54	438	5424
2 processors	44	436	3644
4 processors	50	429	3586
8 processors	54	411	3578

Table 2 shows the acceleration and efficiency data of the developed algorithm.

The tables demonstrate that the highest parallelization efficiency is observed when switching from one stream to two with a large number of cells. The efficiency is not so high with a small number, since the time spent on creating several threads is not justified in the case of a small number of iterations in the cycles.

Table 2. Acceleration and efficiency of the parallel algorithm

	Acceleration			Efficiency		
	10 cells	100 cells	1000 cells	10 cells	100 cells	1000 cells
1 processor	1.0000	1.0000	1.0000	1.0000	1.0000	1.0000
2 processors	1.2273	1.0046	1.4885	0.6137	0.5023	0.7443
4 processors	1.0800	1.0210	1.5125	0.2700	0.2553	0.3781
8 processors	1.0000	1.0657	1.5159	0.1250	0.1332	0.1895

4   Results of a Computational Experiment

A computational experiment is conducted with the selected technological parameters and values corresponding to real conditions for the process of oxidative regeneration of the hydrocracking catalyst given in [3]:

$$M_C = 12 \text{ g/mol}, \; R_C(0) = 0.0025 \text{ m}, \; \rho_C = 1.8 \text{ t/m}^3, \; \gamma_k = 0.6 \text{ t/m}^3, \; \varepsilon_k = 0.3,$$
$$c_k = 1.13 \text{ J/(m}^3\text{·K)}, \; c_0 = 15.72 \text{ mol/m}^3, \; Q_1 = 83.7 \text{ kJ/mol}, \; Q_2 = 394 \text{ kJ/mol},$$
$$Q_3 = 67.6 \text{ kJ/mol}, \; Q_4 = 303 \text{ kJ/mol}, \; Q_5 = 311 \text{ kJ/mol}.$$

Coke sediments burning is carried out with air (the volume fraction of oxygen is 21%), heated to 520 °C. Burning is quite effective, but the catalyst does not overheat at this temperature [3]. The catalyst grain is cooled to room temperature 20 °C at the initial time. The above model takes into account that when heated air passes through the catalyst layer on the surface of the grain and in its pores, exothermic reactions occur. Thus, the heat balance equation reflects the heat transfer from the gas layer to the catalyst layer and the heating of the grain due to reactions.

Figure 2 shows the result of the numerical experiment.

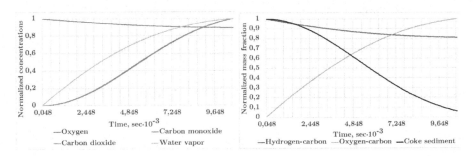

Fig. 2. Graphs of the concentrations of gas mixture components (left) and the mass fractions of coke sediment components (right). (Color figure online)

The graphs are built for normalized values, since the calculated quantities have a different order. The normalization is carried out by dividing each quantity by its maximum value in the integration interval. Figure 2 illustrates the change in the concentrations of substances in the gas phase of the process (left-hand graphs) and the mass fractions of the components of coke sediments (right-hand graphs).

The blue line corresponds to the oxygen concentration in the gas phase of the reaction. The oxygen concentration decreases in accordance with the reaction scheme: in the first stage, oxygen is adsorbed in the layer of coke sediments, in the second and fourth stages, it is consumed during the oxidation of oxygen-carbon and hydrogen-carbon complexes.

The orange line on the graphs indicates the concentration of carbon monoxide. It is formed as a result of oxygen desorption (the third reaction in the scheme) and then remains in the reaction zone.

The gray line corresponds to the concentration of carbon dioxide. During oxidative regeneration, it is formed as a result of the oxidation and recombination of the oxygen-carbon complex. These processes correspond to the second and fourth stages.

The yellow line on the graph indicates the dynamics of water vapor concentration, its increase is associated with the oxidation of the hydrogen-carbon complex.

It can be seen from Fig. 2 that the rate of formation of water vapor exceeds the rate of formation of carbon oxides. This phenomenon is explained by the fact that the hydrogen-carbon complex, which determines the presence of water in the reaction products, is a highly combustible component of coke sediments. The oxidation of the pure carbon surface and the oxygen-carbon complex requires much more time.

The change in the composition of coke sediments reflects the dynamics of their constituents. Coke consists of a hydrogen-carbon complex and pure carbon at the beginning of the process. Low-temperature coal combustion begins with the adsorption of oxygen around the active centers in accordance with its laws [2]. This process is described by the first stage in the reaction scheme, i.e. the formation of an oxygen-carbon complex. The dynamics of its mass fraction is shown on the graph by the green line. At the same time, the combustible hydrogen-carbon complex begins to oxidize and break down, which leads to a decrease in its share (red line).

The main purpose of oxidative regeneration is to burn out coke sediments. A quantitative characteristic of this process is the mass fraction of coke on the catalyst grain (black line in Fig. 2). As can be seen from the graphs, the mass fraction of coke decreases rather quickly, however, with some delay at the beginning of the process. This delay is a consequence of the adsorption of oxygen in the layer of coke sediments.

It should be noted that the above graphs are valid for processes in the area close to the grain surface. Combustion in the center of the grain proceeds extremely slowly for the selected regeneration conditions due to the relatively low diffusion coefficient of air in the pores of the grain and the high heat capacity of the catalyst material. It is necessary to increase the gas flow rate in the reactor to accelerate the removal of coke from the center of the grain.

5   Conclusion

The article presents the parallel algorithm for the numerical modeling of coke sediments burning from the catalyst grain. The process model is a system of partial differential equations reflecting the material and heat balance. The integro-interpolation method is used to construct the computational algorithm. The developed algorithm is implemented in C++ using OpenMP parallel computing technology.

A well-known issue of applying numerical methods to problems that combine diffusion and chemical transformations is the high level of stiffness of the systems of equations included in the model of the phenomenon. The reduction of the computational complexity of the developed algorithms is carried out on the basis of several approaches.

Non-dimensionalization, which reduces the stiffness of the problem, is applied for the mathematical model of the real process.

In turn, the multifactor nature of real practical processes leads to difficulties in the theoretical investigation of the stability and convergence of the developed numerical algorithms, and in the determination of integration steps over time and grid. Multiple-step refinement in space is carried out with stability and convergence checks for each new mesh to solve these issues.

The last step in reducing the computational complexity of the algorithm is the use of parallel computing technology. The computational algorithm includes a large number of iterative processes due to the smallness of the time step and a sufficiently large number of variables in the problem. Parallel computing is used to speed up the cycles. At the same time, the geometry of the problem is quite simple due to the assumptions used in modeling the burning of coke from the catalyst grain, the spherical shape of the grain, and the homogeneity of the distribution of coke over the grain. This causes the use of OpenMP technology, since the interprocessor MPI exchange will lead to significant time costs, which are not justified in this case. An analysis of the efficiency of using parallel technologies shows that the greatest acceleration is achieved when switching from one stream to two with an increase in the number of computational cells. Parallelization does not provide a significant acceleration of calculations with a small number, since the costs of creating several threads are high.

Patterns of the distribution of gas phase components and the mass fractions of coke sediment components are obtained. It describes real processes on the catalyst grain during oxidative regeneration.

An analysis of the obtained patterns demonstrates that, for the selected regeneration conditions, in the area close to the surface of the catalyst grain, coke burning is quite active, however, deep burning requires an increase in the reaction mixture flow rate.

This conclusion will be used in further investigation of the oxidative regeneration process, namely, the development and implementation of algorithms for modeling the catalyst layer.

References

1. Kutepov, B.I.: Kinetics of Formation and Interconversion of Coke Oxidation Products on Modern Cracking Catalysts. Ufa, USSR (1980)
2. Masagutov, R.M., Morozov, B.F., Kutepov, B.I.: Regeneration of catalysts in oil processing and petrochemistry. USSR, Moscow (1987)
3. Gubaydullin, I.M.: Mathematical Modelling of Dynamic Modes of Oxidative Regeneration of Catalysts in Motionless Layer. Ufa, Russia (1996)
4. Gubaydullin, I.M.: Stability of high temperature zones in a motionless catalyst layer. In: Tez.dokl. II Vsesoyuz. konf. molodyh uchenyh po fizkhimii, pp. 232–233. Moscow, USSR (1983)
5. Kuryatnikov, V.V.: Role of the surface properties of dispersed carbon in its inflammation. Combus. Expl. Shock Waves **19**(5), 18–21 (1983)
6. Oran, E., Boris, J.: Numerical Modeling of Reacting Flows. Russia, Moscow (1990)
7. Gubaidullin, I.M., Zhalnin, R.V., Peskova, E.E., et al.: Construction of parallel algorithms of high order of accuracy for modeling the dynamics of reacting flows. In: XI International Conference on Parallel Computing Technologies (PaVT 2017): Short Articles and Descriptions Of Posters, pp. 288–296. Kazan, Russia (2017)
8. Gubaydullin, I.M., Yazovtseva, O.S.: Investigation of the averaged model of coked catalyst oxidative regeneration. Comput. Res. Model. **13**(1), 149–161 (2021). https://doi.org/10.20537/2076-7633-2021-13-1-149-161
9. Zanin, I.K., Ivanchina, E.D., Chuzlov, V.A., Chekancev, N.V.: Optimization of the regeneration process of catalyst of diesel fractions hydrotreating. Oil Refin. Petrochem. **6**, 13–18 (2015)
10. Ivanov, S.Yu., Zanin, I.K., Ivashkina, E.N.: Modeling of the process of regeneration of Pt catalysts for reforming gasoline and dehydrogenation of higher paraffins. Bull. Tomsk Polytech. Univ. 319(3), 96–99 (2011)
11. Budukva, D.V., et al.: Deactivation and oxidative regeneration of last-generation catalysts for deep hydrofining of diesel fuel: Comparison of properties of fresh and deactivated IK-GO-1 catalysts. Russian J. Appl. Chem. vol. **83**(12), 2144–2151 (2010). https://doi.org/10.1134/S1070427210120141
12. Karakhanov, E.A., Lysenko, S.V., Kannut, T., Baranova, S.V., Pushkin, A.N., Bratkov, A.A.: oxidative regeneration of coked cracking catalysts containing heavy metals and a passivator. Petrol. Chem. **38**(1), 58–61 (1998)
13. Baranova, S.V., Kannut, T., Karakhanov, E., A. et al.: Oxidative regeneration of catalysts coked during the cracking of different types of petroleum feedstock. Petrol. Chem. **36**(5), 406–409 (1996)
14. Richard, R., Julcour-Lebigue, C., Manero, M.-H.: Regeneration of coked catalysts by an oxidation process using ozone. In: 1st Trans Pyrenean Meeting in Catalysis (2016)
15. Richard, R., Julcour-Lebigue, C., Manero, M.-H.: A new oxidation process using ozone to regenerate coked catalysts. In: Conference: International Ozone Association - Ozone and Advanced Oxidation for the Water-Energy-Food-Health NexusAt. Swansea, Wales, UK (2016)

16. Daligaux, V., Richard, R., Manero, M.-H.: Deactivation and regeneration of zeolite catalysts used in pyrolysis of plastic wastes – a process and analytical review. Catalysts 11, p. 770 (2021). https://doi.org/10.3390/catal11070770.

17. Brune, A., Geschke, A., Seidel-Morgenstern, A., Hamel, C.: Modeling and simulations of catalyst deactivation and regeneration cycles for propane dehydrogenation - comparison of different modeling approaches. Chem. Eng. Process. 29 (2021) https://doi.org/10.1016/j.cep.2021.108689

18. Vo, P.N.X., Le-Phuc, N., Tran, T.V., Ngo, P.T., Luong, T.N.: Oxidative regeneration study of spent V_2O_5 catalyst from sulfuric acid manufacture. React. Kinet. Mech. Catal. **125**(2), 887–900 (2018). https://doi.org/10.1007/s11144-018-1442-9

19. Sakhibgareev, S.R., Tsadkin, M.A., Badikova, A.D., Osipenko, E.V., Abdrakhmanov, V.A., Mustafin A.G.: Oxidative regeneration of modified metallochloride catalysts. Oil Gas Bus. **6** (2021)

20. Ajamov, K.Y., Huseynova, E.A., Mursalova, L.A., Safarova, S.R.: Some aspects of oxycracking catalysts regeneration. Azerbaijan Chem. J. **1** (2020)

21. Golodets, G.I.: Heterogeneous Catalytic Reactions with the Participation of Molecular Oxygen. Kiev, USSR (1977)

22. Gubaydullin, I.M., Dubinec, O.V.: In: Modeling the oxidative regeneration process taking into account the effect of water vapor. In: Proceedings of the International Scientific "outh School-Seminar Mathematical Modeling, Numerical Methods and Software complexes" named after E.V. Voskresensky, pp. 49–49 (2020)

23. Guldberg, C.M., Waage, P.: Studies concerning affinity. J. Chem. Educ. **63** 1044 (1864)

24. Kohl, A.L., Riesenfeld, F.C.: Gas Purification. Houston, Texas, USA (1985)

MPI-Based PFEM-2 Method Solver for Convection-Dominated CFD Problems

Andrey Popov[1]([⊠]) [iD] and Ilia Marchevsky[1,2] [iD]

[1] Bauman Moscow State Technical University, Moscow, Russian Federation
andreyypopov@bmstu.ru
[2] Ivannikov Institute for System Programming of the RAS,
Moscow, Russian Federation

Abstract. The description of the parallel solver of the Particle Finite Element Method, 2nd generation (PFEM-2), is given. Strategies for the parallelization of both mesh-related and particle-related substeps are outlined. The software implementation is based on the open-source FEM code `deal.II`. The parallel solution of incompressible Navier–Stokes equations with the excluded convective term is performed with the out-of-box tools of deal.II using additional libraries such as `Trilinos` and `p4est`. Several `MPI`-based subroutines are developed for particle transport processing, as well as for particle/mesh field projection operations. The presented PFEM-2 solver allows for simulating convection-dominated flows with a high CFL number on relatively coarse meshes. The submesh resolution of the velocity field is maintained by particles. The results of simulation and speed-up of computations for test problems using multi-core/multi-processor systems are shown.

Keywords: Computational fluid dynamics · finite element method · particle methods · parallel algorithms · MPI

1 Introduction

Contemporary mechanical and engineering problems require complex solutions with numerical simulation, often using considerable computational resources. Mathematically, these problems are often formulated in the 3D case, can have a complicated domain shape, very fine meshes, and take into account various physical effects (in CFD: turbulence, buoyancy, heat transfer, etc.). The problem may also require the application of a multidisciplinary approach. The evolution of numerical methods partially helps to cope with the initial complexity of the problem. In many cases, it turns out that it is possible to build a specific method that has a narrower applicability, but is significantly more efficient for a certain class of problems than a universal approach. In CFD, for a class of convection-dominated problems, such a method, i.e. the Particle Finite Element Method, 2nd generation [1,2], PFEM-2, was proposed in 2013. The main idea behind PFEM-2, which reduces computational costs, is to split the original problem into Eulerian (mesh-related) and Lagrangian (particle-related) parts. In this case, Lagrangian particles simulate convection, and the reduced hydrodynamical problem is solved on a fixed mesh using the conventional finite element method. The mesh remains fixed for the whole process of computing, as opposed to the original Particle Finite Volume Method [3], or PFEM, where it is rebuilt after each time step using particle locations (for a detailed comparison of these two methods see also [4]). Equations solved on the mesh are devoid of the convective term—the one that requires a high-resolution capability to achieve a reasonable accuracy of the result—and, therefore, the mesh can be coarser, and a larger time step is allowed in the case of convection-dominated problems.

Despite this intrinsic potency of the PFEM-2 method, the solution of practical problems often implies the use of a mesh with hundreds of thousands or millions of cells and a large number of particles, which altogether leads to a considerable computational load. It seems natural that the application of parallelization algorithms can speed up computations. However, different parts of the PFEM-2 method (solution on the Eulerian mesh and transport of Lagrangian particles) are completely different algorithmically and, therefore, require specific approaches to parallelization. In this paper, we give a detailed description of these techniques for both parts of PFEM-2 and present the results of their software implementation. It should be noted that there exists only one publicly available implementation of PFEM-2, namely, within the KRATOS software framework [5]. Its parallelization is bounded by the usage of OpenMP technology, and the properties of the solver itself are disputable, based on the authors' experience of its application to the solution of model problems. Thus, the development of a robust parallel implementation of PFEM-2 is an urgent problem.

A general description of the PFEM-2 method is given in Sect. 2, the parallel implementation is covered in Sect. 3. In Sect. 4, we present the results of numerical simulation for a test case of viscous flows past a cylindrical body. The possibilities for further improvement of the parallel solver are outlined in the conclusion.

2 PFEM-2 Method

2.1 Main Concepts and Solution Algorithm

In this paper, flows of incompressible viscous fluids are considered. The governing equations for such flows include the Navier–Stokes equations, as well as the incompressibility equation:

$$
\begin{cases}
\rho \left(\dfrac{\partial \boldsymbol{V}}{\partial t} + (\boldsymbol{V} \cdot \nabla)\boldsymbol{V} \right) = \nabla p + \nabla \cdot \boldsymbol{\tau} + \boldsymbol{f}, \\
\nabla \cdot \boldsymbol{V} = 0,
\end{cases}
\tag{1}
$$

where V and p are the velocity and pressure fields, respectively, $\rho = \text{const}$ is the density, f represents the outer forces, and τ is the deviatoric stress tensor with the following components (μ is the dynamic viscosity):

$$\tau_{ij} = \mu \left(\frac{\partial V_i}{\partial x_j} + \frac{\partial V_j}{\partial x_i} - \frac{2}{3} \delta_{ij} \frac{\partial V_k}{\partial x_k} \right). \tag{2}$$

In the case of flows past cylindrical bodies (as the one for which the results of numerical simulation are presented below), the mathematical model involves a number of typical boundary conditions, including the fixed velocity of the flow at the channel inlet and the no-slip condition on the body surface and channel walls.

The Particle Finite Element Method, 2nd generation, is especially efficient in the case of convection-dominated problems (although it can also be applied to problems where viscosity prevails). For such problems, conventional mesh-based approaches, such as the Finite element method and the Finite volume method, often require excessively fine meshes, as well as small time steps, in order to correctly approximate the convective term in Eq. (1) and yield results of reasonable accuracy. PFEM-2 is a hybrid Eulerian-Lagrangian approach that is based on traditional FEM, but also includes particles moving along velocity streamlines. In this case, particle transport simulates convection in an explicit way, therefore, the convective term is excluded from the momentum equation, and the reduced system of differential equations must be solved using FEM on a mesh. For the same level of accuracy, a coarser mesh is now sufficient, and a larger time step is allowed. This will obviously lead to a certain loss of accuracy for effects simulated on the mesh—viscosity, pressure difference, outer forces (such as buoyancy),—however, for convection-dominated problems, it will not significantly affect the overall accuracy of the results, since their influence on the parameters of the flow is much weaker than that of convection.

The solution for the Eulerian mesh and Lagrangian particles is obtained separately, at different steps of the algorithm. The PFEM-2 method implies that the mesh is fixed and the particles are transported on top of it (this is the main difference between PFEM-2 and the original Particle Finite Element Method, which is purely Lagrangian). It eliminates the need to rebuild the mesh at each time step, but results in two separate sets of variables (namely, velocity fields)—at the mesh nodes and associated with the particles, which have to be kept consistent at each simulation step. For this purpose, two operations are performed: *projection* of the velocity field from the particles onto the mesh nodes and *correction* of the velocities associated with the particles using the values at the mesh nodes.

The whole PFEM-2 solution algorithm includes preliminary steps, as well as a number of operations performed at each simulation time step. The algorithm is shown in Fig. 1 with indication of the Eulerian and Lagrangian steps. The former and latter imply different approaches to parallelization, however, it appears that it can be done efficiently in both cases. The details of these steps are discussed below.

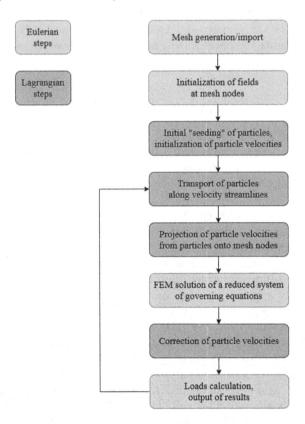

Fig. 1. Implemented PFEM-2 solution algorithm

2.2   FEM Solution on the Eulerian Mesh

Thanks to the utilization of particles simulating convection, the following modified system has to be solved on the fixed Eulerian mesh:

$$\begin{cases} \rho\dfrac{\partial \mathbf{V}}{\partial t} = \nabla p + \nabla \cdot \boldsymbol{\tau} + \boldsymbol{f}, & (3) \\ \nabla \cdot \mathbf{V} = 0. & (4) \end{cases}$$

This system is linear and makes the use of coarser meshes possible. Different methods for its solution can be applied. In the implementation described in this paper, we use a "segregated" approach, which means that the pressure and velocities are decoupled and solved separately. More precisely, the fractional-step approach is used [6]; it includes 3 steps, and only 1 unknown field is obtained per step. For its implementation, the velocity predictor field $\tilde{\mathbf{V}}$ is introduced. It is found as a result of solving the velocity prediction equation (hereinafter $k, l = 1, \ldots, d$, where d is the problem dimension)

$$\rho\frac{\tilde{V}_k - V_k}{\Delta t} = \frac{\partial \tau_{kl}^{n+\theta}}{\partial x_l} + f_k. \tag{5}$$

The pressure field is then obtained as a solution of the pressure equation

$$\frac{\partial^2 \hat{p}}{\partial x_k \partial x_k} = \frac{\rho}{\Delta t}\frac{\partial \tilde{V}_k}{\partial x_k}. \tag{6}$$

The velocity predictor field $\tilde{V}$ is not required to be divergence-free, therefore, the right-hand side of Eq. (6) is generally non-zero. The new velocity field $\hat{V}$ is obtained after the following velocity correction equation is solved:

$$\rho\frac{\hat{V}_k - \tilde{V}_k}{\Delta t} = -\frac{\partial \hat{p}}{\partial x_k}. \tag{7}$$

The whole fractional-step strategy (5), (6), (7) ensures that reduced Navier–Stokes Eqs. (3) are solved, and the resulting velocity field satisfies incompressibility Eq. (4).

A slightly different fractional-step scheme, which includes the known pressure field p in the velocity prediction equation (the pressure equation and the velocity correction equation are modified accordingly), can be used. Although it may appear that extra information will provide better results, it is generally recommended [7] to use Scheme (5)–(7) as a more robust one. Our numerical experiments [8] proved the same.

2.3 Operations with Lagrangian Particles

Particles in PFEM-2 serve the purpose of simulating convection by means of their transport along velocity streamlines. To provide numerical stability, the Courant – Friedrichs – Lewy (CFL) number for this operation should be relatively small (below 0.1..0.15), which leads to the transport of particles being performed in a number of substeps. The velocity field at the mesh nodes is considered "frozen" during this process, and the explicit Euler method is used:

$$\boldsymbol{x}_p^{k+1} = \boldsymbol{x}_p^k + \tau \boldsymbol{v}_p^n(\boldsymbol{x}_p^k), \qquad k = 0, \dots, K-1. \tag{8}$$

$\boldsymbol{v}_p^n(\boldsymbol{x}_p^k)$ here is calculated by interpolating the velocities at the mesh nodes (denoted $\boldsymbol{u}_i^n$) of the cell in which the particle with the index p is currently located ($\boldsymbol{x}_p^k$ being its coordinates):

$$\boldsymbol{v}_p^n(\boldsymbol{x}_p^k) = \sum_{i=1}^{M} \varphi_i(\boldsymbol{x}_p^k)\boldsymbol{u}_i^n, \tag{9}$$

where φ_i are the values of the shape functions of the corresponding mesh cell, M is the number of mesh cell nodes.

Since we use the velocity values at the nodes of the mesh cell surrounding the current particle location in Formula (9), we need to update the ascription of particles to cells after each substep of particle transport. This is a relatively computationally expensive procedure, which implies the analysis of several cases for each particle. The details of the operation of particle resorting will be covered in the next section. After the particles are resorted, we perform a check for each mesh cell whether it contains a sufficient number of particles. If a specific part of the cell is empty, a new particle is created and placed there, with its velocity being initialized using the velocities of the surrounding mesh nodes. At the same time, if the cell part contains too many particles close to each other, this will not enhance the accuracy as their velocities are normally the same, but will inevitably increase computational costs. Therefore, we discard all particles in close adjacency, except a certain number, and delete them from the computation.

Once the particles have been transferred to new locations, we perform the projection of the velocity field from them onto the mesh nodes. Since the particles represent the submesh scale and provide additional information, as opposed to the mesh nodes, we reset the velocities at the mesh nodes to zero and use the velocities associated with the particles for recalculating the former. The velocity of the mesh node with the index j is calculated using the contribution from all particles located in the mesh cells to which this node belongs. Technically, we use the mean value weighted by the shape functions ($\varphi_j(\boldsymbol{x}_p)$ is the value of the shape function corresponding to this mesh node):

$$\boldsymbol{u}_j = \frac{\sum\limits_{p=1}^{P} \boldsymbol{u}_p \varphi_j(\boldsymbol{x}_p)}{\sum\limits_{p=1}^{P} \varphi_j(\boldsymbol{x}_p)}. \tag{10}$$

A similar procedure is performed in the opposite direction after the solution is obtained using FEM on the Eulerian mesh. However, instead of resetting the velocities associated with the particles, we only adjust them by the increment of the velocities at the nodes of the surrounding mesh cell so as not to lose the resolution capability provided by the particles. The correction of particle velocities is done using the following interpolation procedure with the shape function values as coefficients (M is the number of mesh cell nodes):

$$\delta \boldsymbol{u}_p^n(\boldsymbol{x}_p^k) = \sum_{i=1}^{M} \varphi_i(\boldsymbol{x}_p^k)(\boldsymbol{u}_i^{n+1} - \boldsymbol{u}_i^n). \tag{11}$$

3 Parallel Software Implementation of PFEM-2

The original PFEM-2 method algorithm was earlier implemented [9] in a framework based on the deal.II library [10]. The latter is an open-source finite element method toolkit with a wide range of capabilities. For the FEM solution of the hydrodynamic problem (3), (4), the internal features of deal.II were mostly used. The handling of particles also utilizes the mechanisms of this library, however, this functionality was originally intended by the deal.II authors for other classes of problems and required specific modification by the authors of this paper.

The shares of time costs differ for different parts of the PFEM-2 method algorithm. An example for solving the test problem covered further in Sect. 4 in a serial mode is shown in Fig. 2. One can see that among the recurrent operations performed at each time step, the FEM solution and particle transport occupy the majority of the computation time. These procedures, as well as the particle velocities projection and correction, were chosen as primary objects for parallelization. However, as the Eulerian and Lagrangian parts of the PFEM-2 algorithm are very different algorithmically, different approaches to parallelization were applied.

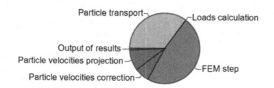

Fig. 2. Shares of time costs of main operations in PFEM-2 (test problem)

3.1   Parallel Version of the FEM Solution in PFEM-2

We implemented a fairly conventional approach to the parallelization of the finite element solution of the hydrodynamic problem. It is mainly based on the features of the deal.II library and a number of auxiliary tools. Running computations on several processor cores leads to the need for domain decomposition, for which the METIS or p4est libraries can be used in compatibility with deal.II. The p4est library was chosen because it is generally recommended as a more "contemporary" alternative to METIS. This library performs the partitioning of the mesh and its storage as a hierarchical arrangement of a forest of quad- or octtrees (hence its name). Partitioning is not aimed to minimize the size of interprocess boundaries, but rather creates subdomains of such form so as to make storing, addressing and manipulating the cells as efficient as possible. This operation is performed by the algorithm within p4est, and the resulting subdomain can even be disconnected and consist of two (but not more) fragments. An example of applying p4est to the mesh from the test problem in Sect. 4 is shown in Fig. 3. For this case, the number of subdomains, which are indicated by different colors, is 16.

The partitioning of the mesh in deal.II has one specific aspect: each process stores its "own" part of the mesh, as well as one adjacent row of its neighboring domains. These cells are called "ghost" cells and are used for auxiliary purposes, which will be shown later.

After the domain is decomposed, the FEM substep of each time step of computation includes the consequent assembly of the system matrix and the right-hand side vector for all unknown fields in Eqs. (5)–(7) (both components of the

Fig. 3. Example of domain decomposition

velocity prediction field, pressure field and both components of the final velocity) and the solution of the corresponding linear systems. During the assembly, each compute node processes cells belonging to its subdomain and calculates its part of the system matrix and the right-hand side. The boundary conditions are also taken into account during this process. After this procedure is finished by all processes, they perform communication with neighboring processes and exchange the necessary data. Handling the vectors and sparse matrices is maintained by the `Trilinos` library [11]. An alternative parallel linear algebra library, `PETSc`, could have been used, but was rejected due to memory leakage issues when used together with `deal.II`. The parallel solution of linear systems is also performed by `Trilinos`, including the solver (the generalized minimal residual method was used with a preconditioner—based on the Jacobi method for velocity fields and the algebraic multigrid for the pressure field).

Despite the computation time for calculating aerodynamic loads being negligibly small (see Fig. 2), it was also parallelized, as different parts of the body surface can belong to different nodes. Therefore, each process calculates its contribution to the drag force F_D and the lift force F_L as parts of the corresponding integrals over their parts of the body surface S:

$$F_D = \int\limits_S \left(\mu \frac{\partial v_t}{\partial \boldsymbol{n}} n_y - P n_x \right) dS, \qquad F_L = -\int\limits_S \left(\mu \frac{\partial v_t}{\partial \boldsymbol{n}} n_x + P n_y \right) dS, \quad (12)$$

where n and t are the normal vector and tangential vector on S, respectively. After these contributions are computed, the summation is performed over all processes using MPI, and then the resulting values of the corresponding aerodynamic coefficients C_D and C_L are output into the file. Although the load of different compute nodes is unbalanced during this operation, it can be neglected because its share in the whole amount of the computation time is incredibly small.

Finally, the output of the results is also performed by all compute nodes in a parallel way. Mostly out-of-box `deal.II` features were used in the case of the FEM solution on a mesh: each node writes out data for its part of the domain to a separate `.vtu` file (XML-type replacement of the legacy VTK format, which is considered more efficient than the latter) in binary form. The governing node then produces a `.pvtu` file that contains a centralized record for the whole group of VTU files for the correct visualization of the global solution.

3.2 Parallel Version of Operations with Particles in PFEM-2

The parallelization of particle handling in PFEM-2 is also connected with domain decomposition. *Particle transport*, which is the main operation, is performed independently by all compute nodes for particles located in the cells of their subdomain. However, this set of particles changes after each substep of particle transport (see Formula (8)) as the particles are resorted. This procedure is different in the parallel case and includes three stages. At first, each process checks all the particles that are currently ascribed to the cells of its subdomain. At this substep, we check whether the particle is still in the cell it was before being transferred. In case the particle has left the cell, we check all its neighboring cells (sorting them according to the direction in which the particle was moved). Some of these cells may be "ghost" cells, i.e. belonging to another process. This check may have three outcomes: the particle is found in another cell belonging to the same compute node; the particle is found in a "ghost" cell or not found in any of the neighboring cells. In the first case, its processing in the resorting procedure is completed; in the second case, it is marked for further data exchange with the corresponding compute node; in the third case, it is deleted from the computation. The latter case mostly happens when the particles leave the entire domain, other cases (such as particle moving across more than one cell at one substep) are extremely rare due to the choice of time steps.

The second stage of the resorting procedure is communication between the nodes and the exchange of respective particle data. Each particle is handed over with its global and local coordinates, as well as the velocity vector. Finally, after the particles received from other processes are placed into the corresponding cells, a check is performed for each cell whether its parts contain at least one particle. If needed, new particles are created and placed in empty cell parts with their velocity initialized using the values at the surrounding mesh cell nodes. This check is done independently by all compute nodes for their subdomains.

The correction of particle velocities is executed in a similar way: each process performs a correction for all particles inside the cells of its subdomain according to Eq. (11). The value required for the adjustment of the particle velocity depends only on the velocities at the nodes of its cell, therefore, no exchange between the neighboring nodes is needed here. The procedure of *the projection of particle velocities* onto the mesh nodes, on the contrary, requires such communication between processes. All compute nodes calculate the sums in the nominator and denominator in Formula (10), but for the mesh nodes belonging simultaneously to two or more processes, the contribution from the latter should also be summed up (see Fig. 4). For this reason, the summation of these two quantities is performed using MPI, and after that the value of the mesh node velocity is finally calculated.

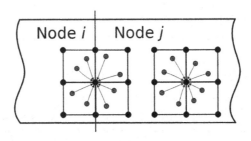

Fig. 4. Projection of particle velocities onto the mesh nodes in the parallel case

The procedure of initial particles "seeding", which precedes the solution cycle over time, is parallelized in a natural way: each compute node performs the placement of the required number of particles inside the cells of its part of the mesh, which is followed by the initialization of the velocities associated with these particles using the velocity values at the mesh nodes.

It should be noted that the ratio between time costs for the FEM solution and particle-related steps does not remain constant throughout the computation. Figure 2 shows only the aggregated shares for different operations over a considerable period of simulation. However, the quantity of particles at a specific time step changes and significantly affects the execution time of different procedures. First, after the initial "seeding" of particles has been performed, they start to move along velocity field streamlines, and free parts of mesh cells or particles are frequently encountered during the check mentioned above. New particles are added, and this process typically continues until the limit of particles per cell (or per cell part) is reached, after which the overall quantity of particles more or less stabilizes (an example of how the number of particles per cell can vary during the computation is shown in Fig. 5). As a result, the share of the FEM step generally decreases for a certain period of time after the start of the computation.

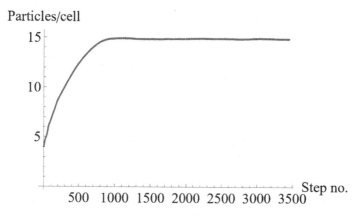

Fig. 5. Number of particles per mesh cell at different time steps of the test computation

4   Numerical Experiment

4.1   Test Problem

The parallel solver for the PFEM-2 method was tested on the model problem for an unsteady viscous flow past the NACA-0012 airfoil, which is a widely known test [12]. A low Reynolds number of 1×10^4 is considered when the flow is laminar, and the airfoil is placed at a small angle of attack $\alpha = 4°$. The physical and numerical parameters of the problem are listed in Table 1.

Table 1. Parameters of the test problem

Parameter		Value
Density	ρ	1
Dynamic viscosity	ν	0.001
Free-stream velocity	V_∞	10
Reynolds number	Re	1×10^4
Time step	Δt	0.001

The configuration of the domain is shown in Fig. 6. Different boundary conditions are applied to the velocity field on different parts of the boundary: Dirichlet-type condition $V = V_\infty$ at the boundaries Γ_1 and Γ_4 and Neumann-type condition $\dfrac{\partial V}{\partial n} = 0$ at the boundaries Γ_2 and Γ_3.

Two different meshes were built using the SALOME Platform containing 174,000 and 562,500 cells. The mesh fragment near the airfoil is demonstrated in Fig. 7. The flow was simulated for 5.0s of model time. The distribution of the velocity field at time $t = 5s$ is shown in Fig. 8. A numerical experiment was

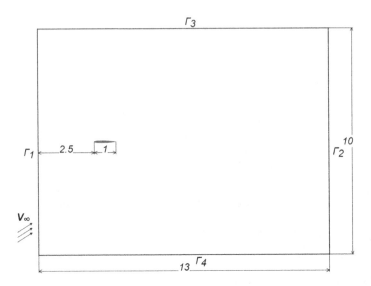

Fig. 6. Domain geometry for the test case

carried out on HPC systems of two different types. The total time, as well as the FEM step time and the particle step time, was measured for all computations (particle transport and projection/interpolation procedures).

Fig. 7. Eulerian mesh near the airfoil

The first series of computations was performed on the multi-core system of Bauman Moscow State Technical University, equipped with two 18-core Intel Xeon Gold 6254 processors and 40 gigabytes of RAM. A coarser mesh (174,000 cells) was used. The speed-up of the computation for a different number n of processor cores is shown in Fig. 9. The total time for a single-core computation in this case was 11 h 40 min. One can see that, despite the use of shared memory, the efficiency of parallelization is far from its theoretical limit. This remains true for different parts of the PFEM-2 algorithm (FEM and particle operations).

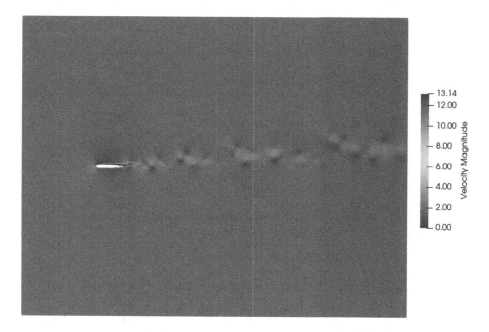

Fig. 8. Velocity field distribution at time $t = 5\,\text{s}$

The second and third series of computations were carried out on a cluster system located at the Applied Mathematics Department of BMSTU. This system comprises 6 compute nodes, each with one 18-core Intel Core i9-10980XE processor and 128 gigabytes of RAM (a total of 108 cores and 768 gigabytes of distributed memory). Communication between the compute nodes is organized via the InfiniBand FDR network (Mellanox SX6036 switch and ConnectX-3 Pro adapters) for data exchange, as well as conventional 5-gigabit Ethernet for control commands. The speed-up of the computation for a different number n of nodes (from 1 to 6) for a coarser mesh and a finer mesh is demonstrated in Fig. 10. Computations on a single 18-core node take up 50 min and 3 h 15 min for these two meshes, respectively. Particle operations scale reasonably well as it can be expected. At the same time, the efficiency of parallelization of the FEM step enhances with an increase in the number of mesh cells per compute node. This results in remarkable overall scalability for the case of the finer mesh, which almost reaches the theoretical limit.

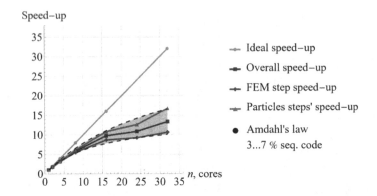

Fig. 9. Speed-up of computations on the multi-core system

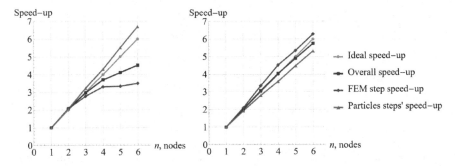

Fig. 10. Speed-up of computations on the cluster system for a coarser mesh (a) and a finer mesh (b)

5   Conclusion

An MPI-based solver for the PFEM-2 method was developed. It is implemented within an open-source software framework with the `deal.II` library at its core. The Eulerian (mesh-related) and Lagrangian (particle-related) steps of the algorithm required different approaches to parallelization. Numerical experiments for a test case show that an acceptable speed-up of computations is achieved. The PFEM-2 method solver scales especially well on a cluster system, and the efficiency of parallelization, as usually, tends to grow together with the size of the problem.

At the same time, the share of time costs for the FEM step remains relatively large compared to other operations. Two ways of improvement can be seen here: optimization of the FEM procedure itself and further parallelization. The FEM step still has a number of possible bottlenecks, with most of the time spent on the assembly of matrices and right-hand side vectors (the solution of linear systems takes considerably less time). Another way to reduce time costs is the application of high-performance computations on GPUs using CUDA technology. The latest versions of `deal.II` already have several classes and subroutines for different operations over CUDA, therefore, it appears to have a certain potential for accelerating manipulations with matrices and vectors during the FEM step and is planned as a stage of further development of the solver.

Acknowledgement. Work of Ilia Marchevsky is supported by the Russian Science Foundation (proj. 17-79-20445).

References

1. Idelsohn, S., Nigro, N., Gimenez, J., Rossi, R., Marti, J.: A fast and accurate method to solve the incompressible Navier-Stokes equations. Eng. Comput. **30**(2), 197–222 (2013). https://doi.org/10.1108/02644401311304854
2. Becker, P.: An enhanced Particle Finite Element Method with special emphasis on landslides and debris flows. Ph.D. thesis, Universitat Politecnica de Catalunya (2015)
3. Idelsohn, S.R., Oñate, E., Del Pin, F.: The particle finite element method: a powerful tool to solve incompressible flows with free-surfaces and breaking waves. Int. J. Numer. Methods Eng. **61**, 964–989 (2004). https://doi.org/10.1002/nme.1096
4. Nigro, N., Gimenez, J., Idelsohn, S.: Recent advances in the particle finite element method towards more complex fluid flow applications. Comput. Methods Appl. Sci. **33**, 267–318 (2014). https://doi.org/10.1007/978-3-319-06136-8_12
5. Dadvand, P., Rossi. R., Oñate, E.: An object-oriented environment for developing finite element codes for multi-disciplinary applications. Arch. Comput. Methods Eng. **17**(3), 253–297 (2010). https://doi.org/10.1007/s11831-010-9045-2
6. Ferziger, J.H., Perić, M.: Computational Methods for Fluid Dynamics. Springer, Cham (2002). https://doi.org/10.1007/978-3-642-56026-2
7. Zienkiewicz, O.C., Taylor, R.L.: The Finite Element Method, vol. 3. Fluid Dynamics (2000)
8. Marchevsky, I.K., Osadchiev, A.A., Popov, A.Y.: Numerical modelling of high-frequency internal waves generated by river discharge in Coastal Ocean. In: Proceedings of the 5th International Conference on Geographical Information Systems Theory, Applications and Management – GISTAM 2019, pp. 384–387 (2019). https://doi.org/10.5220/0007840203840387
9. Popov, A., Marchevsky, I., Serbin, G.: Validation of a newly developed implementation of the PFEM-2 method using an open-source framework. In: Proceedings Ivannikov Ispras Open Conference (ISPRAS), pp. 176–181. IEEE (2021). https://doi.org/10.1109/ISPRAS53967.2021.00031
10. The deal.II Finite Element Library. https://dealii.org
11. Trilinos Home Page. https://trilinos.github.io/
12. Srinath, D.N., Mittal, S.: Optimal aerodynamic design of airfoils in unsteady viscous flows. Comput. Methods Appl. Mech. Eng. **199**, 1976–1991 (2010). https://doi.org/10.1016/j.cma.2010.02.016

Modeling of Two-Phase Fluid Flow Processes in a Fractured-Porous Type Reservoir Using Parallel Computations

Ravil Uzyanbaev[1]([✉]), Yuliya Bobreneva[1,2], Yury Poveshchenko[3],
Viktoriia Podryga[3,4], and Sergey Polyakov[3]

[1] Ufa State Petroleum Technological University, Ufa, Russia
ravil-11@mail.ru
[2] Institute of Petrochemistry and Catalysis of Russian Academy of Sciences,
Ufa, Russia
[3] Keldysh Institute of Applied Mathematics of the Russian Academy of Sciences,
Moscow, Russia
[4] Moscow Automobile and Road Construction State Technical University,
Moscow, Russia

Abstract. The modeling of the mass transfer of a two-phase fluid in a
fractured-porous reservoir is considered. The porous reservoir and fractures have their own filtration-capacity properties, which complicates
filtration processes. To describe the problem, a four-block mathematical
model with splitting by physical processes is used. For the numerical
solution of the problem in the one-dimensional case, an original implicit
difference scheme on a non-uniform grid is proposed. The problem feature
is a large pressure drop, which requires the use of detailed grids and, as
a result, leads to high computational costs. One of the ways to solve the
problem is to use parallel computing. The paper proposes an algorithm
based on the parallel sweep method, which allows one to significantly
speed up calculations and is generalized to the multidimensional case
within the framework of using additional splitting in spatial coordinates.
A series of calculations, confirming the effectiveness of the developed
numerical algorithm and its parallel implementation, are carried out.

Keywords: Mathematical modeling · System of equations for
two-phase filtration · Fractured-porous reservoir · Piezoconductivity
and dual porosity · Implicit difference schemes · Parallel algorithms
based on sweep

1 Introduction

The oil and gas industry is the most important component of the world economy.
The development of the industry requires the solution of issues of a different nature.
One of the main issues is the opening and efficient development of fields. The the-
ory of field development is based on fundamental research in the fields of physics,

L. Sokolinsky and M. Zymbler (Eds.): PCT 2022, CCIS 1618, pp. 276–292, 2022.
https://doi.org/10.1007/978-3-031-11623-0_19

chemistry, mathematics, information technology, geology, as well as applied sciences. It is important to know geological processes, both in a specific oil and gas region and the region as a whole, the physics of oil and gas reservoirs in the reservoir, their structure, physicochemical processes occurring in the reservoir during the development of reserves [1,2]. Modern field development technology is based on a comprehensive study of the properties of productive formations and the fluids contained in them, as well as the study of complex processes occurring in formations during their operation. At this stage, it is crucial to understand the filtration characteristics of the reservoir, the nature of the movement of fluids in the reservoir, the spatial distribution of zones of high and low permeability values. As before, the most significant and important issue is the increase in the completeness of the production of hydrocarbon reserves from deposits. This issue remains especially relevant for carbonate reservoirs, in which the presence of fracturing is confined to the natural geological process of reservoir formation [3]. The relevance of studying filtration processes in fractured reservoirs is due to the fact that more than 60% of the world's proven reserves of hydrocarbons are contained in such fields. The main problem in the development of such reservoirs is a complex structure [4,5], in which, along with intergranular pores, there are always fractures and caverns. The filtration of oil and gas is primarily caused by the presence of fractures and caverns. Despite the presence of a large volume of fractures, the development of such deposits is an extremely complex technological process, often accompanied by difficulties, and can be ineffective [3,6].

A fractured formation is characterized by discrete properties due to the presence of two types of voids. The pore reservoir (or matrix) has smaller pores (voids) and is distinguished by a significant holding capacity, but low filtration properties. The fracture system, on the contrary, is characterized by low capacitive, but high filtration properties.

The process of fluid filtration in fractured reservoirs also changes significantly, since there are two pore systems, which are a system of fractures and a system of matrices with different values of geometric dimensions and reservoir properties. The calculation of flow characteristics under special conditions of sharp reservoir heterogeneity was carried out by different authors [7,8]. However, the most universal model describing the process of mass transfer in these types of reservoirs is the Warren-Root model [7]. According to this model, pores (or matrix) in a fractured-porous reservoir are represented by rectangular parallelepipeds, where the matrix has high porosity and low permeability and is separated by a set of natural fractures that have high permeability and low porosity. The filtration of fluid in the reservoir is carried out along the set of fractures, and the matrix is a reservoir that continuously feeds the set of natural fractures. Thus, the Warren-Root model was chosen to calculate the fractured-matrix fluid exchanges.

The process of fluid filtration in carbonate reservoirs is characterized by a combination of various complex processes and is of a general nature. In this case, computer modeling becomes an integral part of the development of carbonate fields. The features of the problem are a large pressure drop and the presence of a multiphase fluid system (water, oil) in a complex structured fractured-matrix porous medium. Thus, for a two-phase system of immiscible fluids in a fractured-matrix reservoir, taking into account the processes of mass transfer between fractures and the matrix, it is in demand to develop a new mathematical model and a corresponding numerical algorithm for its solution. Even in the spatially one-dimensional case, this leads to a large amount of computation due to the use of detailed grids. One of the ways to overcome this difficulty is to develop an efficient parallel algorithm that adapts to the architecture of modern high-performance systems.

The most common parallel programming technologies are the Message Passing Interface (MPI) and Open Multi-Processing (OpenMP) standards. They are used in the form of library functions (MPI) and special comments (OpenMP) in traditional sequential programming languages C, C++, Fortran, Java and allow one to get efficient parallel programs.

For computers with shared memory, OpenMP technology is more commonly used. The OpenMP interface is conceived as a standard for creating parallel applications for scalable SMP systems (SSMP, ccNUMA, etc.) within the shared memory model. The OpenMP standard includes specifications for a set of compiler directives, helper functions, and environment variables. OpenMP implements parallel computing using multithreading, in which a "master" thread creates a set of "slave" threads, and the task is distributed among them. It is assumed that the threads are executed in parallel on several processors (cores, threads of cores), and the number of processes does not necessarily have to coincide with the number of hardware threads [9].

The MPI standard is one of the most widely used tools for creating parallel and distributed applications using network communications. The MPI standard specifies an interface that both the programming system on each computing platform and the user must follow when creating their programs. Regardless of which physical computing device the MPI program is running on, this technology implements a distributed memory model. Within this model, it is assumed that an MPI program is executed by a group of so-called MPI processes, each of which has its own local memory. All operations in an MPI program are performed in parallel by all MPI processes with each MPI process using data from its own local memory. Obtaining data from the local memory of other processes is organized explicitly with the help of special exchange procedures that constitute the core of MPI technology [9].

The use of parallel technologies significantly reduces the time for solving problems and improves the efficiency of using RAM. In this work, it is proposed to use a more modern version of the above standards, namely, a hybrid that combines distributed parallel computing in a network and multithreading, which is conditionally called as MPI + OpenMP. This option adapts well to the architecture of modern computing clusters. In the work, on its basis, an effective numerical algorithm and its parallel implementation were developed to solve the problem of modeling the processes of the mass transfer of a two-phase system of immiscible liquids in a fractured-porous reservoir.

2   Formulation of the Problem

The mathematical description of the distribution of mass transfer in the "fracture set – matrix" system is presented by differential equations of the second order. The classical functions proposed in the work of Warren-Root [7] are used as the functions of fluid exchange between the set of fractures and the matrix.

$$\frac{\partial(\phi^\alpha \rho_o S_o^\alpha)}{\partial t} + \nabla(\rho_o U_o^\alpha) + q_o^\alpha = \rho_o q_j, q_o^m = -q_o^f = -\rho_o^m \sigma \lambda_o^m (P^f - P^m), \quad (1)$$

$$\frac{\partial(\phi^\alpha \rho_w S_w^\alpha)}{\partial t} + \nabla(\rho_w U_w^\alpha) + q_w^\alpha = \rho_w q_j, q_w^m = -q_w^f = -\rho_w^m \sigma \lambda_w^m (P^f - P^m), \quad (2)$$

$$\lambda_o^m = \frac{k^m k_{ro}(S_o^m)}{\mu_o}, \lambda_w^m = \frac{k^m k_{rw}(S_w^m)}{\mu_w}. \quad (3)$$

The generalized Darcy's law is used to describe the filtration velocity. According to this law, the oil and water filtration velocities are equal to:

$$U_o^\alpha = -\frac{k^\alpha k_{ro}(S_o^\alpha)}{\mu_o} grad P_o^\alpha, U_w^\alpha = -\frac{k^\alpha k_{rw}(S_w^\alpha)}{\mu_w} grad P_w^\alpha. \quad (4)$$

Here $\alpha = f, m$, where f is the fracture system, m is the matrix system, $i = o, w$, where o is the oil, w is the water, P^f is the formation pressure in the fracture system (Pa), P^m is the formation pressure in the matrix (Pa), ϕ^f is the porosity in the fracture system, ϕ^m is the porosity in the matrix, ρ_o is the density of oil (g/m^3), ρ_w is the density of water (g/m^3), S_i^f is the saturation of oil or water in the fracture system, S_i^m is the saturation of oil or water in the matrix, U_i^α is the flow velocity of oil or water, q_j is the fluid rate (m^3/day), q_i^α is the coefficient of redistribution of the fluid between the matrix and the fractures, σ is the coefficient of fractured rock $(1/m^2)$, k^α is the absolute permeability (m^2), k_{rw} and k_{ro} are the relative phase permeabilities of water and oil, μ_o is the viscosity of oil (Pa·s), μ_w is the viscosity of water (Pa·s).

For the problem posed, the following initial and boundary conditions are considered:

$$P^m|_{t=0} = P_0, P^f|_{t=0} = P_0, P^f|_{x=0} = P_w, \frac{\partial P^f}{\partial x}|_{x=l} = 0. \quad (5)$$

System (1)–(4) with initial and boundary conditions (5) is a complex system of equations of mathematical physics of mixed type. At the initial stage, a complete splitting of the system by physical processes is carried out [10]. Splitting occurs into four equations, which include two equations (for the matrix and the system of fractures) with respect to the saturation transfer of one of the phases (namely, water) and two equations (for the matrix and the set of fractures) of piezoconductivity. First, we perform splitting and obtain a system of equations for the first functional block in terms of piezoconductivity. Further, the system of equations is linearized according to the chord method. The resulting differential equations, boundary and initial conditions are approximated by their grid counterparts according to the implicit scheme [11–14]. As a result of the approximation, we obtain a system of linear algebraic equations, which are reduced to the general form [15,16]:

$$- A_{pk}\delta P_{k-1}^f + C_{pk}\delta P_k^f - B_{pk}\delta P_{k+1}^f = \Phi_{pk}, \qquad (6)$$

where the coefficients are as follows:

$$\Phi_{pk} = -F^{fs} - \tau \left\{ \frac{(\rho_w^m \bar{\sigma}\lambda_w^m)^s}{(\rho_w^f)^{(\delta 1 f)\approx}} + \frac{(\rho_o^m \bar{\sigma}\lambda_o^m)^s}{(\rho_o^f)^{(\delta 1 f)\approx}} \right\} \Phi^{ms}, \qquad (7)$$

$$A_{pk} = \frac{\tau}{\left[(\rho_w^f)^{(\delta 1 f)}\right]_k^{\approx}} \left\{ \frac{1}{h_{k-1/2}} \left(\frac{\rho_w^f k^f}{\mu_w^f} \right)_{k-1/2}^s k_{rw(k-1/2)}^{ups} \right\}$$

$$+ \frac{\tau}{\left[(\rho_o^f)^{(\delta 1 f)}\right]_k^{\approx}} \left\{ \frac{1}{h_{k-1/2}} \left(\frac{\rho_o^f k^f}{\mu_o^f} \right)_{k-1/2}^s k_{ro(k-1/2)}^{ups} \right\}, \qquad (8)$$

$$B_{pk} = \frac{\tau}{\left[(\rho_w^f)^{(\delta 1 f)}\right]_k^{\approx}} \left\{ \frac{1}{h_{k+1/2}} \left(\frac{\rho_w^f k^f}{\mu_w^f} \right)_{k+1/2}^s k_{rw(k+1/2)}^{ups} \right\}$$

$$+ \frac{\tau}{\left[(\rho_o^f)^{(\delta 1 f)}\right]_k^{\approx}} \left\{ \frac{1}{h_{k+1/2}} \left(\frac{\rho_o^f k^f}{\mu_o^f} \right)_{k+1/2}^s k_{ro(k+1/2)}^{ups} \right\},$$

$$(9)$$

$$C_{pk} = \frac{(S_w^f)^{(\delta 1 f)\approx}}{(\rho_w^f)^{(\delta 1 f)\approx}} (\bar{\phi}^f \rho_w^f)_{P_f}^{'S} + \frac{(1 - S_w^f)^{(\delta 1 f)\approx}}{(\rho_o^f)^{(\delta 1 f)\approx}} (\bar{\phi}^f \rho_o^f)_{P_f}^{'S}$$

$$+ \frac{\tau}{\left[(\rho_w^f)^{(\delta 1 f)}\right]_k^{\approx}} \left\{ \frac{1}{h_{k+\frac{1}{2}}} \left(\frac{\rho_w^f k^f}{\mu_w^f} \right)_{k+\frac{1}{2}}^s k_{rw(k+\frac{1}{2})}^{ups} + \frac{1}{h_{k-\frac{1}{2}}} \left(\frac{\rho_w^f k^f}{\mu_w^f} \right)_{k-\frac{1}{2}}^s k_{rw(k-\frac{1}{2})}^{ups} \right\}$$

$$+ \frac{\tau}{\left[(\rho_o^f)^{(\delta 1 f)}\right]_k^{\approx}} \left\{ \frac{1}{h_{k+\frac{1}{2}}} \left(\frac{\rho_o^f k^f}{\mu_o^f} \right)_{k+\frac{1}{2}}^s k_{ro(k+\frac{1}{2})}^{ups} + \frac{1}{h_{k-\frac{1}{2}}} \left(\frac{\rho_o^f k^f}{\mu_o^f} \right)_{k-\frac{1}{2}}^s k_{ro(k-\frac{1}{2})}^{ups} \right\}$$

$$+ \left\{ \frac{\tau}{(\rho_w^f)^{(\delta 1 f)}} (\rho_w^m \bar{\sigma}\lambda_w^m)^s (1 - \pi_m^s) \right\}_k + \left\{ \frac{\tau}{(\rho_o^f)^{(\delta 1 f)}} (\rho_o^m \bar{\sigma}\lambda_o^m)^s (1 - \pi_m^s) \right\}_k .$$

$$(10)$$

Here F^{fs} is the difference approximation (multiplied by the time step τ), in grid approximations $a^{\approx}$, the values on the implicit time layer $\hat{t}$ are taken at $s+1$ of the already calculated iteration, $\bar{\phi} = h\phi$, $\delta 1$ is the weight by time, a is the pressure derivative, δP is the pressure increment, $\bar{\sigma} = h\sigma$, $k_{rw\Omega}^{up\Lambda}$ are the relative phase permeabilities of water in the cell Ω taken from the node $\omega(\Omega)$ of this cell, located upstream (up) from the implicit time layer (Λ).

To solve the system of linear algebraic equations with a tridiagonal matrix, the scalar sweep method is used. As a result of solving system (6), we obtain an array of pressures, which describes the dynamics of pressure in time and space in the environment of the well. The obtained pressure values allow one to proceed to the solution of the second block of saturation transfer.

Having constructed the solution for the piezoconductivity block, having determined the pressures in the fractures and the matrix, a transition to the calculation of the second block, which is responsible for the transfer of matter, takes place. It is accepted that the saturations of water and oil add up to one, therefore, the saturation for oil is expressed through the saturation for water, and all calculations are carried out with respect to water. For the numerical solution of this system, the finite difference method is used. An implicit difference scheme is considered. A difference grid is constructed in time and space.

$$-A_{Swk}^f \delta S_{wk-1}^f + C_{Swk}^f \delta S_{wk}^f - B_{Swk}^f \delta S_{wk+1}^f + E_{Swk} \delta S_{wk}^m = 0 - L^{f\approx}, \quad (11)$$

where the coefficients are as follows:

$$A_{Swk}^f = -\tau \left\{ \left[\rho_w^f \frac{k^f}{\mu_w^f} \frac{1}{h} \right]_{k-1/2}^{s+1} (P_k^f - P_{k-1}^f)^{s+1} \left[(k_{rw})'_{S_{wk-1}^f} \right]_{upink}^s \right\}, \quad (12)$$

if $P_k^f < P_{k-1}^f$, $A_{Swk}^f \geq 0$,

$$B_{Swk}^f = \tau \left\{ \left[\rho_w^f \frac{k^f}{\mu_w^f} \frac{1}{h} \right]_{k+1/2}^{s+1} (P_{k+1}^f - P_k^f)^{s+1} \left[(k_{rw})'_{S_{wk+1}^f} \right]_{upink}^s \right\}, \quad (13)$$

if $P_k^f < P_{k+1}^f$, $B_{Swk}^f \geq 0$,

$$C_{Swk}^f = (\bar{\phi}^f \rho_w^f)_k^{s+1} - \tau \left\{ \left[\rho_w^f \frac{k^f}{\mu_w^f} \frac{1}{h} \right]_{k+\frac{1}{2}}^{s+1} (P_{k+1}^f - P_k^f)^{s+1} \left[(k_{rw})'_{S_{wk}^f} \right]_{upink}^s \right\}$$

$$- \tau \left\{ \left[\rho_w^f \frac{k^f}{\mu_w^f} \frac{1}{h} \right]_{k-\frac{1}{2}}^{s+1} (P_k^f - P_{k-1}^f)^{s+1} \left[(k_{rw})'_{S_{wk}^f} \right]_{upink}^s \right\}. \quad (14)$$

Here, the expression in the first square bracket is considered for $P_k^f > P_{k+1}^f$, and the expression in the second square bracket is considered for $P_k^f > P_{k-1}^f$. Obviously, for sufficiently small time steps, the following condition is satisfied

$C_{Swk}^f - A_{Swk}^f - B_{Swk}^f > 0$. L^f is the difference approximation (multiplied by the time step τ), $(k_{rw})'_{S_w^m}$ is the saturation derivative.

The resulting equation is similar to the piezoconductivity equation and is solved using a scalar sweep at each time layer.

3   Parallel Implementation

The computational problem formulated above is highly laborious even in the spatially one-dimensional case. This is especially evident when modeling filtration processes in long reservoirs. In this case, it is necessary to use grids with a large number of nodes. As a result, the computational time can significantly increase. The most general approach to solving this problem is the parallelization of the algorithm and the use of parallel computations [17]. Within the chosen hybrid technology MPI + OpenMP, it is required to monitor the uniform distribution of the computational load of both individual nodes of the cluster (supercomputer) and between threads within each node. This problem can be solved by choosing a suitable distribution of grid nodes between the calculators. This is usually done based on the principle of geometric parallelism.

Since the explicit scheme for solving the formulated problem imposes too stringent requirements on the integration step in time, in this work, an implicit algorithm that presupposes the inversion of the corresponding matrix is chosen. When solving this problem, it is proposed to use the parallel sweep algorithm [18]. To adapt it to the selected problem, we assume that in the space of nodes of a one-dimensional grid, a partition into p adjacent disjoint subdomains is introduced; their number is equal to the number of processes corresponding to the number of hardware threads of all nodes of the computing cluster.

For the convenience of considering the parallel algorithm, we choose the case of a linear discrete equation of type (6). In the operator form, (6) is a linear system of equations with a tridiagonal matrix. A system of this type can be written in the following standard (canonical) form [19]:

$$- A_i y_{i-1} + C_i y_i - B_i y_{i+1} = F_i, 1 \leq i \leq N - 1. \tag{15}$$

At the boundaries, we obtain, respectively:

$$C_0 y_0 - B_0 y_1 = F_0, C_N y_N - A_N y_{N-1} = F_N. \tag{16}$$

To describe the details of the parallel algorithm, we introduce a uniform partition of the set of numbers of grid nodes $\Omega = \{0, 1, ..., N\}$ into adjacent disjoint subsets $\Omega_m = \{i_1^m, ..., i_2^m\}$ ($m = 0, ..., p - 1$ is the logical number of the process).

As a result of such a partition, the process with the number m will process $(i_2^{(m)} - i_1^{(m)} + 1)$ points. Let us represent the solution on each internal process $(0 < m < p - 1)$ in the form:

$$y_i \equiv y_i^{(m)} = y_i^{(I,m)} + y_{i_1^{(m)}} y_i^{(III,m)} + y_{i_2^{(m)}} y_i^{(II,m)}, \tag{17}$$

where $y_i^{(\alpha,m)}(\alpha = I, II, III)$ are defined on Ω_m and play the role of a basis, and the values of the function on the boundary $\Omega_m - y_{i_1^{(m)}}$ and $y_{i_2^{(m)}}$ are not yet known. At the internal nodes Ω_m, the function $y_i^{(I,m)}$ is found from Eq. (15), and the functions $y_i^{(II,m)}$, $y_i^{(III,m)}$ are found from Eq. (15) with zero right-hand side.

The boundary conditions for $y_i^{(\alpha,m)}$ are as follows:

$$y_{i_1^{(m)}}^{(I,m)} = 0, y_{i_2^{(m)}}^{(I,m)} = 0, y_{i_1^{(m)}}^{(II,m)} = 0, y_{i_2^{(m)}}^{(II,m)} = 1, y_{i_1^{(m)}}^{(III,m)} = 1, y_{i_2^{(m)}}^{(III,m)} = 0. \quad (18)$$

On the zero and last processes:

$$y_i^{(0)} = y_i^{(I,0)} + y_{i_2^0} y_i^{(II,0)}, y_i^{p-1} = y_i^{(I,p-1)} + y_{i_1^{(p-1)}} y_i^{(III,p-1)}. \quad (19)$$

The boundary conditions are:

$$C_0 y_0^{(I,0)} - B_0 y_1^{(I,0)} = F_0, y_{i_2^{(0)}}^{(I,0)} = 0, y_{i_1^{(0)}}^{(I,p-1)} = 0,$$

$$C_N y_N^{(I,p-1)} - A_N y_{N-1}^{(I,p-1)} = F_N, C_0 y_0^{(II,0)} - B_0 y_1^{(II,0)} = 0, y_{i_2^{(0)}}^{(II,0)} = 1,$$

$$y_{i_1^{(0)}}^{(III,p-1)} = 1, C_N y_N^{(III,p-1)} - A_N y_{N-1}^{(III,p-1)} = 0. \quad (20)$$

Finding the values at the boundary nodes of subdomains leads us to the so-called "short" system:

$$-A_{i_2^{(m)}} y_{i_2^{(m)}-1} + C_{i_2^{(m)}} y_{i_2^{(m)}} - B_{i_2^{(m)}} y_{i_2^{(m)}+1} = F_{i_2^{(m)}},$$

$$-A_{i_1^{(m+1)}} y_{i_1^{(m+1)}-1} + C_{i_1^{(m+1)}} y_{i_1^{(m+1)}} - B_{i_1^{(m+1)}} y_{i_1^{(m+1)}+1} = F_{i_1^{(m+1)}}. \quad (21)$$

If we take into account the obvious connections in these equations:

$$y_{i_2^{(m)}-1} = y_{i_2^{(m)}-1}^{(I,m)} + y_{i_1^{(m)}} y_{i_2^{(m)}-1}^{(III,m)} + y_{i_2^{(m)}} y_{i_2^{(m)}-1}^{(II,m)}, y_{i_2^{(m)}+1} = y_{i_1^{m+1}},$$

$$y_{i_1^{(m+1)}-1} = y_{i_2^{(m)}}, y_{i_1^{(m+1)}+1} = y_{i_1^{(m+1)}+1}^{(I,m)} + y_{i_1^{(m+1)}} y_{i_1^{(m+1)}+1}^{(III,m)} + y_{i_2^{(m+1)}} y_{i_1^{(m+1)}+1}^{(II,m)}.$$

we get:

$$-\tilde{A}_{i_2^{(m)}} y_{i_1^{(m)}} + \tilde{C}_{i_2^{(m)}} y_{i_2^{(m)}} - \tilde{B}_{i_2^{(m)}} y_{i_1^{(m+1)}} = \tilde{F}_{i_2^{(m)}},$$

$$-\tilde{A}_{i_1^{(m+1)}} y_{i_2^{(m)}} + \tilde{C}_{i_1^{(m+1)}} y_{i_1^{(m+1)}} - \tilde{B}_{i_1^{(m+1)}} y_{i_2^{(m+1)}} = \tilde{F}_{i_1^{(m+1)}}, \quad (22)$$

with the coefficients

$$\tilde{A}_{i_2^{(m)}} = A_{i_2^{(m)}} y_{i_2^{(m)}-1}^{(III,m)}, \tilde{B}_{i_2^{(m)}} = B_{i_2^{(m)}}, \tilde{C}_{i_2^{(m)}} = C_{i_2^{(m)}} - A_{i_2^{(m)}} y_{i_2^{(m)}-1}^{(II,m)},$$

$$\tilde{F}_{i_2^{(m)}} = F_{i_2^{(m)}} + A_{i_2^{(m)}} y_{i_2^{(m)}-1}^{(I,m)}, \tilde{A}_{i_1^{(m+1)}} = A_{i_1^{(m+1)}}, \tilde{B}_{i_1^{(m+1)}} = B_{i_1^{(m+1)}} y_{i_1^{(m+1)}+1}^{(II,m+1)},$$

$$\tilde{C}_{i_1^{(m+1)}} = C_{i_1^{(m+1)}} - B_{i_1^{(m+1)}} y_{i_1^{(m+1)}+1}^{(III,m+1)}, \tilde{F}_{i_1^{(m+1)}} = F_{i_1^{(m+1)}} + B_{i_1^{(m+1)}} y_{i_1^{(m+1)}+1}^{(I,m+1)}.$$

As a result, we obtain the following system of $2p-2$ equations for $2p-2$ unknowns

$$- \tilde{A}_i y_{i-1} + \tilde{C}_i y_i - \tilde{B}_i y_{i+1} = \tilde{F}_i, i \in \tilde{\Omega} = \{i_2^{(0)}, i_1^{(1)}, i_2^{(1)}, ..., i_1^{(p-1)}\}, \quad (23)$$

where the index $i \pm 1$ means the transition to the corresponding neighboring element from the set $\tilde{\Omega}$. At the boundary nodes $i_2^{(0)}$ and $i_1^{(p-1)}$, Eq. (23) take a form similar to (16). Let us now note the properties of the basis functions [20]:

$$\|y^{(I,m)}\|_C \le \|D^{-1}F\|_C, 0 \le y^{(II,m)} \le 1, 0 \le y^{(III,m)} \le 1, m = 0, ..., p-1, \quad (24)$$

$0 \le y_i^{(II,m)} + y_i^{(III,m)} \le 1$, for all i, m.

These properties ensure the stability of calculations by formulas (17).

Due to the properties of basis (24), the coefficients of the short system of equations also satisfy the conditions of the maximum principle. Therefore, the solution to system (23) exists and is unique. Having determined it by the conventional sweep method, the solution of the original problem can be calculated using formulas (17).

Let us present the sequence of actions of the parallel sweep algorithm.

1. Each calculator using the sequential sweep algorithm solves three (or two) problems to find the basis functions $y^{(\alpha,m)}$.
2. Each calculator finds its part of the coefficients of the short system relative to the unknowns $y_{i_1}^{(m)}, y_{i_2}^{(m)} (m = 0, ..., p-1)$.
3. All calculators carry out a collective exchange of the coefficients of the short system.
4. Each calculator solves the short system and chooses the $y_{i_1}^{(m)}$ and $y_{i_2}^{(m)}$ values that it needs.
5. Each calculator uses the $y_{i_1}^{(m)}$ and $y_{i_2}^{(m)}$ values to calculate its part of the solution by formulas (17).

The general algorithm for solving the problem is that an explicit-implicit scheme (explicit in terms of nonlinearity and implicit in the spatial operator) is used in a cycle in time and is implemented using the parallel sweep method.

To study the properties of the developed parallel algorithm and compare it with the sequential algorithm, we use such characteristics as speedup (S_m) and efficiency (E_m) coefficients.

$$S_m = \frac{T_1}{T_m}, \quad (25)$$

$$E_m = \frac{S_m}{m} \cdot 100\%, \quad (26)$$

where S_m is the speedup, E_m is the efficiency, T_1 is the execution time of the sequential program, T_m is the execution time of the parallel program on m processes.

When theoretically estimating the speedup (usually done before the development of the program), one can use the approximate formula

$$S_m \approx \frac{Q_1}{Q_m}, \tag{27}$$

where Q_1 is the number of generalized arithmetic operations (GAO) of the sequential algorithm, Q_m is the maximum number of generalized arithmetic operations of one calculator when implementing the algorithm on m devices.

When solving a dynamic problem, it is sufficient to estimate the speedup and efficiency for one time step, since further these calculations are repeated many times according to the same scheme. Therefore, the quantities Q_1 and Q_m will be related to one step of the cycle in time.

Each step of the time cycle consists of two main steps:

- calculation of the coefficients of the discrete problem (15), (16);
- calculation of the solution at a step using the sweep algorithm.

Considering these circumstances, we estimate the values Q_1 and Q_m. We assume that the first stage of calculations in the sequential algorithm is estimated by the value $C_0 N$, where C_0 is the number of operations per element of the computational grid. The second stage of the sequential algorithm is estimated by the value $C_1 N$. As a result, the value is $Q_1 = (C_0 + C_1)N$.

When executing one time step of the algorithm in parallel mode, the first stage is estimated by the value $C_0 N/m$. The second stage is estimated by the value $3C_1 N/m + C_2 m \log_2 m + C_1(2m-2) + C_3 N/m$. In the latter case, it is taken into account that each calculator first determines 3 basis functions using the sequential sweep algorithm, then calculates 8 or 4 coefficients of the short system, participates in the collective exchange of these coefficients, and finally solves the short problem (also using the sequential sweep algorithm) and calculates the final solution. It should be noted that the constants C_1 and C_3 are related by the ratio 7:5, and they can conditionally be considered equal. The constant C_2 depends on the frequency of processors and the throughput of network communications. Therefore, in the end, the value is $Q_m = 4C_1 N/m + 2C_1 m + C_2 m \log_2 m$.

If we now evaluate the theoretical speedup, then we get

$$S_m \approx \frac{(C_0 + C_1)N}{(C_0 + 4C_1)N/m + 2C_1 m + C_2 m \log_2 m} =$$
$$\frac{(1+\alpha)m}{[1 + 4\alpha + 2\alpha m^2/N + m^2 \beta \log_2 m/N]}, \tag{28}$$

where $\alpha = C_1/C_0$, $\beta = C_2/C_0$.

The analysis of formula (28) shows that for a very large number of grid nodes, the speedup is estimated from above by the value $S_{m,max} = (1+\alpha)m/(1+4\alpha)$, i.e., the proposed algorithm has the necessary asymptotics. The value of the parameter α in the worst case (a problem with constant coefficients and a linear right-hand side) takes the value $7/4$, but most often the situation $\alpha \ll 1$ is realized. The value of the coefficient β can be small, but it can also exceed 1 (when using low-speed communications). However, more often than not, the overall speedup is affected by the entire combination $m^2/N(2\alpha + \beta \log_2 m)$. Therefore, in specific calculations, the effect of limited maximum speedup is manifested. The consequence of this fact is that for a fixed number of grid nodes, there is an optimal number of nodes of a particular computing system.

To implement the parallel algorithm, a C language program was developed using the MPI standard [9]. Multithreading was ensured by placing additional MPI processes inside the compute nodes of the cluster. The main calculations were performed on the K100 supercomputer at the Center for Collective Usage of the Keldysh Institute of Applied Mathematics of the RAS [21].

When developing a parallel program, in addition to the main part of the application, auxiliary functions were written, they are mentioned below.

Here are the main stages of work and sections of the parallel program.

Stage 1. Initialization of the parallel part of the application.
The initialization is carried out in the MyNetInit function, including:

- initialization of the MPI application (MPI_Init);
- determination of the total number of parallel processes in the group (MPI_Comm_size);
- determination of the process number in the group (MPI_Comm_rank);
- returning the name of the processor on which the call was made (MPI_Get_processor_name);
  and other auxiliary actions.

Stage 2. Initialization of the data for the applied problem.
The initialization is carried out by the Initia_Data function, including:

- opening, reading and closing the initial data file (parameters of Eq. (1)–(5) and parameters of the numerical method) on the master process ($m == 0$);
- filling in the fields of the data structure and broadcast (MPI_Bcast) to other processes.

Stage 3. Subdivision of the computational domain.
The subdivision is carried out using the MyRange function, allocating memory for arrays of the grid and coefficients of system (6), as well as buffers for data exchange, including:

- the range of numbers of nodes of the computational grid is $(i_1^{(m)}, i_2^{(m)})$;
- the number of calculation points for each process is $(n = i_2^{(m)} - i_1^{(m)} + 1)$;
- memory allocation for arrays with length of n and clipboards;
- filling the arrays with initial data.

Stage 4. Time Loop.
It is carried out in the body of the main program and includes the following at each step:

- data exchange of the process m with neighboring processes $(m-1)$ and $(m+1)$ using the BndAExch1D procedure;
- calculation of the coefficients A, B, C, F of scheme (6) on the next layer in time;

- calling the algorithm of the right sequential (prog_right_s) or right parallel (prog_right_p) sweep depending on the number of processes;
- calculation of pressure on a new layer in time according to the increment obtained from the run;
- saving the next portion of the results to the disk (output_solution);
- checking the conditions of the end of the time cycle.
  Note that in the function (BndAExch1D) the following happens:
- receiving/sending messages without blocking between neighboring processors (MPI_Isend/MPI_Irecv);
- blocking the work of processes until all exchange operations are completed (MPI_Waitall).

  Thus, using the BndAExch1D function, the values $\rho_o^f, \rho_w^f, k^f, \mu_o^f, \mu_w^f, P^f, S_i^f$ from (7)–(10) will be transferred.

In the parallel sweep procedure, the collective interaction of processes is carried out using the MPI_Allreduce function.

4   Calculation Results

The mathematical model (1)–(5) is implemented numerically so far only for the one-dimensional case. Table 1 lists the parameters required for the calculation for all processors.

Having set the parameters and initial conditions of the model (see Table 1), the space-time dynamics of the pressure change processes was obtained and analyzed. Figure 1 shows the pressure dynamics versus time in the matrix and the fracture system. It is noted that after the well is put into operation, the pressure in the fractures decreases faster than in the matrix. However, after 80 min, the drop curves approach each other, this is due to the fact that there is a redistribution of fluid from the matrix into the fractures, and the pressure is equalized between them.

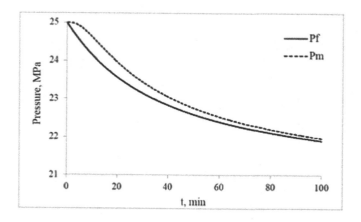

Fig. 1. Dynamics of pressure in time in the fractures (Pf) and the matrix (Pm)

Figure 2 shows the dynamics of pressure in space at different points in time. With an increase in the operating time of the well, the drawdown funnel increases, which is associated with fluid withdrawals.

Table 1. Model parameters

Name of parameter	Variable	Value (dimension)
Well radius	Xa	0.1 (m)
Research radius	Xb	10...100 (m)
Time step	tau	0.01 (s)
Time	time	1000...10000 (s)
Accuracy	Epst	0.001
Polynomial coefficients for determining the relative permeability of water	kr_wi, i=1,...,3	$0.03, 0.002, 0.0002$
Polynomial coefficients for determining the relative permeability of oil	kr_oi, i=1,...,4	$7.7, -12.1, 6.9, -1.8$
Density of oil at the surface	Ro0	730 (kg/m^3)
Density of oil in the reservoir	Ro1	870 (kg/m^3)
Density of water at the surface	Rw0	1000 (kg/m^3)
Density of water in the reservoir	Rw1	1118 (kg/m^3)
Initial pressure in the fracture set	P0	25 (MPa)
Pressure on the left in the fracture set	P0l	22 (MPa)
Atmosphere pressure	Pa	101325 (Pa)
Weight coefficient	d1f	0.5
Porosity	m_1	0.01
Fracture permeability	kf_1	$10^{-12}(m^2)$
Matrix permeability	km_1	$10^{-16}(m^2)$
Water viscosity	Mw_1	$0.67 \cdot 10^{-3}$ $(Pa \cdot s)$
Oil viscosity	Mo_1	$0.86 \cdot 10^{-3}$ $(Pa \cdot s)$
Water saturation	Sw_1	0.36
Number of points in space	Nx	1000...10000

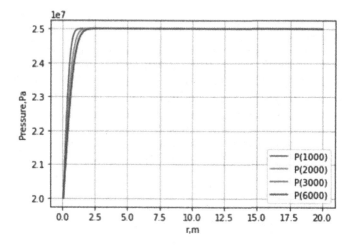

Fig. 2. Dynamics of pressure in space at different times

In order to be convinced of the expediency of solving the problem using parallel technologies, let us consider the calculation time for a small number of time steps $ntv = 100000$. Table 2 shows the calculation time for a different number of parallel processes (m) for the variant with $Time = 100$ seconds and the number of points in space $N_x = 1000$ (the physical grid step in this case is 10 m). The data in Table 2 illustrate that at $m <= 12$ the calculation time decreases, and at $m > 12$ it starts to increase. Thus, the optimal number of processes with this choice of the spatial grid is 12.

Table 2. Calculation time for a different number of parallel processes

Number of processors	Time, s
1	2.193175e+01
2	1.089155e+01
3	7.157851e+00
6	4.692821e+00
8	4.125761e+00
12	3.493805e+00
13	6.374054e+00
14	3.542320e+00
16	7.087328e+00
24	7.430083e+00

Figures 3 and 4 show the graphs of speedup and efficiency depending on the number of processes. We see that up to $m = 12$ the speedup increases, and the efficiency decreases moderately. Then the situation deteriorates significantly.

Therefore, it is inappropriate to divide the calculation area by the number of processes more than 12.

Note that if the grid is more detailed, then, in accordance with our theoretical estimates (see Sect. 3), the results of parallelization improve significantly. For example, if, for methodological purposes, we take the dimensions Nx = 10000 and 100000, then the optimal speedup value will be achieved in 18 and 48 processes. Another thing is that in real calculations it is more important to consider already two-dimensional and three-dimensional versions of the problem, where the practically significant sizes of different-scale grids will be, respectively, on the order of 10000 × 100 and 10000 × 100 × 100 and more.

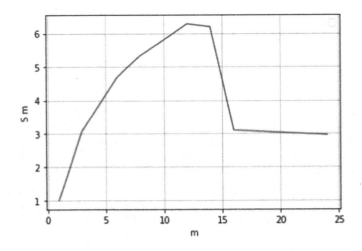

Fig. 3. Parallel speedup graph

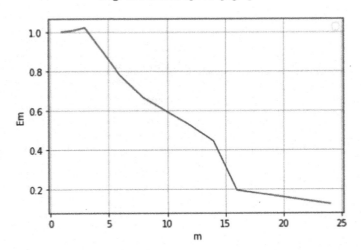

Fig. 4. Graph of parallelization efficiency

5   Conclusion

Thus, using the methods of mathematical physics, a system of mass-energy balances, which describes the process of the mass transfer of a two-phase fluid in a fractured-porous reservoir, was studied. To describe mass transfer in a reservoir with dual porosity, a four-block mathematical model with splitting by physical processes was used. For the numerical solution of the mathematical problem, an original implicit finite-difference scheme on a non-uniform spatial grid was proposed. The resulting system of equations was solved using the parallel scalar sweep algorithm. To test the proposed approach, a series of computational experiments were carried out. The calculation results confirmed the effectiveness of the developed numerical algorithm and its parallel implementation. Graphs of the speedup and efficiency of parallel algorithms were given depending on the number of processors. The optimal number of processors (equal to 12) was obtained for the considered formulation problem. As a result of the calculation, pressure curves were obtained as a function of time in the matrix and fractures, they showed the behavior of pressure after the well was put into operation. In addition, pressure curves depending on the spatial coordinate were plotted, they demonstrated the behavior of pressure at a distance from the well at different points in time.

Acknowledgments. The work was funded by the Russian Science Foundation (project № 21-71-20047). The calculations were performed on the K100 hybrid supercomputer installed at the Center for Collective Usage of the KIAM RAS.

References

1. Tugarova, M.A.: Reservoir Rocks: Properties, Petrographic Features, Classifications. Educational and Methodical manual. St. Petersburg University, Saint Petersburg (2004). (in Russian)
2. Kovaleva, L.A.: Physics of the Oil and Gas Reservoir. RIO BSU, Ufa (2008). (in Russian)
3. Golf-Racht, T.D.: Fundamentals of Fractured Reservoir Engineering. Elsevier Scientific Publishing Company, Amsterdam - Oxford - New York (1982)
4. Chernitskii, A.V.: Geological Modeling of Oil Fields in Massive Type of Carbonate Fractured Reservoirs. RMNTK Nefteotdacha, Moscow (2002). (in Russian)
5. Denk, S.O.: Problems of Fractured Productive Objects. Electronic Publishing, Perm (2004). (in Russian)
6. Barenblatt, G.I., Entov, V.M., Ryzhik, V.M.: The Flow of Liquids and Gases in Natural Reservoirs. Nedra, Moscow (1984). (in Russian)
7. Warren, J.E., Root, P.J.: The behavior of naturally fractured reservoirs. J. Soc. Petrol. Eng. **3**(03), 245–255 (1963). https://doi.org/10.2118/426-PA
8. Odeh, A.S.: Unsteady-state behavior of naturally fractured reservoirs. J. Soc. Petrol. Eng. **5**(1), 60–66 (1965). https://doi.org/10.2118/966-PA
9. Antonov, A.S.: Parallel Programming Using MPI Technology: A Textbook. MSU, Moscow (2004). (in Russian)

10. Rahimly, P.I., Poveshchenko, Yu.A., Rahimly, O.R., Podryga, V.O., Kazakevich, G.I., Gasilova, I.V.: The Use of Splitting with Respect to Physical Processes for Modeling the Dissociation of Gas Hydrates. Math. Models Comput. Simul. **10**(1), 69–78 (2018). https://doi.org/10.1134/S2070048218010118

11. Samarskii, A.A., Nikolaev, E.S.: Numerical Methods for Grid Equations. Nauka, Moscow (1978). (in Russian)

12. Tikhonov, A.N., Samarskii, A.A.: Equations of Mathematical Physics. Nauka, Moscow (1972). (in Russian)

13. Samarskii, A.A., Gulin, A.V.: Numerical Methods. Nauka, Moscow (1989). (in Russian)

14. Sikovskii, D.F.: Methods of Computational Heat Transfer. Extended Lecture Notes, Novosibirsk (2007). (in Russian)

15. Bobreneva, Yu.O., Rahimly, P.I., Poveshchenko, Yu.A., Podryga, V.O., Enikeeva, L.V.: Numerical modeling of multiphase mass transfer processes in fractured-porous reservoirs. J. Phys. Conf. Ser. **2131**, 022002 (2021). https://doi.org/10.1088/1742-6596/2131/2/022002

16. Bobreneva, Yu.O., Rahimly, P.I., Poveshchenko, Yu.A., Podryga, V.O., Enikeeva, L.V.: On one method of numerical modeling of piezoconductive processes of a two-phase fluid system in a fractured-porous reservoir. J. Phys. Conf. Ser. **2131**, 022001 (2021). https://doi.org/10.1088/1742-6596/2131/2/022001

17. Klochkov, M.A., Markov, K.Yu., Mitrokhin, Yu.S., Chirkova, L.S.: Organization of Parallel Calculations for Solving Differential Equations on the Blade Server. Udmurt University, Izhevsk, Educational and Methodical Manual (2011). (in Russian)

18. Konovalov, A.N.: Introduction to Computational Methods of Linear Algebra. Siberian Publishing Firm, Novosibirsk, VO Nauka (1993). (in Russian)

19. Samarskii, A.A.: Theory of Difference Schemes. Nauka, Moscow (1983). (in Russian)

20. Kudryashova, T.A., Polyakov, S.V.: On some methods for solving boundary value problems on multiprocessor computing systems. In: Proceedings of the Fourth International Conference on Mathematical Modeling, vol. 2, pp. 134–145. Publishing House "STANKIN", Moscow (2001). (in Russian)

21. Center for Collective Usage of the Keldysh Institute of Applied Mathematics of RAS. http://ckp.kiam.ru

Kinetic Modeling of Isobutane Alkylation with Mixed C4 Olefins and Sulfuric Acid as a Catalyst Using the Asynchronous Global Optimization Algorithm

Irek Gubaydullin[1,2], Leniza Enikeeva[2,3] ⓘ, Konstantin Barkalov[4(✉)] ⓘ,
Ilya Lebedev[4] ⓘ, and Dmitry Silenko[4]

[1] Institute of Petrochemistry and Catalysis – Subdivision of Ufa Federal Research
Centre of the RAS, Ufa, Russia
[2] Ufa State Petroleum Technological University, Ufa, Russia
[3] Novosibirsk State University, Novosibirsk, Russia
[4] Lobachevsky State University of Nizhny Novgorod, Nizhny Novgorod, Russia
{konstantin.barkalov,ilya.lebedev}@itmm.unn.ru

Abstract. The paper considers the application of parallel computing
technology to the simulation of a catalytic chemical reaction, which is
widely used in the modern automobile industry to produce gasoline with
a high octane number. As a chemical reaction, the process of alkylation of
isobutane with mixed C4 olefins, catalyzed by sulfuric acid, is assumed.
To simulate a chemical process, it is necessary to develop a kinetic model
of the process, i.e., to determine the kinetic parameters. To do this, the
inverse problem of chemical kinetics is solved; it predicts the values of the
kinetic parameters based on laboratory data. From a mathematical point
of view, the inverse problem of chemical kinetics is a global optimization
problem. A parallel asynchronous information-statistical global search
algorithm was used to solve it. The use of the asynchronous algorithm
significantly reduced the search time to find the optimum. The found
optimal parameters of the model made it possible to adequately simulate
the process of alkylation of isobutane with mixed C4 olefins catalyzed
by sulfuric acid.

Keywords: Global optimization · Multi-extremal functions · Parallel
computing · Chemical kinetics · Inverse problems

1 Introduction

Currently, there is a tendency to improve the environmental characteristics of
automobile fuel while maintaining a high octane number. Sulfuric acid alkylation
of isobutane with olefins makes it possible to obtain a high-octane component of
gasoline with a minimum content of aromatic hydrocarbons. The alkylate, which
is produced by alkylation of isobutane with C3 – C5 olefins in the presence of

L. Sokolinsky and M. Zymbler (Eds.): PCT 2022, CCIS 1618, pp. 293–306, 2022.
https://doi.org/10.1007/978-3-031-11623-0_20

strong acid, has the advantages of a high octane number, low vapor pressure, and zero content of olefins and aromatics, making it a desirable blending component for high-quality gasoline. Alkylates will continue to act as a desirable blending component for high-quality gasoline as the quality of gasoline continues to increase [3]. Therefore, it is a significant process for a modern refinery. To optimize the chemical process in industry, it is necessary to develop first its model, which in this case means building a mathematical model of the chemical process, and then its kinetic model, i.e., to numerically calculate the kinetic constants of the reaction.

As a rule, it is impossible to find out the kinetic constants of reactions analytically. Therefore, there is a need in the development and application of numerical methods for finding the kinetic constants (see, e.g., [5–7,13,22–24]). In this case, the quality criteria of the solution found (objective function) do not have an explicit analytical description, but enable an algorithmic representation and require considerable computational resources. Moreover, in the inverse problems of chemical kinetics, the objective function can be essentially multi-extremal, i.e., can have many local extrema along with the global one.

Numerical methods for solving such multi-extremal problems (global optimization methods) differ significantly from local search methods (see, e.g., [16,19]). As a rule, local optimization methods cannot escape the local extremum attraction region and do not find the global optimum. At the same time, the use of model parameters corresponding to the found local solution may appear to be insufficient since the global solution can provide a considerable advantage over local ones.

The diversity of emerging global optimization problems entails various approaches to their solution. Methods for solving global optimization problems can be divided into two classes: metaheuristic and deterministic. Metaheuristic algorithms are usually based on the simulation of processes occurring in nature. Some examples of metaheuristic algorithms are simulated annealing, evolution and genetic algorithms, etc. (see, e.g., [2,4]). Due to their relative simplicity, metaheuristic algorithms are more popular among researchers than deterministic methods. However, the problem solution found by the metaheuristic algorithm is, generally speaking, local and may be far from the global solution [14].

The possibility to construct deterministic global search methods different from grid search and metaheuristic methods is related to the availability and consideration of some *a priori* assumption on the properties of problem functions. Such assumptions play a key role in the development of efficient global optimization algorithms and serve as the main mathematical tool for estimating global solutions.

The assumption on limited relative variations of objective function values is one of the natural assumptions of the problem. Such an assumption is related to the ratio of the function increment to the respective increment of its argument, which is usually limited by some threshold defined by the limited energy of variations in the simulated system. In this case, the functions are known as

Lipschitz ones, and the problem itself is called the Lipschitz global optimization problem.

This paper presents the results of applying parallel Lipschitz optimization methods for solving the inverse problems of chemical kinetics. The main part of the paper has the following structure. The description of the mathematical model of the investigated chemical reaction is presented in Sect. 2. The formal statement of Lipschitz global optimization problems and the asynchronous parallel algorithm for solving them are described in Sect. 3. The results of the numerical solution of the inverse problem of chemical kinetics are discussed in Sect. 4.

2   Problem Statement

Let us consider a mathematical model of the isobutane alkylation reaction with olefins in the presence of sulfuric acid, which is a system of ordinary nonlinear differential equations (1)–(12).

$$\frac{dc_1}{dt} = -k_1 c_1 + k_2 c_3 - k_3 c_1 c_3 - k_7 c_1 c_2 c_4 - k_{11} c_1 + k_{14} c_{11} \tag{1}$$

$$\frac{dc_2}{dt} = -k_4 c_2 c_4 - k_6 c_2 c_5 - k_7 c_1 c_2 c_4 - k_{15} c_{11} c_2 c_4 \tag{2}$$

$$\frac{dc_3}{dt} = k_1 c_1 + k_4 c_2 c_5 - k_3 (c_1 + c_{11}) c_3 - k_5 c_{12} c_3 - k_2 c_3 + k_7 c_1 c_2 c_4 + k_{15} c_{11} c_2 c_4 \tag{3}$$

$$\frac{dc_4}{dt} = k_3 (c_1 + k_{11}) c_3 - k_4 c_2 c_4 - k_7 c_1 c_2 c_4 - k_{15} c_{11} c_2 c_4 \tag{4}$$

$$\frac{dc_5}{dt} = k_5 c_{12} c_3 - k_6 c_2 c_5 \tag{5}$$

$$\frac{dc_6}{dt} = k_4 c_2 c_4 \tag{6}$$

$$\frac{dc_7}{dt} = k_6 c_2 c_5 - k_{10} c_7 \tag{7}$$

$$\frac{dc_8}{dt} = k_7 c_1 c_2 c_4 + k_{15} c_{11} c_2 c_4 + k_9 c_9 c_{10} - k_8 c_8 \tag{8}$$

$$\frac{dc_9}{dt} = k_8 c_8 - k_9 c_9 c_{10} \tag{9}$$

$$\frac{dc_{10}}{dt} = k_8 c_8 - k_9 c_9 c_{10} \tag{10}$$

$$\frac{dc_{11}}{dt} = -k_3 c_{11} c_3 - k_{15} c_{11} c_2 c_4 + k_{11} c_1 + k_{12} c_{12} - k_{13} c_{11} - k_{14} c_{11} \tag{11}$$

$$\frac{dc_{12}}{dt} = -k_5 c_{12} c_3 + k_{13} c_{11} - k_{12} c_{12} \tag{12}$$

The initial conditions are $t = 0, c_1 = c_1^0; c_2 = c_2^0; c_3 = 0; c_4 = 0; c_5 = 0; c_6 = 0; c_7 = 0; c_8 = 0; c_9 = 0; c_{10} = 0; c_{11} = c_{11}^0; c_{12} = c_{12}^0$. The corresponding species in Eqs. (1)–(12) are 1, iC4H8; 2, iC4, 3, iC4+; 4, TMPs+; 5, DMHs+; 6, TMPs; 7, DMHs; 8, HEs; 9, iCx+; 10, iCy=; 11, 2-C4H8; 12, 1-C4H8.

Information that represents a change in the concentrations of the reaction components over time at different temperatures is taken as experimental data from [3]; the data in Table 1 are presented as an example of experimental data at a temperature of 276.2 K.

Table 1. Experimental data

time, min	1	2	5	10	15	20
DMH	0.12	0.11	0.1	0.1	0.095	0.09
TMP	0.54	0.65	0.69	0.69	0.7	0.705

Thus, solving the system (1)–(12) with the corresponding initial data, we will get a change in the calculated concentrations of the reaction components over time.

However, it is necessary to take into account the fact that the reaction rate constants $k_1, k_2, ..., k_{15}$ included in Eqs. (1)–(12) are parameters depending on the reaction temperature, this dependence is the Arrhenius equation and has the following form:

$$k_i(T) = k_i^0 \exp\left(-\frac{E_i}{RT}\right), \tag{13}$$

where $k_i(T)$ is the constant of the i-th stage of the reaction rate, k_i^0 is the pre-exponential factor of the i-th reaction stage, E_i is the activation energy, J/mol, R is the universal gas constant, J · (K·mol), T is the temperature, K. Thus, to fully develop the kinetic model of the reaction, it is necessary to calculate the activation energies E_i and the pre-exponential factors k_i^0 of all stages of the chemical reaction. There are two formulations of the problems of searching for kinetic parameter data E and k^0. The first one is to solve the inverse problem of selecting the kinetic parameters, included in Eq. (13), which during the solution allow us to calculate all the reaction rate constants k_i. With the found rate constants of the reaction stages, the system of differential equations (1)–(12) is solved, then the calculated concentrations are compared with the corresponding experimental data. Mathematically, this problem has the following formulation: it is necessary to minimize the following objective function

$$F_1 = \sum_{i=1}^{I}\sum_{j=1}^{J}\sum_{k=1}^{K}\left|c_{ijk}^{exp} - c_{ijk}^{calc}\right| \longrightarrow \min, \tag{14}$$

where c_{ijk}^{exp} and c_{ijk}^{calc} are the experimental and calculated values of the k-th observed component at the i-th experiment, respectively, I is the number of observed temperatures for the reaction, ($I = 4$ in this case), K is the number of experiments conducted at one temperature $(K = 3)$, M is the number of observed components of the reaction $(M = 2)$.

The second formulation of the inverse problem of chemical kinetics implies the search for the rate constants of the stages k_i included in the system (1)–(12), separately for each temperature, then on the basis of Arrhenius equation (13), the activation energies E_i and the pre-exponential multipliers k_i^0 are calculated using the least squares method. Mathematically, this statement of the problem coincides with Eq. (14), except for the first summation by temperatures:

$$F_2 = \sum_{j=1}^{J} \sum_{k=1}^{K} \left| c_{ijk}^{exp} - c_{ijk}^{calc} \right| \longrightarrow \min. \tag{15}$$

Thus, both formulations of the problem (14) and (15) are optimization problems, and the next section will describe the method used to solve these minimization problems.

3 Parallel Algorithm for Solving Global Optimization Problems

3.1 Global Optimization Problem

As mentioned above, from a formal point of view, we consider the inverse problem of chemical kinetics as a global optimization problem. In the specific problem under consideration, the values of the objective function are calculated by solving the stiff ODE system (1)–(12). Since the right parts of the system are continuous functions with bounded derivatives, theoretically its solution will also be continuous and bounded. Therefore, discrepancy (15) will satisfy the Lipschitz condition with a priori unknown constant.

In the general form, the problem of the class specified above can be formulated mathematically as follows:

$$\varphi^* = \varphi(y^*) = \min \{\varphi(y) : y \in D\}, \tag{16}$$
$$D = \{y \in R^N : a_i \le y_i \le b_i,\ 1 \le i \le N\}, \tag{17}$$

where a, b are the given vectors, $a, b \in R^N$, and the objective function $\varphi(y)$ satisfies the Lipschitz condition

$$|\varphi(y_1) - \varphi(y_2)| \le L \|y_1 - y_2\|,\ y_1, y_2 \in D. \tag{18}$$

The function $\varphi(y)$ is assumed to be multi-extremal and defined in the form of "black box" (i.e., in the form of some computing procedure, into the input of which the vector of parameters is supplied, and the corresponding function value is taken from the output). Moreover, each *trial* (i.e., the computation of the function value at a point of the search domain) is assumed to be a time-consuming operation. As noted in Introduction, such a problem statement corresponds to the inverse problem of chemical kinetics completely.

Lipschitz condition (18) can be utilized to estimate the global minimum of a function within an interval, and knowing the Lipschitz constant allows constructing global search algorithms and proving the convergence conditions for them (see, e.g., [21]).

The growth of computational costs with increasing the problem dimensionality is one of the main difficulties in solving multidimensional global optimization problems. Decreasing the number of trials at preserving the solution accuracy is possible by the complete utilization of some *a priori* assumptions on the objective function, which leads to adaptive serial optimization algorithms.

For example, the non-uniform space covering method [9] and the simplicial partitions method [17] are such methods. These approaches were successfully applied for the development of parallel optimization methods as well [8,18]. Another adaptive approach to solving multidimensional problem (16) is its reduction to a single one-dimensional problem or to several ones followed by the application of one-dimensional algorithms. Such a reduction can be made, for example, using the nested optimization scheme [10] or Peano-Hilbert curves [1]. The latter approach was used in the present work.

Using the continuous unambiguous mapping (Peano-Hilbert curve) $y(x)$ of the interval $[0, 1]$ of the real axis on the hypercube D from (17), one can reduce multidimensional problem (16) to a one-dimensional problem

$$\varphi(y^*) = \varphi(y(x^*)) = \min\{\varphi(y(x)) : x \in [0, 1]\},$$

where the function $\varphi(y(x))$ will satisfy the uniform Hölder condition

$$|\varphi(y(x_1)) - \varphi(y(x_2))| \leq H\,|x_1 - x_2|^{1/N}$$

with the Hölder constant H linked to the Lipschitz constant L by the relation $H = 2L\sqrt{N+3}$. The issues of the numerical construction of various approximations of the Peano-Hilbert curve were considered in [20,21].

So far, a search trial at some point $x' \in [0, 1]$ will include first the construction of the image $y' = y(x')$ and then the computation of the value of the function $z' = \varphi(y')$.

3.2   Parallel Asynchronous Global Search Algorithm

In the approach proposed, the parallelization scheme corresponds to the "master/worker" principle. In the master process, the global search algorithm is executed, it accumulates search information, evaluates the Lipschitz constant for the objective function on its base, determines new trial points and distributes them among worker processes.

Worker processes receive the trial points from the master process, perform new trials at these points and send the trial results to the master process.

Let us assume that the master process computes one point of the next trial at each iteration and sends it to the worker process for executing the trial. At the same time, the execution of the trial by the worker process is a much more computationally expensive operation than the choice of a new trial point by the master that excludes idle worker processes. In this case (unlike synchronous parallel algorithms), the total number of trials executed by each worker process will depend on the computational costs of executing a particular trial and cannot be estimated in advance.

In the description of the parallel algorithm, let us assume that $p + 1$ computational processes are at our disposal: one master process and p worker ones.

At the beginning of the search, the master process (let us assume it to be Process No 0) initiates the parallel execution of p trials at p different points of the search domain. Two of these points are boundary, while the rest are internal, i.e., at the points $\{y(x^1), y(x^2), ..., y(x^p)\}$ where $x^1 = 0$, $x^p = 1$, $x^i \in (0,1), i = 2, ..., p-1$.

Now let us assume that $k \geq 0$ trials (in particular, k can be equal to 0) are completed, and worker processes perform trials at the points

$$y(x^{k+1}), \ y(x^{k+2}), ..., \ y(x^{k+p}).$$

Each worker process, having completed its trial at some point (without any loss of generality, let us assume this point to be $y(x^{k+1})$ corresponding to Process No 1), sends the trial result to the master process. In turn, the master process selects a new trial point x^{k+p+1} for the worker process according to the rules described below. Note that in this case we will have a set of preimages of the trial points

$$I_k = \left\{ x^{k+1}, x^{k+2}, ..., x^{k+p} \right\},$$

at which the trials have already started, but have not yet been completed.

Step 1. Renumber the set of preimages of the trial points

$$X_k = \left\{ x^1, x^2, ..., x^{k+p} \right\},$$

containing all preimages at which the trials either have been completed or underway in the increasing order (by the lower index) so that

$$0 = x_1 < x_2 < ... < x_{k+p} = 1.$$

Step 2. Compute the values

$$M_1 = \max \left\{ \frac{|z_i - z_{i-1}|}{(x_i - x_{i-1})^{1/N}} : x_{i-1} \notin I_k, x_i \notin I_k, 2 \leq i \leq k+p \right\},$$

$$M_2 = \max \left\{ \frac{|z_{i+1} - z_{i-1}|}{(x_{i+1} - x_{i-1})^{1/N}} : x_i \in I_k, 2 \leq i < k+p \right\},$$

$$M = \max\{M_1, M_2\},$$

where $z_i = \varphi(y(x_i))$ if $x_i \notin I_k$, $1 \leq i \leq k+p$. The values z_i at the points $x_i \in I_k$ are undefined since the trials at the points $x_i \in I_k$ have not yet been completed. If the value of M equals 0, then set $M = 1$.

Step 3. Juxtapose each interval (x_{i-1}, x_i), $x_{i-1} \notin I_k$, $x_i \notin I_k$, $2 \leq i \leq k + p$ to the quantity $R(i)$, which is called the characteristic of the interval and is computed according to the formula

$$R(i) = rM\Delta_i + \frac{(z_i - z_{i-1})^2}{rM\Delta_i} - 2(z_i + z_{i-1}), \tag{19}$$

where $\Delta_i = (x_i - x_{i-1})^{1/N}$ and $r > 1$ is the reliability parameter of the method.

Step 4. Select the interval $[x_{t-1}, x_t]$, which the maximum characteristic corresponds to, i.e.,

$$R(t) = \max \left\{ R(i): \ x_{i-1} \notin I_k, x_i \notin I_k, \ 2 \leq i \leq k + p \right\}.$$

Step 5. Define a new trial point $y^{k+p+1} = y(x^{k+p+1})$, the preimage of which is $x^{k+p+1} \in (x_{t-1}, x_t)$ according to the formula

$$x^{k+p+1} = \frac{x_t + x_{t-1}}{2} - \text{sign}(z_t - z_{t-1})\frac{1}{2r}\left[\frac{|z_t - z_{t-1}|}{M}\right]^N.$$

Upon computing the next trial point, the master process adds it to the set I_k and sends it to the worker process, which initiates a new trial at this point.

The master process terminates the algorithm if one of two conditions is satisfied: $\Delta_t < \epsilon$ or $k + p > K_{max}$. The real number $\epsilon > 0$ and the integer number $K_{max} > 0$ are the parameters of the algorithm and correspond to the solution search precision and to the maximum number of trials, respectively.

The parallel asynchronous algorithm described above is based on the serial information global search algorithm. The theoretical substantiation of the algorithm convergence is given in [21]. The synchronous parallelization schemes used earlier in solving a number of applied problems [12,15] are also presented here. The novelty of the present work lies in the practical implementation and application of the asynchronous parallelization scheme featured by a higher efficiency in solving problems with different computational costs for performing trials at different points of the search domain. It was confirmed by the results of the experiments described in the next section.

4   Numerical Experiments

According to problem statements (14) and (15), the corresponding calculations were carried out in this work. The UNN supercomputer "Lobachevsky" (CentOS 7.2, SLURM, two CPUs Intel Sandy Bridge E5-2660 2.2 GHz and 64 Gb RAM on the node) was used for numerical experiments. The asynchronous global optimization algorithm was implemented using C++ (GCC 5.5.0 and Intel MPI were used); the objective function values were computed using Python 3.9. The accuracy of solving the ODE system (1)–(12) was set small enough so that the final error of the solution was much less than the accuracy of the stopping criterion of the optimization method and did not affect the method used.

4.1 Search for Activation Energies and Pre-exponential Multipliers of the Reaction

First, the problem of searching for activation energies and pre-exponential multipliers of all reaction stages was solved. The number of optimized parameters is 30, i.e., two parameters for each of the fifteen reaction stages. For the activation energies, the search range was set to $0 \leq E_i \leq 100$ kJ/mol, and $0 \leq E_i \leq 10^{12}$ for the pre-exponential multipliers based on physicochemical considerations. However, based on the stiffness of the system of differential equations (1) and (12), no solution was found in such a wide range; this is due to the too high degree of pre-exponential multipliers included in the Arrhenius equation. Therefore, during the calculations, the value of the upper bound of the pre-exponential multipliers was reduced, and the solution was obtained at the upper bounds of 10^5. The kinetic parameters found are presented in Table 2.

Table 2. Calculated rate constants of the reaction

	k_1	k_2	k_3	k_4	k_5	k_6	k_7
E, kJ / mol	98.60	98.22	99.07	2.29	97.61	94.30	8.67
k^0	$1.46 \cdot 10^3$	$1.53 \cdot 10^2$	$1.03 \cdot 10^4$	1.10	$4.99 \cdot 10^2$	$1.31 \cdot 10^2$	$5.45 \cdot 10^2$

	k_8	k_9	k_{10}	k_{11}	k_{12}	k_{13}	k_{14}	k_{15}
	11.57	73.16	65.54	13.86	4.93	2.69	21.19	0.63
	$2.60 \cdot 10^2$	$3.95 \cdot 10^4$	$3.24 \cdot 10^4$	$1.73 \cdot 10$	3.43	1.78	$1.42 \cdot 10^3$	$5.57 \cdot 10$

To evaluate the efficiency of the implemented optimization method, the results obtained were compared applying the serial algorithm, the parallel synchronous and parallel asynchronous algorithms with the use of 8 nodes when solving the problem in the above statement. The minimum values of the objective function found by the respective methods, the time of solving the problem (in hours), and the values of speedup in time are presented in Table 3. During the experiments, the parameter of the method $r = 3.0$ from (19) and the accuracy $\epsilon = 10^{-3} \|b - a\|$ in the termination condition were used. Once the global search method achieved the preset accuracy, the solution was refined by the Hook-Jeeves local method [11] with the accuracy $\epsilon = 10^{-5} \|b - a\|$.

The results show that both parallel algorithms demonstrated a moderate speedup, but found better solutions than the serial method. At that, the asynchronous algorithm found a better solution than the synchronous one. This also explains a smaller speedup of the asynchronous algorithm as compared with the synchronous one, since the asynchronous method executed more trials in the course of search for the optimal kinetic parameters of the problem.

Table 3. Indicators achieved when solving the problem with 30 parameters

Method	Minimum	Time (h.)	Speedup
Serial	7.6	3.8	—
Synchronous	5.9	0.9	4.3
Asynchronous	4.8	1.1	3.6

With the help of the obtained kinetic parameters, the direct problem of chemical kinetics was solved. However, the calculated kinetic curves poorly described the experimental data, which is confirmed by Fig. 1. It can be seen that the character of the calculated curve does not match the experimental dependence.

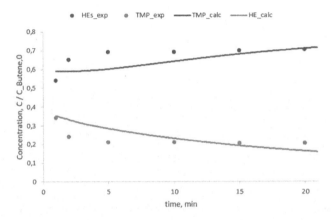

Fig. 1. Concentration profiles of key components when calculating the activation energies and pre-exponential reaction multipliers according to problem statement 14. Temperature: 276.2 K. Symbols, experimental data; line, calculated values.

Therefore, it was decided to carry out calculations according to the second formulation of the problem (15), namely, to calculate the constants of each reaction stage separately, then, according to the Arrhenius dependence, find the kinetic parameters E_i and k_i^0.

4.2   Searching for Rate Constants Separately for Each Temperature

Next, the problem of finding the constants k_i of the reaction stages included in the system (1)–(12) was solved. Velocity constants were calculated for each of the temperatures (Table 4).

When solving this problem, the operation performances of the serial algorithm, of the parallel synchronous and parallel asynchronous algorithms were also compared. The minimum values of the objective function found by the

Table 4. Calculated rate constants

T, K	k_1	k_2	k_3	k_4	k_5	k_6	k_7
276.2	1.66	0.13	2.09	0.08	0.11	1.83	8.82
279.2	1.94	0.33	2.19	0.32	0.16	1.96	14.15
282.2	2.14	0.99	5.43	2.77	0.56	2.13	45.85
286.2	2.43	0.99	5.51	2.81	0.56	2.35	58.97

k_8	k_9	k_{10}	k_{11}	k_{12}	k_{13}	k_{14}	k_{15}
0.87	13.38	13.71	12.57	4.20	18.54	2.70	58.61
1.05	13.39	14.50	24.26	7.67	19.41	3.86	74.64
1.09	18.92	17.41	33.73	6.07	19.24	9.61	77.37
1.50	24.09	17.88	34.22	4.35	23.04	16.38	94.45

respective methods, the time of solving the problem (in hours), and the speedup in time with the use of 8 nodes are presented in Table 5. All the parameters of the method were the same as in the previous run.

Table 5. Indicators achieved when solving the problem with 15 parameters

Method	Minimum	Time (h.)	Speedup
Serial	0.35	3.4	—
Synchronous	0.36	0.4	8.6
Asynchronous	0.35	0.2	16.6

The results show that all algorithms found good solutions (in the values of the objective function). At that, the asynchronous algorithm demonstrated twice as much speedup than the synchronous one. The good speedup of the asynchronous algorithm remains with a larger number of nodes; the results of its work are presented in Table 6.

Note that when solving the global optimization problem, the number of iterations of the parallel algorithm (and hence its speedup) significantly depends on the estimation of the Lipschitz constant of the objective function. The constant is adaptively estimated during the work of the algorithm and may vary depending on the accumulated search information. With a correct estimate of the Lipschitz constant, the method can converge to the global optimum point faster than in the case of its incorrect estimate. This explains the effect of superlinear speedup observed in the experiments.

Table 6. Speedup of the asynchronous parallel algorithm

Nodes	Minimum	Time (h.)	Speedup
1	0.35	3.4	—
8	0.35	0.2	16.6
16	0.36	0.1	34.3
32	0.35	0.06	59.5

The direct problem of chemical kinetics was solved with the found rate constants, the results of comparison with the experimental data are shown in Fig. 2 (an experiment at a temperature of 276.2 K is presented). We see that this time the description of the data turned out to be rather accurate.

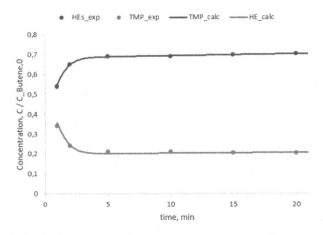

Fig. 2. Concentration profiles of key components when calculating the rate constants according to problem statement 15. Temperature: 276.2 K. Symbols, experimental data; line, calculated values.

After calculating the rate constants for different temperature values, it is possible to calculate the parameters E_i and k_i^0. Thus, for example, for the first stage of the reaction $E_1 = 24.65$ kJ/mol, $k_1^0 = 6.85 \cdot 10^4$ min^{-1}, for the third stage $E_3 = 75.57$ kJ/mol, $k_3^0 = 2.62 \cdot 10^{14}$ kg $\cdot$mol^{-1}$\cdot$min^{-1}. However, for some stages, the parameter values k^0 were fairly high: for the second stage $k_2^0 = 8.52 \cdot 10^{25}$ min^{-1}, for the seventh stage $k_7^0 = 2.82 \cdot 10^{26}$ kg mol^{-2} min^{-2}. Therefore, in future works, the constants corresponding to these kinetic parameters will be recalculated. Since the problem is multidimensional, there may be several solutions that describe experimental data within a certain deviation error. The solution may change if, for example, additional experimental data are found. However, the algorithm proposed in the paper provides a single solution within the search range, and the high values of the pre-exponential multipliers explain the presence of complex stages, which, in turn, consist of several stages that can be refined by chemists. The traditional scheme of assessing the quality of the problem solution as a deviation of the found solution from the exact one is not applicable here since the exact solution is not known.

5 Conclusions and Future Work

The article describes the search for the kinetic parameters of the industrial chemical reaction of isobutane alkylation with olefins in the presence of sulfuric acid. The search was carried out for the rate constants of all reaction stages, and the activation energies and pre-exponential multipliers were calculated. The optimization method allowed us to find a fairly accurate description of the experimental data. In the future, it is planned to use this method and parallelization to eliminate the high values of the pre-exponential reaction multipliers and search for optimal conditions for the alkylation reaction using the developed kinetic model.

Acknowledgments. This study was supported by the Russian Science Foundation, project No. 21-11-00204, and the Russian Foundation for Basic Research, project No. 19-37-60014.

References

1. Barkalov, K., Strongin, R.: Solving a set of global optimization problems by the parallel technique with uniform convergence. J. Global Optim. **71**(1), 21–36 (2017). https://doi.org/10.1007/s10898-017-0555-4
2. Battiti, R., Brunato, M., Mascia, F.: Reactive Search and Intelligent Optimization. Springer, New York (2009). https://doi.org/10.1007/978-0-387-09624-7
3. Cao, P., Zheng, L., Sun, W., Zhao, L.: Multiscale modeling of isobutane alkylation with mixed c4 olefins using sulfuric acid as catalyst. Indus. Eng. Chem. Res. **58**(16), 6340–6349 (2019). https://doi.org/10.1021/acs.iecr.9b00874
4. Eiben, A., Smith, J.: Introduction to Evolutionary Computing. Springer, Heidelberg (2015). https://doi.org/10.1007/978-3-662-44874-8
5. Enikeev, M., et al.: Analysis of corrosion processes kinetics on the surface of metals. Chem. Eng. J. **383**, 123, 131 (2020). https://doi.org/10.1016/j.cej.2019.123131
6. Enikeeva, L., Marchenko, M., Smirnov, D., Gubaydullin, I.: Parallel gravitational search algorithm in solving the inverse problem of chemical kinetics. In: Voevodin, V., Sobolev, S. (eds.) RuSCDays 2020. CCIS, vol. 1331, pp. 98–109. Springer, Cham (2020). https://doi.org/10.1007/978-3-030-64616-5_9
7. Enikeeva, L.V., et al.: Gravitational search algorithm for determining the optimal kinetic parameters of propane pre-reforming reaction. React. Kinet. Mech. Catal. **132**(1), 111–122 (2021). https://doi.org/10.1007/s11144-021-01927-8
8. Evtushenko, Y., Malkova, V., Stanevichyus, A.A.: Parallel global optimization of functions of several variables. Comput. Math. Math. Phys. **49**(2), 246–260 (2009). https://doi.org/10.1134/S0965542509020055
9. Evtushenko, Y., Posypkin, M.: A deterministic approach to global box-constrained optimization. Optim. Lett. **7**, 819–829 (2013). https://doi.org/10.1007/s11590-012-0452-1

10. Grishagin, V., Israfilov, R., Sergeyev, Y.: Convergence conditions and numerical comparison of global optimization methods based on dimensionality reduction schemes. Appl. Math. Comput. **318**, 270–280 (2018). https://doi.org/10.1016/j.amc.2017.06.036

11. Hooke, R., Jeeves, T.: "Direct search" solution of numerical and statistical problems. J. ACM **8**(2), 212–229 (1961). https://doi.org/10.1145/321062.321069

12. Kalyulin, S., Shavrina, E., Modorskii, V., Barkalov, K., Gergel, V.: Optimization of drop characteristics in a carrier cooled gas stream using ANSYS and Globalizer software systems on the PNRPU high-performance cluster. Commun. Comput. Inf. Sci. **753**, 331–345 (2017). https://doi.org/10.1007/978-3-319-67035-5_24

13. Koledina, K.F., et al.: Kinetics and mechanism of the synthesis of Benzylbutyl ether in the presence of copper-containing catalysts. Russian J. Phys. Chem. A **93**(11), 2146–2151 (2019). https://doi.org/10.1134/S0036024419110141

14. Kvasov, D., Mukhametzhanov, M.: Metaheuristic vs. deterministic global optimization algorithms: the Univariate case. Appl. Math. Comput. **318**, 245–259 (2018). https://doi.org/10.1016/j.amc.2017.05.014

15. Modorskii, V., Gaynutdinova, D., Gergel, V., Barkalov, K.: Optimization in design of scientific products for purposes of cavitation problems. AIP Conf. Proc. **1738**, 400013 (2016). https://doi.org/10.1063/1.4952201

16. Paulavičius, R., Žilinskas, J.: Simplicial Global Optimization. Springer, New York (2014). https://doi.org/10.1007/978-1-4614-9093-7

17. Paulavičius, R., Žilinskas, J., Grothey, A.: Investigation of selection strategies in branch and bound algorithm with simplicial partitions and combination of Lipschitz bounds. Optim. Lett. **4**(2), 173–183 (2010). https://doi.org/10.1007/s11590-009-0156-3

18. Paulavičius, R., Žilinskas, J., Grothey, A.: Parallel branch and bound for global optimization with combination of Lipchitz bounds. Optim. Method. Softw. **26**(3), 487–498 (2011). https://doi.org/10.1080/10556788.2010.551537

19. Sergeyev, Y.D., Kvasov, D.E.: Deterministic global optimization: an introduction to the diagonal approach. Springer, New York (2017). https://doi.org/10.1007/978-1-4939-7199-2

20. Sergeyev, Y.D., Strongin, R.G., Lera, D.: Introduction to global optimization exploiting space-filling curves. Springer Briefs in Optimization, Springer, New York (2013). https://doi.org/10.1007/978-1-4614-8042-6

21. Strongin R.G., Sergeyev Y.D.: Global Optimization With Non-convex Constraints. Sequential and Parallel Algorithms. Kluwer Academic Publishers, Dordrecht (2000). https://doi.org/10.1007/978-1-4615-4677-1

22. Uskov, S., et al.: Fibrous alumina-based Ni-MOx (M=Mg, Cr, Ce) catalysts for propane pre-reforming. Mater. Lett. **257**, 126, 741 (2019). https://doi.org/10.1016/j.matlet.2019.126741

23. Uskov, S.I., Potemkin, D.I., Enikeeva, L.V., Snytnikov, P.V., Gubaydullin, I.M., Sobyanin, V.A.: Propane pre-reforming into methane-rich gas over Ni catalyst: experiment and kinetics elucidation via genetic algorithm. Energies **13**(13) (2020). https://doi.org/10.3390/en13133393

24. Zaynullin, R.Z., Koledina, K.F., Gubaydullin, I.M., Akhmetov, A.F., Koledin, S.N.: Kinetic model of catalytic gasoline reforming with consideration for changes in the reaction volume and thermodynamic parameters. Kinet. Catal. **61**(4), 613–622 (2020). https://doi.org/10.1134/S002315842004014X

Simulation of Nonstationary Thermal Fields in Permafrost Using Multicore Processors

Elena N. Akimova[1,2]([✉]) [iD] and Vladimir E. Misilov[1,2] [iD]

[1] Krasovskii Institute of Mathematics and Mechanics, Ural Branch of the RAS,
16 S. Kovalevskaya Street, Ekaterinburg, Russia
aen15@yandex.ru, v.e.misilov@urfu.ru
[2] Ural Federal University, 19 Mira Street, Ekaterinburg, Russia

Abstract. The paper is aimed to develop and investigate efficient parallel algorithms for solving heat-transfer equations in a three-dimensional domain. Applying the alternating-direction finite-difference scheme, the problem is reduced to solving multiple SLAEs with tridiagonal matrices. In this work, several approaches to computing the coefficients of these systems are implemented. To solve the systems, the sweep method is used. Parallel algorithms are implemented for multicore processors using OpenMP technology. The results of numerical experiments and the evaluation of the algorithms efficiency are presented. A comparison of the computing times shows that the new implementation is up to two times faster than the earlier one.

Keywords: Heat Transfer · Stefan Problem · Mathematical Modeling · Parallel Computing · OpenMP

1 Introduction

This paper aims to construct efficient parallel algorithms for solving the initial boundary problem for a heat equation considering a phase change [1] (also known as the Stefan problem). This problem can be utilized for simulating engineering constructions in the Arctic region, for example, the thawing of the permafrost soil around oil and gas production wells. To capture various factors, such as heat exchange at the Earth's surface and engineering constructions, specifics of the soil structure, complicated boundary conditions should be considered [2–7].

The problem is described by a three-dimensional heat equation with discontinuous coefficients. It is approximated using the implicit three-point difference scheme and reduced to solving a set of systems of linear algebraic equations with tridiagonal matrices for each spatial direction at each subsequent time step. The long-term simulation of real objects requires time and spatial grids of large size, which leads to the large computing time. One way to reduce it is to use parallel computing [8–11]. Several parallel implementations are developed for simulating

thermal fields in the permafrost soil [12–14]. In [15], an approach to parallelization using OpenMP technology is proposed. It is based on the possibility to solve
several SLAEs independently, allowing one to distribute work between OpenMP
threads.

In this work, we present a new efficient approach to the distribution of the
work of forming and solving SLAEs, which allows utilizing the vectorization
and SIMD instruction of modern processors, as well as multiple cores, using
OpenMP technology. We present the results of computational experiments, compare the new approach with the previous one, and estimate the parallel algorithm
effectiveness.

The paper is organized as follows. In Sect. 2, the mathematical model is
presented, and the considered problem is formulated. Section 3 describes the
numerical methods used for solving the problem. In Sect. 4, parallel algorithms
are constructed and implemented, the results of numerical experiments are presented, and the performance of parallel implementations is studied. Section 5
concludes our work.

2   Problem Statement and Mathematical Model

To simulate heat propagation processes, an adequate mathematical model is
needed. This model should take into account multiple factors, such as soil composition, yearly weather changes, and the characteristics of technical systems.
These factors are taken into account in the model developed in [6,15].

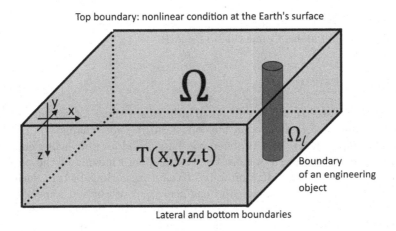

Fig. 1. Computational domain.

Let us describe this model. Consider a Carthesian grid with the x and y axes
parallel to the ground surface and the z axis directed upwards as shown in Fig. 1.
The computational domain Ω is a rectangular parallelepiped of sizes L_x, L_y, L_z.

Thus, $\Omega = \{x, y, z\} : 0 \leqslant x \leqslant L_x, 0 \leqslant y \leqslant L_y, -L_z \leqslant z \leqslant 0$. $T = T(t, x, y, z)$ is the sought soil temperature at the point (x, y, z) at the instant t.

The two-phase Stefan problem in the area Ω can be formulated as a single generalized nonlinear heat equation [1]

$$\rho\left(c_v(T) + \kappa\delta(T - T^*)\right)\frac{\partial T}{\partial t} = \operatorname{div}(\lambda(T)\operatorname{grad}T), \tag{1}$$

where $\rho = \rho(x, y, z)$ is the density [kg/m^3], $T^* = T^*(x, y, z)$ is the phase transition temperature, $\kappa = \kappa(x, y, z)$ is the specific heat of phase transition, δ is the Dirac delta function.

The specific heat capacity $c_v(T)$ [J/(kg $\cdot$ K)] and the thermal conductivity $\lambda(T)$ [W/(m·K)] depend on the phase and are defined by discontinuous functions

$$c_v(T) = \begin{cases} c_1(x, y, z), & \text{for } T < T^*, \\ c_2(x, y, z), & \text{for } T > T^*, \end{cases}$$

$$\lambda(T) = \begin{cases} \lambda_1(x, y, z), & \text{for } T < T^*, \\ \lambda_2(x, y, z), & \text{for } T > T^*. \end{cases}$$

The initial condition is

$$T(0, x, y, z) = T_0(x, y, z), \quad x, y, z \in \Omega, \tag{2}$$

and the boundary conditions are

$$T(t, x, y, z) = g(t, x, y, z), \quad x, y, z \in \delta\Omega \quad t_0 \leqslant t \leqslant \overline{t}. \tag{3}$$

In this formulation, the explicit phase transition boundary is not considered. Heat release or absorption during phase transition is represented by the delta function term. The most popular approach to construct numerical methods for solving problem (1)–(3) is to smooth the coefficients. The delta function $\delta(u)$ is approximated by some function $\widetilde{\delta}(u, \Delta)$ that has a zero value outside the interval $[-\Delta, \Delta]$ and satisfies $\int_{-\Delta}^{\Delta} \widetilde{\delta}(u, \Delta)du = 1$. In our implementation, we use the piecewise linear function $\widetilde{\delta}(u, \Delta) = \max\left\{0, \dfrac{\Delta - |u|}{\Delta^2}\right\}$. The discontinuous coefficient $\lambda(T)$ can also be approximated by some function $\widetilde{\lambda}(T, \Delta)$. The accuracy of the solution of (1) does not depend on the choice of a specific approximation function, however, it depends on the smoothing parameter Δ.

Thus, we reduce (1) to the classical heat equation

$$\rho \cdot \widetilde{c}(T)\frac{\partial T}{\partial t} = \operatorname{div}(\lambda(T) \cdot \operatorname{grad}T), \tag{4}$$

where $\widetilde{c}(T) = c_v T + \kappa\widetilde{\delta}(T - T^*, \Delta)$ is the effective thermal capacity. These coefficients ρ, k, c_v, λ can vary inside the domain due to soil heterogeneity and the presence of engineering structures.

The system of boundary conditions (3) is constructed as follows. On the lateral and lower boundaries of the domain, we have

$$\left.\frac{\partial T}{\partial x}\right|_{x=\pm L_x} = 0, \quad \left.\frac{\partial T}{\partial y}\right|_{y=\pm L_y} = 0, \quad \left.\frac{\partial T}{\partial z}\right|_{z=-L_z} = 0. \tag{5}$$

At the ground surface (upper boundary), we need to balance several heat fluxes, namely, incoming solar radiation, internal heat, air conduction, and soil emission. This leads to the condition

$$\alpha q + b(T_{\text{air}} - T|_{z=0}) = \varepsilon\sigma T_{z=0}^4 + \lambda\left.\frac{\partial T}{\partial z}\right|_{z=0}, \tag{6}$$

where $q(t)$ is the total incoming solar radiation, $\alpha(t,x,y)$ is the absorption coefficient, $T_{\text{air}}(t)$ is the air temperature, $b(t,x,y)$ is the heat exchange coefficient, σ is the Stefan–Boltzmann constant, $\varepsilon(t,x,y)$ is the emissivity coefficient. These coefficients can represent climatic and weather conditions, as well as the characteristics of the surface layer of soil.

To represent engineering objects as heat sources, we consider their surfaces as internal boundaries $\Omega_l, l \in \{1, ..., L\}$. This gives us more boundary conditions

$$T|_{\Omega_l} = T_l(t), \quad l \in \{1, ..., L\}. \tag{7}$$

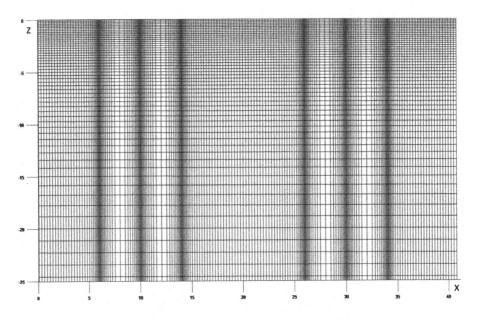

Fig. 2. Example of computing the grid in the XZ plane.

3   Numerical Method

To solve the initial boundary problem for Eq. (4) with initial condition (2) and boundary conditions (5)–(7), we use the finite difference method with splitting by spatial variables [1,6]. A non-uniform orthogonal grid $\{x_i, y_j, z_k\}$: $i \in \{0, ..., N_x\}$, $j \in \{0, ..., N_y\}$, $k \in \{0, ..., N_z\}$ is introduced for the domain Ω. The grid points are condensed near the boundaries $\Omega|_{z=0}$ and Ω_l as shown in Fig. 2. Denote the temperature values $T_{i,j,k} = T(x_i, y_j, z_k)$, and let us use a similar notation for the coefficients ρ, $\lambda(T)$, $\tilde{c}(T)$. An implicit additive locally one-dimensional finite difference three-point scheme is used for each spatial direction for each subsequent instant $t = t_0 + r\tau$, $r \in \{0, ..., N_t\}$, $\tau = (\bar{t} - t_0)/N_t$.

For clarity, let us consider the x direction. We need to construct and solve a system of difference equations for each fair pair (j, k), iterating over the index i.

$$
\begin{bmatrix}
b_0 & c_0 & & & & \\
a_1 & b_1 & c_1 & & & \\
& \ddots & \ddots & \ddots & & \\
& & a_{(N_x-2)} & b_{(N_x-2)} & c_{(N_x-2)} & \\
& & & a_{(N_x-1)} & b_{(N_x-1)}
\end{bmatrix}
\cdot
\begin{bmatrix}
T_{0,j,k} \\
T_{1,j,k} \\
\vdots \\
T_{(N_x-2),j,k} \\
T_{(N_x-1),j,k}
\end{bmatrix}
=
\begin{bmatrix}
d_0 \\
d_1 \\
\vdots \\
d_{(N_x-2)} \\
d_{(N_x-1)}
\end{bmatrix}. \tag{8}
$$

The coefficients for the inner points $i \in \{1, ..., (N_x - 2)\}$ are found by the following formulae

$$
a_i = \frac{\lambda_{(i-0.5),j,k}}{2\delta_i \Delta_{i-1}}, \quad b_i = \frac{\rho_{i,j,k} \cdot \tilde{c}_{i,j,k}}{\tau} + a_i + c_i,
$$
$$
c_i = \frac{\lambda_{(i+0.5),j,k}}{2\delta_i \Delta_{i+1}}, \quad d_i = \frac{T_{i,j,k} \cdot \rho_{i,j,k} \cdot \tilde{c}_{i,j,k}}{\tau}, \tag{9}
$$

where

$$
\Delta_{i-1} = x_i - x_{i-1}, \quad \Delta_{i+1} = x_{i+1} - x_i, \quad \delta_i = \min\{\Delta_{i-1}, \Delta_{i+1}\}/2,
$$
$$
\lambda_{(i\pm0.5,j,k)} = \lambda(T(x_i \pm \delta_i, y_j, z_k), x_i \pm \delta_i, y_j, z_k).
$$

The coefficients $\lambda_{(i\pm0.5),j,k}$ for the internodal points are obtained by linear interpolation. Note that this interpolation also approximates the discontinuous function $\lambda(T)$, relieving us from doing this explicitly.

The boundary points $i = 0$ and $i = (N_x - 1)$ correspond to condition (5). Therefore, the coefficients are

$$
\begin{aligned}
a_0 &= 0, & b_0 &= 1, & c_0 &= -1, & d_0 &= 0, \\
a_{(N_x-1)} &= -1, & b_{(N_x-1)} &= 1, & c_{(N_x-1)} &= 0, & d_{(N_x-1)} &= 0.
\end{aligned}
$$

To solve systems (8), the sweep method [16] (also known as the Thomas algorithm) is used. Again, for clarity, let us consider the x direction and iterate over the index i. The sweep method consists of two stages. In the forward sweep, we calculate the coefficients α_i, β_i by recursive formulae

$$
\alpha_0 = -\frac{c_0}{b_0}, \qquad \beta_0 = \frac{d_0}{b_0},
$$
$$
\alpha_{i+1} = -\frac{c_i}{b_i + \alpha_i a_i}, \quad \beta_{i+1} = \frac{d_i - \beta_i a_i}{b_i + \alpha_i a_i}, \tag{10}
$$
$$
i \in \{0, ..., (N_x - 2)\}.
$$

Then, the sought values are found by backward substitution

$$
T_{(N_x-2),j,k} = \beta_{N_x-1},
$$
$$
T_{i,j,k} = \alpha_{i+1} T_{(i+1),j,k} + \beta_{i+1}, \tag{11}
$$
$$
i \in \{(N_x - 2), ..., 1\}.
$$

For the z direction, when we iterate over the index k, the last equation in system (8) corresponds to the ground surface $z_{(N_z-1)} = 0$. From condition (6), we obtain

$$
-\frac{\lambda_{i,j,(N_z-1)}}{\Delta N_{z-1}} T_{i,j,(N_z-2)} + \left(b + \frac{\lambda_{i,j,(N_z-1)}}{\Delta N_{z-1}}\right) T_{i,j,(N_z-1)} + \varepsilon\sigma T^4_{i,j,(N_z-1)}
$$
$$
= \alpha q + b T_{\text{air}}. \tag{12}
$$

After the forward sweep, we should find the value T_{N_z-1} from this nonlinear equation. The iterative Newton method is used to solve it. Then, other values are computed by backward substitution (11).

To take into account condition (7), dummy nodes are introduced at the intersections of the boundary of Ω_l and the scanline $\{x, y, z\} : x \in \mathbb{R}$, $y = y_j$, $z = z_k$. For example, let the body Ω_l begin exactly at $\overline{x}$. We have some grid point x_h, such as $x_{h-1} < \overline{x} < x_h$, $\{x_h, y_j, z_k\} \in \Omega_l$. Then, for calculating the coefficients a_{h-1}, b_{h-1}, c_{h-1}, d_{h-1}, we replace the value x_h with $\overline{x}$. The coefficients for the index h will be $a_h = 0$, $b_h = 1$, $c_h = 0$, $d_h = T_l$.

4   Parallel Implementation and Numerical Experiments

Let us describe the test problem. The size of the domain is $L_x = 41$ m, $L_y = 21$ m, $L_z = 26$ m. The grid size is $200 \times 96 \times 56$. The time interval $t_0 = 0$, $\overline{t} = 10$ years with a step $\tau = 86\,400$ s (one day). The smoothing coefficient is $\Delta = 1$ K.

The thermal characteristics of soil are

$$
\lambda_1 = 1.82 \text{ W/(m} \cdot \text{K)}, \ c_1 = 2.13 \cdot 10^6 \text{ J/(kg} \cdot \text{K)} \text{ for frozen soil;}
$$
$$
\lambda_2 = 1.58 \text{ W/(m} \cdot \text{K)}, \ c_2 = 3.14 \cdot 10^6 \text{ J/(kg} \cdot \text{K)} \text{ for melted soil;}
$$
$$
\rho = 1.6 \cdot 10^3 \text{ kg/m}^3, \ \kappa = 1.386 \cdot 10^8 \text{ J/(kg} \cdot \text{K)}, \quad T^* = 0\,°\text{C}.
$$

Two object configurations are considered. The former one consists of two vertical boreholes with the internal temperature $T_1 = T_2 = 50\,°\mathrm{C}$ with a diameter of 1 m going vertically through the entire domain $z \in [0, L_z]$. The latter one adds four vertical cooling devices around each borehole. They have the temperature $T_2 = -20\,°\mathrm{C}$, a diameter of 0.2 m and end at the depth of 12 m.

Figures 3 and 4 show the 3D voxel images of thermal fields after 10 years of simulation. Figures 5 and 6 illustrate the sections at $y = 10$. For the first configuration, almost the entire area is melted, while cooling devices in the second configuration keep shallow layers frozen.

The experiments are performed on the 8-core Intel i7-10700k CPU. The program is written in C++ and compiled using Intel C++ Compiler 19.2.

The simplest approach for implementing a parallel algorithm using OpenMP technology is proposed in [15,17,18]. For each direction, we need to form and solve a set of SLAEs, one SLAE per one "scanline". Apparently, these SLAEs can be formed and solved independently. Thus, to parallelize the computational algorithm, we just need to place '#pragma omp for' for the outer loop.

Note that in this approach, each thread forms and solves SLAEs one by one. This way, the usage of SIMD capabilities of modern processors is limited, since the sweep method (10)–(11) has flow dependencies (the coefficients α_{i+1} and β_{i+1} depend on the values α_i and β_i).

In this work, to avoid this issue, we form multiple systems at once and solve them simultaneously. This means that we calculate the coefficients $a_{i,(j,k)}$, $b_{i,(j,k)}$, $c_{i,(j,k)}$, $d_{i,(j,k)}$ using formulae (9) and store them in three-dimensional arrays. Then, we solve the systems using formulae (10)–(11), also storing the auxiliary coefficients $\alpha_{i,(j,k)}$ and $\beta_{i,(j,k)}$ in three-dimensional arrays. Note that the coefficients for different (j, k) do not depend on each other. If we arrange the index order as $[i]$ $[k]$ $[j]$ for storing the coefficients, then all these calculations and memory accesses can be vectorized automatically. To provide the optimized storage alignment and efficient automatic vectorization, we use the Intel SDLT library [19] instead of standard C arrays or C++ containers.

Note that we can use any of these approaches for each direction x, y, or z. For a particular direction, we will use the approach that gives the best performance, obtaining a combined algorithm. Let us further investigate these two approaches by performing numerical experiments.

We want to study the performance of the most expensive part of the algorithm, which is the formation and solution of systems (8). Thus, we do not consider the time taken by solving nonlinear equation (12) or modifying the coefficients for the dummy nodes.

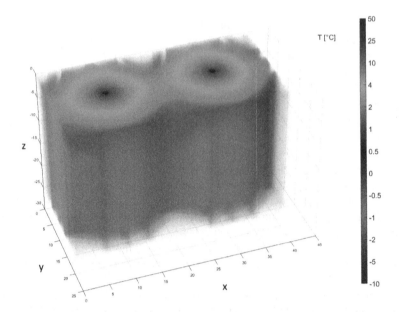

Fig. 3. Simulation results. Temperature around the boreholes without cooling devices after 10 years.

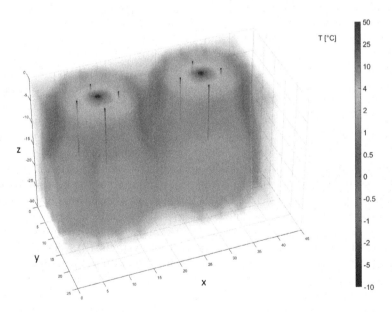

Fig. 4. Simulation results. Temperature around the boreholes with 8 cooling devices after 10 years.

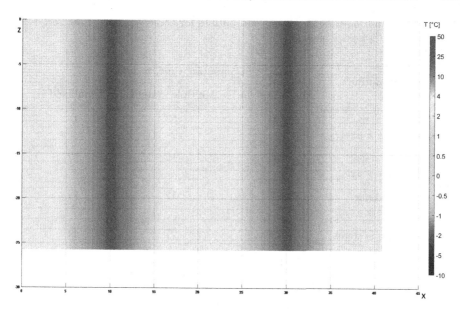

Fig. 5. Simulation results. Temperature around the boreholes without cooling devices after 10 years.

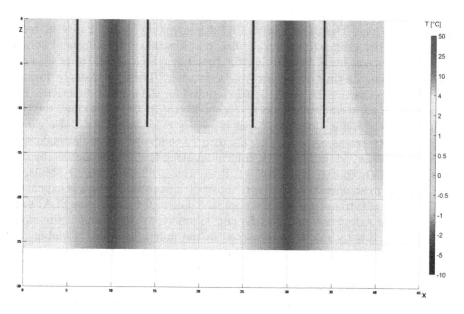

Fig. 6. Simulation results. Temperature around the boreholes with 8 cooling devices after 10 years.

Table 1. Computing time of various subroutines for three variants of the serial algorithm on the $200 \times 96 \times 56$ grid

Subroutine	Computing time, seconds		
	Single system	Multiple systems	Combined
Form systems along the x axis	6	55	6
Form systems along the y axis	16	12	12
Form systems along the z axis	27	12	12
Solve the systems	79	27	44
Total	128	106	74

Table 1 shows the computing time for solving the test problems using three variants of the serial algorithm. It also demonstrates the time taken by individual subroutines of the algorithm. The second column ("Single system") shows the results of the simplest algorithm implemented in [15] – forming and solving the system one by one. The third column ("Multiple systems") illustrates the result of the algorithm that attempts to utilize vectorization – forming and solving multiple systems at once. We see that the time taken by a SLAE solver is nearly 3 times less than the time of the unvectorized variant. The time taken by forming the systems and saving the results is also reduced for the y and z directions. This is caused by a more efficient memory access pattern. At the same time, the time of forming the systems along the x axis is greatly increased. This is also caused by the memory access pattern. The 3D array of temperatures is flattened with the index order $[k]\,[j]\,[i]$. Thus, when forming along the x direction one by one, memory access is contiguous. However, if we want to form several systems, we need to perform an operation similar to matrix transposition, which is expensive.

The solution is to use a combined approach, i.e., to form and solve SLAEs one by one for the x direction and use the new approach for the y and z directions. The result of this technique is presented in the fourth column ("Combined"). The total computing time using this approach is 1.7 times less than using the naive one.

Table 2 shows the results of the parallel algorithms. The table presents the results of the naive approach, as well as the new combined approach described above. It contains the computing times T_n by a various number n of OpenMP threads. It also contains the speedup $S_n = T_1/T_n$ and efficiency $E_n = S_n/n$ coefficients. The performance is limited by the memory bandwidth, therefore, the maximal speedup is less than 4 for both methods.

Table 2. Computing time, speedup and efficiency for parallel variants of the algorithm on the 200×96×56 grid

Number n	Single system			Combined		
of threads	Time, s	Speedup	Efficiency	Time, s	Speedup	Efficiency
1	128	—	—	74	—	—
2	68.1	1.88	0.94	43.5	1.7	0.85
4	43.2	2.96	0.74	24.4	2.8	0.7
8	33.1	3.87	0.48	21	3.52	0.44

5 Conclusion

Parallel algorithms for solving the three-dimensional heat equation are implemented for multicore processors using OpenMP technology. The algorithm is based on the three-point difference scheme for each spatial direction. This reduces the process of finding the sought temperature distribution to solving a set of systems of linear algebraic equations with tridiagonal matrices. In this work, a more memory-efficient algorithm for forming and solving these systems is constructed. Numerical experiments are performed to evaluate the performance of the developed algorithms. The new implementation is up to 2 times faster than the previous one. The parallel program achieves up to 4 times speedup using an 8-core processor.

References

1. Samarsky, A.A., Vabishchevich, P.N.: Computational Heat Transfer, vol. 2, The Finite Difference Methodology. Wiley, Chichester (1995)
2. Romanovsky, V.E., Smith, S.L., Christiansen, H.H.: Permafrost thermal state in the polar Northern 430 Hemisphere during the International Polar Year 2007–2009: a synthesis. Permafr. Periglac. Proces. **21**, 106–116 (2010). https://doi.org/10.1002/ppp.689
3. Gornov, V.F., Stepanov, S.P., Vasilyeva, M.V., Vasilyev, V.I.: Mathematical modeling of heat transfer problems in the permafrost. AIP Conf. Proc. **1629**, 424–431 (2014). https://doi.org/10.1063/1.4902304
4. Stepanov, S.P., Sirditov, I.K., Vabishchevich, P.N., Vasilyeva, M.V., Vasilyev, V.I., Tceeva, A.N.: Numerical simulation of heat transfer of the pile foundations with permafrost. In: Dimov, I., Faragó, I., Vulkov, L. (eds.) Numerical Analysis and Its Applications. NAA 2016. LNCS, vol. 10187, pp. 625–632. Springer, Cham (2017). https://doi.org/10.1007/978-3-319-57099-0_71
5. Kong, X, Doré, G, Calmels, F.: Thermal modeling of heat balance through embankments in permafrost regions. Cold Reg. Sci. Technol. **158**, 117–127 (2019). https://doi.org/10.1016/j.coldregions.2018.11.013
6. Vaganova, N.A., Filimonov, M.Y.: Computer simulation of nonstationary thermal fields in design and operation of northern oil and gas fields. AIP Conf. Proc. **1690**, 020016 (2015). https://doi.org/10.1063/1.4936694

7. Filimonov, M., Vaganova, N.: Permafrost thawing from different technical systems in arctic regions. IOP Conf. Ser. Earth Environ. Sci. **72**, 012006 (2017). https://doi.org/10.1088/1755-1315/72/1/012006

8. Voevodin, V. V., Antonov S. A., Dongarra, J.: AlgoWiki: an open encyclopedia of parallel algorithmic features. Supercomput. Front. Innov. **2**(1), 4–18 (2015). https://doi.org/10.14529/jsfi150101

9. Ortega, J. M.: Introduction to Parallel and Vector Solution of Linear Systems. Springer Science & Business Media, New York (2013). https://doi.org/10.1007/978-1-4899-2112-3

10. Rodrigue, G. (Ed.): Parallel Computations, vol. 1. Elsevier, Amsterdam (2014)

11. Chandra, R., Dagum, L., Kohr, D., Menon, R., Maydan, D., McDonald, J.: Parallel Programming in OpenMP. Morgan Kaufmann, Burlington (2001)

12. Pavlova, N.V., Vabishchevich, P.N., Vasilyeva, M.V.: Mathematical modeling of thermal stabilization of vertical wells on high performance computing systems. In: Lirkov, I., Margenov, S., Waśniewski, J. (eds.) LSSC 2013. LNCS, vol. 8353, pp. 636–643. Springer, Heidelberg (2014). https://doi.org/10.1007/978-3-662-43880-0_73

13. Pepper, D. W., Lombardo, J. M.: High-Performance Computing for Fluid Flow and Heat Transfer. Advances in Numerical Heat Transfer, vol. 2. Routledge, Milton Park (2018)

14. Orgogozo, L., et al.: Water and energy transfer modeling in a permafrost-dominated, forested catchment of central Siberia: the key role of rooting depth. Permafr. Periglac. Process. **30**(2), 75–89 (2019). https://doi.org/10.1002/ppp.1995

15. Akimova, E.N., Filimonov, M.Y., Misilov, V.E., Vaganova, N.A.: Application of high performance computations for modeling thermal fields near the wellheads. In: Sokolinsky, L., Zymbler, M. (eds.) PCT 2020. CCIS, vol. 1263, pp. 266–278. Springer, Cham (2020). https://doi.org/10.1007/978-3-030-55326-5_19

16. Samarskii, A.A., Nikolaev, E.S.: Methods of Solving Finite-Difference Equations. Moscow (1978). (in Russian)

17. Vaganova, N., Filimonov, M.: Parallel splitting and decomposition method for computations of heat distribution in permafrost. In: CEUR Workshop Proceedings, vol. 1513, pp. 42–49 (2015)

18. Akimova, E.N., Filimonov, M.Y., Misilov, V.E., Vaganova, N.A.: Simulation of thermal processes in permafrost: parallel implementation on multicore CPU. In: CEUR Workshop Proceedings, vol. 2274, pp. 1–9 (2018)

19. Intel Corporation: Introduction to the SIMD Data Layout Templates. https://www.intel.com/content/www/us/en/develop/documentation/cpp-compiler-developer-guide-and-reference/top/compiler-reference/libraries/introduction-to-the-simd-data-layout-templates.html. Accessed 14 Feb 2022

High-Performance Calculations for Modeling the Propagation of Allergenic Plant Pollen in an Atmospheric Boundary Layer

Olga Medveditsyna[1] , Sergey Rychkov[2] , and Anatoly Shatrov[1,2]([envelope])

[1] Kirov State Medical University, Kirov, Russia
avshatrov1@yandex.ru
[2] Vyatka State University, Kirov, Russia

Abstract. Pollen grains contained in the atmosphere have the ability to cause allergic diseases. Plant pollen is a strong allergen: sensitization to it is registered in 30–75% of cases. People who are allergic to pollen usually use plant flowering tables. Our work is in the way of studying the transfer of allergenic pollen using mathematical modeling methods, more exactly, modeling atmospheric fluxes from plant pollen sources on the surface boundary layer. The quasi-two-dimensional model of impurity propagation, early designed elsewhere, is modified to transport allergenic plant pollen from spreader forested areas in the vicinity of a large city. The model includes the consideration of mesoscopic scale hydro- and thermodynamic processes in the lower atmosphere with account for the thermal nonuniformity of the underlying surface in the urban and suburban environs. Some results of numerical calculations are presented. The parallel computational algorithm is implemented on Intel Fortran 12 in Intel Cluster Studio for Linux. The calculations are carried out on the basis of a system of equations with initial and boundary conditions. The great expenditure of processor time, on the one hand, and the natural parallelism of the processed data, on the other hand, have led to building a parallel version of the computer program.

Keywords: High-performance calculations · Transfer of impurity · Atmospheric boundary layer · Allergenic plant pollen

1 Introduction

This paper discusses mesoscale models of the transfer of biological aerosol components, both for individual species of plant pollen and in the aggregate with inert impurities. For calculations, the equations of momentum transfer, temperatures, impurity concentrations are used. In the calculations of concentrations, we use a quasi-two-dimensional model of the pollen grain transfer of various fractions representing the most common types of plant aerosol allergens: birch, alder, poplar, maple, willow, at micro- and mesoscales. For a numerical implementation, a finite-difference explicit calculation method is used. The software implementation of the model is made to analyze and predict the state of pollution in Kirov and its environs on a 20×20 km area with a resolution of up to 200 m. The parallel implementation of the calculation algorithm is made on Intel Fortran 12 in Intel Cluster Studio for Linux in Open MP. The parallel version of the calculation algorithm is built on the basis of the principle of geometric decomposition of the grid region. At the same time, the entire calculation area is divided into parts equal in the number of grid nodes, in which the calculations are carried out simultaneously and independently. The results are given as distributions of pollen concentrations at different time periods, taking into account seasonality.

2   Medical Aspects for the Problem of the Propagation of Allergenic Plant Pollen

The problem of spreading allergic diseases among children is very acute. Table 1 presents WHO data on allergic diseases (AD).

Table 1. Distribution of ADs in various countries over the past 30 years, percent

Country	Children	Adults
Russia	2–4	1–6
Norway	12	10
Sweden	5	—
Switzerland	—	17
Italy	3–6	8
Finland	6	14
Germany	10	9–19
Great Britain	12	11
Portugal	—	7
USA	11	19
Ukraine	3–5	8–10

First of all, the inaccuracy of the data is due to significant divergence between the registered cases and the actual ones. Thus, if one relies on official information, the cases of allergic diseases in our country do not exceed 1.5%, while according to the Institute of Immunology of Russia this figure reaches 30%. Judging by the number of visits to medical institutions, no more than 0.4% of the population suffers from allergic rhinitis, and only every 100 Russians suffer from asthma.

The following diagrams (Figs. 1 and 2) show the dynamics of allergic diseases in the Kirov region for three population groups: children, teenagers and adults.

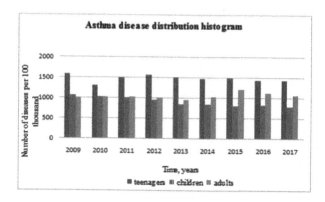

Fig. 1. Dynamics of the asthma prevalence and asthmatic status among teenagers, children, adults of the Kirov region for 2009–2017 (per 100 thousand of the corresponding population).

3   Analysis of the Methods of Propagating Allergenic Plant Pollen

Moreover, there are much fewer people with allergies among villagers, while in Moscow every third suffers from hay fever, in Berlin – every fourth, in New York – every sixth. The reason is that allergies are caused not so much by the plants themselves as by their pollen, which absorbs all the harmful emissions and polluting particles that are presented in catastrophic amounts in the air of the metropolis. A sharp increase in the number of ADs occurs in April-May in the conditions of central Russia, when the flowering of alder, birch, willow, maple and poplar begins. During this period, pollen calendars are formed for most large cities, the patterns of the pollen content of certain plant species in the atmosphere are investigated, the influence of meteorological factors is determined, a network of permanently operating stations for monitoring pollen is created [4,18].

The most informative services for users are special sites [18], however, these sites function irregularly and not for all regions. The well-known information search engine Yandex daily publishes a map of the distribution of pollen emissions of various origins in the vicinity of large cities. Yandex.Pogoda generates a special map for those who are allergic to pollen. The map covers the European part of Russia, Moldova, as well as certain regions of Belarus, Ukraine and Kazakhstan.

People who are allergic to pollen usually use plant flowering tables. However, they provide only approximate data. Plants bloom not strictly according to the calendar, but in the presence of appropriate conditions. Birch catkins begin to intensively secrete pollen when a positive temperature is established; it happens in different years at different times.

The flowering time also depends on the region: earlier in the south, later in the north. The map contains data for 15 common allergen plants: ragweed,

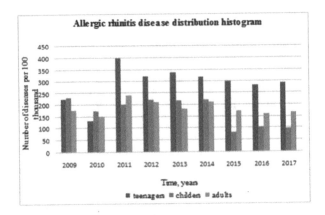

Fig. 2. Dynamics of the allergic rhinitis prevalence among teenagers, children, adults of the Kirov region for 2009–2017 (per 100 thousand of the corresponding population).

birch, elm, oak, spruce, cereals, willow, maple, nettle, alder, hazel, wormwood, weed grass, pine and ash.

However, these distributions are not confirmed numerical parameters and can be considered as an illustrative material of possible occurrences of aerosol pollen components. An important factor in assessing the degree of pollution of aerosol pollen is the knowledge of physical parameters during the transfer of pollen. Data on the mass proportion of grains of various tree species and the procedure of measuring them are given in [11]. Table 2 shows the data on the distribution of masses of grains and the corresponding proportion of the main tree species for the European part of Russia.

Table 2. Pollen grains parameters of various wood species

Wood species	Mass of grains, ng	Percent in distribution
Fir	82,4	0,06
Spruce	63,1	0,24
Pine	15,5	0,18
Linden, oak, maple, elm	10,7	0,02
Aspen	4	0,1
Birch	3,9	0,26
Alder	3,5	0,09
Poplar	3,5	0,03
Willow	2,5	0,02

One can see that the presented data are grouped by grain weight in three main groups: heavy (spruce, fir, pine), medium (linden, oak, maple, elm) and light (aspen, birch, alder, poplar, willow). Taking into account the presented data, attention should be paid to the fact that the mass of allergenic pollen grains has the greatest influence on transfer processes, and this is a group of light fractions. It is the group that represents the most dangerous impact on the development of ADs in large cities.

If we define a certain, rather small neighborhood of the impurity distribution region over a finite period of time, then it is quite reasonable to use simplified (including stationary) models that allow exact solutions. But it is necessary to take into account the complex dynamics of the velocity and temperature fields, surface inhomogeneity and boundary conditions in the case of problems with extended geometry or with sufficiently powerful pollutant sources, for example, when estimating emissions from large industrial enterprises. In [1,7], mesoscale models of the bioaerosol component transport are considered both for individual types of plant pollen [1] and in the aggregate of inert impurities [7]. The equations of momentum, temperature, impurities and moisture transfer are used for calculations. In [21], the mesoscale model of the surface layer is used to calculate the transfer of fungal mold and estimate its interaction with atmospheric flow moisture. This work presents a mesoscale quasi-two-dimensional model of the transfer of pollen grains of various fractions, which are the most common types of plant aerosol allergens: birch, alder, poplar, maple, willow, on micro- and mesoscales [20]. A finite-difference explicit calculation method is used for a numerical implementation.

The construction of a parallel version of the calculation algorithm is based on the principle of geometric decomposition of the grid domain.

4   Mathematical Model and Its Computer Implementation of the Problem

Let us consider the lower-atmosphere boundary layer restricting ourselves to mesoscale processes for which the layer height D and the horizontal scale L satisfy the relation much less than 1. Take the three-dimensional equations of the hydrothermodynamics of dry atmosphere in a rotating Cartesian coordinate system as the original equations [2–15]

$$\frac{\partial u}{\partial t} + u\frac{\partial u}{\partial x} + v\frac{\partial u}{\partial y} + w\frac{\partial u}{\partial z} = -\frac{\partial \Phi}{\partial x} + lv + A_M \Delta u + \frac{\partial}{\partial z}k_M\frac{\partial u}{\partial z}, \qquad (1)$$

$$\frac{\partial v}{\partial t} + u\frac{\partial v}{\partial x} + v\frac{\partial v}{\partial y} + w\frac{\partial v}{\partial z} = -\frac{\partial \Phi}{\partial y} - lu + A_M \Delta v + \frac{\partial}{\partial z}k_M\frac{\partial v}{\partial z}, \qquad (2)$$

$$\frac{\partial w}{\partial t} + u\frac{\partial w}{\partial x} + v\frac{\partial w}{\partial y} + w\frac{\partial w}{\partial z} = -\frac{\partial \Phi}{\partial z} + \beta\theta + A_M \Delta w + \frac{\partial}{\partial z}k_M\frac{\partial w}{\partial z}, \qquad (3)$$

$$\frac{\partial u}{\partial x} + \frac{\partial v}{\partial y} + \frac{\partial w}{\partial z} = 0, \tag{4}$$

$$\frac{\partial \theta}{\partial t} + u\frac{\partial \theta}{\partial x} + v\frac{\partial \theta}{\partial y} + w\frac{\partial \theta}{\partial z} = A_T \Delta\theta + \frac{\partial}{\partial z} k_T \frac{\partial \theta}{\partial z}, \tag{5}$$

$$\frac{\partial \varphi}{\partial t} + u\frac{\partial \varphi}{\partial x} + v\frac{\partial \varphi}{\partial y} + w\frac{\partial \varphi}{\partial z} + \sigma\varphi = A_S \Delta\varphi + k_S \frac{\partial^2 \varphi}{\partial z^2}. \tag{6}$$

The initial and boundary conditions are as follows:

$$u = -c_g \sin(dd), \quad v = -c_g \cos(dd), \quad \theta = \theta_S, \quad \varphi = 0, \quad t = 0, \tag{7}$$

$$\frac{\partial u}{\partial z} = \frac{\partial v}{\partial z} = w = 0, \quad \frac{\partial \theta}{\partial z} = 0, \quad \frac{\partial \varphi}{\partial z} = 0, \quad z = D, \tag{8}$$

$$u = v = w = 0, \quad \frac{\partial \theta}{\partial z} = \gamma(\theta - \theta_S), \quad \frac{\partial \varphi}{\partial z} = \alpha\varphi - f_S, \quad z = 0. \tag{9}$$

In Eqs. (1–9), t is the time, Δ is the Laplace operator, Ox, Oy, and Oz are the eastward, northward, and upward coordinate axes, (u, v, w) is the air flow velocity vector, $\Phi = RT_m p'/p$ is the geopotential fluctuation, where R is the specific gas constant and T_m is the mean air temperature in the layer, p is the atmospheric pressure, $p' = p - p_0$, where p is the potential pressure dependent only on the altitude, l is the Coriolis parameter, $\beta = g/\theta$ is the buoyancy parameter, $\theta = T(p_0/p)^{\frac{R}{C_p}}$ is the potential temperature, where T is the air temperature, p_0 is the atmospheric pressure near the ground, and C_p is the specific heat at constant pressure; φ is the impurity concentration, σ is the impurity absorption coefficient in the atmosphere, θ_S is the air temperature at the roughness level of the underlying surface, c_g is the geostrophic wind velocity [3] at the upper free boundary of the atmospheric boundary layer, dd is the geostrophic wind azimuth, γ is the heat transfer coefficient, α is the coefficient of impurity absorption by the underlying surface, A_M, A_T, A_S, k_M, k_T, k_S are the coefficients of gorizontal and vertical turbulent diffusion and $f_S = \sum_{i=1}^{m} f_i \delta(x - x_i)\delta(y - y_i)$ is the intensity of impurity sources, x_i and y_i are the source coordinates, m is the number of sources.

Consider an $L \times L$ area. The geostrophic wind velocity c_g above the atmospheric boundary layer and its direction, as well as the boundary layer height D, are assumed to be known. The horizontal wind velocity fields are calculated from the formulae [3] $u = -c_g \sin(dd)$ and $v = -c_g \cos(dd)$, where $dd = 0$ corresponds to the north wind and $dd = \pi/2$ to the east wind. The wind can also be preassigned as the layer-average velocity field (mean across the layer). At the lateral boundaries, it is assumed that

$$\frac{\partial \mathbf{v}}{\partial n} = 0, \quad \frac{\partial \theta}{\partial n} = 0, \quad \frac{\partial \varphi}{\partial n} = 0, \tag{10}$$

n is the external normal vector. For the mathematical modeling of the impurity transport from a ground source, we introduce a quasi-two-dimensional model based on the locally equilibrium approach. This technique is presented in [2, 15, 16, 20]. Restricting our consideration to mesoscale processes, we assume that $t \gg t_r$, where t is the characteristic time of equilibrium states, and t_r is the time of air flow relaxation to the equilibrium state when the external conditions are varied. Introduce the dimensionless variable $\zeta = z/D$, denote the layer-average quantity as

$$\langle g \rangle = \int\limits_0^1 g(t, x, y, \zeta) \, d\zeta \tag{11}$$

and integrate Eqs. (1–6) using boundary conditions (7–10). Then, with account for the condition of air incompressibility in the lower atmosphere, we obtain

$$\frac{\partial \langle u \rangle}{\partial t} + \frac{\partial \langle uu \rangle}{\partial x} + \frac{\partial \langle uv \rangle}{\partial y} = -\frac{\partial \langle \Phi \rangle}{\partial x} + l\langle v \rangle + A_M \Delta \langle u \rangle + \frac{k_M}{D^2} \frac{\partial u}{\partial \zeta} \Big|_{\zeta=0}^{\zeta=1}, \tag{12}$$

$$\frac{\partial \langle v \rangle}{\partial t} + \frac{\partial \langle uv \rangle}{\partial x} + \frac{\partial \langle vv \rangle}{\partial y} = -\frac{\partial \langle \Phi \rangle}{\partial y} - l\langle u \rangle + A_M \Delta \langle v \rangle + \frac{k_M}{D^2} \frac{\partial v}{\partial \zeta} \Big|_{\zeta=0}^{\zeta=1}, \tag{13}$$

$$\frac{\partial \langle \theta \rangle}{\partial t} + \frac{\partial \langle u\theta \rangle}{\partial x} + \frac{\partial \langle v\theta \rangle}{\partial y} = A_T \Delta \langle \theta \rangle - \frac{\gamma k_T}{D}(\theta|_{\zeta=0} - \theta_S), \tag{14}$$

$$\frac{\partial \langle \varphi \rangle}{\partial t} + \frac{\partial \langle u\varphi \rangle}{\partial x} + \frac{\partial \langle v\varphi \rangle}{\partial y} + \sigma \langle \varphi \rangle = A_S \Delta \langle \varphi \rangle - \frac{k_S}{D}(\alpha \varphi|_{\zeta=0} - f_S). \tag{15}$$

To close the system of equations (12–15), it is necessary to express $\langle uu \rangle$, $\langle uv \rangle$, $\langle vv \rangle$, $\langle u\theta \rangle$, $\langle v\theta \rangle$, $\langle u\varphi \rangle$, $\langle v\varphi \rangle$, $\frac{\partial u}{\partial \zeta}\Big|_{\zeta=0}^{\zeta=1}$, $\langle v\varphi \rangle$, $\frac{\partial v}{\partial \zeta}\Big|_{\zeta=0}^{\zeta=1}$, $\theta|_{\zeta=0}$, and $\varphi|_{\zeta=0}$ in terms of the layer-average impurity concentration $\langle \varphi \rangle$ and the mean velocity $\langle u \rangle$ and $\langle v \rangle$ and temperature $\langle \theta \rangle$ fields. For this purpose, we use the exact solution of the original problem, which can be obtained for a linear air temperature distribution at the roughness level of the underlying surface. We seek the solution in the form: $u = u(\zeta)$, $v = v(\zeta)$, $w = 0$, $\theta = \theta_S + \theta(\zeta)$, and $\varphi = \varphi(\zeta)$. Then the problem from Eqs. (1–6, 8–10) becomes a linear boundary value problem for ordinary differential equations with constant coefficients. Its solution gives the following representation for the velocity

$$M(\zeta) = f_1(\zeta)\langle M \rangle - 2f_2(\zeta)U, \tag{16}$$

where

$$f_1 = \frac{1}{1 - \tanh(\lambda)/\lambda}\left[1 - \frac{\cosh(\lambda(\zeta))}{\cosh(\lambda)}\right], \tag{17}$$

$$f_2 = f_1(\zeta)\left[\frac{\cosh(\lambda) - 1}{\lambda^2 \cosh(\lambda)}\right] - \frac{\sinh(\lambda\zeta)}{\lambda \cosh(\lambda)} + \zeta. \tag{18}$$

The mean values of these functions $\langle f_1 \rangle = 1$ and $\langle f_2 \rangle = 0$. Here $\lambda = (1+i)/\sqrt{2Ek}$ is a parameter dependent on the Ekman number $Ek = k_M/lD^2$, $M(\zeta) = u(\zeta) + iv(\zeta)$, $U = u_x + iv_y$, $U_x = -\beta D \frac{\partial \langle \theta \rangle}{\partial y}$, $U_y = \beta D \frac{\partial \langle \theta \rangle}{\partial x}$, $i = \sqrt{-1}$. The subscripts denote the partial derivatives in regard to x and y, respectively. Assume that the potential temperature $\theta = \langle \theta \rangle$

$$\varphi = \langle \varphi \rangle + \frac{f_S D}{\alpha D \cosh(S) + S \sinh(S)} \left[\cosh(S(1-\zeta)) - \frac{\sinh(S)}{S} \right], \quad (19)$$

where $S^2 = (\sigma D^2)/k_S$ is the dimensionless parameter.

In [7,21], similar solutions are called locally equilibrium. Assuming that provided the conditions of Eqs. (1) and (12) are fulfilled, formulae (16)–(21) fairly adequately (asymptotically correctly in the small parameter δ_1) describe the structure of a thermally nonuniform mesoscale air flow at each point of the layer and at each moment of time [16], we use these conditions as closing relations of the system of Eqs. (12–15). Applying the curl operation to Eqs. (12) and (13), we arrive at an evolutionary equation for the vorticity

$$\omega(t,x,y) = \frac{\partial \langle v \rangle}{\partial x} - \frac{\partial \langle u \rangle}{\partial y}. \quad (20)$$

Bearing in mind that the layer-average velocity is divergence-free,

$$\frac{\partial \langle u \rangle}{\partial x} + \frac{\partial \langle v \rangle}{\partial y} = 0,$$

we introduce the stream function $\psi(t,x,y)$ such that

$$\langle u \rangle = -\frac{\partial \psi}{\partial y}, \quad \langle v \rangle = -\frac{\partial \psi}{\partial x}, \quad (21)$$

$$\frac{\partial \omega}{\partial t} + k_1\{\psi,\omega\} + k_3 Rt[\{\theta,\omega\} + \{\psi,\Delta\theta\}] - k_5 Rt^2\{\theta,\Delta\theta\} = \frac{1}{Re}\Delta\omega - \mu(k_7\omega - k_8 Rt\Delta\theta), \quad (22)$$

$$\Delta\psi = \omega, \quad (23)$$

$$\frac{\partial \theta}{\partial t} + \{\psi,\theta\} = \frac{1}{Pe}\Delta\theta - \bar{q}(\theta - \bar{\theta}_S), \quad (24)$$

$$\frac{\partial \varphi}{\partial t} + \{\psi,\varphi\} = \frac{1}{Pe_S}\Delta\varphi - \bar{\sigma}\varphi + A\sum_{i=1}^{m} \bar{f}_i\delta(x-x_i)\delta(y-y_i). \quad (25)$$

We take the quantities L, c_g, L/c_g, $\theta_0 = \max \theta_S$, and φ_{MPC} (maximum permissible impurity concentration) as length, velocity, time, temperature, and impurity concentration scales. Then in terms of the vorticity ω, the stream function ψ, the layer-average potential temperature taken in the units of the stream function, $\theta_*(t, x, y) = (\beta d)/(2l)\langle\theta\rangle$, and the layer-average concentration $\varphi_*(t, x, y) = \langle\varphi\rangle\varphi_{MPC}$ (for brevity, the symbols "*" will be omitted), the equation of the model describing mesoscale processes in the lower atmosphere can be brought into the following dimensionless form.

Here in Eqs. (22–25):

$$\{\psi, \omega\} = \frac{\partial\psi}{\partial x}\frac{\partial\omega}{\partial y} - \frac{\partial\psi}{\partial y}\frac{\partial\omega}{\partial x}$$

is the Jacobian operator;

$$Rt = \frac{\beta D\theta_0}{2lc_g L}$$

is the counterpart of the thermal Rossby number [15];

$$Re = \frac{c_g L}{A_T}$$

is the Reynolds number;

$$\mu = \frac{lc_g}{L}$$

is the dimensionless coefficient of the friction on the underlying surface,

$$Pe = \frac{c_g L}{A_T}$$

is the Peclet number;

$$\bar{q} = qc_g/L$$

is the dimensionless coefficient of cooling, where $q = \gamma k_T/D$;

$$Pe_S = \frac{c_g L}{A_S}$$

is the solutal Peclet number;

$\bar{\sigma} = \sigma_1 L/c_g$ is the dimensionless impurity absorption coefficient, where $\sigma_1 = \sigma + \alpha k_S/D$;

$$\bar{f}'_S = \frac{f'_S k_S L}{\varphi_{MPC} c_g D};$$

$$A = 1 - \frac{\alpha D}{\alpha D\cosh(S) + S\sinh(S)}\left(\cosh(S) - \frac{\sinh(S)}{S}\right);$$

and $k_1 = \Re(\langle f_1 f_1\rangle)$, $k_3 = \Re(\langle f_1 f_2\rangle)$, $k_5 = \Re(\langle f_2 f_2\rangle)$, $k_7 = \Re(f'_1)$, $k_8 = \Re(f'_2)$ are the Ekman-number-dependent coefficients (here $\Re$ is the real part of the number).

In the case under consideration $Ek = 1$, and these coefficients are as follows: $k_1 = 1.199$, $k_3 = 0.00077$, $k_5 = 0.0005909$, $k_7 = 3.0057$, and $k_8 = 0.000952$. In terms of the vorticity ω, the stream function ψ, and the reduced, layer-average potential temperature, the initial and boundary conditions are brought into the form:

$$t = 0 : \psi = y\sin(dd) - x\cos(dd), \quad \omega = 0, \quad \theta = \theta_S, \quad \phi = 0, \quad (26)$$

$$\frac{\partial\psi}{\partial n} = 0, \quad \omega = 0, \quad \frac{\partial\theta}{\partial n} = 0, \quad \frac{\partial\phi}{\partial n} = 0. \quad (27)$$

The discretization of the continuous model (22–25) is described in [13].

The finite-difference approximation of differential equations on a two-dimensional grid is represented by a five-point template.

The analysis of transport models in a turbulent boundary layer using parallel calculations is given in [19].

The one-dimensional decomposition of the grid domain for three processor elements is shown in Fig. 3.

5   Results of Modeling

The parallel computational algorithm is implemented on Intel Fortran 12 in the Intel Cluster Studio Package for Linux, installed on the Vyatka State University HPC Enigma X000 cluster supercomputer. The calculations are carried out on the basis of the system of Eqs. (22–25) with initial and boundary conditions (26–27). The explicit difference scheme [14] is used on a 1000×1000 grid. The program complex used is based on certificate of the Russian State Registration for Computer Programs No. 2015662922 on 07.12.2015 (Rychkov S.L. et al.).

In accordance with the theory of Monin and Obukhov [6,12,18], the coefficients of vertical and horizontal turbulent viscosity, thermal conductivity, and diffusion for mesoscale turbulent processes in the lower atmosphere are assumed the same, namely, $k_M, T, S = lD^2$, where $D = 400$ m and $A_M, T, S = 400\,\mathrm{m^2/s}$.

In the selected reference frame, the westward wind blew from left to right. The wind velocity c_g varied from 1 to 10 m/s. In most calculations, the velocity was 2–5 m/s; in this case, the temperature inhomogeneity effect on the wind flow in the vicinity of a heat source is most clearly expressed. The interaction between aerosol impurity and the underlying surface was taken into account on the basis of information on the nonuniformities of the temperature and absorption coefficient distributions from the map of land utilization of the computational domain. The air temperature θ_S varied from $18\,°C$ outside populated areas to $23\,°C$ in the city of Kirov. The minimum temperature was observed at the north boundary of the area. The coefficient of impurity absorption by the underlying surface was assumed to be $\alpha = 0.0139\,\mathrm{mm^{-1}}$ outside populated areas and $\alpha = 0.00139\,\mathrm{m^{-1}}$ on their territories. A point impurity source was located on the underlying surface, in the center of the region under consideration (within the city territory). In the calculations, it was also taken that $l = 1.24 \times 10^{-4}\,\mathrm{s^{-1}}$, $\sigma = 5.67 \times 10^{-8}\,\mathrm{s^{-1}}$, $\gamma = 0.25 \times 10^{-3}\,\mathrm{m^{-1}}$, $f_S = 0.9996 \times 10^{-7}\,\mathrm{kg/m^4}$, and $\varphi_{MPC} = 0.5 \times 10^{-7}\,\mathrm{kg/m^3}$.

The results of pollen concentration distribution calculations for some wind directions are presented in Figs. 4–5.

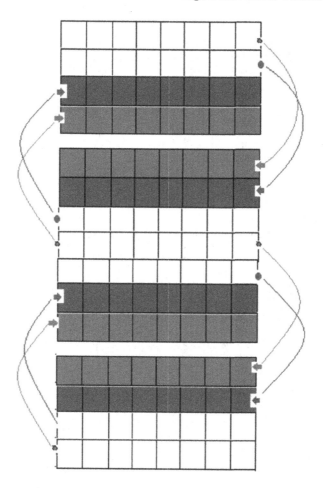

Fig. 3. Decomposition of the grid domain

Figure 6 shows the distribution of birch pollen concentration (number of grains per cubic meter) in the vicinity of Kirov in the period from April 20 to May 30.

An increase in the number of disease cases in the period April – June is revealed.

A visible increase in concentration in May correlates with an increase in the number of diseases at this time.

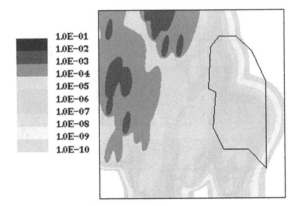

Fig. 4. 20-km zone near the city of Kirov, south wind

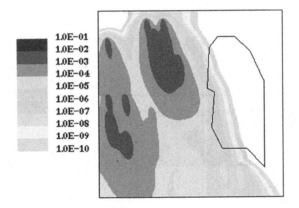

Fig. 5. 20-km zone near the city of Kirov, north wind

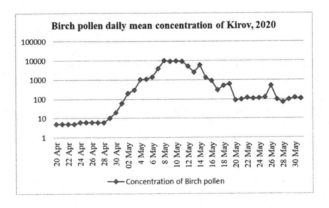

Fig. 6. Distribution of birch pollen concentration

6   Conclusion

Our work is in the way of studying the transfer of allergenic pollen using mathematical modeling methods, more exactly, modeling atmospheric fluxes from plant pollen sources on the surface boundary layer.

A detailed description of these methods is presented, for example, in [5,8–10]. In [10], a model of the propagation of pathogenic strains by atmospheric flows is considered. The authors assess the impact of the pathogen phenotype on the environment and the relationship of spatial sources with the anthropogenic environment. This paper also takes into account the effects of the interaction of various pathogenic strains with each other. The authors consider that such mechanisms can work in many natural systems.

The continuation and development of such an approach is in [5]. This paper presents a three-dimensional model of the atmospheric transportation of plant pollen, taking into account the flow turbulence.

The problem of impurity propagation in the interaction of the flow in the atmospheric boundary layer with a homogeneous forest canopy is numerically studied on the basis of the method of large vortices simulation (LES). The impurity contained in the atmosphere can not only be carried away by the flow and spread due to diffusion, but also enter the flow due to the interaction of the flow with the plant elements of the forest canopy and the "leaching" of the accumulated impurity.

With regard to these publications, it should be noted that when using a three-dimensional model for elliptic differential equations, the question of setting boundary conditions remains open, especially on the upper boundary.

It is well known that incorrectly set boundary conditions result in errors within the computational domain, sometimes exceeding many times the errors at the boundaries. In the works mentioned above, "soft" boundary conditions, meaning that the derivatives are equal to zero, are used.

Extensive and detailed information about the use of cartographic and biophysical data in mathematical modeling is provided in [8,9]. These papers describe a mathematical model for the transfer of allergens (birch pollen) and fungal impurities based on the WRF climate model. The proposed model is considered to be mesoscale, however, its suitability for regional forecasts is limited by the minimum size of the calculation cell of 15 km, which does not allow obtaining reliable regional forecasts.

The aim of our work is to create a computational set of programs that allow us to obtain a forecast of the spread of allergenic pollen based on the mathematical modeling of the transfer processes of allergenic impurities on a regional scale.

For example, there are given the results of calculating the distribution of birch pollen concentration in the period of the highest emission from April 20 to May 30 in the vicinity of the city of Kirov, located in the Volga Federal District of the Russian Federation.

As follows from the previous section, data of most web sites designed to monitor the distribution of plant pollen do not provide a detailed analysis of the distribution and production of impurities.

They mainly provide estimated information based on palynological bioindication methods, which reflect the local characteristics of the place where the precipitating impurity is measured.

Other methods use allergen sensitivity coefficients, which means that the data are based on individual feelings of allergy sufferers.

Below is a brief overview of some specialized sites in the Russian segment of the Internet that provide information on the situation with the transfer of allergenic pollen.

The Allergotop.com website (www.allergotop.com/files/terms-of-use.pdf) is created by practicing allergic doctors and employees of the Faculty of Biology of Moscow State University named after M.V. Lomonosov. The Pollen.club website (www.pollen.club) is based on health indicators provided by service users themselves. The forecast of the dust level for the current day, according to the site, is carried out on the basis of mathematical modeling taking into account the weather factors of the SILAM model [17]. The creators of the site notify about the limited possibilities of forecasts for which data are taken from the national pollen monitoring sites www.pollenwarndienst.at, www.norkko.fi, www.silam.fmi.fi. All information is of evaluation nature. There may be omissions and inaccuracies in the data due to the irregular nature of observations.

The www.silam.fmi.fi website [17] is developed by the Finnish Meteorological Institute and offers forecasts of pollen distribution for 3 days. At the same time, the developers warn that all forecasts are created for scientific use only and cannot be used as accurate data. The Polleninfo.org website is developed by the Medical University of Vienna and is multifunctional. Polleninfo.org includes several indicators: the average risk of an allergy to pollen based on the intensity of the dusting of several allergens and weather parameters (including air pollution); a symptom map that enables a comparison of the intensity of reactions manifested in patients; dust maps in Europe that show the dynamics of the pollen content of more than 300 monitoring stations across Europe.

References

1. Aloyan, A.: Dynamics and kinematics of gas impurities and aerosols in the atmosphere. Institute of Computational Mathematics, A textbook, Russian Academy of Sciences, Moscow (2002). (in Russian)
2. Aristov, S., Frik, P.: Dynamics of large-scale flows in thin fluid layers, preprint [in Russian]. Technical report, Ural Division of the Russian Academy of Sciences, Institute of Continuum Mechanics, Perm, Russia (1987)
3. Aristov, S., Frik, P.: Large-scale turbulence in a thin layer of nonisothermal rotating fluid. Fluid Dyn. **23**(4), 522 (1988)
4. Belov, P., Shcherbakov, A.: Numerical modeling of the diurnal course of meteorological elements in a large city [in Russian]. Meteorol. Gidrol. **7**, 45 (1983)
5. Gavrilov, K., Morvan, D., Accary, G., Lyubimov, D., Meradji, S.: Numerical modeling of coherent structures attendant on impurity propagation in the atmospheric boundary layer over a forecast canopy. Fluid Dyn. **46**(1), 138–147 (2011). https://doi.org/10.1134/S0015462811010169

6. Golovko, V.V., Zueva, G.A., Kiseleva, T.I.: Anemophilous plant pollen grains entering the atmosphere: cluster composition. Atmosp. Ocean. Opt. **34**(5), 483–490 (2021). https://doi.org/10.1134/S1024856021050092

7. Kibel, I.: Hydrodynamic short-term forecasts in the problems of meteorology [in Russian]. Tr. Gidrometeotsentr SSSR **48**, 3 (1970)

8. Kurganskiy, A., et al.: Incorporation of pollen data in source maps is vital for pollen dispersion models. Atmosph. Chem. Phys. **20**(4), 2099–2121 (2020). https://doi.org/10.5194/acp-20-2099-2020

9. Kurganskiy, A., et al.: Enviro-HIRLAM birch pollen modeling for northern Europe. Rep. Ser. Aeros. Sci. **163**, 229 (2015)

10. Loos, C., Seppelt, R., Meier-Bethke, S., Schiemann, J., Richter, O.: Spatially explicit modelling of transgenic maize pollen dispersal and cross- pollination. J. Theor. Biol. **225**(3), 241–255 (2003). https://doi.org/10.1016/s0022-5193(03)00243-1

11. Penenko, V., Aloyan, A.: Models and Methods for the Problems of Environmental Control. Nauka, Novosibirsk (1985). (in Russian)

12. Rychkov, S., Shatrov, A., Shvarts, K.: Mathematical modeling of aerosol transport in the atmosphere. In: Proceedings of All-Russian Scientific Conference "Environment and Stable Development of Regions: New Research Methods and Technologies, Vol. III, Modeling in the Environmental Control. General Ecology and Control of Biovariety, p. 84. Kazan, Russia (2009). (in Russian)

13. Shatrov, A., Shvarts, K.: Numerical modeling of mesoscale atmospheric impurity transport processes in the environs of the city of Kirov. Fluid Dyn. **46**(2), 333–340 (2011). https://doi.org/10.1134/S0015462811020165

14. Shvarts, K.: Models of geophysical hydrodynamics. A textbook [in Russian]. Technical report, Perm University Press, Perm (2006)

15. Shvarts, K., Shklyaev, V.: Modeling impurity transport processes in the free atmosphere on the basis of a quasi-three-dimensional model. Meteorol. Gidrol. **8**, 44 (2000)

16. Shvarts, K., Shklyaev, V.: Numerical modeling of mesoscale vortex structures near an intense hot impurity source in the atmospheric boundary layer. Vych. Mekh. Sploshnykh Sred **1**, 96 (2009)

17. Sofiev, M., Siljamo, P., Valkama, I., Ilvonen, M., Kukkonen, J.: A dispersion modelling system SILAM and its evaluation against ETEX data. Atmosph. Environ. **40**, 674–685 (2006). https://doi.org/10.1016/j.atmosenv.2005.09.069

18. Starchenko, A., Danilkin, E., Prohanov, S., Leshchinsky, D.: Numerical prediction of local meteorological processes above a city with a supercomputer. J. Phys. Conf. Ser. **1740**, 012071 (2021). https://doi.org/10.1088/1742-6596/1740/1/012071

19. Starchenko, A., Danilkin, E., Prohanov, S., Leshchinsky, D.: Parallel implementation of a numerical method for solving transport equations for the mesoscale meteorological model TSUNM3. J. Phys. Conf. Ser. **1715**, 012073 (2021). https://doi.org/10.1088/1742-6596/1715/1/012073

20. Tarnopolskii, A., Shnaidman, V.: Modeling the atmospheric boundary layer for an urban built-up area and a suburban zone. Meteorol. Gidrol. **1**, 41 (1991). (in Russian)

21. Veltishcheva, N.: Three-dimensional nonhydrostatic model describing circulation over an urban heat island. Tr. Gidrometeotsentr SSSR. **219**, 6 (1979). (in Russian)

Author Index

Printed in the United States
by Baker & Taylor Publisher Services